In recent years, there has been much debate over the extent to which under-graduate textbook macroeconomic models are theoretically well grounded and whether they adequately reflect the latest developments in the field. The aim of *Macroeconomic Theory and Macroeconomic Pedagogy* is to encourage and advance this debate, with a specific view to improving macroeconomics education.

The book contains sixteen essays from internationally renowned scholars working in the field of macroeconomics. Contributions examine teaching models in light of recent developments in theory, with an eye to promoting a better understanding of real-world issues. Topics include the three-equation New Consensus model, extensions and alternatives to this model, and endo-genous money and finance.

Macroeconomic Theory and Macroeconomic Pedagogy

Edited by

Giuseppe Fontana
University of Leeds, UK, and University of Sannio, Italy

and

Mark Setterfield
Trinity College, Hartford, USA

First published 2009
Published in paperback 2010 by
PALGRAVE MACMILLAN

Palgrave Macmillan in the UK is an imprint of Macmillan Publishers Limited, registered in England, company number 785998, of Houndmills, Basingstoke, Hampshire RG21 6XS.

Palgrave Macmillan in the US is a division of St Martin's Press LLC, 175 Fifth Avenue, New York, NY 10010.

Palgrave Macmillan is the global academic imprint of the above companies and has companies and representatives throughout the world.

Palgrave® and Macmillan® are registered trademarks in the United States, the United Kingdom, Europe and other countries.

ISBN 978–0–230–20203–0   hardback
ISBN 978–0–230–27763–2   paperback

This book is printed on paper suitable for recycling and made from fully managed and sustained forest sources. Logging, pulping and manufacturing processes are expected to conform to the environmental regulations of the country of origin.

A catalogue record for this book is available from the British Library.

A catalog record for this book is available from the Library of Congress.

10 9 8 7 6 5 4 3 2
19 18 17 16 15 14 13 12 11 10

Printed and bound in Great Britain by
CPI Antony Rowe, Chippenham and Eastbourne

Contents

List of Figures

List of Appendices

Notes on the Contributors

Philip Arestis (University of Cambridge, UK; E-mail: pa267@cam.ac.uk) is University Director of Research, Cambridge Centre for Economics and Public Policy, Department of Land Economy, University of Cambridge, UK; Professor of Economics, Department of Applied Economics V, University of the Basque Country, Spain; Distinguished Adjunct Professor of Economics, Department of Economics, University of Utah, US; Senior Scholar, Levy Economics Institute, New York, US; Visiting Professor, Leeds University Business School, University of Leeds, UK; and Professorial Research Associate, Department of Finance and Management Studies, School of Oriental and African Studies (SOAS), University of London, UK. He is Chief Academic Adviser to the UK Government Economic Service (GES) on Professional Development in Economics. He has published as sole author or editor, as well as co-author and co-editor, a number of books, contributed in the form of invited chapters to numerous books, produced research reports for research institutes, and has published widely in academic journals.

Robert J. Barbera (ITG, USA; E-mail: Bob.Barbera@itg.com) is Managing Director and Chief Economist at ITG. He is responsible for ITG's global economic and financial market forecasts. He has spent the last twenty-six years as a Wall Street economist, earning a wide institutional following. He is a regular guest on CNBC and is frequently quoted in the *New York Times* and the *Wall Street Journal*. He currently also serves as a Fellow in the Economics Department of the Johns Hopkins University. He is also a member of the Johns Hopkins Center for Financial Economics Advisory Board. He has been teaching applied macroeconomics at Johns Hopkins for the last five years. Before joining ITG, he was Chief Economist and Director of Economic Research at Lehman Brothers, and prior to that was Chief Economist at E.F. Hutton. Dr Barbera also lectured at MIT. He earned both his BA and PhD from Johns Hopkins University.

Emiliano Brancaccio (University of Sannio, Italy; E-mail: emiliano.brancaccio@unisannio.it) is a researcher in political economy and lecturer on macroeconomics and labour economics in the Faculty of Economic Sciences and Business Studies of the University of Sannio in Benevento (Italy). He is the author of a synthesis of two of the primary schools in the critique of economic theory, namely the 'surplus' approach and 'monetary circuit' approach. His area of study also encompasses banking systems, financial markets and European economic policy.

Wendy Carlin (University College London, UK; E-mail: w.carlin@ucl.ac.uk) is Professor of Economics at University College London (UCL). She is co-managing editor of *Economics of Transition*. Her research focuses on macroeconomics, institutions and economic performance, and the economics of transition. She has published papers with a number of co-authors on subjects including economic restructuring in transition; ownership, finance and growth; competitiveness and export performance; competition and growth in transition; the political economy of Germany; and New Keynesian macroeconomics. She has co-authored with David Soskice two macroeconomics books: *Macroeconomics and the Wage Bargain* and *Macroeconomics: Imperfections, Institutions and Policies*). She is a Council member of the Royal Economics Society and the European Economics Association and a Trustee of the Anglo-German Foundation.

Jagjit S. Chadha (University of Kent, UK; E-mail: jsc@kent.ac.uk) is Professor of Economics at Kent University. He is also Professorial Fellow at the Centre for International Macroeconomics and Finance at the University of Cambridge and Visiting Fellow of Clare College Cambridge. He is Fellow of the European Area Business Cycle Network and of the European Monetary Forum. He has previously worked at the Bank of England and at BNP Paribas Investment Bank, where he continues to hold an advisory role. He has provided advice to the UK's Parliamentary Treasury Committee and is on the Advisory Panel at the Royal Institute of Chartered Surveyors. He works with dynamic stochastic general equilibrium models and in the broad area of macroeconomics and finance and has published extensively in this field. He was educated at University College London and the London School of Economics.

David Colander (Middlebury College, USA; E-mail: colander@middlebury. edu) received his PhD from Columbia University and has been the Christian A. Johnson Distinguished Professor of Economics at Middlebury College, Middlebury, Vermont since 1982. In 2001–02 he was the Kelly Professor of Distinguished Teaching at Princeton University. He has authored, co-authored, or edited over 40 books and 100 articles on a wide range of topics. His books have been, or are being, translated into a number of different languages, including Chinese, Bulgarian, Polish, Italian and Spanish. He has been president of both the Eastern Economic Association and History of Economic Thought Society and is, or has been, on the editorial boards of numerous journals, including the *Journal of Economic Perspectives* and the *Journal of Economic Education*.

Jesus Ferreiro (Universidad del País Vasco, Spain; E-mail: jesus.ferreiro@ ehu.es) is Associate Professor in Economics at the University of the Basque Country, in Bilbao, Spain. He has a PhD from the University of the Basque

Country. His research interests are in the areas of macroeconomic policy, labour market and international financial flows. He has published a number of articles on those topics in edited books and in academic journals such as *Economic and Industrial Democracy, Économie Appliquée, Ekonomia, European Planning Studies, International Review of Applied Economics* and the *Journal of Post Keynesian Economics*.

Giuseppe Fontana (University of Leeds, UK; E-mail: gf@lubs.leeds.ac.uk) is Professor of Monetary Economics at the University of Leeds (UK); Associate Professor at the Università del Sannio (Italy); Life Member Fellow at Clare Hall (University of Cambridge, UK); and Visiting Research Professor at the Centre for Full Employment and Price Stability (University of Missouri, Kansas City, USA), and the Cambridge Centre for Economic and Public Policy (University of Cambridge, UK). He has recently been awarded the 2008 G.L.S. Shackle Prize, St Edmund's College, Cambridge (UK). He has published in the *Cambridge Journal of Economics*, the *International Review of Applied Economics*, the *Journal of Economic Psychology*, the *Journal of Post Keynesian Economics*, *Metroeconomica, Revue Economie Politique*, and the *Scottish Journal of Political Economy*, among others. He has recently co-edited two books with Palgrave Macmillan and published *Money, Time, and Uncertainty* with Routledge.

Eckhard Hein (Berlin School of Economics and Law, Germany; Email: eckhard.hein@hwr-berlin.de) is Professor of Economics at the Berlin School of Economics and Law. Previously he was Senior Researcher at the Macroeconomic Policy Institute (IMK), Hans Boeckler Foundation, Duesseldorf, and a Visiting Professor at Carl von Ossietzky University Oldenburg, the University of Hamburg and at the Vienna University of Economics and Business Administration. He is a member of the coordination committee of the Research Network Macroeconomics and Macroeconomic Policies and a managing co-editor of *Intervention: European Journal of Economics and Economic Policies*. His research focuses on money, financial systems, distribution and growth, on European economic policies and on Post Keynesian economics. He has published in the *Cambridge Journal of Economics*, the *European Journal of the History of Economic Thought*, the *International Review of Applied Economics, Metroeconomica*, and *Structural Change and Economic Dynamics*, among others. *Money, Distribution Conflict and Capital Accumulation: Contributions to 'Monetary Analysis'* was published by Palgrave Macmillan.

Peter Howells (University of the West of England, UK; E-mail: peter.howells@uwe.ac.uk) is Professor of Monetary Economics in the Centre for Global Finance at the Bristol Business School. He is the author (with Keith Bain) of *Monetary Economics: Policy and its Theoretical Basis,* as well as the popular textbook, *The Economics of Money, Banking and Finance.* His research interests are in central banking and monetary policy, and he has published extensively in major international journals, often with Iris Biefang-Frisancho Mariscal. He is also the editor of the Royal Economic Society's *Newsletter*.

Marc Lavoie (University of Ottawa, Canada; E-mail: marc.lavoie@uottawa.ca) is Professor in the Department of Economics at the University of Ottawa, where he started teaching in 1979. He has written a number of books, including *Foundations of Post-Keynesian Economic Analysis* (1992), *Introduction to Post-Keynesian Economics* (2006) and *Monetary Economics: An Integrated Approach to Money, Income, Production and Wealth* (2007) with Wynne Godley. With Mario Seccareccia, he has been the co-editor of a book on the works of Milton Friedman (1993) and of *Central Banking in the Modern World: Alternative Perspectives* (2004), in addition to writing the Canadian edition of the Baumol and Blinder first-year textbook (2009). Lavoie was also the associate editor of the *Encyclopedia of Political Economy* (1999), and he has been a visiting professor at the universities of Bordeaux, Nice, Rennes, Dijon, Grenoble, Limoges, Lille, Paris-Nord and Paris-1, as well as Curtin University in Perth (Australia). He has lectured at the Post Keynesian summer schools in Kansas City and Berlin.

Casey Rothschild (Middlebury College, USA; E-mail: crothsch@middlebury.edu) received an AB in physics from Princeton University in 1999 and immediately began teaching economics at the Advanced Placement level at the Roxbury Latin School in Boston. After returning to school and earning his PhD from MIT in 2006, he joined the Economics faculty at Middlebury College as an assistant professor. His research focuses on applied micro theory, with a particular emphasis on insurance and pension annuity markets. He is also deeply interested in economic pedagogy, and he teaches courses in macroeconomics, public finance, game theory, and decision theory. His research has been published or is forthcoming in the *Journal of Economic Theory*, the *Journal of Financial Economics*, the *Journal of Pension Economics and Finance* and *Geophysical Research Letters*. He currently serves on the editorial board of the *Journal of Economic Education*.

Malcolm Sawyer (University of Leeds, UK; Email: mcs@lubs.leeds.ac.uk) is Professor of Economics, University of Leeds, UK, and formerly Pro-Dean for Learning and Teaching for the Faculty of Business. He is managing editor of *International Review of Applied Economics* and the editor of the series *New Directions in Modern Economics* published by Edward Elgar. He is the author of 11 books, has edited 22 books and published 90 papers in refereed journals, and has contributed chapters to over 100 books. His research interests are in macroeconomics, fiscal and monetary policy, the political economy of the European Monetary Union, nature of money, causes and concepts of unemployment and the economics of Michal Kalecki.

Felipe Serrano (Universidad del País Vasco, Spain; E-mail: felipe.serrano@ehu.es) is Professor in Economics at the University of the Basque Country, in Bilbao, Spain. He is the head of the Department of Applied Economics V at the University of the Basque Country. His research interests are in the areas of social security, the welfare state, the labour market, innovation and economic policy. He is the author of a number of articles on these topics in edited books and in academic journals such as *Economies et Sociétés, Ekonomia, European Planning Studies, Industrial and Labour Relations Review, International Review of Applied Economics* and the *Journal of Post Keynesian Economics*.

Mark Setterfield (Trinity College, USA; E-mail: mark.setterfield@trincoll.edu) is Professor of Economics in the Department of Economics at Trinity College, Hartford, Connecticut; Associate Member of the Cambridge Centre for Economic and Public Policy (Cambridge University, UK); and Senior Research Associate at the International Economic Policy Institute (Laurentian University, Canada). His main research interests are macrodynamics (particularly the development and application of concepts of path dependence) and Post Keynesian economics. He is the author or editor of five books and has an extensive record of publication in academic journals. He serves on several editorial boards, including that of the *Journal of Economic Education*.

John Smithin (York University, Canada; E-mail: jsmithin@yorku.ca) is Professor of Economics in the Department of Economics and the Schulich School of Business, York University, Toronto, Canada. He holds a PhD from McMaster University, has previously taught at the University of Calgary and Lanchester Polytechnic (now Coventry University) in England, and is former Bye Fellow at Robinson College, Cambridge. His main research interests are in the fields of macroeconomics, monetary theory and the philosophy of money and finance. He is the author/editor (or co-author/co-editor) of *Keynes and Public Policy after Fifty Years, Macroeconomics after Thatcher and Reagan, Economic Integration between Unequal Partners, Macroeconomic Policy and the Future of Capitalism, Money, Financial Institutions and Macroeconomics, What is Money?, Globalization and Economic Growth, Controversies in Monetary Economics, Fundamentals of Economics for Business* and *Money, Enterprise and Income Distribution*.

David Soskice (University of Oxford, UK and Duke University, USA; E-mail: soskice@duke.edu) taught macroeconomics, econometrics and labour economics at Oxford from 1968 to 1990 before becoming Research Director at the Wissenschaftszentrum in Berlin (WZB), where he remained until 2007 working in collaboration with Peter Hall (Harvard) on *Varieties of Capitalism*. In 2004 he was the Mars Visiting Professor of Political Science at Yale and Visiting Professor of Government at Harvard in 2006. He is currently Research Professor of Comparative Political Economy at Oxford and Senior Research Fellow of Nuffield College, and since 2001 has spent each spring semester in the Political Science department at Duke. He has published two macroeconomic textbooks with Wendy Carlin, most recently *Macroeconomics: Institutions, Imperfections and Policies*. In a series of publications with Torben Iversen (Harvard) he has sought to develop models linking wage bargaining, welfare states and the political system in advanced economies, (*Quarterly Journal of Economics* 2000, *American Political Science Review* 2001, 2006, 2007); they were co-winners of the Luebbert Prize of the American Political Science Association for the 2006 *APSR* article.

Engelbert Stockhammer (School of Economics, Kingston University, UK; E-mail: E.Stockhammer@kingston.ac.uk) is Senior Lecturer in Economics at Kingston University and research associate at the Political Economy Research Institute at the University of Massachusetts at Amherst. He has held visiting positions at the Sabanci University, Istanbul, Bilkent University, Ankara, and the Deutsches Institut für Wirtschaftsforschung, Berlin, and is a member of the coordination committee of the Research Network Macroeconomics and Macroeconomic Policies. His research areas include macroeconomics, applied econometrics, European integration, financialization, and heterodox economics. He has published a book on *The Rise of Unemployment in Europe* and articles in *the Cambridge Journal of Economics,* the *Journal of Post Keynesian Economics,* the *International Review of Applied Economics, Metroeconomica,* the *Journal of Economic Issues, Empirica,* and *Structural Change and Economic Dynamics.*

Roberto Tamborini (Università di Trento, Italia; E-mail: roberto.tamborini@economia.unitn.it) is Full Professor of Political Economy at the University of Trento. He received a Laurea in Economics from the University of Modena (Italy), an MPhil from the University of Cambridge (UK), and a PhD from the European University Institute in Florence (Italy). His current research is mainly on macroeconomic theories and policies, money and financial markets, policies and institutions. In the field of macroeconomic theories, he has devoted particular attention to microeconomic foundations, with particular regard to decision-making under uncertainty, incomplete information, bounded rationality. In the monetary and financial field, his research has focused on new theories of imperfect capital markets, based on asymmetric information or on bounded rationality, and their implication for economic activity. His macro policy research has mainly concerned the debate on the Maastricht Treaty and the creation of the European Monetary Union. He has produced national and international publications in the form of monographs, contributions to collective books, and articles in academic journals.

Eric Tymoigne (Lewis and Clark College, Portland, Oregon, USA; E-mail: etymoigne@lclark.edu) received his PhD from the University of

Missouri-Kansas City (USA) with a specialization in monetary theory and financial macroeconomics. His BA and MA degrees in economic theory and policy are respectively from the Université de Bretagne Occidentale (France) and from the Université Paris-Dauphine (France). His current research agenda includes money matters (nature, history, and theory), the detection of aggregate financial fragility and its implications for central banking, and the theoretical analysis of monetary production economies. He has published in the *Journal of Post Keynesian Economics* and the *Journal of Economic Issues*, and has contributed to several edited books. He recently published a book on central banking, asset prices and financial fragility.

Charles L. Weise (Gettysburg College, USA; E-mail: cweise@gettysburg.edu) is Associate Professor of Economics at Gettysburg College in Gettysburg, Pennsylvania. He received his PhD in economics from the University of Wisconsin–Madison in 1993. He has also held positions as Assistant Professor of Economics at the College of William and Mary and visiting lecturer at Lancaster University, Lancaster, UK. He has published papers on a variety of topics in macroeconomics including nonlinear vector autoregressions, inflation episodes in OECD countries, credibility of disinflation episodes in the OECD, and the response of the Federal Reserve to signals from public pressure groups. His current research projects include political sources of the Great Inflation of the 1970s and the integration of Minskyan ideas into Wicksellian macroeconomic models.

L. Randall Wray (University of Missouri Kansas City, USA; E-mail: WrayR@umkc.edu) is senior scholar, Levy Economics Institute, a professor of economics at the University of Missouri-Kansas City and director of research at the Center for Full Employment and Price Stability. He is currently working in the areas of monetary policy, employment, and social security. Wray has published widely in journals and is the author of *Money and Credit in Capitalist Economies: The Endogenous Money Approach* and *Understanding Modern Money: The Key to Full Employment and Price Stability*. He is also the editor of *Credit and State Theories of Money: The Contributions of A. Mitchell Innes* and co-editor of *The Continuing Relevance of The General Theory: Keynes for the 21st Century*. Wray received a BA from the University of the Pacific and an MA and a PhD from Washington University in St Louis.

Simon Wren-Lewis (University of Oxford, UK; E-mail: simon.wren-lewis@ economics.ox.ac.uk) is a professor at Oxford University and a Fellow of Merton College. He began his career as an economist in H.M. Treasury. In 1981, he moved to the National Institute of Economic and Social Research, where as a Senior Research Fellow he constructed the first versions of the world model NIGEM, and as Head of Macroeconomic Research he supervised development of this and the Institute's domestic model. In 1990, he became a professor at Strathclyde University (UK), and built the UK econometric model COMPACT. From 1995 to 2006, he was a professor at Exeter University. He has published papers on macroeconomics in a wide range of academic journals including the *Economic Journal*, *European Economic Review*, and *American Economic Review*. He also wrote one of the background papers for the Treasury's 2003 assessment of its five economic tests for joining the EMU and advised the Bank of England on the development of its new macromodel. His current research focuses on the analysis of monetary and fiscal policy in small calibrated macromodels, and on equilibrium exchange rates.

Foreword

Carl E. Walsh

The last half century has seen a dramatic evolution in macroeconomics, from old-style Keynesianism, to the rational expectations revolution, to the rise of new classical economics, to the resurgence of new Keynesianism. Throughout it all, Hicks's *IS–LM* model, augmented since the 1960s by some variant of a Phillips curve, remained the dominant pedagogical device for teaching macroeconomics to undergraduates. There were good reasons for its longevity. Despite being at odds with the emphasis on micro foundations of mainstream macro theory, the *IS–LM* had two very big strengths. First, as a pedagogical device, it lent itself to a graphical presentation that fit well with the supply and demand diagrams that are the bread and butter of undergraduate microeconomic courses. With an upward sloping *LM* curve and a downward sloping *IS* curve, Hicks's framework provided a convenient structure for illustrating how financial (money market) and demand side (goods market) disturbances affected the macroeconomy.

Second, the outcomes of comparative static exercises using the *IS–LM* framework matched with most economists' understanding of the empirical evidence. Increases in the money supply produced a liquidity effect, lowering interest rates. With prices (or inflation) slow to react, the real interest rate was also reduced, stimulating aggregate demand and output. Increases in autonomous spending led to a rise in output and interest rates. Many micro-founded, equilibrium models lacked both these strengths.

The advent of the new Keynesian framework (also known as the new Neoclassical Synthesis or the New Consensus) has provided macroeconomists with a framework whose microfoundations are clear but which offers the pedagogical simplicity of the *IS–LM–AS* framework. Critically, it offers a more realistic treatment of monetary policy by treating an interest rate as the policy instrument.

This new framework will eventually dominate the way economists teach macroeconomics to undergraduates. One clear advantage of the framework, besides being more consistent with the models actually used in research and monetary analysis, is its recognition that major central banks do not determine policy by setting a path for the supply of money, as is assumed in the *IS–LM* framework. Instead, major central banks determine short-term interest rates. Since students are familiar with debates over whether the Fed, the ECB, or the Bank of England should raise or lower rates, the new framework fits with what students read in the paper, and the instructor can focus on the more critical issues: Why does a central bank raise or lower rates, and how do these rate changes affect the macroeconomy?

One consequence of treating the interest rate, rather than the money supply, as the instrument of monetary policy is that doing so makes clear that the quantity of money is an endogenous variable, an interpretation long stressed by Post Keynesian economists. More importantly, as noted above, treating the interest rate as the instrument of policy aligns the classroom model with the practice of central banks, allowing students to see better how theory can help them understand actual economic developments.

Transitions from a tried and true teaching tool to a new one, even if the new one offers significant advantages, are always difficult. Old frameworks continue to dominate most textbooks, though in recent years, several introductory and intermediate textbooks have been organized around the *IS*, Phillips curve, and interest rate policy rule framework.

Fortunately, the essays in this volume offer a clear exposition of the new approaches as well as critical appraisal of the basic model and suggestions for extension. In addition to setting out the framework, the essays offer instructors significant new tools for teaching students a macroeconomics that is relevant for understanding real-world developments, yet still accessible.

Of course, despite the great advantages of dropping the *LM* curve, models will always be too simple to capture all that is going on in real economies, a point the present financial crisis illustrates quite dramatically. Just as the oil price hikes of the 1970s led to an integration of inflation into undergraduate textbook models, the next major step will be to incorporate credit markets and risk, moving away from the single interest rate implicit in current models. Many of the essays in this volume offer ways to bring back the money and credit markets that were dropped along with the *LM* curve in the basic new Keynesian model.

CARL E. WALSH
Department of Economics
University of California
Santa Cruz, USA

Macroeconomic Theory and Macroeconomic Pedagogy: An Introduction

Giuseppe Fontana and Mark Setterfield

The purpose of this book, as its title suggests, is to reflect on the relationship between contemporary macroeconomic theory and prevailing techniques and practices in undergraduate macroeconomics education. Its primary concern is with the development of simple macroeconomic teaching models in light of recent developments in macroeconomic theory, with an eye to promoting a better understanding of current real world issues. As such, the chapters that follow focus on 'content', i.e. what students are taught and its relationship to macroeconomics as it is currently perceived and practised by the profession, rather than methods of and strategies for instruction.

Many of the chapters are intended for direct consumption by students, and are suitable for explicit introduction into the classroom. Others are aimed at instructors, with a view to influencing the way instructors think about macroeconomic theory, and hence what they will subsequently seek to teach to their students. Our hope is that the collection as a whole will inspire academic economists to reflect on the relationship between contemporary macroeconomic theory and the teaching models that they use in the classroom.[1] Put bluntly, our ambition is to influence macroeconomics education by affecting both the material that instructors currently seek to present in their classrooms, and the contents of future generations of macroeconomics textbooks.

In many ways, this is a timely project. Macroeconomics has a long and venerable history of revolutions and counter-revolutions, and since the symposium devoted to macroeconomic pedagogy that appeared in the *Journal of Economic Education* in 1996 (volume 27, issue 2), the discipline has undergone another revolution of sorts. This is associated with the emergence of the 'New Neoclassical Synthesis' or 'New Consensus' in macroeconomics, benchmark statements of which can be found in Clarida *et al.* (1999), and Woodford (2003). In its simplest form, the New Consensus is a three-equation model consisting of an *IS* curve, an accelerationist Phillips curve, and a Taylor rule. It is this last feature that points to the key innovation of the New Consensus, namely the fact that it practises 'macroeconomics without the *LM* curve' (Romer, 2000). Hence, in *IS–LM* analysis, which has been the workhorse teaching model in undergraduate textbooks for several decades, one of the foundations of the *LM* curve is an exogenously given quantity of money in circulation, determined by the central bank. In the New Consensus, however, the interest rate is understood to be the instrument of monetary policy, and as the central bank manipulates the interest rate, the quantity of money in circulation is determined as an endogenous residual.[2] In light of all this, a debate has recently emerged regarding the extent to which current undergraduate macroeconomics teaching models are well grounded in and adequately reflect the latest developments in the field. Several well known and widely cited papers – including those by Allsopp and Vines (2000), Romer (2000), Taylor (2000), Walsh (2002), Carlin and Soskice (2005), Bofinger, Mayer and Wollmerhäuser (2006), and Turner (2006) – have already attempted to 'translate' the New Consensus into forms suitable for presentation to undergraduates at either the introductory or intermediate levels. Indeed, the New Consensus has already begun to influence the content of macroeconomics textbooks, as evidenced by Sørensen and Whitta-Jacobsen (2005), Carlin and Soskice (2006), DeLong and Olney (2006), and Jones (2008).

Not surprisingly, then, much of this book is concerned with the presentation, further development and/or critique of the 3-Equation New Consensus macroeconomic model. Part I begins with an aptly-titled chapter by Wendy Carlin and David Soskice, showing how the central ideas of the New Consensus can be presented in a form that is accessible to an undergraduate audience. Drawing on their recent works (2005, 2006) the authors provide a simplified diagrammatical exposition of the 3-Equation New Consensus model. They show how this model can be used to analyse a broad range of phenomena, including current commodity price shocks. In so doing, they draw attention to two key features of the New Consensus, namely (1) its emphasis on the forward-looking behaviour of the central bank; and (2) the necessity of appealing to underlying behavioural relations when using the model for comparative static exercises. The latter is seen as a major pedagogical advantage of the model relative to its *IS–LM* based predecessor.

In Chapter 2, Simon Wren-Lewis builds on the diagrammatical exposition of the 3-Equation New Consensus model of Carlin and Soskice. He argues that current undergraduate macroeconomics can and should be updated: central to this project is expunging the *LM* curve from teaching models and re-focusing discussion of monetary policy on manipulation of the interest rate. The author shows that, in conjunction with an up-dated presentation of the *IS* curve and an expectations-augmented Phillips curve, the resulting model permits more intuitive discussion of macroeconomic outcomes and policy interventions. The result, then, is an approach that not only modernizes undergraduate macroeconomics, but also makes teaching macroeconomics easier and more effective.

The development of simple diagrams that can be used by undergraduate students to understand interest rate setting by policy-makers is also the purpose of Chapter 3 by Jagjit Chadha. The author constructs a simple monetary-macro teaching model in keeping with the principles of the New Consensus, and shows how graphical representations of this model can be used to demonstrate the appropriate monetary policy responses to a variety of demand and supply shocks, as well as dislodged inflation expectations. Particular attention is paid to the ways in which the zero lower bound problem and the operation of private financial markets may complicate these policy responses.

Chapter 4 by Roberto Tamborini is devoted to the development of a basic macroeconomic model that conveys clear and theoretically consistent ideas about the relationship between different monetary policy strategies, and the levels of output and inflation. In a break with earlier chapters, Tamborini comes to the rescue of the *LM* curve. More precisely, he seeks to re-integrate a fuller account of the monetary sector – of the sort that was common when the *LM* curve was in vogue – into a New Consensus model. This gives rise to a macro teaching model that admits both 'exogenous money' and 'endogenous money' regimes, depending on the policy choices and objectives of the central bank. Tamborini argues that this model better integrates macroeconomic theory with the material taught in monetary economics and finance, without giving up the advances in macroeconomics associated with the New Consensus.

The last two chapters of Part I provide a critical appraisal of the main theoretical, empirical and methodological propositions of the New Consensus. In Chapter 5, Philip Arestis assesses the theoretical structure and policy implications of the New Consensus model. The author focuses on six key issues of which teachers and students of the 3-Equation macroeconomics model should be explicitly aware: (1) the emphasis on inflation targeting as the main objective of central banks; (2) the purported long-run neutrality of money and monetary policy; (3) the single-minded focus on excess aggregate demand as the source of inflationary pressure in the economy; (4) the relative neglect of open-economy issues; (5) the assumed desirability of low inflation; and (6) the relative neglect of the destabilizing effects of asset price inflation. Arestis is also critical of the empirical basis of the New Consensus model, especially the interest (in)sensitivity of aggregate expenditure, and the effects of inflation targeting on observed rates of inflation. The author argues that a discussion of these theoretical and empirical issues associated with the 3-Equation New Consensus model helps to highlight the ever-evolving nature of macroeconomic theory and macroeconomic teaching.

This last point is further developed in Chapter 6 by David Colander and Casey Rothschild, who relate the evolving nature of macroeconomic theory and pedagogy to the complex nature of modern economies. Their point of departure is the oft-noted methodological inconsistency between macroeconomics education at the undergraduate and graduate levels – an inconsistency that would persist even if the content of undergraduate education were modernized along the lines recommended in preceding chapters. The authors argue that the methods and models characteristic of *both* undergraduate *and* graduate macroeconomics overlook the complexity of real-world economies. Their thesis is that, nevertheless, macroeconomics education can be rendered consistent. Specifically, Colander and Rothschild argue that both undergraduate and graduate teaching models should be presented as different but complementary approaches to the same set of issues and challenges that are presented by the intrinsic complexity of modern economies.

One major issue with the New Consensus model, an issue first discussed in Friedman's (2003) 'The *LM* Curve: A Not-So-Fond Farewell' and echoed in several of the contributions in Part I, is the disappearance of the banking sector from the standard 3-Equation New Consensus model. The New Consensus has rejected the *LM* curve and its unrealistic assumption that the central bank controls monetary aggregates. But, in so doing, it has discarded many interesting research questions about the functioning of the banking system and credit markets more generally. In the New Consensus, the central bank controls the short-run nominal interest rate. But how does it affect the myriad real interest rates in the economy? And how do these real rates influence the interest-sensitive components of aggregate demand? These questions – and answers to them – are the cornerstone of endogenous money theory, which is at the heart of the contributions to Part II of the book.

Chapter 7 by Malcolm Sawyer starts with a simple observation: treating money as an endogenous rather than exogenous variable (as in the old *IS–LM* model) has consequences for macroeconomic analysis that extend well beyond the change it imposes on the policy instrument of the central bank. The author identifies and discusses six broad themes that are affected by the endogeneity of money: (1) the measurement of money and the interest rate; (2) the operations of the banking sector; (3) the operations of the central bank; (4) the formation of aggregate demand; (5) the role of the demand for money; and (6) the nature of the inflation process. The main point that emerges from this chapter is that each of these themes must be satisfactorily addressed in order to teach successfully macroeconomics in an endogenous money environment.

Chapter 8 by Giuseppe Fontana and Mark Setterfield takes up most of Sawyer's themes. The authors build a teaching model which is a further development of both the old *IS–LM* model and the modern 3-Equation New Consensus model. In their resulting endogenous money model, the interest rate is the instrument of monetary policy, and both the behaviour in the credit market of commercial banks and the non-bank private sector, and of the behaviour of the central bank in the reserve market, are explicitly described. The model embodies a Keynesian hierarchy of markets, in which monetary and financial factors impact the goods market, which in turn determines outcomes in the labour market. In addition, the model generates both Classical and Keynesian adjustment dynamics in response to downwardly-flexible nominal wages. Fontana and Setterfield claim that these features lend their model greater generality than ostensibly similar models based on the New Consensus, making it a better teaching tool.

Chapter 9 by Peter Howells draws Part II to a close in appropriate fashion. Inspired by the work of Fontana (2003, 2006) and the diagrammatic representation of the monetary sector in Carlin and Soskice (2006), Howells aims to integrate a fully developed account of the banking sector into the standard 3-Equation New Consensus macroeconomic model. The result is an amended version of the New Consensus model, which explicitly draws on endogenous money theory. Howells puts to the test his amended New Consensus model by examining its response to shocks emanating from the real economy and the financial sector. Both types of shocks are shown to produce plausible macroeconomic outcomes. Howells concludes that these results recommend the underlying model as a tool for teaching macroeconomics in a manner that explicitly and realistically captures the structure and functioning of the banking sector and of the macro economy more generally.

A second major issue with the New Consensus – and one that is closely related to the themes raised by endogenous money theory discussed in Part II – is the absence of financial markets from the standard 3-Equation New Consensus model (Goodhart and Tsomocos, 2007; Canzoneri *et al.*, 2008). In the face of the recent turmoil in US and world financial markets, ignoring the origin of speculative excesses and panic in financial markets, together with the related probability of default and bankruptcy and its implications for banks and other major financial institutions, makes teaching undergraduate macroeconomics almost embarrassing. Certainly, this state of affairs only makes it harder for students to effect the transition from the macroeconomics of the press to the macroeconomics of the classroom. The contributions to Part III of the book seek to remedy this situation by drawing on (among other things) the contributions of the late Hyman Minsky (2008).

Chapter 10 by Marc Lavoie shows how the 3-Equation New Consensus macroeconomic model can be amended to incorporate financial issues as well as other fundamental Keynesian concerns (such as different configurations of the Phillips curve and hysteresis effects in the labour and capital markets), all of which call into question the centrality to the New Consensus of supply-determined equilibrium in the real economy. In addressing financial issues, the author focuses on the difference between the overnight rate charged by the central bank and the market interest rate charged by commercial banks. His particular interest is in the Minskyan potential for the latter to change relative to the former – as, for example, during financial crises – and the consequences of this for policy-making and aggregate activity.

This last set of issues is the starting point for Chapter 11 by Charles Weise and Robert Barbera. The aim of this chapter is to introduce the analysis of financial intermediation between borrowers, commercial and investment banks, and the central bank into the standard 3-Equation New Consensus model. Specifically, Weise and Barbera focus their attention on a major Minskyan insight, namely, the evolution of risk perceptions over the course of the business cycle as reflected in credit spreads. The result is an ingenious teaching model that places financial market dynamics between the overnight rate set by the central bank and the risk-laden commercial rate at which households and firms borrow. In this way, the chapter introduces students to the importance of finance in generating business cycles.

As is clear from what has been said above, the first two chapters of Part III seek to amend and extend New Consensus-type models by introducing financial themes that are closely related to the work of Hyman Minsky. It is fitting, then, that Chapter 12, by L. Randall Wray and Eric Tymoigne, is devoted to a fuller exploration of the financial theory of investment developed by Minsky. This theory highlights the centrality of money and finance to the dynamics of modern capitalist economies, and thus provides an alternative to contemporary teaching models, which take for granted the long-run neutrality of money and finance. Wray and Tymoigne show how the financial theory of investment gives rise to the possibility that booms will 'sow the seeds of their own destruction', possibly culminating in financial crises. The chapter thus shows how increasing financial instability can arise in the ordinary course of economic growth. This possibility is illustrated with reference to developments in the US economy.

In the standard 3-Equation New Consensus model, the central bank is supposed to change the short-run nominal interest rate with the purpose of changing the output gap so as to achieve the desired rate of inflation. This means that by changing the short-run nominal interest rate the central bank aims to affect real financial conditions in credit markets, which should, in turn, influence interest-responsive components of aggregate demand and hence current output. But perceptive students may wonder whether or not these continuous changes in real financial conditions will have long-lasting effects on the earnings of financial institutions, in addition to their expected short-run countercyclical effects? Students are taught that profits are the reward for entrepreneurial activities while wages are the compensation for labour services. Is it not the case, then, that real financial conditions are the remuneration of financial institutions for the use of their accumulated financial capital? Any answer to this question brings forth discussion of income distribution, and the potential role of the central bank as a disguised arbiter of the income claims of firms, wage-earners and financial institutions (the 'rentiers' of Classical economics). The contributions to Part IV of the book deal with this and other issues related to the basic orientation and 'message' of macroeconomic teaching models.

Chapter 13 by John Smithin has a twofold aim: to present a teachable variant of the New Consensus, and to show that a plausible alternative to this model, which differs fundamentally from the New Consensus in its description of the wage and price setting behaviour of workers and firms, results in macroeconomic outcomes and associated policy conclusions that are very much at variance with those derived from the standard 3-Equation model. The chapter also serves a valuable pedagogical purpose by demonstrating that, the current 'consensus' in monetary macroeconomics notwithstanding, there is still room in undergraduate macroeconomics for debate over how the economy operates and how policy-makers should respond to new economic conditions.

A similar pedagogical purpose characterizes Chapter 14 by Eckhard Hein and Engelbert Stockhammer. The aim of this chapter is to construct a teachable alternative to the New Consensus model that nevertheless accounts for short-run, supply-side limits to the extent of real activity. The income-generating process is demand-driven, but the inflation process – which is based on the competing claims on real income of workers, firms and rentiers, and which determines *both* the equilibrium rate of inflation *and* the functional distribution of income – imposes an upper limit on the level of activity in the short run. As in the New Consensus, this limit is only reached by virtue of the proper conduct of monetary policy, but unlike the New Consensus, it is endogenous in the medium run. Ultimately, the authors show that a portfolio of fiscal, monetary and incomes policies is required for effective macroeconomic stabilization.

Chapter 15 by Emiliano Brancaccio shows how the emerging New Consensus teaching model can be amended to broaden the horizons of undergraduates. The immediate concern of this chapter is with the increasing hegemony of 'the textbook view' in undergraduate macroeconomics, which identifies 'modern' macro as a linear outgrowth of the old Neoclassical Synthesis. This view, Brancaccio argues, admits no place for competing schools of thought in macroeconomics, inhibiting the development of critical thinking by students – and potentially concealing the distributional role of the central bank. Brancaccio shows how this can be remedied using standard teaching tools – namely, the 3-Equation New Consensus model *plus* Solow's growth theory – simply by altering the choice of exogenous and endogenous variables. The result is two very different representations of the economy and the role of policy-makers, derived from the same core analytical structure.

The book ends with Chapter 16 by Jesus Ferreiro and Felipe Serrano. These authors are concerned with the standard assumptions about decision-making and the availability of information that undergird the majority of macroeconomic models and their teaching variants. The authors highlight the fact that, in a world of full information and rational expectations, aggregate demand is irrelevant in anything other than a strictly short-run context, and the only institutions that matter (apart from competitive markets) are those that bind the state to consistent, and therefore predictable, policy interventions. Ferreiro and Serrano show that once the existence of fundamental uncertainty is recognized, both the importance of aggregate demand and the role of institutions in the economy are radically revised. Ultimately, then, their chapter serves to draw the attention of students to the vital role played by the most basic premises of macroeconomic theory in the determination of its central results and policy prescriptions.

In concluding this introduction, a few additional words about the general approach and intent of this book are in order. A core belief that runs through all of its chapters is that macroeconomics is a useful – indeed, essential – academic discipline. As the book goes to print, global finance is in the process of being torn apart. Giants of the housing market, investment banking, and the insurance sector have collapsed: Fannie Mae and Freddie Mac, Lehman Brothers, AIG, and HBOS are now household names, and for all the wrong reasons. Macroeconomic theory can help to explain the events that led to this crisis, and how policy-makers should respond. It can also suggest solutions for other current problems – from reconciling stable inflation with rapid growth and low unemployment, to revitalizing real income growth for the majority of wage-earners. But there is much more to macroeconomics besides its capacity for explaining current real-world issues. It is a fascinating and engaging subject in its own right, that can open minds to new perspectives and ideas. It can help to develop the skills associated with critical thinking, as well as contribute to the moulding of personal points of view. In short, students should be encouraged to learn macroeconomics for their own enjoyment and satisfaction, as well as to enhance their understanding of the world around them. The long-lasting ambition of this book is to contribute to the process of making macroeconomics a subject that can be read for pleasure as well as for its real-world relevance.

Notes

1. This is (or should be), of course, an on-going project for macroeconomists, and we are by no means the first to recommend it. See, for example, Froyen (1996).
2. The 'old' and the 'new' Neoclassical Syntheses may therefore appear to be diametrically opposed, but this is not altogether true. Both can be seen as emerging from essentially the same framework of analysis, under different assumptions about what the central bank chooses to make the instrument of monetary policy (the interest rate or the monetary base), as in the work of Poole (1970).

   Note, moreover, that the essential 'novelty' of the New Consensus, namely that central banks manipulate the interest rate while the private sector determines the quantity of money in circulation, is not, in fact, new, there being a long history of endogenous money theory in macroeconomics (see, for a classic statement, Moore, 1988). As will become clear in the chapters that follow, there exists a *variety* of macroeconomic traditions, and hence teaching models, that are consistent with the observation that the interest rate (rather than the quantity of money in circulation) is the instrument of monetary policy.

References

Allsopp, C. and Vines, D. (2000), 'The assessment: macroeconomic policy', *Oxford Review of Economic Policy*, 16(4), 1–32.

Bofinger, P., Mayer, E., and Wollmerhäuser, T. (2006), 'The BMW model: a new framework for teaching monetary economics', *Journal of Economic Education*, 37(1), 98–117.

Canzoneri, M., Cumby, R.E., Diba, B., and Lopez-Solido, D. (2008), 'Monetary aggregates and liquidity in a Neo-Wicksellian framework', *NBER Working Paper Series*, n. 14244.

Carlin, W. and Soskice, D. (2005), 'The 3-Equation New Keynesian Model – a graphical exposition', *Contributions to Macroeconomics*, 5(1), 1–27.

Carlin, W. and Soskice, D. (2006), *Macroeconomics: Imperfections, Institutions and Policies*, Oxford: Oxford University Press.

Carlin, W. and Soskice, D. (2005), *Macroeconomics Imperfections, Institutions and Policies*, Oxford: Oxford University Press.

Clarida, R., Galí, J., and Gertler, M. (1999), 'The science of monetary policy: a new Keynesian perspective', *Journal of Economic Literature*, 37(4), 1661–707.

DeLong, J. Bradford and Olney, Martha L. (2006), *Macroeconomics*, 2nd edn, Boston: McGraw-Hill Irwin.

Fontana, G. (2003), 'Post Keynesian approaches to endogenous money: a time framework explanation', *Review of Political Economy*, 15(3), 291–314.

Fontana, G. (2006), 'Telling better stories in macroeconomic textbooks: monetary policy, endogenous money and aggregate demand', in M. Setterfield (ed.), *Complexity, Endogenous Money and Macroeconomic Theory: Essays in Honour of Basil J. Moore*, Cheltenham, Edward Elgar, 353–67.

Friedman B.M. (2003), 'The *LM* Curve: A Not-so-fond Farewell', *NBER Working Paper Series*, n. 10123.

Froyen, R.T. (1996), 'The evolution of macroeconomic theory and implications for teaching intermediate macroeconomics', *Journal of Economic Education*, 27(2), 108–15.

Goodhart, C.A.E and Tsomocos, D.P. (2007), 'Analysis of financial stability', *Oxford Financial Research Centre*, Financial Economics WP Series, no. 4.

Jones, C.I. (2008), *Macroeconomics*, London: W.W. Norton.

Minsky, H.P. (2008; orig. 1986), *Stabilizing an Unstable Economy*, New York: McGraw-Hill.

Moore, B.J. (1988), *Horizontalists and Verticalists: The Macroeconomics of Credit Money*, Cambridge: Cambridge University Press.

Poole, W. (1970), 'Optimal choice of monetary policy instrument in a simple stochastic macro model', *Quarterly Journal of Economics*, 84(2), 197–216.

Romer, D. (2000), 'Keynesian macroeconomics without the *LM* curve', *Journal of Economic Perspectives*, 14(2), 149–69.

Sørensen, P.B. and Hans Jørgen Whitta-Jacobsen (2005), *Introducing Advanced Macroeconomics: Growth and Business Cycles*, Maidenhead: McGraw-Hill.

Taylor, J.B. (2000), 'Teaching macroeconomics at the Principles level', *American Economic Review*, 90(2), 90–4.

Turner, P. (2006), 'Teaching undergraduate macroeconomics with the Taylor-Romer model', *International Review of Economics Education*, 5(1), 73–82.

Walsh, C.E. (2002), 'Teaching Inflation Targeting: An Analysis for Intermediate Macro', *Journal of Economic Education*, 33(4): 330–46.

Woodford, M. (2003), *Interest and Prices: Foundations of a Theory of Monetary Policy*, Princeton: Princeton University Press.

Part I
The 3-Equation New Consensus Macroeconomic Model

1

Teaching Intermediate Macroeconomics using the 3-Equation Model

Wendy Carlin and David Soskice

Much teaching of intermediate macroeconomics uses the *IS−LM−AS* or *AD−AS* approach. This is far removed both from the practice of interest rate setting, inflation-targeting central banks and from the models that are taught in graduate courses. Modern monetary macroeconomics is based on what is increasingly known as the 3-equation New Keynesian model: *IS* curve, Phillips curve and interest rate-based monetary policy rule (*IS−PC−MR*). This is the basic analytical structure of Michael Woodford's book *Interest and Prices* published in 2003 and, for example, of the widely cited paper 'The New Keynesian Science of Monetary Policy' by Clarida *et al.* published in the *Journal of Economic Literature* in 1999. A recent graduate textbook treatment is Galí (2008). Much of this literature is inaccessible to undergraduates and non-specialists. Our aim is to show how this divide can be bridged in a way that retains the tractability and policy-friendliness of the old approach yet fits the institutional realities of contemporary policy-making and opens the way to the more advanced literature.

Our contribution is to develop a version of the 3-equation model that can be taught to undergraduate students and can be deployed to analyse a broad range of policy issues, including the recent credit/banking crisis and the oil and commodities price shock.[1] It can be taught using diagrams and minimal algebra. The *IS* diagram is placed vertically above the Phillips diagram, with the monetary rule shown in the latter along with the Phillips curves. We believe that our *IS−PC−MR* graphical analysis is particularly useful for explaining the optimizing behaviour of the central bank. Users can see and remember readily where the key relationships come from and are therefore able to vary the assumptions about the behaviour of the policy-maker or the private sector. In order to use the model, it is necessary to think about the economics behind the processes of adjustment. One of the reasons *IS−LM−AS* got a bad name is that it too frequently became an exercise in mechanical curve-shifting: students were often unable to explain the economic processes involved in moving from one equilibrium to another. In the framework presented here, in order to work through the adjustment process, the student has to engage in the same forward-looking thinking as the policy-maker.

The model we propose for teaching purposes is New Keynesian in its 3-equation structure and its modelling of a forward-looking optimizing central bank. A significant problem for most students in the more formal versions of the New Keynesian model is the assumption that both households (in the IS equation) and price-setting firms (in the Phillips curve) are forward looking. Our approach focuses just on a forward-looking central bank (in the Monetary or Taylor Rule) but does not incorporate forward-looking behaviour in either the *IS* curve or the Phillips curve.[2]

1 The 3-Equation Model

In this section, we set out the Carlin–Soskice (C–S) simplified version of the 3-equation model to show how it can be taught to undergraduates. Before showing how the central bank's problem-solving can be illustrated in a diagram, we set out the algebra.

1.1 Equations

The 3 equations are the IS equation $y_1 = A - ar_0$ in which real income y is a positive function of autonomous expenditure A and a negative function of the real interest rate r; the Phillips curve $\pi_1 = \pi_0 + \alpha(y_1 - y_e)$, where π is the rate of inflation and y_e, equilibrium output; and the central bank's Monetary Rule. Equilibrium output is the level of output associated with constant inflation. In a world of imperfect competition it reflects the mark-up and structural features of the labour market and welfare state.[3] We shall see that in order to make its interest rate decision, an optimizing central bank must take into account the lag in the effect of a change in the interest rate on output – the so-called policy lag – and any lag in the Phillips curve from a change in output to inflation. The key lags in the system relevant to the central bank's interest rate decision are shown in Figure 1.1. In the *IS* curve, the choice of interest rate in period zero r_0 will only affect output next period y_1 as it takes time for interest rate changes to feed through to expenditure decisions. In the Phillips curve, this period's inflation π_1 is affected by the current output gap $y_1 - y_e$ and by last period's inflation π_0. The latter assumption of inflation persistence can be justified in terms of lags in wage- and or price-setting or by reference to backward-looking expectations.

The central bank minimizes a loss function, where the government requires it to keep next period's inflation close to the target whilst avoiding large output fluctuations:

$$L = (y_1 - y_e)^2 + \beta(\pi_1 - \pi^T)^2 \quad \text{(central bank loss function)} \quad (1.1)$$

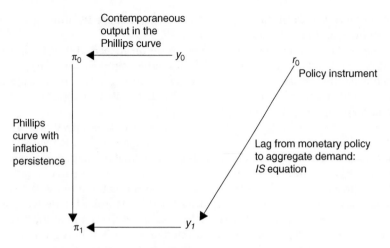

Figure 1.1 The lag structure in the C–S 3-equation model

Any deviation in output from equilibrium or inflation from target – in either direction – produces a loss in utility for the central bank. The lag structure of the model explains why it is π_1 and y_1 that feature in the central bank's loss function: by choosing r_0, the central bank determines y_1, and y_1 in turn determines π_1. This is illustrated in Figure 1.1. The critical parameter in the central bank's loss function is β: $\beta > 1$ will characterize a central bank that places less weight on output fluctuations than on deviations in inflation, and vice versa. A more inflation-averse central bank is characterized by a higher β.

The central bank optimizes by minimizing its loss function subject to the Phillips curve:

$$\pi_1 = \pi_0 + \alpha(y_1 - y_e) \quad \text{(inertial Phillips curve: PC equation)} \quad (1.2)$$

By substituting the Phillips curve equation into the loss function and differentiating with respect to y_1 (which, as we have seen in Figure 1.1, the central bank can choose by setting r_0), we have:

$$\frac{\partial L}{\partial y_1} = (y_1 - y_e) + \alpha\beta(\pi_0 + \alpha(y_1 - y_e) - \pi^T) = 0 \quad (1.3)$$

Substituting the Phillips curve back into this equation gives:

$$(y_1 - y_e) = -\alpha\beta(\pi_1 - \pi^T) \quad \text{(monetary rule: MR–AD equation)} \quad (1.4)$$

This equation is the 'optimal' equilibrium relationship in period 1 between the inflation rate chosen indirectly and the level of output chosen directly by the central bank in the current period 0 to maximize its utility given its preferences and the constraints it faces.

Here is the logic of the central bank's position in period 0: it knows π_0 and hence it can work out via the Phillips curve (since $\pi_1 = \pi_0 + \alpha(y_1 - y_e)$) what level of y_1 it has to get to – by setting the appropriate r_0 in the current period – for this equilibrium relation to hold. We shall see that there is a natural geometric way of highlighting this logic.

We can either talk in terms of the Monetary Rule or alternatively the Interest Rate Rule (sometimes called the optimal Taylor Rule), which shows the short term real interest rate relative to the 'stabilizing' or 'natural' real rate of interest, r_S, that the central bank should set now in response to a deviation of the current inflation rate from target. To find out the interest rate that the central bank should set in the current period, as well as to derive r_S we need to use the *IS* equation. The central bank can set the nominal short-term interest rate directly, but since the expected rate of inflation is given in the short run, the central bank is assumed to be able to control the real interest rate indirectly. We make use here of the Fisher equation, $i \approx r + \pi^E$. The *IS* equation incorporates the lagged effect of the interest rate on output:

$$y_1 = A - ar_0 \quad \text{(IS equation)} \tag{1.5}$$

A key concept is the stabilizing interest rate r_S, which is the interest rate that produces equilibrium output. This is defined by

$$y_e = A - ar_S \tag{1.6}$$

So subtracting this from the *IS* equation we can rewrite the *IS* equation in output gap form as:

$$y_1 - y_e = -a(r_0 - r_S) \quad \text{(IS equation, output gap form)} \tag{1.7}$$

If we substitute for π_1 using the Phillips curve in the *MR–AD* equation, we get

$$\pi_0 + \alpha(y_1 - y_e) - \pi^T = -\frac{1}{\alpha\beta}(y_1 - y_e)$$

$$\pi_0 - \pi^T = -\left(\alpha + \frac{1}{\alpha\beta}\right)(y_1 - y_e) \tag{1.8}$$

and if we now substitute for $(y_1 - y_e)$ using the *IS* equation, we get

$$(r_0 - r_S) = \frac{1}{a\left(\alpha + \frac{1}{\alpha\beta}\right)}(\pi_0 - \pi^T) \quad \text{(interest-rate rule, } IR \text{ equation)} \tag{1.9}$$

As a simple case, let $a = \alpha = \beta = 1$, so that

$$(r_0 - r_S) = 0.5(\pi_0 - \pi^T) \tag{1.10}$$

This tells the central bank how to adjust the interest rate (relative to the stabilizing interest rate) in response to a deviation of inflation from its target.

By setting out the central bank's problem in this way, we have identified the key role of forecasting: the central bank must forecast the Phillips curve and the *IS* curve it will face next period. Although the central bank observes the shock in period zero and calculates its impact on current output and next period's inflation, it cannot offset the shock in the current period because of the lagged effect of the interest rate on aggregate demand. We therefore have a 3-equation model with an optimizing central bank in which *IS* shocks affect output. As we shall see in Section 1.2, the *MR–AD* equation is the preferred formulation of policy behaviour in the graphical illustration of the model. We return to the relationship between the *MR–AD* equation and the Taylor Rule in Section 3.

1.2   Diagram: the example of an *IS* shock

We shall now explain how the 3-equation model can be set out in a diagram. A graphical approach is useful in bringing out the economic intuition at the heart of the model. It allows students to work through the forecasting exercise of the central bank and to follow the adjustment process as the optimal monetary policy is implemented.

The first step is to present two of the equations of the 3-equation model. In the lower part of Figure 1.2, the vertical Phillips curve at the equilibrium output level, y_e, is shown. We think of labour and product markets as being imperfectly competitive so that the equilibrium output level is where both wage- and price-setters make no attempt to change the prevailing real wage or relative prices. Each Phillips curve is indexed by the pre-existing or inertial rate of inflation, $\pi^I = \pi_{-1}$.

As shown in Figure 1.2, the economy is in a constant inflation equilibrium at the output level of y_e; inflation is constant at the target rate of π^T. Figure 1.2 shows the *IS* equation in the upper panel: the stabilizing interest rate, r_S, will produce a level of aggregate demand equal to equilibrium output, y_e. We now need to combine the three elements: *IS* curve, Phillips curve and the central bank's loss function to show how the central bank formulates monetary policy. To see the graphical derivation of the monetary rule equation (labelled *MR–AD*), it is useful to begin with an example.

In Figure 1.3 we assume that as a consequence of an *IS* shock the economy is initially at point *A* with output above equilibrium, i.e. $y > y_e$, and inflation of 4% above the 2% target. The central bank's job is to set the interest rate, r_0, in response to this new information about economic conditions. In order

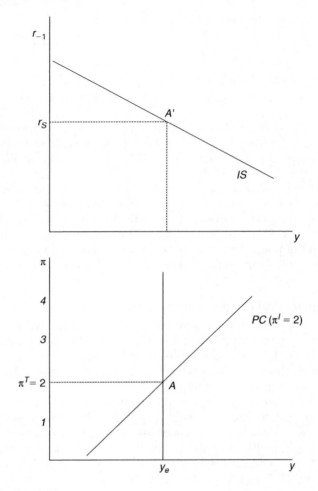

Figure 1.2   IS and *PC* curves

to do this, it must first make a forecast of the Phillips curve next period, since this will show the menu of output–inflation pairs that it can choose from by setting the interest rate now. Given that inflation is inertial, its forecast of the Phillips curve in period one will be $PC(\pi^I = 4\%)$ as shown by the dashed line in the Phillips curve diagram. The only points on this Phillips curve with inflation below 4% entail lower output. Hence, disinflation will be costly.

How does the central bank make its choice from the combinations of inflation and output along the forecast Phillips curve ($PC(\pi^I = 4\%)$)? Its choice will depend on its preferences: the higher is β the more averse it is to inflation

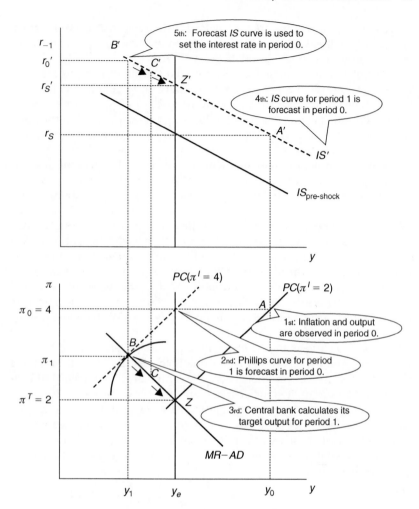

Figure 1.3 How the central bank decides on the interest rate

and the more it will want to reduce inflation by choosing a larger output gap. We show in the Appendix how the central bank's loss function can be represented graphically by loss circles or ellipses. In Figure 1.3, the central bank will choose point B at the tangency between its 'indifference curve' and the forecast Phillips curve: this implies that its desired output level in period one is y_1. In other words, y_1 is the central bank's aggregate demand target for period 1 as implied by the monetary rule. The $MR-AD$ line joins point B and the zero loss point at Z where inflation is at target and output is at equilibrium. The fourth step is for the central bank to forecast the IS curve for period one. In the example in Figure 1.3 the forecast *IS* curve is shown by the dashed line. With this *IS* curve, if an interest rate of r'_0 is set now, the level of output in period one will be y_1 as desired.

To complete the example, we trace through the adjustment process. Following the increase in the interest rate, output falls to y_1 and inflation falls. The central bank forecasts the new Phillips curve, which goes through point C in the Phillips diagram and it will follow the same steps to adjust the interest rate downwards so as to guide the economy along the *IS* curve from C' to Z'. Eventually, the objective of inflation at $\pi^T = 2\%$ is achieved and the economy is at equilibrium unemployment, where it will remain until a new shock or policy change arises. The *MR–AD* line shows the optimal inflation–output choices of the central bank, given the Phillips curve constraint that it faces.

An important pedagogical question is the name to give the monetary rule equation when we show it in the πy–diagram. What it tells the central bank at $t = 0$ is the output level that it needs to achieve in $t = 1$ if it is to minimize the loss function, given the forecast Phillips curve. Since we are explaining the model from the central bank's viewpoint at $t = 0$, what we want to convey is that the downward-sloping line in the πy–diagram shows the aggregate demand target at $t = 1$ implied by the monetary rule. We therefore use the label *MR–AD*.[4]

The *MR–AD* curve is shown in the Phillips rather than in the *IS* diagram because the essence of the monetary rule is to identify the central bank's best policy response to any shock. Both the central bank's preferences shown graphically by the indifference curve (part of the loss circle or ellipse) and the trade-off it faces between output and inflation appear in the Phillips diagram. Once the central bank has calculated its desired output response by using the forecast Phillips curve, it is straightforward to go to the *IS* diagram and discover what interest rate must be set in order to achieve this level of aggregate demand.

2   Using the Graphical Model

We now look briefly at different shocks so as to illustrate the role the following six elements play in their transmission and hence in the deliberations of policy-makers in the central bank:

(1) the inflation target, π^T
(2) the central bank's preferences, β
(3) the slope of the Phillips curve, α
(4) the interest sensitivity of aggregate demand, a
(5) the equilibrium level of output, y_e
(6) the stabilizing interest rate, r_S

A temporary aggregate demand shock is a one-period shift in the *IS* curve, whereas a permanent aggregate demand shock shifts the *IS* curve and hence r_S, the stabilizing interest rate, permanently. An inflation shock is a temporary (one-period) shift in the short-run Phillips curve. This is sometimes referred to as a temporary aggregate supply shock. An aggregate supply shock refers to a permanent shift in the equilibrium level of output, y_e. This shifts the vertical Phillips curve.

2.1 *IS* shock: temporary or permanent?

In Figure 1.3, we analysed an *IS* shock – but was it a temporary or a permanent one? In order for the central bank to make its forecast of the *IS* curve, it has to decide whether the shock that initially caused output to rise to y_0 is temporary or permanent. The terms 'temporary' and 'permanent' should be interpreted from the perspective of the central bank's decision-making horizon. In our example, the central bank took the view that the shock would persist for another period, so it was necessary to raise the interest rate to r_0' above the new stabilizing interest rate, r_s'. Had the central bank forecast that the *IS* would revert to the pre-shock *IS*, then it would have initially raised the interest rate by less since the stabilizing interest rate would have remained equal to r_S, i.e. its chosen interest rate would have been on the $IS_{\text{pre-shock}}$ curve in Figure 1.3 rather than on the *IS'* curve. This highlights one of the major forecasting problems faced by the central bank.

2.2 Supply shock

One of the key tasks of a basic macroeconomic model is to help illuminate how the main variables are correlated following different kinds of shocks. We can appraise the usefulness of the $IS-PC-MR$ model in this respect by looking at a positive aggregate supply shock and comparing the optimal response of the central bank and hence the output and inflation correlations with those associated with an aggregate demand shock. A supply shock results in a change in equilibrium output and therefore a shift in the vertical Phillips curve. It can arise from changes that affect wage- or price-setting behaviour such as a structural change in wage-setting arrangements, a change in taxation or in unemployment benefits or in the strength of product market competition, which alters the mark-up.

Figure 1.4 shows the analysis of a positive supply-side shock, which raises equilibrium output from y_e to y_e'. The vertical Phillips curve shifts to the right as does the short-run Phillips curve corresponding to inflation equal to the target (shown by the $PC(\pi^I = 2, y_e')$). The first consequence of the supply shock is a fall in inflation (from 2% to zero) as the economy goes from *A* to *B*. To decide how monetary policy should respond to this, the central bank forecasts the Phillips curve constraint ($PC(\pi^I = 0, y_e')$) for next period and chooses its optimal level of output as shown by point *C*. To raise output to this level, it is necessary to cut the interest rate in period zero to r' as shown

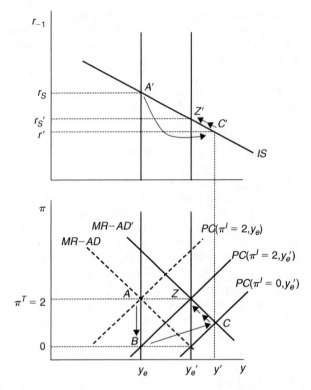

Figure 1.4   Response of the central bank to a positive supply-side shock, a rise in equilibrium output

in the *IS* diagram. (Note that the stabilizing interest rate has fallen to r_S'.) The economy is then guided along the *MR–AD'* curve to the new equilibrium at *Z*. The positive supply shock is associated initially with a fall in inflation and a rise in output – in contrast to the initial rise in both output and inflation in response to the aggregate demand shock.

2.3 Applying the model to recent macro-economic events

The economic conjuncture from August 2007 poses a good test for a macro model at the intermediate level. Two major developments affected the world economy: the credit and housing crisis emanating from the sub-prime lending behaviour of US banks and the dramatic increase in oil and commodities prices. We look first at each development in turn. The credit crisis is a negative aggregate demand shock: credit became more expensive and some classes of borrowers were excluded entirely from the market. Hence, at a given central bank interest rate, *r*, interest-sensitive spending is lower and the *IS* curve is shifted to the left. As we have seen, this requires the central bank to reduce the interest rate in order to guide the economy back to equilibrium output at target inflation. The use of temporary expansionary fiscal measures as adopted in the US in 2008 will – if successful in boosting consumption expenditure – also help to offset the leftward shift of the *IS* curve and reduce the extent to which the interest rate has to be cut. The simplest way of modelling this is as an increase in the autonomous component of aggregate demand captured in the *A* term in the *IS* equation.

Analysis of the oil and commodity price shock can also be undertaken using the 3-equation model. There are two elements to the shock: its implications for aggregate demand and for the supply-side. For countries that are net importers of oil and commodities, the price increase represents a negative aggregate demand shock: at any real interest rate, aggregate demand is depressed by the higher import bill and the *IS* curve shifts to the left. The simplest way of depicting the supply-side effects of the oil price rise is as a temporary inflation shock: the Phillips curve is shifted upwards for one period. An inflation shock requires the central bank to raise the interest rate since a spell of output below equilibrium is required to squeeze the increased inflation out of the system. In the context of an oil price shock, since aggregate demand is depressed by the higher import bill, the central bank will need to raise the interest rate by less than it otherwise would.

In the circumstances of 2008, the central bank is faced with a forecast deterioration of both constituents of its loss function. Aggregate demand and output are depressed both by the credit crisis and the oil shock, which points to a cut in the interest rate. However, the inflation shock points to the need for the interest rate to be raised. The 3-equation model illustrates the conflicting pressures on the central bank and highlights that whether it should raise or lower the interest rate depends on its judgement of the relative size and persistence of the *IS* and inflation shock effects.

The modelling of the supply-side consequences of an oil shock as a temporary inflation shock hinges on the willingness of wage- and/or price-setters in the economy to accept the reduction in real income implied by the exogenous deterioration in the economy's terms of trade. Higher real oil and commodity prices mean that output per worker available for domestic agents is lower. If domestic profit margins and or domestic real wages do not adjust to this, then the oil shock represents a supply shock that reduces equilibrium output, rather than a temporary inflation shock. This can be modelled using the supply shock analysis presented above: the *MR−AD* curve and the vertical Phillips curve shift to the left. The implications for the economy of a negative supply shock are more pessimistic than for an inflation shock because the inflation target can now only be met at higher equilibrium unemployment and lower output. In the contemporary discussion of the oil shock, the question has been discussed as to whether 'second round effects' have emerged. If wage- and/or price-setters do not accept the reduction in real

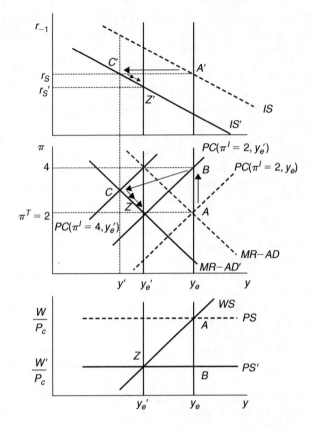

Figure 1.5 Combined credit crisis and oil price shock: lower equilibrium output

income associated with the shock, the Phillips curve for a given inertial inflation rate will shift upward as it is now indexed by the new higher equilibrium
unemployment. This is a way of illustrating such second round effects.

We use Figure 1.5 to show how the combined effect of the credit crunch
and the oil price shock can be modelled graphically. There are three panels:
the labour market is introduced as the lowest panel, with the real consumption wage on the vertical axis. The utility of wage-setters is defined in terms
of the real consumption wage, i.e. the money wage deflated by the consumer
price index. Wage-setters' behaviour is shown by the positively sloped *WS*
curve: they require a higher real consumption wage at higher employment
(output). A simple way of thinking about the wage-setting curve is that it represents a mark-up reflecting workers' bargaining power over the competitive
labour supply curve, which slopes upward to reflect the disutility of work.
By contrast, firms or price-setters care about their profits defined in terms of

the product price. On the assumption of constant labour productivity and a constant mark-up, the price-setting curve is horizontal. It shows the real consumption wage that is consistent with firms getting their required profit margin, given labour productivity and the size of the wedge between the real consumption and product wages.[5] The wedge will be affected by a change in the price of imported oil and commodities because this affects the difference between the consumer price index and the producer price index. An increase in the wedge caused by higher oil and commodity prices will be reflected in a downward shift in the price-setting real wage curve in Figure 1.5 to *PS'*.

In Figure 1.5, we analyse the case in which wage- and/or price-setters do not accept the reduction in available real income per worker implied by the higher oil prices. Had they done so, either the *WS* curve would have shifted downwards to go through point *B* or the *PS* curve would have remained unchanged at *PS* with profit margins squeezed (or some combination of the two). The failure of the real wage and profit claims of wage- and price-setters to adjust (or adjust fully) means that the oil shock leads to a fall in equilibrium output: this is shown by the shift from y_e to y'_e in Figure 1.5. The lower level of equilibrium output indicates that the only way constant inflation can prevail in the economy is to reduce the real wage claims of wage-setters by a higher level of unemployment.

As noted above, the *IS* curve in Figure 1.5 shifts to the left for two reasons – on the one hand because of the impact of the credit crisis on aggregate demand and, on the other, because of the implications for aggregate demand of the higher prices of oil and commodities. For illustrative purposes, the combined effect is shown by *IS'*. In the example shown in the diagram, the *IS* shift is sufficiently large that the central bank does not have to change the interest rate in order to achieve its desired level of output *y'* on the *MR–AD'* at point *C*, and is therefore at point *C'* on the *IS'* curve. The central bank will then lower the interest rate on the path from *C'* to the new stabilizing interest rate, r'_s. In the central panel, inflation will gradually fall back its target level (*C* to *Z*) and output will stabilize at the new lower equilibrium level (point *Z*).[6]

In Figure 1.6 the combined effect of the credit crisis and oil shock is illustrated using the more optimistic assumption that there is no deterioration in equilibrium output. This is shown graphically in the lower panel, where in contrast to Figure 1.5, there is a downward shift of the wage-setting curve to *WS'*. This may be the result of an agreement amongst unions to exercise wage restraint or alternatively, if the wage-setting curve is vertical (e.g. inelastic labour supply), there will also be no change in equilibrium output. The impact of the oil shock on the supply side takes the form of a one-off upward shift in the Phillips Curve to $PC(\pi^I = 2\%; \varepsilon = 2\%)$, where ε is the inflation shock. This is illustrated in the middle panel. By comparing the middle panel of Figure 1.5 with that of Figure 1.6, one can see that in each case there is a new Phillips curve going through point *B* with an inflation rate of 4% at

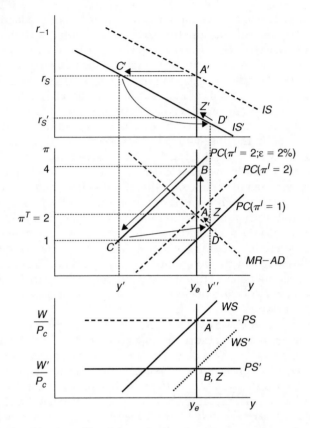

Figure 1.6 Combined credit crisis and oil price shock: unchanged equilibrium output

the initial output level. As before, the effects on aggregate demand are illustrated by the shift of the *IS* curve to *IS'*. As a consequence of the combined shocks, output falls to y' and inflation drops from 4% to 1%. The economy is at point *C* in the middle panel. The central bank forecasts the new Phillips curve to be the one labelled $PC(\pi^I = 1\%)$. It must therefore cut the interest rate (below r'_s in the upper panel) so as to steer the economy from point *D* back to target inflation and equilibrium output at point *Z*, which coincides with the economy's starting point at *A*.

For both cases illustrated in Figures 1.5 and 1.6, it is a useful exercise to experiment with a combination where the *IS* shift is smaller relative to the Phillips curve shift than the one shown. This highlights the debates in the various central banks around the world as to whether interest rates should be raised or lowered in response to the credit crisis and oil shock.

In the example shown, the *IS* shift is substantial and squeezes inflation hard; with a smaller negative *IS* shock, the central bank would have to do more to eliminate the rise in inflation and a rise in interest rates would be observed.

We see that the initial consequences for the economy of the credit and oil crises are lower output and higher inflation in both of the cases illustrated in this section. Given the presence of an inflation-targeting central bank, target inflation is regained in each case but unless the implications for real incomes of the oil shock are accepted by private sector agents, a higher rate of unemployment will be required to ensure constant inflation at the target rate.

2.4   IS shock: the role of the interest-sensitivity of aggregate demand

In the next experiment (Figure 1.7), we keep the supply side of the economy and the central bank's preferences fixed and examine how the central bank's response to a permanent aggregate demand shock is affected by the sensitivity of aggregate demand to the interest rate. It is assumed that the economy starts off with output at equilibrium and inflation at the target rate of 2%. The equilibrium is disturbed by a positive aggregate demand shock such as improved buoyancy of consumer expectations, which is assumed by the central bank to be permanent. Two post-shock *IS* curves are shown in the upper panel of Figure 1.7: the more-interest sensitive one is the flatter one labelled *IS''*.

The consequence of output above y_e is that inflation rises above target – in this case to 4% (point B). This defines the Phillips curve ($PC(\pi^I = 4)$) along which the central bank must choose its preferred point for the next period: point C. The desired level of aggregate demand depends only on the aspects of the economy depicted in the Phillips diagram, i.e. the supply side and the central bank's preferences and hence is the same for each economy. However, by going vertically up to the *IS* diagram, we can see that the central bank must raise the interest rate by less in response to the shock if aggregate demand is rather responsive to a change in the interest rate (as illustrated by the flatter *IS* curve).

2.5   How central bank inflation aversion and the slope of the Phillips curve affect interest rate decisions

To investigate how structural features of the economy such as the degree of inflation aversion of the central bank and the responsiveness of inflation to the output gap impinge on the central bank's interest rate decision, we look at the central bank's response to an inflation shock. A one-period shift in the Phillips curve could occur as a result, for example, of an agricultural disease outbreak that temporarily interrupts supply and pushes inflation above the target level.

We focus attention on the consequences for monetary policy of different degrees of inflation aversion on the part of the central bank (β) and on the

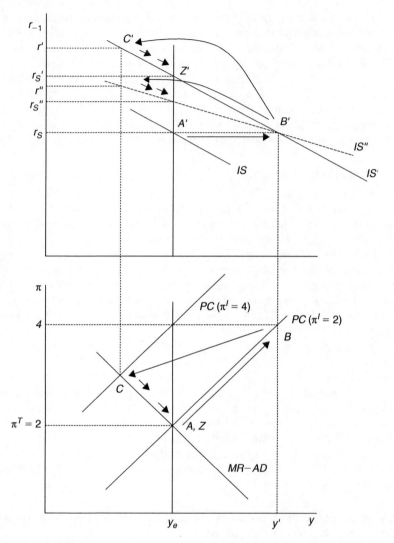

Figure 1.7 The monetary policy response to a permanent *IS* shock: the role of the slope of the *IS* curve

responsiveness of inflation to output as reflected in the slope of the Phillips curve (α). We assume the economy is initially in equilibrium with inflation at the central bank's target rate of 2% and experiences a sudden rise in inflation to 4%. The Phillips curve in Figure 1.8 shifts to $PC(\pi^I = 4\%)$.

From the *MR–AD* equation ($(y_1 - y_e) = -\alpha\beta(\pi_1 - \pi^T)$) and from the geometry in Figure 1.8, it is clear that if the indifference curves are circles (i.e. $\beta = 1$)

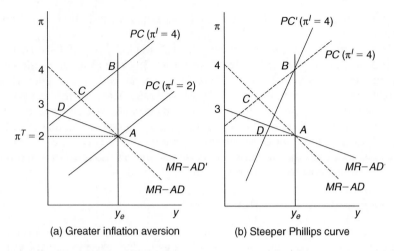

Figure 1.8 Inflation shock: the effect of (a) greater inflation aversion of the central bank and (b) steeper Phillips curve

and if the Phillips curve has a gradient of one (i.e. $\alpha = 1$), the *MR–AD* line is downward sloping with a gradient of minus one. It follows that the *MR–AD* line will be *flatter* than this either if the weight on inflation in the central bank's loss function is greater than one ($\beta > 1$) or if the Phillips curves are steeper, i.e. if inflation is more responsive to a change in output ($\alpha > 1$). This is illustrated in Figure 1.8 where the flatter *MR–AD* line, labelled *MR–AD'*, in the left hand panel reflects a more inflation-averse central bank and in the right hand panel, a steeper Phillips curve. In each case the comparison is with the neutral case of $\alpha = \beta = 1$.

Using the diagram underlines the fact that although the *MR–AD* curve is flatter in both cases, the central bank's reaction to a given inflation shock is quite different. In each case, the inflation shock takes the economy to point *B* on the vertical Phillips curve. In the left hand panel, the flatter *MR–AD* curve is due to greater inflation-aversion on the part of the central bank. Such a central bank will always wish to cut output by more in response to a given inflation shock (choosing point *D*) as compared with the neutral case of $\beta = 1$ (where point *C* will be chosen).

In the right hand panel, we keep $\beta = 1$ and examine how the central bank's response to an inflation shock varies with the steepness of the Phillips curve. When $\alpha = 1$, the central bank's optimal point is *C*, whereas we can see that if the Phillips curve is steeper (labelled *PC'*), the central bank cuts aggregate demand by *less* (point *D*). The intuition behind this result is that a steeper Phillips curve means that the central bank has to 'do less' in response to a given inflation shock since inflation will respond sharply to the fall in output associated with tighter monetary policy.

The examples in Figure 1.8 and Figure 1.7 highlight that if we hold the central bank's preferences constant, common shocks will require different optimal responses from the central bank if the parameters α or a differ. This is relevant to the comparison of interest rate rules across countries and to the analysis of monetary policy in a common currency area. For example, in a monetary union, unless the aggregate supply and demand characteristics that determine the slope of the Phillips curve and the *IS* curve in each of the member countries are the same, the currency union's interest rate response to a common shock will not be optimal for all members.

3   Lags and the Taylor Rule

An optimal Taylor Rule is a policy rule that tells the central bank how to set the current interest rate in response to shocks that result in deviations of inflation from target or output from equilibrium or both in order to achieve its objectives. In other words, $(r_0 - r_S)$ responds to $(\pi_0 - \pi^T)$ and $(y_0 - y_e)$, for example:

$$r_0 - r_S = 0.5(\pi_0 - \pi^T) + 0.5(y_0 - y_e) \quad \text{(Taylor rule)} \tag{1.11}$$

We have already derived the optimal Taylor-type rule for the 3-equation C–S model:

$$(r_0 - r_S) = \frac{1}{a\left(\alpha + \frac{1}{\alpha\beta}\right)}(\pi_0 - \pi^T) \quad \text{(IR equation, C–S model)} \tag{1.12}$$

which with $a = \alpha = \beta = 1$, gives

$$r_0 - r_S = 0.5(\pi_0 - \pi^T) \tag{1.13}$$

Two things are immediately apparent: first, only the inflation and not the output deviation is present in the rule and, second, as we have seen in the earlier examples, all the parameters of the 3-equation model matter for the central bank's response to a rise in inflation. If each parameter is equal to one, the weight on the inflation deviation is one half. For a given deviation of inflation from target, and in each case, comparing the situation with that in which $a = \alpha = \beta = 1$, we have

- a more inflation averse central bank ($\beta > 1$) will raise the interest rate by more
- when the *IS* is flatter ($a > 1$), the central bank will raise the interest rate by less

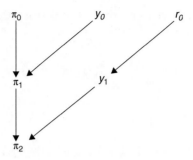

Figure 1.9 Double lag structure in the 3-equation model

- when the Phillips curve is steeper ($\alpha > 1$), the central bank will raise the interest rate by less.

In order to derive a Taylor Rule in which both the inflation and output deviations are present, it is necessary to modify the lag structure of the three equation C–S model. Specifically, it is necessary to introduce an additional lag: in the Phillips curve, i.e. the output level y_1 affects inflation a period later, π_2. This means that it is y_0 and not y_1 that is in the Phillips curve for π_1.

The double lag structure is shown in Figure 1.9 and highlights the fact that a decision taken today by the central bank to react to a shock will only affect the inflation rate two periods later, i.e. π_2. When the economy is disturbed in the current period (period zero), the central bank looks ahead to the implications for inflation and sets the interest rate r_0 so as to determine y_1, which in turn determines the desired value of π_2. As the diagram illustrates, action by the central bank in the current period has no effect on output or inflation in the current period or on inflation in a year's time.

Given the double lag, the central bank's loss function contains y_1 and π_2 since it is these two variables it can choose through its interest rate decision:[7]

$$L = (y_1 - y_e)^2 + \beta(\pi_2 - \pi^T)^2 \tag{1.14}$$

and the three equations are:

$$\pi_1 = \pi_0 + \alpha(y_0 - y_e) \quad \text{(Phillips curve)}$$
$$y_1 - y_e = -a(r_0 - r_S) \quad \text{(IS)} \tag{1.15}$$
$$\pi_2 - \pi^T = -\frac{1}{\alpha\beta}(y_1 - y_e) \quad \text{(MR–AD)}$$

By repeating the same steps as we used to derive the interest rate rule in section 2, we can derive a Taylor rule:

$$(r_0 - r_S) = \frac{1}{a\left(\alpha + \frac{1}{\alpha\beta}\right)}[(\pi_0 - \pi^T) + \alpha(y_0 - y_e)] \qquad (1.16)$$

If $a = \alpha = \beta = 1$, then

$$(r_0 - r_S) = 0.5(\pi_0 - \pi^T) + 0.5(y_0 - y_e) \qquad (1.17)$$

Implicitly, the Taylor Rule incorporates changes in the interest rate that are required as a result of a change in the stabilizing interest rate (in the case of a permanent shift in the *IS* or of a supply-side shift): r_S in the rule should therefore be interpreted as the post-shock stabilizing interest rate.

It is often said that the relative weights on output and inflation in a Taylor Rule reflect the central bank's preferences for reducing inflation as compared with output deviations. However, we have already seen in the single lag version of the model that although the central bank cares about both inflation and output deviations, only the inflation deviation appears in the interest rate rule. Although both the output and inflation deviations are present in the *IR* equation for the double lag model, the *relative* weights on inflation and output depend only on α, the slope of the Phillips curve. The relative weights are used *only* to forecast next period's inflation. The central bank preferences determine the interest rate response to next period's inflation (as embodied in the slope of the *MR* curve). Another way to express this result is to say that the output term only appears in the *IR* equation because of the lag from a change in output to a change in inflation.

4 Conclusions

The graphical 3-equation (C–S) model is a replacement for the standard *IS*–*LM*–*AS* or *AD*–*AS* model and has a number of features that distinguish it from other models that replace the *LM* with a monetary policy rule.[8] It conforms with the view that monetary policy is conducted by forward-looking central banks and provides undergraduate students and non-specialists with the tools for analysing a wide range of macroeconomic disturbances. The graphical approach helps illuminate the role played by the structural characteristics on the aggregate supply and demand sides of the economy and by the central bank's preferences in determining the central bank's optimal interest rate response to shocks.

By setting out a simple version of the three-equation model, we can see the role played by frictions in the economy. An inflation shock entails costly adjustment in the economy when inflation is inertial. When aggregate demand responds to interest rate changes with a lag and inflation is inertial, the central bank will not be able to offset aggregate demand and aggregate supply shocks immediately and adjustment will therefore be costly. If, in addition, the response of inflation to output is lagged, the central bank will have to forecast the Phillips curve a further period ahead and the Taylor Rule will take its familiar form to include contemporaneous inflation and output shocks. The 3-equation (C–S) model provides access to contemporary debates in the more specialized monetary macroeconomics literature. As shown in Carlin and Soskice (2005), it is straightforward to demonstrate the origin of the time-inconsistency problem using the graphical approach.

All modelling in economics needs to be taken with a pinch of salt. Our purpose is to provide a simple tool-kit for analysing most common situations. Three concluding remarks are important: (1) In this chapter, we do not discuss in any detail how y_e is derived: the example shown in Figure 1.5 indicates how changes in the real cost of raw materials, including food and energy, are reflected in the interaction of price-setting and wage-setting real wage curves. The structural effects of tax changes can be shown in a similar way, as can shifts in productivity and institutional and policy characteristics of the labour and product markets. (2) Autonomous demand A is probably the most difficult component to forecast particularly when household and business expectations are changing. And the ability of the CB to 'pick' future output by current changes in r is most suspect under such volatile conditions. Finally (3) the chapter focuses on the closed economy. Although we have introduced the analysis of an oil price shock, we have not presented a full model of the open economy to include the role of exchange rate determination. As we show in our textbook (2006), the role of the real exchange rate in the open economy leads to some important changes in analysis.

Appendix 1.1   The central bank's loss function: graphical representation

The geometry of the central bank's loss function can be shown in the Phillips curve diagram. The loss function

$$L = (y_1 - y_e)^2 + \beta(\pi_1 - \pi^T)^2 \tag{1.18}$$

is simple to draw. With $\beta = 1$, each 'indifference curve' is a circle with (y_e, π^T) at its centre (see Figure 1.10(a)). The loss declines as the circle gets smaller. When $\pi = \pi^T$ and $y = y_e$, the circle shrinks to a single point (called the 'bliss point') and the loss is at a minimum at zero. With $\beta = 1$, the central bank is indifferent between inflation 1% above (or below) π^T and output 1% below (or above) y_e. They are on the same loss circle.

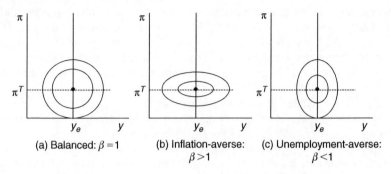

Figure 1.10   Central bank loss functions: utility declines with distance from the 'bliss point'

Only when $\beta = 1$, do we have indifference *circles*. If $\beta > 1$, the central bank is indifferent between (say) inflation 1% above (or below) π^T and output 2% above (or below) y_e. This makes the indifference curves ellipsoid as in Figure 1.10(b). A central bank with less aversion to inflation ($\beta < 1$) will have ellipsoid indifference curves with a vertical rather than a horizontal orientation (Figure 1.10(c)). In that case, the indifference curves are steep indicating that the central bank is only willing to trade off a given fall in inflation for a smaller fall in output than in the other two cases.

Notes

1. This chapter is based on a section of Carlin and Soskice (2005).
2. Both extensions are provided in Chapter 15 of Carlin and Soskice (2006).
3. A more detailed discussion is provided in Carlin and Soskice (2006) Chapters 2, 4 and 15.
4. It would be misleading to label it *AD* thus implying that it is the *actual AD* curve in $\pi_1 y_1$–space because the actual *AD* curve will include any aggregate demand shock in $t = 1$. If aggregate demand shocks in $t = 1$ are included, the curve ceases to be the curve on which the central bank bases its monetary policy in $t = 0$. On the other hand, if an aggregate demand shock in $t = 1$ is excluded – so that the central bank can base monetary policy on the curve – then it is misleading to call it the *AD* schedule; students would not unreasonably be surprised if an *AD* schedule did not shift in response to an *AD* shock.
5. A formal derivation of the price-setting curve to reflect imported materials is provided in Carlin and Soskice (2006) footnote 7, pp. 396–7.
6. Note that if the central bank does not recognize that the equilibrium level of output has fallen and continues to target an output level of y_e, the economy will end up at the intersection of vertical line above y_e' and the initial *MR–AD* curve. Inflation will be constant but it will be higher than the target rate. This is an example of so-called inflation bias and is examined in more depth in Carlin and Soskice (2005).

7. For clarity when teaching, it is probably sensible to ignore the discount factor, i.e. we assume $\delta = 1$.
8. The differences are set out in Carlin and Soskice (2005).

References

Carlin, W. and Soskice, D. (2005), 'The 3-Equation New Keynesian Model – A Graphical Exposition', *Contributions to Macroeconomics*, 5(1), art. 13, 1–36.

Carlin, W. and Soskice, D. (2006), *Macroeconomics: Imperfections, Institutions and Policies*, Oxford: Oxford University Press.

Clarida, R., Galí, J., and Gertler, M. (1999), 'The Science of Monetary Policy: A New Keynesian Perspective', *Journal of Economic Literature*, 37(4), 1661–707.

Galí, J. (2008), *Monetary Policy, Inflation, and the Business Cycle: An Introduction to the New Keynesian Framework*, Princeton: Princeton University Press.

Woodford, M. (2003), *Interest and Prices: Foundations of a Theory of Monetary Policy*, Princeton: Princeton University Press.

2
Bringing Undergraduate Macroeconomics Teaching Up to Date

Simon Wren-Lewis[1]

1 Introduction

I have taught a core graduate macroeconomics course ever since I became an academic in 1990, and I often start it by saying that the subject matter is pretty similar to undergraduate macroeconomics: what determines inflation, output, the exchange rate, etc. The difference, I suggest, is that the macroeconomics you learn as a graduate student is only slightly out of date, whereas the macroeconomics taught at undergraduate level is 30 years out of date. I say this in a joking way, but unfortunately the statement contains more than a grain of truth.

I find teaching *IS/LM* to undergraduate students embarrassing. At best I can say that a monetary policy that involved a fixed value for money is how some monetary authorities *tried* to operate for a few years in the 1980s. To good students I can say that it's similar to what would happen if the monetary authorities had a price level target. But why subject students to what is at best a piece of economic history, when it is actually quite difficult to learn.[2]

We have to throw out the *LM* curve. When we do this, a lot of other outdated and unhelpful apparatus must also either disappear, or at least be downgraded in importance. The *AS/AD* framework is an inferior tool to the Phillips curve, and survives in part because the *AD* curve can be derived from the *LM* curve. The Mundell–Fleming model, with its confusing three curve diagrams, becomes largely redundant once the *LM* curve disappears.

One feature of all these pieces of apparatus is that students find it difficult to connect with them. I am sure it turns many off macroeconomics. In contrast, the undergraduate lectures of mine that are always well received (and exam answers best written) involve intertemporal consumption, which is at the heart of modern macroeconomics. So we teach outdated stuff that is difficult and remote for students, and we sideline what is modern, relevant, and easy for students to relate to. No wonder there is a shortage of macroeconomists. Teaching macroeconomics – as the profession currently sees the subject – need not be difficult, it can be fun and engage students.

In this essay I want to suggest how undergraduate macroeconomics can be taught in a way that is not 30, or even 10 years out of date. However, I have to begin in Section 2 by outlining in rather more detail why the *LM* curve has to go, and what the consequences of this might be. These arguments appear to me compelling, and similar points have been put forward by far more eminent practitioners (see Romer (2000) and Taylor (2000) for example). However they raise an obvious question, which is why the *LM* curve continues to survive. Section 3 is more positive, and makes a number of suggestions about what should take the place of *IS/LM* at the undergraduate level. The discussion is based around the 'three-equation model' in Carlin and Soskice (2006), but it contains a number of ideas about how this framework can be augmented and improved, in the context of both introductory and more advanced undergraduate macro courses. Section 4 concludes with a summary in the form of ideal course outlines.

2   Why the *LM* Curve has to Go

There have been numerous attacks on, and defences of, *IS/LM* over the years, which raise many interesting and important issues (see, for example, Solow (1984)). In the present context I do not believe it is necessary to address these issues, because I would argue that my primary concern – that the *LM* curve does not reflect what monetary authorities actually do – is fatal enough.

For the last two decades, most monetary authorities have used a short term interest rate as their main policy instrument. They have moved interest rates in an effort to control inflation and output. At best, changes in the stock of money have been one of a number of indicators that they might have looked at as a guide to what might happen to output and inflation in the future. They have not targeted the money stock.

Even the die-hard monetarists that I occasionally meet do not suggest that we should go back to targeting the money supply. (Instead, they tell me that monetarism was really all about inflation targeting using monetary policy, and that we are all monetarists now.) Yet with *IS/LM*, the first macro model that most students are taught assumes that the money stock is targeted, and targeted successfully. It's a bit like teaching medics in their first year the advantages and techniques of blood letting for curing various diseases.[3]

Teaching *IS/LM* has two additional drawbacks, besides its irrelevance. First, I find it tends to obscure the fact that monetary policy involves a choice – in the case of the *IS/LM* model a choice of whether to change the money supply or not. Thus, too many students end up believing that fiscal policy is always and inevitably crowded out by higher interest rates. Second, students find it understandably difficult to translate the analysis into one where inflation is positive rather than zero. This problem becomes particularly acute when we move to traditional *AS* and *AD* curves.

AS/AD implies that policy just needs to match aggregate demand to the position of the vertical *AS* curve, and the economy will stabilize. Prices have reached a new steady state, so inflation is back to zero. They later learn using a Phillips curve that returning output to its natural rate will just stabilize the inflation rate, so some deflation may be required to return inflation to target. Once again, we needlessly confuse. (Guest (2003) makes a similar point.) For a significant minority of students, I also find that *AS/AD* curves encourage them to make illegitimate links between macroeconomics and the supply and demand curves of a simple market.

Confusion is again encouraged when we open the economy out, and teach 'Mundell–Fleming' with three curves in interest rate output space (the third typically being a horizontal Uncovered Interest Parity line). The student has to remember which curve is endogenous, and therefore which has to shift to go through the equilibrium defined by the other two. In one case (fixed exchange rates) this needlessly complicates a very simple story, while in the other it can be pretty misleading. Under fixed exchange rates, Uncovered Interest Parity (UIP) implies world interest rates tie down domestic rates, so output just depends on the position of the *IS* curve. Why use three curves, when one will do? Is it that important what happens to the money supply? Under floating rates, the *IS* curve first moves out, as we undertake an expansionary fiscal policy (say), and then moves back, as an appreciation crowds this out. This is, of course, a result that depends crucially on the assumption of a fixed money supply, yet the danger is that students remember 'fiscal policy is ineffective', without this crucial caveat. (It is also a result that can be demonstrated by just writing down a money demand equation, and noting that if you fix all the variables besides output, then output cannot change.)

From the above it might seem that by abandoning the *LM* curve, we lose a good deal of standard macro theory: i.e. *AS/AD* analysis and Mundell–Fleming. In fact we lose even more – the money multiplier also goes, for reasons succinctly put in Goodhart (2008). But, as I will suggest below, we already have an apparatus which can, at least in principle, replace it – it is the apparatus that we actually use when teaching graduate students macro and in advising on policy.

The *IS* curve, in contrast, tells a basic truth and therefore survives. Of course, there is a lot that is left out when we draw an inverse relationship between the current interest rate and the current level of output, although at least without the *LM* curve we can make this the real interest rate on the vertical axis. However, I do wonder whether the standard approach to deriving the *IS* curve is both too formalistic and potentially misleading.

The way the majority of students first encounter the *IS* curve is a combination of interest rate sensitive investment, and a multiplier. There are two problems with this account in relation to how we actually think economies work: multipliers are at best small, and consumption also depends on interest rates. Below I advocate using the two-period consumption problem as an alternative derivation of the *IS* curve, which I believe students would understand much more easily.

There is one more charge that I would level at the door of *IS/LM* , and that is that its opaqueness diverts first year students and their teachers away from a far more important feature of Keynesian economics, which is that aggregate demand determines output when prices are sticky. If we spent more time explaining why this might be, I think it would be easier for students to understand the relationship between short-run and medium-run analysis.

If the case against the *LM* curve is so strong, two related questions naturally arise: why do many good macroeconomists continue to teach it, and why does it dominate first year texts and almost dominate second year texts? (Even the textbook by Carlin and Soskice, which in my view uses a far more appropriate model, feels obliged to also go through *IS/LM*, and retains Mundell–Fleming.) Probably the second question answers the first. It is very difficult, and possibly foolish, to attempt to teach macroeconomics to first- and second-year undergraduates without strong back-up from a textbook.

Of course, if using the *LM* curve totally distorted macroeconomic theory, then macroeconomists at the forefront of the discipline, like Mankiw, would not write textbooks that are based on it. In a sense the problem is that using the *LM* curve gives us answers that are kind of OK most of the time. Consider a positive demand shock. With *IS/LM* output increases, and interest rates go up. As shocks to the *IS* curve are in reality not killed immediately through monetary policy, using the *LM* curve gives us a realistic answer (both interest rates *and* output rise). So, for much of what we do in the classroom, pretending that the authorities fix money gives us results which are not grossly misleading.

But, as I argue below, there is a clearly superior apparatus that does a better job in a simpler way. So why in textbooks like Mankiw does this apparatus appear in a piecemeal fashion *after IS/LM*, *AS/AD*, etc. In Carlin and Soskice, where it does play a much more central role, it still appears after a chapter on *IS/LM*! I do not know the answer to this question, perhaps because I have never written a textbook. However, I suspect that if I ever did write a textbook, my publisher would be the first to point out that by not leading with *IS/LM* I was in danger of seriously diminishing the market for my book. Even if a significant segment of the market was made up of active macroeconomics researchers who were pained by the lack of correspondence between the macro they taught and the macro they used, would this group outweigh the market segment made up of teachers who were not primarily macroeconomists and learnt their macro 30 years ago?

3 The Alternative to *IS/LM*

To teach basic business cycle macro, I believe we need just two relationships: the *IS* curve and the Phillips curve. If we want to endogenize monetary policy we could add a monetary rule. This is the three-equation model that should replace *IS/LM* and *AS/AD*. Guest (2003) calls this the Taylor–Romer model, after Romer (2000) and Taylor (2000).

For anyone unconvinced that this model can do the job better than *IS/LM*, I can only refer them to the textbook *Macroeconomics: Markets, Imperfections and Institutions* by Carlin and Soskice. Rather than repeat what is there, I want in this section to attempt to move the discussion one step forward by outlining different aspects of that model, and the issues that teaching it brings to the fore. Inevitably this will involve me in some cases suggesting how I would do things differently from this text, but I want to emphasize that I'm only able to do this because their presentation – unlike *IS/LM* – represents a clear and sensible starting point. I use Carlin and Soskice as the main text in the second-year lectures I give to Oxford undergraduates.

The core piece of apparatus in Carlin and Soskice's presentation is in fact two diagrams, one above the other. The lower diagram draws a Phillips curve and a monetary policy rule in inflation and output space, and a diagram above draws an *IS* curve in output/interest rate space. I think this works better than attempting to utilize one diagram (as in Guest (2003) or Turner (2006)), because the clarity this brings outweighs any advantage that trying to do everything in a single diagram might have.

The following discussion starts by going through each of the equations in this three-equation model: the *IS* curve, the Phillips curve and the monetary rule. I then talk about the problems that arise in opening up this model. Finally I deal with how to locate this Keynesian model of the business cycle within a medium term analysis of the macroeconomy. At each stage I try and distinguish what I would teach as part of a first year course, and what should be part of a more advanced undergraduate course.

3.1 Microfounding the *IS* curve

I noted above my misgivings about the traditional Keynesian derivation of the *IS* curve. In particular, I think students find it difficult to relate to investment decisions, or even aggregate output. In contrast, I find that students enjoy lectures on intertemporal consumption, and can easily relate to the ideas there. The obvious conclusion is to replace the former by the latter, particularly as intertemporal consumption is perhaps the central relationship in modern macroeconomics.

Of course what I have in mind here is not the multi-period version of the model solved using dynamic optimization techniques, but the simple two-period model. This model is finding its way into macro texts (e.g. Mankiw (2007)) but it is not normally given the prominence that I am suggesting here. Let me elaborate on why I think it would be good to start students off in this way.

Only the keenest of students regularly read the *Financial Times*. Almost none have ever had to find a full time job, and encountered the difference between a strong and weak labour market. The business cycle is something that, at best, they have heard their parents talk about. They have never had to decide whether to undertake an investment project, and therefore compared returns to the cost of capital.

However, nearly every student has had to take out a large student loan. Most are concerned about this debt 'hanging over them', and many are having to decide on whether to undertake additional borrowing. Should they be running up an overdraft in anticipation of that highly paid job that awaits them, or should they not? So the idea of borrowing or lending to smooth out consumption directly relates to something that is central to their current experience.

I often start teaching the two-period consumption model (at whatever level) with a little quiz. Imagine you have just heard that a previously unknown relative has left you £10,000. Would you spend it all this year, half this year and half next, etc etc. I always get a full range of responses from the class, and I promise that after a lecture or two they will know whether their response was rational or not. Although we may only formally go through the two-period case, students easily see the generalization to their life cycle, and they can also grasp the impact of credit constraints on the model, because most of them are subject to these constraints.

I also like starting this way because it shows up a key limitation of the basic model: it sidesteps the problem of uncertainty. For a large number of students consumption smoothing is constrained not by lack of credit, or low expectations of future income, but by a risk averse attitude to the uncertainty of future income. I think it is good if students can easily remember a model's deficiencies as well as its advantages.

So my suggestion is that the two-period consumption model forms the basis for the *IS* curve. Of course, to do this we need to undertake what is probably the most difficult piece of analysis with the two-period model, which is to tilt the budget line. And what if the income effect dominates the substitution effect? There are three points to make here. First, the net effect of interest rates on current consumption is not just the combination of income and substitution effects, but also the impact of interest rates on total wealth. In other words, we pivot the budget constraint not at an axis, but at the current endowment. (See Figure 2.1.) Second, to use this model for the *IS* curve, period 2 is clearly much longer than period 1 (which is the 'current period'), so the pivot point is much closer to the period 2 axis. In this case, almost certainly current consumption falls. Third, if students are taught this two-period model before they are familiar with income and substitution effects, there is no necessity to invoke them in order to motivate a downward sloping *IS* curve.

I see no reason why this analysis could not be an early part of a first-year macroeconomics course. The analysis can then be revisited in subsequent years, perhaps formally adding credit constraints by drawing a kinked budget

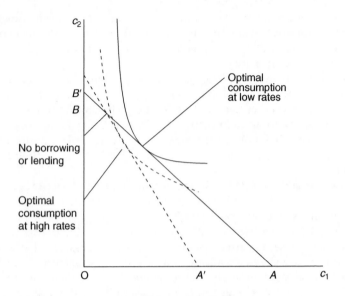

Figure 2.1   Using the two-period model to get an *IS* curve

line, and/or presenting the optimization problem in algebraic terms using a simple (e.g. log) utility function.

In Figure 2.1, the solid lines represent a low interest rate case, and the dashed lines a high interest rate case. The length OA or OA' represents total discounted wealth (human capital plus any initial financial wealth) in the first period, and length OB or OB' is this times the real interest rate. Where the two budget lines intersect represents the outcome if they undertake no borrowing or lending: it is close to the vertical axis to indicate that the first period is short relative to the second. The diagram is drawn so that in both cases consumers want to borrow to consume more than their income in period 1, but this borrowing is less at high interest rates.

3.2   The Phillips curve and expectations in macroeconomics

The core analysis in Carlin and Soskice uses what can be described simply as a 'backward looking' Phillips curve, where inflation depends on lagged inflation as well as the output/unemployment gap. I think this is appropriate for two reasons. First, it is easier to teach than its New Keynesian counterpart, as we will discuss shortly. Second, it does help explain two important stylized facts, which are that disinflations have invariably been costly, and the appearance of Phillips curve loops in the data.

A key problem arises, however, in microfounding this relationship. The story that is easiest to tell is some variant of Friedman's original model involving persistently mistaken expectations by workers, but this is incompatible with rational expectations. Ideally it would be better to provide a microfoundation for inflation inertia that was compatible with rational expectations. While there is a number of candidates kicking around, I'm not sure which will be regarded as both plausible and relevant in 20 years' time.

However, I think it would be treating microfoundations as a straightjacket if this prevented us from giving prominence to the backward looking Phillips curve. In any case, the microfoundations of the New Keynesian Phillips curve (such as Calvo contracts) are hardly gilt edged. In my own lectures, I present the Phillips curve first as an aggregate equation with empirical support. I then discuss the Friedman story. Having used the Phillips curve to discuss the costs of reducing the rate of inflation, I then ask where these costs come from, and this provides a spring board for a presentation of rational expectations, and then an analysis of the New Keynesian Phillips curve (NKPC).

The NKPC raises a basic difficulty in teaching undergraduate macroeconomics – how do we incorporate rational expectations? The two dimensional, two variable diagram is the basic tool we use in teaching undergraduates. We shift curves and move along curves. This already raises a problem for a subject that is inherently dynamic. We cope with this problem by shifting curves through time, and students are able to handle this in the case of the backward looking Phillips curve, because time works in the intuitive direction: we start with some shock or exogenous change, and work forwards through time.

With rational expectations, we have to work backwards, from the future to the present. With one-off shocks in models without inertial dynamics there is not much of a problem, because the second period is the steady state. If shocks are at all persistent, then I fear trying to shift curves backwards through time may be too much. An example is given in the discussion of Uncovered Interest Parity (UIP) below. (The dynamic structure of UIP and the NKPC are very similar: replace inflation by the exchange rate and the output gap by the interest rate differential.) But perhaps I am underestimating the ability of students here.

When I teach the NKPC I prefer to use timelines: two dimensional diagrams with time on one axis. This can bring out the symmetry between the backward looking and New Keynesian Phillips curves (if we ignore discounting in the latter). Suppose we consider a shock to the output gap that lasts a few periods, and is equal in each period. Figure 2.2 illustrates the two relationships under the assumption that once the shock occurs, its duration and size are also known. The rectangle represents a period where the output gap is positive, at some constant level. The solid, downward sloping line represents the behaviour of inflation under a NKPC with a credible inflation target: inflation jumps up on news of the positive output gap (and knowledge of its size and persistence), and then falls gradually back to its target level. The dashed line represents inflation when the Phillips curve is backward looking: inflation gradually rises from its initial level, and settles at a new higher level when the positive output gap disappears. We can complete the symmetry

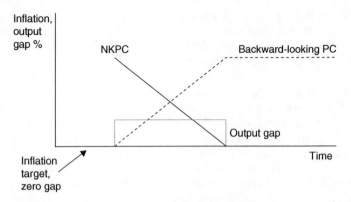

Figure 2.2   Forward- and backward-looking Phillips curves

by looking at an anticipated demand shock with a New Keynesian Phillips curve.

The Phillips curve is so central to macroeconomics that I think it should be part of any first-year macroeconomics course. However, in the first year I think there is no need to tell the Friedman story about mistaken expectations. Instead the Phillips curve can be presented as an empirically useful relationship that reflects the interaction between price setting in goods and labour markets. The key point to stress at this early stage is why excess demand leads to a change in inflation rather than some particular level of inflation, and why this makes macroeconomic sense. I would leave a discussion of the NKPC to a second or third year course.

3.3   Monetary policy

One of my objections to *IS/LM* was that it allowed students to forget that monetary policy was something governments or central banks choose, and that this was significantly different from the choices of an atomistic private sector. For this reason, I prefer to think of the three-equation model as the 2 + 1 equation model.

Why is this important? Consider, for example, an anticipated demand shock. Here, the appropriate behaviour for the monetary authority is not to follow some rule, but to simply kill the demand shock. The *IS* curve tells us how. Now of course demand shocks are rarely anticipated, so we might not want to dwell on this case, but failure to understand this basic point will lead students to get confused later on.

The case most often considered in Carlin and Soskice is of a completely unanticipated demand shock, which is either one-off, or permanent. After the first period, the nature of the shock is known. This case is more realistic than a completely anticipated demand shock, but it still has awkward features. Once the shock is known, we immediately move on to the monetary rule, so if the initial shock raised output, then in the second period output falls, as higher inflation expectations are unwound. In subsequent periods we move along the monetary rule line. My worry here is that students take this too literally, and think that once shocks are known, output immediately reverses sign. In reality, of course, it is many periods before a significant positive output shock is followed by a period with a negative output gap. When lecturing at this point I wave my hands and talk about responses to uncertainty, but I wish I had a more formal way of representing (potentially optimal) inertia in monetary policy.

Carlin and Soskice spend some time showing how a monetary rule may be optimally derived from preferences over output and inflation and the parameters of the Phillips curve. I think this is useful, but it has clear limitations, because the optimization presented is always for one period only. Any central bank that knows about the (backward looking) Phillips curve, for example, will be much more inflation averse than a one-period optimizer, because they recognize that inflation today has implications for inflation tomorrow.

The point becomes particularly important when we look at inflation bias. If we define inflation bias as steady state inflation above target, then it is possible to get inflation bias with a completely backward looking Phillips curve when the central bank is myopic in its preferences. Here the monetary rule apparatus and its associated central bank preferences come into their own, and this can all be nicely show in a two dimensional diagram. However, if we replace a myopic central bank by one that does not discount at all, then this inflation bias disappears (see Kirsanova *et al.*, 2009). Inflation bias here is just a consequence of a short-sighted policy-maker (although policy-makers may well be short-sighted). It is a rather different kind of inflation bias from that coming from time inconsistency under rational expectations.

For all these reasons, I prefer to play down the role of the monetary rule in the three-equation model. For much the same reason, I would not want to replace the *LM* curve by a 'monetary policy curve', as in Turner (2006). The approach I take is to use – where necessary – a Taylor rule as a possible empirical description of what central banks do, and address the issue of optimality on a case by case basis. However, this is a point about emphasis more than anything else.

3.4 An open economy

Nearly all textbooks, whether for undergraduates or graduates, start off with a closed economy model, and then move to an open economy. If our focus is a medium term, flex price economy with intertemporal consumption decisions at its heart, then there is a very good case for doing things the other way round. In a simple small open economy in a one good world with perfect capital mobility, real interest rates are exogenous because they are determined overseas, and so we can focus on consumption smoothing and tilting without worrying about interest rate endogeneity. This idea is at the core of Obstfeld and Rogoff's (1996) excellent graduate text.

In a short term, Keynesian world, the model is all about how policy varies real interest rates, so the open economy is more complicated than the closed economy. In one sense this is a pity, because as I noted above the structure of the UIP relationship and the New Keynesian Phillips curve are so similar, but from experience I believe students generally find it easier to connect with the former.

A great advantage of UIP is that, because the underlying relationship is so simple, it enables us to focus on how to solve models under rational expectations. The static relationship is trivial: if we double the interest rate differential, holding the expected future exchange rate constant, we double the expected change in the exchange rate. This simplicity makes it easier to move away from the two variable graph to time lines. The issue I remain unsure about is whether to attempt to analyse UIP in interest rate/exchange rate space.

Compare the following two expositions. We are interested in the impact of a one point, multi-period change in the interest rate differential on the exchange rate. One representation would be as in Figure 2.3, which is like one half of the diagram for the Phillips curve above.

The diagram shows the exchange rate response to an initially unexpected, but subsequently known, multi-period increase in interest rates. It is very easy to show the algebraic equivalent to this: by forward substitution in

$$e_t = E[e_{t+1}] + rd_t \tag{2.1}$$

(where e is the logged exchange rate, rd the interest rate differential, and E the expectations operator) we get

$$e_t = rd_t + E[rd_{t+1} + rd_{t+2} + \ldots + rd_{t+n}] + E[e_{t+n+1}] \tag{2.2}$$

We can relate this formula to the diagram: because it's so simple, we can focus on the idea of a stable medium term equilibrium exchange rate, and whether interest changes are expected or not. We can then talk about speculation, uncertainty about equilibrium rates, and a lot more.

A different representation would look at interest rate, log exchange rate space, as shown in Figure 2.4. Suppose the interest rate differential lasts for two periods. We start off with the UIP line one period ahead, where the expected exchange rate is the equilibrium rate. This passes through zero on

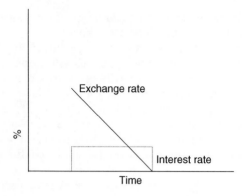

Figure 2.3 A time-line representation of UIP

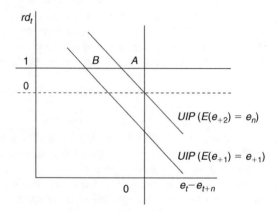

Figure 2.4 UIP in interest rate, exchange rate space

both axes (where the horizontal axis measures deviations from the long run rate). With a 1% interest rate differential, this gives us point *A*, which is the starting point for the current period UIP line. This then gives us point B, which is the initial jump in the exchange rate: i.e. a 2% change in the exchange rate.

Comparing these two expositions, I think there is no contest for which is easier to understand, and easier to manipulate. Nevertheless it is tempting to try the second approach when we integrate UIP into the transmission mechanism. Ideally we would like to combine the demand side relationship between aggregate demand and the real exchange rate with UIP to show how a transmission mechanism that worked through the exchange rate might operate. Drawing a positive, and static, relationship between competitiveness and aggregate demand makes sense, but linking competitiveness with interest rates encounters the difficulties illustrated above.

It may be simpler not to try. As a starting point in an open economy, we can work with exactly the same apparatus as a closed economy: an *IS* curve and a Phillips curve. If we are willing to work with a Phillips curve that is specified in terms of output price inflation rather than consumer price inflation (for reasons discussed in Kirsanova *et al.*, 2006, for example), then that curve is unchanged. At its simplest, the relationship between interest rates, the exchange rate and net exports makes the *IS* curve flatter. The essential lessons learnt from the closed economy go through to the open economy.

The complication that UIP makes evident is that expectations of future monetary policy influences the position of the *IS* curve. We can address this graphically by shifting the *IS* curve. In addition, we could note that if the relationship between current and future interest rate changes were predictable then this would in effect flatten the *IS* curve still further. But a key point to make here is that these complications can equally well occur in a closed economy, because future real interest rate changes will also impact on today's consumption and investment decisions through expectations.

A diagram that puts an *IS* curve on top, and a Phillips curve below, is useful because it expresses a recursive structure. For given interest rates, shocks to the *IS* curve lead to changes in output and inflation. Monetary policy then decides what combination of output and inflation to aim for, given the constraint of the Phillips curve. The *IS* curve then tells policy-makers how to achieve this combination using monetary policy.

While it is natural to want to generalize this apparatus to include the exchange rate in an open economy, I'm not sure what doing so would achieve in terms of new lessons learnt. Students should certainly understand that the transmission mechanism from interest rates to output is more complicated in an open economy because of movements in the exchange rate, but I'm not sure showing them a number of interlinked and inevitably partial diagrams is required to make this point.

What about the fiscal policy ineffectiveness proposition so central to textbook Mundell–Fleming? If we are talking about temporary changes in government spending that are not counteracted by monetary policy, then the ineffectiveness proposition disappears. The *IS* curve shifts, and if real interest rates stay unchanged then output moves. (There is no change in the real exchange rate: because the change in government spending is temporary, everything on the right-hand side of the extended UIP equation above is unchanged.) However, a permanent increase in spending, even if it is not crowded out by falling consumption because of (anticipated) tax increases, will be crowded out by an immediate appreciation in the real exchange rate. This is difficult to understand if students have yet to come across how the open economy works in a flex price medium term. I want to argue next that this should not be the case.

3.5   Placing this model in context

The three-equation model is not the only innovative feature of the Carlin and Soskice textbook. Another is the centrality of imperfect competition, with labour supply and demand curves replaced by wage-setting and price-setting curves. I like this for three reasons. First, it allows an explicit analysis of how imperfect competition impacts on the macroeconomy. Second, it makes a treatment of how the real exchange rate influences output much more natural. Third, an imperfectly competitive world makes it much easier to discuss both why prices might be sticky, and more importantly why under sticky prices output is demand determined. It fits very well with the microfounded New Keynesian models that we currently use.

However, in many respects an imperfectly competitive flex price economy works just like a perfectly competitive flex price economy. As a good deal of the micro students learn assumes perfect competition, it is foolish to appear to throw this away. We probably also want to talk about real business cycle models (see below). So I think it is essential to relate wage-setting and price-setting curves (drawn in real wage, employment (or output) space) to labour demand and labour supply curves at every opportunity.[4]

The issue I want to address here is how to fit a Keynesian short run into whatever longer run perspective we may choose. In simple terms, what is the best way to relate the Keynesian model to the Classical model from a pedagogical point of view? Should we start with the Keynesian short run, as is traditional, or should we start from the 'other end', with the long run based around the Solow growth model?

My own view is that things are a lot clearer if a Keynesian analysis comes after a reasonably thorough discussion of the medium term, which we could call a 'flex price equilibrium'. I think this has one major advantage. It makes clear that modern Keynesian analysis is not an alternative to the Classical model, but an augmentation of it, where prices are sticky. In particular, the flex price equilibrium becomes the natural target for monetary policy-makers in a Keynesian world. In addition, real business cycle analysis, although it might be regarded as an alternative explanation of cycles, does not disappear once we take this modern Keynesian view. There are similar advantages when it comes to analysing an open economy. Let me elaborate each of these points in turn.

A key aspect of stabilization policy with Phillips curves is that there is a short run inflation/output trade-off, which policy-makers need to take decisions about. We represent their preferences in terms of, typically quadratic, deviations from some inflation and output target. But students often fail to understand why output above target is a bad thing, besides its impact on inflation. Surely more output is better in itself? This mistake would occur less often if the output target were seen as the outcome of another trade-off: that between consumption and leisure. Too much output means too little leisure. Once this is clear, it is also much easier to motivate discussions of inflation bias, particularly if we work with both labour supply and demand curves as well as their imperfectly competitive equivalent.

The discussion of real business cycle theory in undergraduate texts varies considerably. This may reflect a significant problem – RBC dynamics are complex, and depend on parameter values in a way that simple Keynesian models do not. However, I think we can convey the basic ideas of RBC theory by exploiting a simple version of the first order condition relating labour supply to consumption and real wages. For example

$$Max \quad U(C,L) = \ln(C) - \kappa \frac{L^{\psi}}{\psi}$$
$$subject\ to\ C = wL(1-t) + Z \tag{2.3}$$

where C is consumption, L labour supply, t is the income tax rate, w the real wage, and Z are all other elements of the budget constraint, including saving, implies the following first order condition for labour:

$$L^{\psi-1} = \frac{w(1-t)}{\kappa C} \tag{2.4}$$

If real wages move roughly in line with any productivity movements, then the behaviour of labour supply will depend crucially on how consumption changes. Consumption is likely to rise less than wages for two reasons which, given the right course structure, can already be familiar to students: real interest rates will be higher because of the additional demand for capital, and because of consumption smoothing. I think this way of telling the story is a bit more intuitive than looking at relative wages in a two-period model.

Turning to an open economy, one of the advantages of working with a supply side based on imperfect competition is that an aggregate demand curve relating domestic output to competitiveness becomes quite natural. This is where I do draw aggregate supply and aggregate demand curves, but in real output/competitiveness space (the Swan diagram).[5] As my discussion of UIP above shows, it is much easier to understand the short term analysis of shocks in a Keynesian framework if this medium term analysis is already firmly embedded.

So to summarize, I would present Keynesian macroeconomics after a fairly comprehensive analysis of a medium-term, flex price economy. This applies to both closed economy and open economy macroeconomics. Where growth theory, or more generally the macroeconomics of the long run, fits in is both less obvious and I believe less important. While starting with the long run, moving to the medium run and ending with the short run has a certain elegance, I do not think there is a clear pedagogical case for doing this.

4 Summary

In the introduction, I related how I used to tell masters students that they would learn about the same issues they learnt about as undergraduates, but now the analysis would no longer be 30 years out of date. What I have tried to do in this chapter is to make suggestions to change that situation. Let me try and bring these threads together by outlining the essentials of what I would like to teach undergraduates, both in their first-year course, and in a subsequent specialized macroeconomics course.

I would start with a medium term, flex price economy, which we could describe as the Classical model. In the first year I would focus on labour supply and labour demand curves, while in subsequent years I would add wage-setting and price-setting curves, and add a formal discussion of labour/leisure optimization. In either case I would try and motivate this analysis as much as possible with the empirical and policy implications of this framework, such as attitudes to immigration, or the Laffer curve.

I would then present the two-period consumption model, along the lines discussed in the previous section. This would be of value in its own right, but also as a motivation for the *IS* curve. Consideration of other demand components like investment could be added to taste. At this stage I would include a discussion of international competitiveness, net trade and capital mobility. We could then consider how aggregate demand equals aggregate supply in two cases: a closed economy, through real interest rates, and an open economy, through the real exchange rate. This could be explored, particularly after the first year, by looking at various permanent 'shocks', including an increase in productivity. In later years I would discuss the current account, drawing links with intertemporal consumption.

A natural transition is then to examine temporary but persistent shocks, and the Real Business Cycle model for a closed economy. However, I personally would not give this more than a passing mention in a first-year course. Something that I would also reserve for a second year course would be a discussion of monetary policy under flexible prices e.g. nominal anchors compared to interest rate rules.

A first-year course should include a basic discussion of the government's budget constraint and problems associated with deficit bias and government debt. More advanced courses can discuss Ricardian Equivalence, and the 'twin deficits' in an open economy.

Now we can move to a Keynesian world. A first-year course can simply outline some reasons for price rigidity, and discuss why output might follow aggregate demand in a sticky price world. More advanced courses could explore the microfoundations of Keynesian analysis in more depth, including for example the role of wage setting, with reference back to the labour supply curve in RBC models.

This provides enough background for the core Keynesian analysis: the Phillips curve and *IS* curve, as in the Carlin and Soskice text. As I discussed in the previous section, a second-year course would add to the basic backward looking model by talking about rational expectations and a New Keynesian Phillips curve. For reasons discussed above, I would downplay the role of a monetary rule curve. In the first year I would just talk about the control problem faced by a central bank in general terms, while in the second year I would talk about Taylor rules as empirical regularities, and then discuss the extent to which this did or did not represent an optimal response to expected or unexpected shocks.

Uncovered Interest Parity seems sufficiently important to appear in a first-year macroeconomics course, although any subsequent course can formalize the analysis along the lines discussed in the previous section. It is important in part because it allows us to say something about why exchange rates can be volatile, and these ideas can be easily extended to asset prices. It would be a shame if a student completed a first-year macro course without knowing anything about why certain prices were prone to self-fulfilling type behaviour. As my earlier remarks indicated, I am less sure how useful it is to formalize the discussion of the transmission mechanism of monetary policy under floating exchange rates. The motivations for fixed exchange rates or monetary unions, the sustainability of the former and how policy operates within them comes here. A second-year course could also discuss countercyclical fiscal policy at this point: why it is only occasionally used under floating rates, and possible conflicts with longer run concerns discussed earlier in the course.

A discussion of inflation bias must be concentrated in a second/third-year course, because of the central role played by rational expectations. I would also add a discussion of stabilization bias, using simple examples to illustrate why optimal policy may be time inconsistent. This allows a discussion of credibility and transparency that goes a bit beyond hand waving. Finally a second/third-year course should include a reasonable chunk of growth theory. I think this can appear at a number of points in the sequence outlined above.

All this, without a mention of *LM* curves, money demand, traditional *AS* and *AD* curves, or Mundell–Fleming. Actually I exaggerate. In a second/third-year course, I would use an *LM* curve once. In discussing Taylor rules, I would raise the possibility that interest rates might not react to output and inflation directly, but indirectly via some intermediate target. After recalling the use of money as a possible nominal anchor, and the briefest discussion of money demand, I would show how money-targeting gives rise to a Taylor type rule for price level targeting. I would describe how this approach was tried in the past, and why it was quickly abandoned. In doing this, the main problem

I would have is keeping students' interest for what is, after all, a rather small piece of macroeconomic history that happened before they were born.

Notes

1. My thanks to Giuseppe Fontana, John Maloney, Mark Setterfield, David Vines, and John Vickers for helpful comments on an earlier draft, but all probably disagree with at least some of the views expressed here.
2. That students find it difficult is a personal view, although one that is not uncommon (e.g. Turner, 2006). Turner (2006) suggests that difficulty may be justified if the apparatus is rich in possibilities, but he shares my misgivings on its relevance to current policy.
3. From the perspective of the history of economic thought, a particularly interesting question is why the *LM* curve was believed to be such an essential part of Keynesian theory. Perhaps the need for comparisons with more Classical theory, and with the concept of neutrality in particular, was critical here. (I'm indebted to David Vines for his knowledge and thoughts on this point.) The revival of the ideas of Wicksell in Woodford (2003) is also interesting from this perspective.
4. In this respect, I have a major problem with Carlin and Soskice, which is that the default position for their price setting curve is horizontal. This makes the comparison I've just suggested much trickier than it should be. It is so easy to model a downward sloping price-setting curve, and relate it to a labour demand curve, using monopolistic competition, so why throw this away with a story about customer markets or rule of thumb behaviour?
5. My aggregate supply curve is what Carlin and Soskice call an ERU curve. My preference is to draw this supply curve almost vertical, because I'm not sure we have the empirical evidence to do otherwise, and the 'special case' of a vertical supply curve is pedagogically useful.

References

Carlin, W. and Soskice, D. (2006), *Macroeconomics: Markets, Imperfections and Institutions*, Oxford: Oxford University Press.

Goodhart, C. A. E. (2008), 'The continuing muddles of monetary theory: a steadfast refusal to face facts', mimeo.

Guest, R. (2003), 'Modifying the Taylor–Romer Model of Macroeconomic Stabilisation for Teaching Purposes', *International Review of Economics Education*, 2, 58–68.

Kirsanova, T., Leith, C., and Wren-Lewis, S. (2006), 'Should Central Banks Target Consumer Prices or the Exchange Rate?', *Economic Journal*, 116, 208–31.

Kirsanova, T., Vines, D., and Wren-Lewis, S. (2009), 'Inflation Bias with Dynamic Phillips Curves and Impatient Policy Makers', *B.E. Journal of Macroeconomics*, Berkeley Economic Press, 9(1).

Mankiw, G. (2007), *Macroeconomics*, 6th edn, Worth.

Obstfeld, M. and Rogoff, K. (1996), *Foundations of International Macroeconomics*, Cambridge, MA: MIT Press.

Romer, D. (2000) 'Keynesian macroeconomics without the *LM* curve', *Journal of Economic Perspectives*, 14(2), 149–69.

Solow, R. (1984), 'Mr. Hicks and the Classics', *Oxford Economic Papers*, 36, 13–25.

Taylor, J. B. (2000), 'Teaching modern macroeconomics at the principles level', *AER Papers and Proceedings*, 90(2), 90–4.

Turner, P. (2006) 'Teaching Undergraduate Macroeconomics with the Taylor–Romer Model', *International Review of Economics Education*, 5.

Woodford, M. (2003), *Interest and Prices: Foundations of a Theory of Monetary Policy*, Princeton: Princeton University Press.

3
Monetary Policy Analysis: An Undergraduate Toolkit[1]

Jagjit S. Chadha

1 Introduction

The nuts and bolts of setting monetary policy are often hard to get across to students. There are a number of key hurdles to overcome. First, the conceptual idea of how setting interest rates may (or may not) act to stabilize an economy comprising many households, firms, financial institutions and a significant government sector. Secondly, there are a host of institutional details to convey such as the framework for monetary policy, the relationship between the Finance Ministry and the central bank and what might be the ultimate objectives of stabilization policy. Thirdly, the theory of monetary policy is itself really developing into a branch of 'robust' control theory and so is subject to severe technical barriers at the frontier.[2] And finally, there is the aspect of the real data: how do we convey the idea that the observed economy is not some clearly identifiable mass but a construct based upon a myriad of observations or surveys announced on a daily basis? The mixture of institutional detail, high theory, data and, at times, low politics makes monetary policy courses a daunting mix for instructor and student alike.

We tend to start monetary policy courses with an analogy related to one of driving cars, steering ships or taking a shower! In which, the policy-maker is cast as the driver, pilot or bather in question. But the user has severe information problems, he (or she) cannot know with a high degree of certainty where he might currently be compared to where he would like to be. He also does not quite know how the machine will react when he asks it to help him get to where he would like to be. Finally, it may also be some time before he realizes that he is or is not where he thinks he would like to be and so he may frequently under- or even overshoot his final destination. Should your head be reeling, you will now be pleased to know that I have chosen to side-step almost entirely these kinds of control issues in this chapter.

What will concern us mostly in this chapter is the rather prosaic set of issues to do with where should interest rates go if the economy has a demand-induced boom, a supply-induced contraction or indeed if inflation expectations become dislodged.[3] These questions will be considered within the context of a simple two-quadrant and then four-quadrant diagram that I will develop and use to explore directly two further monetary policy issues: how might the zero bound for interest rates complicate the monetary policy problem and how might money market shocks complicate monetary policy choices? The level of exposition is appropriate for good undergraduates and I introduce many key readings in modern macroeconomics. In Section 2, I write down a standard New Keynesian model appended with both a supply side, money market clearing condition and a term for the price level as well as inflation. I develop the simple conditions for the determinacy of this system and show that it implies a monetary policy reaction where policy rates rise more than equiproportionally with inflation, the so-called 'Taylor Principle' of active monetary policy. Once the existence of an equilibrium for this economy has been established I return to the policy experiments. For the more technically grounded students the Appendix gives a fuller derivation.

In Section 3, I represent the key relationships diagrammatically for an inflation targeting central bank and consider the appropriate responses to three static problems of a positive demand shock, a negative supply shock and an increase in inflation expectations. In each case, I show that policy (interest) rates will have to rise temporarily to bring inflation back to target. In Section 4, I consider two special cases: what happens to the monetary policy reaction function when nominal rates are bounded at zero and when the money market may directly provide perturbations because the economy may be considered more or less risky over time. In the former case, policy rates are shown to be unable to drive real rates lower as inflation falls and thus there appear to be 'real' limits to the efficacy of interest rates as a stabilization device under a low and/or falling inflation. In the latter case, I show that a disconnect between interest rates set in the private money markets and policy rates can set up independent deviations of aggregate demand from potential and so require some offsetting in monetary policy.

With this background exposition in the student's toolkit I conclude that it becomes easier to consider the questions of diagnosis of any given monetary policy problem, institutional development, to track real-time data developments and to consider more complicated games that the policy-makers may have to play with their various (ir)rational counterparts. I leave that analysis to more advanced courses.

2   The Basic New Keynesian Model with Money

The point of departure for a simple macroeconomic model suitable for monetary policy analysis has become the New Keynesian (NK) framework (see McCallum (2001) and King (2002)), which is essentially an aggregate model with dominant supply side dynamics but where sticky prices mean that output may deviate temporarily from its flex-price long run level. The possibility of temporary deviations in output from its flex-price level creates a role for the monetary policy-maker. In brief, the basic NK story is that the capacity of output is set by a production function based on usual arguments in land and capital with its accumulation of efficiency shocks (the so-called Solow residuals: see, for example, 1987) and short-run output is determined by a monopolistically competitive supply side faced with Calvo time dependent price setting.

The NK structure means that the full capacity level of output in this economy lies at a point behind the perfectly competitive frontier, which in principle provides an incentive to push the economy above its full capacity level.[4] Secondly, with prices adjusting only gradually to an optimal mark-up over evolving marginal costs, short-run output can deviate from this capacity level. Following any shocks, prices can only be reset in each period by the fraction of firms who are sent an exogenous (Calvo) signal to re-price – with the fraction given by $1 - \alpha$ in each time period. And so all other firms, α, are faced with having to accept a sub-optimal price for their output for at least one period and the overall price level, which is a linear combination of all firms' prices, is also sub-optimal, which means that there are both distributional and output consequences from sticky prices.

Inflation is driven by both the difference between capacity and the short-run aggregate level of production chosen by all firms and expected inflation. And so inflation, at least in its temporary deviations from target, is not a monetary phenomenon in this model but really an output gap phenomenon, which is itself controlled by interest rate choices. But nevertheless to this basic model we can also consider appending a simple model of money demand (in which the supply of money by the monetary policy-maker is implicitly perfectly elastic), where we assume that households need to hold money balances to meet a given level of planned nominal expenditures. The role of the policy-maker is to set interest rates so that output stabilizes at the capacity level, that is the so-called output gap is closed, at which point inflation is also stabilized. In the remainder of this section I list and explain the key dynamic equations and examine the policy-makers' problem in terms of the determinacy of equilibrium.

The simple New Keynesian model expresses each variable as its log deviation from steady-state. Equation (3.1) gives aggregate demand, y_t, as a function of this period's expectation, E_t, of demand next period, y_{t+1}, and of the expected real interest rate, where R_t is the policy rate, $E_t \pi_{t+1}$ is the next period expectation of inflation and σ is the intertemporal rate of substitution in output.[5] Equation (3.2) is the forward-looking New Keynesian Phillips curve that relates current inflation, π_t, to discounted expected next period inflation, where β is the subjective discount factor, and is proportional to the deviation of aggregate demand from supply, where κ is the slope of the Phillips curve.[6] The term κ is related to two deep parameters in the underlying Calvo–Yun model (see Yun, 1996): the probability of firms maintaining a fixed price in the next period, α, and the subjective discount factor, β. In inflation space κ can be shown to be equal to $[(1 - \alpha)(1 - \alpha\beta)]/\alpha$ and thus in price space, with the deviation in the price level proportional to inflation (see equation (3.6), the Phillips curve becomes: $p_t = E_t p_{t+1} + (1 - \alpha\beta)(y_t - \hat{y}_t) + (\alpha/1 - \alpha)\varepsilon_{A,t}$. Under either formulation inflation or the price level is less responsive to the output gap as $\alpha \to 1$.

Equation (3.3) says that real balances, $m_t - p_t$, are held in proportion to demand, y_t, and inversely with the opportunity cost of holding non-interest paying money, R_t, with a semi-elasticity, η. Equation (3.4) is a simple interest rate-based rule that is used to stabilize inflation about its steady state value with the weight on inflation given by φ_π. The supply side of the economy, $\tilde{y}_t$, which we interpret as the flex-price, or steady-state, level of output is given by equation (3.5). The shocks to this equation account for changes in the short-run deviation of flex-price output from its steady-state and can typically be interpreted as productivity, or efficiency, shocks. Finally, the forward looking Phillips curve, (3.2), determines the split between current and expected inflation as a function of the current output gap but we can use the current inflation rate to back out the price level: α is the fraction of firms that hold prices fixed and so $(1 - \alpha)$ is the fraction which are given a signal to re-price as a mark-up over marginal costs (see Yun, 1996), thus inflation is simply the ratio of firms that re-price at the new price level, p_t, relative to those that cannot re-price, (3.6).[7]

The system is subject to stochastic shocks, $\varepsilon_{A,t}$, $\varepsilon_{B,t}$, $\varepsilon_{C,t}$, $\varepsilon_{D,t}$, which are respectively to demand, mark-up, monetary policy and to aggregate supply:

$$y_t = E_t y_{t+1} - \sigma(R_t - E_t \pi_{t+1}) + \varepsilon_{A,t} \tag{3.1}$$

$$\pi_t = \beta E_t \pi_{t+1} + \kappa(y_t - \tilde{y}_t) + \varepsilon_{B,t} \tag{3.2}$$

$$m_t - p_t = y_t - \eta R_t \tag{3.3}$$

$$R_t = \varphi_\pi \pi_t + \varepsilon_{C,t} \tag{3.4}$$

$$\tilde{y}_t = \varepsilon_{D,t} \tag{3.5}$$

$$\pi_t = \frac{1 - \alpha}{\alpha} p_t \tag{3.6}$$

We can substitute (3.4) into (3.1) and into (3.3), (3.5) into (3.2) and solving (3.6) for p_t into (3.3) to give us a system of four difference equations that can be written in vector form, if we suppress the stochastic errors, as:

$$E_t \mathbf{x}_{t+1} = \mathbf{\Lambda} \mathbf{x}_t \qquad (3.7)$$

where the transpose of the vector of state variables $\mathbf{x}_t$ is:

$$\mathbf{x}_t' \equiv [\, \pi_t \quad y_t \quad m_t \quad p_t \,]$$

where $\mathbf{\Lambda}$ is a 4×4 matrix of parameters. And so the basic NK model can be boiled down to a set of equations linking output and inflation to money and prices via the determination of nominal interest rates.

2.1 Understanding the model dynamics

A question that first concerns macroeconomists when faced with such a model are the 'Blanchard–Kahn local stability conditions',[8] to locate a rational expectations solution to a forward looking macroeconomic model. In fact much modern macroeconomic theory is concerned with the conditions under which a given model has a solution, or analogously can be thought to be stable following economic shocks. The existence or not of a unique solution for $\mathbf{X}_t$, given the forcing processes, $\mathbf{\varepsilon}_t$,[9] and will depend upon matching the number of eigenvalues (or roots) of the matrix $\mathbf{\Lambda}$ within the unit circle (less than absolute value of 1) with the number of predetermined state variables.[10]

Predetermined variables are those that we might think of as backward looking and depend upon shocks in previous periods or decisions in previous periods for the attainment of their current levels. On the other hand non-predetermined variables (also known as forward looking, or jump, variables) depend upon expectational terms for the current value. Note from equations (3.1) and (3.2) that both inflation and output are determined with reference to expectations of their own future values and so are non-predetermined variables. This is a key feature of NK macroeconomics, that many of the key variables behave like asset prices rather than traditionally sluggish prices and quantities. This means that the NK economy is somewhat more flexible, faster adjusting, than an examination of the data on a typical economy might suggest.[11] One way to think of the policy problem is that it is necessary to set the coefficients of the policy rule, (3.4), to ensure local determinacy of the whole system, and this setting is affected by the extent to which key variables are forward looking.[12]

We can see from inspection of equations (3.1) to (3.6) how the structure of this economy responds to shocks. Demand and mark-up shocks, $\varepsilon_{A,t}$ and $\varepsilon_{B,t}$, immediately impact on output and inflation, respectively, and shocks to the policy rate and supply side, $\varepsilon_{C,t}$ and $\varepsilon_{D,t}$, also work their way through output and inflation. We can thus see that providing some conditions are met so that inflation and output stabilize after shocks, by which I mean return to their steady-state or target values, then money and prices will also be stabilized. Equation (3.3) shows that the demand for real balances will be satisfied providing output and the interest rate is stable, which itself is a function of inflation in this simple model. Furthermore equation (3.6) tells us that a stable path for inflation will also stabilize the price level.

The model is therefore recursive (see the Appendix for a fuller proof) and consequently monetary policy-makers have concentrated on determining stability by concentrating on the output gap and inflation dynamics. And arguing that the traditional 'bread and butter' of monetary policy, monetary aggregates, impart little or no further information because the observed market clearing levels of money supply are equilibrium outcomes, reflecting stable paths for output and inflation contingent on the policy rule, which therefore have no further information to impart about the state of the economy. The idea that our observations on the economy, that is the time series we have on money, output, inflation and interest rates, are always equilibrium outcomes begs the very difficult question of what models we can use that will simultaneously produce market clearing in all markets and still match the data.

2.2 Inflation–output dynamics

Let us examine the conditions (somewhat loosely) for the determination of monetary stability.[13] First suppress the stochastic terms from equations (3.1) and (3.2):

$$y_t = E_t y_{t+1} - \sigma(R_t - E_t \pi_{t+1}) \tag{3.8}$$

$$\pi_t = \beta E_t \pi_{t+1} + \kappa y_t \tag{3.9}$$

Solve (3.2) for $E_t \pi_{t+1}$ and substitute out the policy rate from (3.4) to give:

$$y_t = E_t y_{t+1} - \sigma(\varphi_\pi \pi_t - \beta^{-1}(\pi_t - \kappa y_t)) \tag{3.10}$$

Now simplify the expression by assuming that $\sigma = 1$ and that $\beta \approx 1$:

$$y_t = E_t y_{t+1} - \varphi_\pi \pi_t + \pi_t - \kappa y_t \tag{3.11}$$

At steady-state the growth rate of output around the trend will be zero and so:

$$E_t y_{t+1} - y_t = (\varphi_\pi - 1)\pi_t + \kappa y_t = 0 \tag{3.12}$$

which means that output will be at steady-state providing the following condition is satisfied:

$$y_t = \frac{(1 - \varphi_\pi)}{\kappa} \pi_t \tag{3.13}$$

which we note will be positively sloped if $\varphi_\pi < 1$ and negatively sloped if the weight on inflation in the interest rate rule is greater than one. We can think of these alternate rules for monetary policy as passive and active, respectively (see Leeper, 1991). Note that under a passive rule a positive shock to inflation will imply that output will rise and hence through the Phillips curve will generate higher inflation in this and subsequent periods, i.e. inflation will not be stabilized and will continue to escalate.[14] But the active rule will imply that higher inflation will be associated with lower output and this will continue to drive down future inflation until it is also back to target. In this way the crucial aspect of this system's determinacy is the adoption of an *active* rule in the monetary policy-maker's reaction function.

To sum up, in this section, I have set out a modern macroeconomic model. There is an important but largely hidden supply side based on a Cobb–Douglas production function and the Solow residual to provide a measure of productivity growth, which is basically treated as exogenous. Inflation is set by a Phillips curve and demand responds to the expected path of real interest rates. The stability of this economy depends on the monetary policy reaction function, which moves to stabilize inflation via the output gap. The stability of this system can also be said to be recursive in that as long as inflation and output are pinned down to a unique solution path then the money stock and the price level are also determined in each period. I have also explored a simple exposition of how the adoption of an active rule will stabilize this economy. In the following section, I will create some simple toolkit diagrams, which can be used to understand the setting of monetary policy.

3 Toolkit Policy Diagrams

I can now represent the key elements of this model within the context of a simple set of quadrant style diagrams in which the target inflation rate is determined by a monetary policy-maker using the interest rate as a tool of stabilization. In this section we will develop this diagram and also consider the appropriate policy response to a positive demand shock, a negative supply shock and the possibility of dislodged (from fundamentals) inflation expectations.

3.1 Basic steady-state equations

The simple model outlined in equations (3.1) to (3.6) explained the dynamics of an economy around some steady-state or target level. In this section, we briefly outline those steady-states so that we can depict the economy in a diagrammatic form. At steady-state or target values there will be no expected deviation of output, y_t, from its flex-price level and so $y_t = E_t y_{t+1}$, and inflation will equal expected inflation, which in turn will equal the target level of inflation, $\pi_t = E_t \pi_{t+1} = \pi^T$ and assuming that $\sigma = 1$ and $\beta \approx 1$, we can examine the steady-state as follows:

$$0 = E_t y_{t+1} - y_t = \sigma (R_t - E_t \pi_{t+1})$$
$$R = \pi^T \tag{3.14}$$

$$0 = E_t \pi_{t+1} - \pi_t = \kappa (y_t - \tilde{y}_t)$$
$$y = \tilde{y} \tag{3.15}$$

Equations (3.14) and (3.15) tell us that at steady-state, where there is no expected deviation of inflation or output from its target, π^T, or potential value, $\tilde{y}$, the nominal interest rate will deviate from the long-run real rate of interest (the so-called *Wicksellian rate of interest*)[15] by the inflation target and output will be equal to its potential with the output gap at zero. The money market will thus clear as follows:

$$m - p = \tilde{y} - \eta \pi^T$$
$$m = \tilde{y} + \tilde{p} - \eta \pi^T \tag{3.16}$$

Equation (3.16) tells us that money will be held to finance steady-state demand for steady-state output, $\tilde{y}$, and in direct proportion to the price level minus an 'inflation tax' term, $\eta \pi^T$, because for any positive inflation target there is a steady-state disincentive to hold money balances. This is because the negative of the target inflation rate, $\eta \pi^T$, is equal to return on money holdings, when money balances yield no monetary return. We are now in a position to draw our two quadrant diagram for interest rate determination and for output determination. For the moment let us put money on one side and concentrate on policy rates, inflation and output.

3.2   Inflation and interest rates

Figure 3.1 shows the determination of equilibrium in the interest rate–inflation space. There are two lines. The first, labelled, *FE*, is the Fisher equation and relates nominal interest rates to expected inflation equiproportionally and so has a slope of 1 (see equation (3.13)). The *FE* lines cuts the interest rate axis at the natural, or Wicksellian, rate of interest where nominal interest rates equal real interest rates as inflation is zero at this point. It might be argued that at this point there might be a limited degree of money illusion as at zero inflation equilibrium real and nominal changes are identical and so this is a possible long-run solution for a monetary economy. The *FE* line also cuts the inflation axis when nominal rates are zero and inflation is equal to the negative of the real interest rate, $-\pi = R^{nat}$. At this point money balances gives a return equal to the R^{nat} because inflation is negative, which is the so-called Friedmanite maximum, at which point money holdings would be maximized as they do not suffer an opportunity cost in terms of returns relative to bonds.[16]

The second line is called *IRR* and represents the reaction of the monetary policy-maker to inflation above or below his or her target. I draw the line as an *active* policy rule. As illustrated in Section 2, equation (3.13), the slope of this curve is greater than 1 and means that policy rates rise by more than any increase (decrease) in inflation implying that real interest rates rise (fall) in order to induce aggregate demand to move back to the full employment level. As drawn there is a unique equilibrium at the inflation target, π^T, which is also equal to the level of inflation expectations, π^e. In this economy what we would therefore expect to see is that, with inflation expectations at target or credibility, interest rates, inflation and output would move in unison around the steady-state: rising and falling together.

In some sense, the equilibrium suggested by Figure 3.1 is arbitrary as the central bank could easily choose an alternate inflation target and set interest rates to stabilize inflation around that level. There is a wide-ranging debate in monetary economics about the appropriate level of inflation target and although there appears to be have been an advanced country consensus for a numerical statement of something in the region of 2%, it is not at all clear whether that consensus will persist. There is a conceptual trade-off that involves deciding, on the one hand, upon a level of inflation that is not so high that prices lose their signalling power and introduce a significant degree of uncertainty into the economy, which will lead to economizing on monetary balances and also on the divergence of resources to mitigating that uncertainty. And, on the other hand, to bear in mind that inflation should not be set at so low a level that it starts to impact on the ease of relative

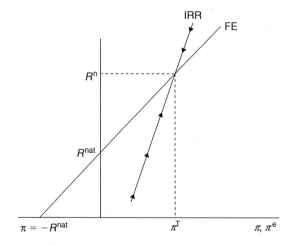

Figure 3.1 Interest rates and inflation targets

price adjustment, as some wages and prices are downwardly rigid, or that the zero bound on nominal interest rates may start to become a significant constraint.[17]

3.3   Aggregate dynamics revisited

Figure 3.2 appends a lower quadrant to the earlier interest rate–inflation space. It shows the aggregate supply curve, which is determined by equation (3.5), and Phillips curve (PC), which for a fixed level of inflation expectations shown in the top quadrant, slopes upwards with the parameter, κ (see equation (3.2)). I can now assess what happens to this economy in response to three comparative static shocks: aggregate demand, aggregate supply and inflation expectations.

3.3.1   *A positive shock to demand*

Points A and B show the initial equilibrium in Figure 3.2. Now imagine that there has been a shock to output demand from something like an increase in wealth, fiscal expenditure or some relaxation of credit conditions.[18] Aggregate demand is now in excess of supply at some point C and inflation has increased by $\kappa(C - B)$. With fixed inflation expectations, which is really what is meant by the attainment of credibility, the central bank simply raises interest rates to E, given by the *IRR* slope and at this point real rates are $(E-D)$ higher than the natural rate, R^{nat}. The increase in real rates bears down on aggregate demand and the demand converges back to point B with interest rates and inflation determined at A. The demand shock leads to a temporary

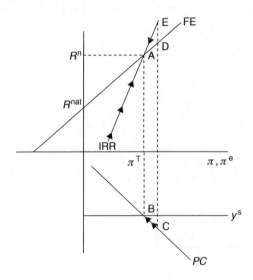

Figure 3.2   Two-quadrant diagram – demand shock

inflation, boom and increase in policy rates but at the end of the cycle we are back to where we started from in terms of the level of interest rates and inflation.

3.3.2   A negative aggregate supply shock

Figure 3.3 helps us understand the correct NK policy response to a negative supply shock. From the initial equilibrium at *A* and *B*, a negative supply shock shifts the horizontal line in the lower quadrant upwards and takes with it the locus for aggregate demand which also then goes through the new equilibrium point *C*. Despite the movements in the *AS* and *AD* schedules that lead to the determination of a new steady-state level for supply, the level of demand initially remains at point *B*, which is clearly in excess of capacity. Excess demand drives inflation up and because inflation can jump in this model (see equation (3.2)), inflation will move to *D* at the same level of excess demand. At *D* inflation is above target, policy rates are moved up to *E*, where again real rates are set in excess of the natural rate. The economy then slides down the locus *D−C* and policy rates fall from *E* to *A*. In this cycle policy rates and inflation are back to where we started from after a temporary escalation in both but output lies at a permanently lower level.

3.3.3   An escalation in inflation expectations

In Figure 3.4 we add to the two-quadrant diagram a vertical line in the upper quadrant that represents inflation expectations formed today for inflation in

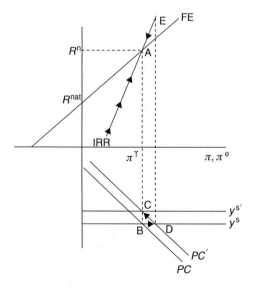

Figure 3.3   Two-quadrant diagram – supply shock

the next period, $E_t\pi_{t+1}$. They can also be interpreted as longer run inflation expectations and so reflect the level of monetary policy credibility, which is some inverse function of $|E_t\pi_{t+1} - \pi^T|$. Initially the economy is at the equilibrium A and B. Now let us suppose that inflation expectations shift to the right because of changes in the monetary constitution such that it is no longer judged that the marginal benefit and the marginal cost of inflation are equalized at the target. In other words, it is perceived that the monetary policy-maker derives some benefit from elevated inflation.[19] In this case, inflation expectations will be in excess of actual inflation at D and actual real rates will diverge from expected real rates, which have fallen, and output will start to expand towards E from B as there has been an effective loosening of policy.

There are two possible solutions. First, the increase in inflation expectations are accommodated and a new inflation target is set equal to the elevated level of inflation expectations and PC slides up AS to cut it at the higher inflation target. That is, the economy moves to an equilibrium of D and C. At this new inflation target, the economy continues to operate at full capacity and the higher inflation expectations lead to a change in the inflation rate and ultimately to the inflation target. The alternative is more difficult and costly as it requires a significant monetary policy response but also illustrates the importance of having some well understood target for monetary policy. First note that at the new equilibrium CD expected real rates are equal to the natural real rate. And the problem is how to deflate

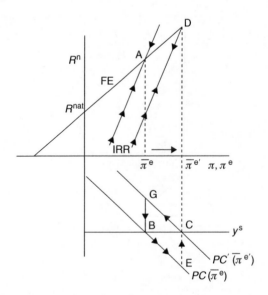

Figure 3.4 Inflation expectation accommodated

inflation and inflation expectations back to the original target. The central bank could have chosen to treat the initial increase in inflation expectations as one of inflation and raised rates along the original *IRR* to a point vertically above D and this would have acted to reduce demand from E to B and inflation back to the original equilibrium, A. If on the other hand now that the economy has settled at CD a shift to the old *IRR* curve will entail a sharp rise in real rates and the maximum size of the recession from this policy, CGB, will occur if inflation expectations are sluggish and there is little credibility. On the other hand, in the event that such a policy quickly restores credibility, the economy may jump back quickly from C to B.[20]

4 Two Extensions

Within the context of the framework outlined in the previous section, I can also examine two ongoing monetary policy dilemmas. The first is exactly how the zero-lower bound for monetary policy constrains the scope of interest rate reaction with low inflation or even deflation. The second is how exactly a disconnect between money market interest rates and policy rates leads to complications for monetary policy-makers.

4.1 An application to non-linearity

The difference between the *FE* line and the *IRR* line represents the deviation of the real policy rate from the natural rate of interest. And so the triangle *ABC* in Figure 3.5 represents the force acting on the economy via the choice of the level of interest rates when inflation is below target. As interest rates can rise as high as policy-makers wish to place them, the opportunity for deflationary impetus is reasonably unconstrained. But once nominal rates start to fall they are constrained to remain at or above a lower bound of zero.

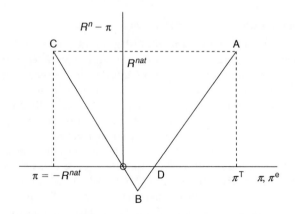

Figure 3.5   The zero bound problem

And so I plot the possible triangle of real rate choices faced by a policy-maker who pursues his or her interest rate paths in a piece-wise linear fashion, with policy rates falling first to zero and then staying there as inflation falls. The x-axis shows inflation and the y-axis shows the real interest rate, essentially I simply plot the difference between the *FE* and *IRR* curves in inflation-real rate space. Note that at initial equilibrium, *A*, and at the Friedmanite maximum for money holdings, *C*, real rates equal the natural or Wicksellian rate.

At the origin, *O*, nominal rates are zero since both inflation and the real rate is zero. Triangle *OBD* represents the region over which negative interest rates pertain. The policy-maker is able to drive real rates down only to point *B*, after which real rates will rise, as inflation can fall but nominal rates cannot. But note that real rates along *ABC* are all below the natural rate and are therefore acting to stimulate the economy. The issue then is whether inflation will fall below – R^{nat} after which it will act to further bear down on demand and whether the increasing real rates over the range *BC* will be sufficient to stabilize a deflating economy. If not then other monetary policy tools will have to be considered. The Japanese experience since the collapse of the asset price bubble in the early 1990s led to a prolonged debate about how to deal with deflation and led to the suggestion of a number of complementary tools to monetary policy, for example, exchange rate devaluation or the underfunding of government fiscal deficits. The question for policy-makers is thus simply does the triangle *ABC* place sufficient stabilization policy in the hands of the policy-maker when inflation lies in the range $\pi = -R^{nat}$ to π^T? Or should more extreme responses be engendered early in any deflationary episode, so that the slope of the line *AB* is even more negative i.e. real rates are pushed down very quickly so as to minimize the possibility of a increasing real rates as inflation falls i.e. *BC*. I leave it to the reader to draw his or her preferred path for rates but it may well not be linear.

4.2   An application to the money market

As the name suggests the two quadrant diagram can be extended with two further quadrants. In Figure 3.6 we add one quadrant for determining market interest rates with a premium over the policy rate and the second as a clearing condition for the money market based on market rather than policy rates. Let us first suggest that the market interest rate has an external finance premium, *efp*, over the policy rate and so we draw an *efp* line in the top left-hand quadrant, which simply states that the market interest rate, $R^m = R^n + efp$. The magnitude of the *efp* has been explored in various papers and is likely to vary cyclically over the business cycle to reflect market risk.[21] Note that in an NK framework the risk premium can be directly linked to the state of the economy and can be thought of as reflecting the marginal costs of loan supply to the private sector and may well be highly correlated with the business cycle such that financial intermediaries may perceive their costs of loan supply to

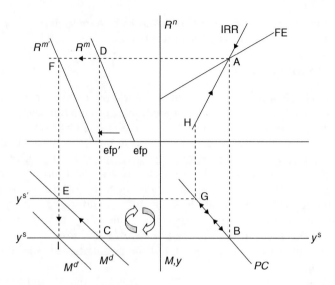

Figure 3.6 The four-quadrant diagram

fall in an expansion and rise in a recession, meaning that risk premia are counter-cyclical and act to amplify the business cycle.[22]

In equilibrium the supply of money is set by the full employment level of output (see equation (3.18)) and money demand is decreasing in the level of market interest rates with a slope term reflecting the interest rate elasticity of demand for money, η. At equilibrium, point *ABCD*, inflation is at target, $\pi = \pi^T$, output is at its full employment level, $y = \tilde{y}$, and money demand equals money supply, $M^d = M^s$ at the policy rate and the market interest rate, R^n and R^{efp}.

Now let us suppose that the external finance premia is driven upwards as perceptions of risk in the market economy increase and this reduces the supply of money (or liquidity) at each given market rate. The *efp* then jumps up with a new intercept, where *efp'* > *efp*. In the absence of a fall of velocity induced by higher market interest rates, which would drive the demand curve outwards, the money market will now clear at a higher level of market rates and a lower level of observed nominal money supply, i.e. *EF*. But the higher market interest rates and lower money supply will set up a deflationary impetus to the economy as scarce liquidity will drive demand down relative to capacity, *G*, and inflation will fall. The policy rate is thus cut to *H* in order to offset the increase in market interest rates, which induces a temporary inflation and ought to cause both the money supply and demand curves to shift out to a new equilibrium, *I*, at the higher market interest rate. So when money markets disconnect policy rates, output and inflation may eventually return to their long-run level but there has to be a temporary offset of the higher market interest rates by the policy-maker.

5   Concluding Remarks

In this chapter, I have outlined a simple macroeconomic model that underpins much of modern macroeconomic analysis. Although not developed here at great length, the main equations (3.1) to (3.6) can all be derived from the first principles of household constrained optimization. I have shown that the paths for output and for inflation are determined by the arguments in the central bank's policy rule. Under such a rule we also show that money and the price level are well determined. One key feature of this model is that output and inflation are forward looking and respond to the expected path of real interest rates and output respectively. I also show that the monetary policy reaction function does imply a trade-off between output and inflation because increasing (reducing) output has an inflationary (deflationary) implication.

I then transfer the key elements of this model to a series of simple diagrammatic expositions that are suitable for undergraduate study. Specifically, we analyse the equilibrium for interest rates and inflation and the slope of the monetary policy reaction function. We are also able to use the diagram to illustrate the multiplicity of possible equilibria, for example, an inflation target can be set at any point from the Freidmanite minimum upwards, and the relationship from this space to that of inflation–output, which is simultaneously determined. The correct policy response to demand and supply shocks are considered as is that to the possibility that inflation expectations may become dislodged from target and I leave to the student the analysis of what to do if the natural rate of interest changes. Finally we examine some limitations of this tool by considering the limits to the correct policy response as a result of a zero bound constraint on the nominal interest rate and also the possibility that disruption to money markets may cause market rates to disconnect from policy rates.

This chapter takes the intermediate student to the point of understanding more fully many of the issues currently occupying monetary theorists and practitioners. That is, what are the key equations required to understand more fully the aggregate economic system and how the choice of monetary policy rule plays a crucial role in the system's dynamics. Underpinning much of this work is the observation that it is not possible to understand aggregate dynamics of a monetary economy without reference to monetary policy and the level of credibility it has bestowed upon it. The model structure thus outlined takes the Lucas (1996) critique seriously. Ultimately the student who understands the key role of policy rules, targets and beliefs in determining a monetary equilibrium is better equipped to understand how issues such as learning, uncertainty, robust rules, min–max objectives and so forth play their way out of a basic New Keynesian macroeconomic model.

Appendix to Section 2

A3.1 Block triangularity

We note that the 4×4 matrix, Λ, can be written in block form, where each block $(\mathbf{A}, \mathbf{0}, \mathbf{C}, \mathbf{D})$ is a 2×2 matrix:

$$\Lambda = \begin{bmatrix} \frac{1}{\beta} & -\frac{\kappa}{\beta} & 0 & 0 \\ \sigma\varphi_\pi - \frac{\sigma}{\beta} & \kappa\frac{\sigma}{\beta} + 1 & 0 & 0 \\ \Gamma_1 & \Gamma_2 & 1 & 0 \\ \Gamma_3 & \Gamma_4 & 0 & 1 \end{bmatrix} = \begin{bmatrix} \mathbf{A} & \mathbf{0} \\ \mathbf{C} & \mathbf{D} \end{bmatrix}$$

where Γ_i are composite parameters. The block triangularity, or recursiveness, of matrix Λ, with a null matrix in the upper right hand block, means that the eigenvalues of the whole matrix are simply given by the eigenvalues of $\mathbf{A}$, referring to $[\pi_t \ y_t]$ and $\mathbf{D}$, referring to $[m_t \ p_t]$. Also in this case the determinacy of Λ follows from the determinacy of $\mathbf{A}$ given $\mathbf{D}$ is the identity matrix. In other words by locating a stable path for inflation and output around steady-state or target values then both the money stock and the price level will follow recursively in each period. This is a key result, in that in this model it is the case that controlling the economy at the top level of output and inflation is sufficient to control other aggregate quantities and prices, in this case the money stock and the price level.

A3.2 Determinacy

The determinacy of this system will depend on the stability of $\mathbf{A}$. The dynamics of a first order system depend on the eigenvalues, λ_1 and λ_2, of matrix $\mathbf{A}$ which determines the equation of motion for $\mathbf{x}$ in equation (3.7). And so for the equation of motion for $\mathbf{A}$ this case, with both inflation and output non-predetermined, then determinacy will require matrix A to have two eigenvalues outside the unit circle.

A3.2.1 $\lambda_{1,2} > |1|$ i.e. eigenvalues both outside the unit circle

When the roots are both positive, as they will be in this case (see de la Fuente (2000)), the conditions for both eigenvalues to be outside the unit circle are easy to derive. Note first that for all square matrices the eigenvalues, $\lambda_1 \ldots \lambda_n$, of the matrix will be related to its trace and determinant in the following way:

$$Det(A) = \lambda_1 \lambda_2 \tag{3.17}$$

$$Trace(A) = \lambda_1 + \lambda_2 \tag{3.18}$$

And so now note that for a matrix where both roots are outside the unit circle:

$$Det(A) = \lambda_1 \lambda_2 > 1 \tag{3.19}$$

$$Trace(A) = \lambda_1 + \lambda_2 > 2 \qquad (3.20)$$

Because both roots must be greater than 1, then the following condition must also hold:

$$(\lambda_1 - 1)(\lambda_2 - 1) > 0 \qquad (3.21)$$

which expands to:

$$\lambda_1\lambda_2 - (\lambda_1 + \lambda_2) + 1 > 0$$

And thus:

$$Det(A) - Trace(A) > -1$$

$$\left[\frac{1}{\beta}(\kappa\sigma\varphi_\pi + 1)\right] - \left[\frac{1}{\beta} + \kappa\frac{\sigma}{\beta} + 1\right] > -1$$

$$\kappa\frac{\sigma\varphi_\pi}{\beta} + \frac{1}{\beta} - \frac{1}{\beta} - \kappa\frac{\sigma}{\beta} - 1 > -1$$

$$\kappa\frac{\sigma\varphi_\pi}{\beta} - \kappa\frac{\sigma}{\beta} > 0$$

$$\kappa\frac{\sigma\varphi_\pi}{\beta} > \kappa\frac{\sigma}{\beta}$$

$$\varphi_\pi > 1 \qquad (3.22)$$

And so providing the nominal interest rate increases by more than any inflationary shock, the economy can be stabilized around any given inflation target. In other words given an inflationary shock, providing the real interest rate increases, inflation can be brought back to target by inducing a reduction in demand and so a closing of any output gap. I have illustrated this form on monetary policy response, which is termed *active*, in Figure 3.1 of the main text.

A3.3   Optimality

Let us append a simple loss function to the trade-off between output and inflation:

$$L^{mp} = \frac{1}{2}\left[\omega_\pi\pi^2 + \omega_y\left(y\right)^2\right] \qquad (3.23)$$

This form of loss function for equal weights on $\omega_y = \omega_\pi$ will imply indifference curves that are a series of concentric circles around the point where inflation is at target and output is equal to its flex-price level, the so-called 'bliss point'. Typically the bliss point used to be thought to lie to the right of the flex-price level of output, thereby bringing about a bias into monetary policy to try and get to a higher indifference curve. The so-called 'inflation bias' stemmed from this perception (Nordhaus, 1995).

We can also use the loss function in (3.14) alongside the Phillips curve, which we can interpret as setting the rate of exchange between current period inflation and output, to analyse the slope of the monetary policy reaction function in output–inflation space. Let us start from some point where there is a negative output gap, $y < 0$, and evaluate the gain from increasing y,[23] which will be simply given by $-\omega_y y \Delta y$. The resulting loss from increasing output will increase inflation, via the Phillips curve, which will be given by $\omega_\pi \pi \kappa \Delta y$. Now equating the marginal cost to the marginal benefit any outcome for inflation and output must satisfy the following constraint:

$$y = -\kappa \frac{\omega_\pi}{\omega_y} \pi \qquad (3.24)$$

Equation (3.15) thus shows the slope of the optimal monetary policy reaction function in inflation–output space. The rate of transformation, or slope, is given by the slope of the Phillips curve, κ, and the relative weight on output or inflation in the loss function, (3.14). Finally note that the form of the loss function will determine the optimal monetary policy reaction function in output–inflation space. For example if we only worry about large deviations of output or inflation from target rather than all deviations, the policy reaction function will be flat over some range and then react aggressively when it is in some danger of being breached – this is a form of min–max reaction.

Notes

1. I thank my students and colleagues for their patience and understanding while I developed some of the ideas contained in this chapter. I also thank William Collier, the Fellows and Master of Clare College, Cambridge for their hospitality and Luisa Corrada, Sean Holly and Charles Nolan for allowing me to draw upon our joint work and ideas. Finally I thank the editors for their kind and helpful comments and Qi Sun for research assistance.

2. As well as the hurdle of deriving aggregate relationships from first principles (so-called micro-foundations), the resulting equations need to be understood and manipulated to examine issues such as determinacy and learnability, and various solutions for the policy rule can be examined according to various loss functions for the monetary policy-maker. For example, rather than the well known quadratic loss function which seeks to minimize the deviations of a variable from its target, a policy-maker may seek to minimize the losses from the worst possible (probable) outcome and act more like a portfolio manager with a so-called min-max loss function. Appendix A.3.3 illustrates the connection between the choice of loss function and the optimal monetary policy rule. See Alan Greenspan (2004) for an introduction to how risk management issues impact on simple monetary policy decisions.

3. By which I mean dislodged from their (model-based) connection with the state of the economy.
4. The implications of this incentive, i.e. an inflation bias, will not concern me greatly in this chapter.
5. This intertemporal equation also operates as the basic asset pricing equation, or kernel, in a New Keynesian model.
6. This compares to various specifications of the Phillips curve through time, relating firstly the inflation rate to the unemployment rate and then the change in inflation to various measures of capacity. The key difference here is that the impact of the output gap is split between current and expected inflation. It is worth reading Bill Phillips' (1958) original paper.
7. Equation (3.6) is the deviation of inflation and prices from steady state and results from the observation that $P_{t+n} = f[\alpha P_{t-1+n}, (1-\alpha)P_{t+n}]$ and so if prices are at steady state in the initial period under Calvo pricing they will move by the ratio of those who can re-price to those who cannot.
8. See Blanchard and Kahn (1980).
9. Which is an analagous 4×1 vector for the shocks.
10. I shall not continue with much matrix algebra in this section but the interested reader is directed to the Appendix for more details.
11. For example, a rule of thumb for central banks is that the economy responds most actively with a lag of 4–8 quarters to a monetary policy shock but that tends to be considerably longer than that suggested by a typical NK model.
12. See Woodford (2003) for a comprehensive treatment of this problem.
13. For a full account see Appendix A.3.3.
14. The argument is the same for a negative inflation shock whereby the active policy rule will ensure that output is higher in future periods but there is a downward constraint as nominal interest rates cannot go below zero. I discuss this lacuna in the section on the zero-bound.
15. The Wicksellian rate of interest is explored in other chapters in this volume but essentially is the real rate of interest consistent with (flex-price) equilibrium fluctuations in output.
16. See Friedman (1969) on this suggestion.
17. A good introduction to the debate on optimal inflation can be found in Feldstein (1979).
18. See Chadha and Nolan (2007), for an examination of the interactions between monetary and fiscal policy.
19. See Kydland and Prescott (1977).
20. Sargent (1981) outlines a nice illustration of the benefits of credibility.
21. See Chadha *et al.* (2008) for an examination of the possible links between the money markets and interest rate spreads. Other chapters in this volume also consider this question.
22. This endogenous interpretation of business cycle generated risk premia is quite different to the exogenous view taken by the followers of Minsky.
23. I am grateful to Walsh (2002) for this simple thought experiment. In this simple example, I have implicitly set $\tilde{y} = 0$.

References

Blanchard, O. J. and C. M. Kahn (1980), 'The Solution of Linear Difference Models under Rational Expectation', *Econometrica*, 48, 1305–11.

Chadha, J. S. and Nolan, C. (2007), 'Optimal Simple Rules for the Conduct of Monetary and Fiscal Policy', *Journal of Macroeconomics*, 29, 665–89.

Chadha, J. S., Corrado, L. and Holly, S. (2008), 'Reconnecting Money to Inflation: the Role of the External Finance Premium'. Cambridge Working Papers in Economics, 0852.

Feldstein, M. S. (1979), 'The Welfare Cost of Permanent Inflation and Optimal Short-Run Economic Policy', *Journal of Political Economy*, 87, 749–68.

Friedman, M. (1969), *The Optimal Quantity of Money and Other Essays*, Chicago: Aldine.

de la Fuente, A. (2000), *Mathematical Methods and Models for Economists*, Cambridge: Cambridge University Press.

Greenspan, A. (2004), 'Risk and Uncertainty in Monetary Policy', Remarks made to the AEA meetings in San Diego, California.

King, M. (2002), 'No Money, No Inflation – The Role of Money in the Economy', *Bank of England Quarterly Bulletin*, 42, 162–77.

Kydland, F. E. and Prescott, E.C. (1977), 'Rules Rather than Discretion: The Inconsistency of Optimal Plans', *Journal of Political Economy*, 85, 473–92.

Leeper, Eric M. (1991), 'Equilibria under "active" and "passive" monetary and fiscal policies', *Journal of Monetary Economics*, 27, 129–47.

Lucas, R. E. Jr (1996), 'Nobel Lecture: Monetary Neutrality', *Journal of Political Economy*, 104, 661–82.

McCallum, B. T. (2001), 'Monetary Policy Analysis in Models without Money', *Review*, Federal Reserve Bank of St. Louis, 83, 145–64.

Nordhaus, W. D. (1995), 'Policy Games: Co-ordination and Independence in Monetary and Fiscal Policies', *Brookings Papers on Economic Activity* 2, 139–216.

Phillips, A. W. H. (1958), 'The Relation between Unemployment and the Rate of Change of Money Wage Rates in the United Kingdom, 1861–1957', *Economica*, 2, 283–99.

Sargent, T. J. (1981), 'Stopping moderate inflations: the methods of Poincaré and Thatcher', Federal Reserve Bank of Minneapolis Working Paper.

Solow, R. M. (1987), 'Growth Theory and After', Nobel Prize Lecture.

Walsh, C. (2002), 'Teaching Inflation Targeting: An Analysis for Intermediate Macroeconomics', *Journal of Economic Education*, Fall, 333–46.

Woodford, M. (2003), *Interest and Prices: Foundations of a Theory of Monetary Policy*, Princeton: Princeton University Press.

Yun, T. (1996), 'Nominal Price Rigidity, Money Supply Endogeneity, and Business Cycles', *Journal of Monetary Economics*, 37, 345–70.

4

Rescuing the *LM* Curve (and the Money Market) in a Modern Macro Course

Roberto Tamborini

1 Introduction

The diffusion of direct control of the interest rate among central banks, and the parallel development of consensus on the so-called 'New Neoclassical Synthesis' blending New Classical and New Keynesian insights (Goodfriend and King, 1997; Blanchard, 2000; Woodford, 2003), have paved the way for the idea that macro-modelling can benefit greatly if it starts directly from the 'fundamental three equations' consisting of aggregate demand (*IS*), aggregate supply (*AS*) and a Taylor rule (*TR*) representative of interest-rate-based monetary policy. Taylor (2000), Romer (2000), Allsopp and Vines (2000), Carlin and Soskice (2004) provide examples of introductory-level treatments. Aside from the theoretical innovations in the aggregate demand and supply functions (which can be introduced at higher levels of sophistication), the main difference between this new workhorse and the one on duty to date (generally known as *IS–AS–LM*) is that the *TR* replaces the *LM* function as a means to determine the nominal interest rate and to link the monetary block with the real block of the economy.

As argued by Romer (2000), dispensing with the *LM* apparatus altogether has several advantages. First, in its traditional static version the *LM* function is notoriously faulty in various respects (see also Leijonhufvud, 1983, for early warnings). To mention only a few: the *LM* function is derived from money *stock* equilibrium while being embedded in a *flow* equilibrium setup; the *LM* schedule is drawn with respect to the *nominal* interest rate whereas its counterpart, the *IS* function, depends on the *real* interest rate; when the *real* money stock is made explicit as the determinant of the *LM* schedule, the relevant variable is the *general price level* (GPL) whereas the key variable in the macroeconomic debate is the *inflation rate*. Second, from the point of view of monetary policy, the *LM* schedule implies that the central bank controls the level of the money stock in the economy, whereas today the general practice of central banking is based on direct control of interest rates. By contrast, starting from scratch with output, inflation and the interest rate, as with the *TR*, is quite attractive and may ease the transition of students from the economics of the press to the economics of the classroom. And yet, as Romer himself notes, the diffusion of the *IS–AS–TR* model in textbooks is rather slow, much slower than one might expect from its academic dominance.

One reason may be that, as is often the case, the change of workhorse has both advantages and drawbacks. Friedman (2003) has pointed some of them out. In his view, a major defect on the side of the bare *IS–AS–TR* framework is that it completely hides the concept of monetary equilibrium from view, transmitting the faulty idea that the central bank can set the interest rate at will, with no connection at all with money demand and supply.[1] This idea is blatantly at variance with the claim that modern macroeconomics should be taught as a discipline firmly rooted in general-equilibrium principles. It may be added that, at the same time, this representation of the monetary sector conveys the equally faulty idea that, were the central bank not to intervene on the interest rate, the latter would be totally unrelated to changes in the state of the economy. No less problematic is the hazardous shortcut taken by Romer (2000) and Taylor (2000), who posit that the central bank directly sets the *real* interest rate. This seems hardly viable as a solution to the problem that the old *IS–LM* system failed to distinguish between the nominal and real interest rates owing to the missing link of expected inflation.

These are serious problems, since they do not concern the unavoidable pros and cons of simplifying assumptions and their proper dosages, but rather fundamental points of conceptual consistency that may distort the learner's conception of the macroeconomy. As a personal example of someone who teaches macroeconomics as part of a finance curriculum, the disappearance of the *LM* apparatus makes it hard for students to recollect the macroeconomic role of the credit and asset markets that they study in other courses. Even more importantly, blurring the relationship between monetary policy, the money market and asset markets bears some responsibility for today's poor understanding of the genesis and control of financial boom–bust episodes at the highest level of scholarship, as well as in policy-making circles (e.g. Borio and Lowe, 2002; Leijonhufvud, 2008).

One can only agree with Romer's criticisms of the traditional treatment of the *LM* apparatus that still survives even in modern textbooks. Nevertheless, ideally, we would like to have a basic macroeconomic model that conveys clear and theoretically consistent ideas about the relationships among monetary policy, the nominal interest rate, output and inflation in the context of short-run business cycles by amending the *LM* block rather than suppressing it. That is the aim of this chapter. It may be read as a guide to structuring a macro course around a basic New Keynesian model, although its main focus is restricted to the monetary block of the economy.

Section 2 overviews the foundations of the macro model. It provides the background for the treatment of the monetary block subsequently expounded, and introduces the *AD* and *AS* functions in a form that, according to current practice, relates 'output gaps' to 'inflation gaps' with respect to general-equilibrium trend values. Section 3 deals with the foundations of the role of money in the model, and shows how to derive a consistent *LM* 'gap function' in relation to output gaps and inflation gaps. Section 4 expands upon the monetary block, highlighting that it admits of two monetary policy regimes, the 'exogenous-money regime' where the central bank controls the rate of growth of the money stock, and the 'endogenous-money regime' where the central bank sets the nominal interest rate. The latter leads quite naturally to the Taylor rule, while making it clear that this is a particular choice of the central bank, and that it implies an endogenous path of the money stock determined by the underlying money market equilibrium. It can therefore be seen that, when properly re-worked in an inflationary set-up, the *LM* apparatus has no faults, and that the exogenous and endogenous monetary regimes are formally equivalent because they are both consistent with monetary equilibrium. Section 5 concludes.

2 Overview of the Macroeconomic Model

This section summarizes the building blocks of a simple macroeconomic model of New Keynesian inspiration providing the basic elements for understanding business cycles, that is to say, *short-run fluctuations of output and inflation*. The introductory elements presented in this section provide the background for the treatment of the monetary block set out subsequently.

The approach considered here rests on the idea that output fluctuations occur around a given growth trend, and that the two phenomena (growth and fluctuations) are produced by sets of causes that can be analysed separately. Though this idea has been criticized by important scholars and different schools of thought, both past (e.g. Keynes, 1937) and present (e.g. the 'Real Business Cycle' school introduced by, among others, Lucas, 1977), today it is nonetheless part of the 'new consensus' in macroeconomics, which is also known as the 'New Neoclassical Synthesis' (e.g. Blanchard, 2000). The development of this view has led all major official statistical agencies to provide estimated time series of the trend value of GDP, or *'potential output'*, Y_t^*. This measure of output is generally time-varying. Yet, in accordance with the idea of fluctuations set forth at the beginning, the data show further deviations of actual output from its potential level at any point in time.[2] The rate of deviation of actual output Y_t from potential output Y_t^* at each point in time t is usually called the *'output gap'* (i.e. $\hat{Y}_t = Y_t/Y_t^* - 1$).

Like output, the general price level (GPL) typically increases over time at an uneven pace, so that it, too, can be decomposed into fluctuations and the underlying trend. As long as the GPL is on the trend, prices are growing at the *historical inflation rate*. Whenever the GPL is above (below) the trend, prices are growing faster (slower) than the historical inflation rate. Macroeconomic principles have long been taught with reference to the GPL: it is common to read in textbooks that as a result of an increase (reduction) of aggregate demand the GPL *rises (falls)*. This practice is somewhat confusing to the average person, who has no experience of falling absolute prices (as a matter of fact, this is a rare phenomenon that may only occur in connection with severe general economic crises). If one wants to stick to the tradition, then the correct concept is that the GPL P_t, at a given point in time t, may rise *above* (or fall *below*) its trend value P_t^* at that point in time. Yet, the inflation rate, not the absolute GPL, is the centre of attention for central banks, as well as governments, economists and public opinion. Hence, it seems desirable that the inflation rate is introduced into the picture from the outset.

The core of the foregoing general view is usually represented by means of two simple log-linear relationships, one for aggregate supply (*AS*), y_t^s, and the other for aggregate demand (AD), y_t^d, both referred to the current time period t:

$$y_t^s = y_t^* + y_w(\pi_t - \pi_t^e) \tag{4.1}$$

$$y_t^d = -y_r(i_t - \pi_{t+1}^e) + u_t^d \tag{4.2}$$

where y_t^* is potential output, π_t is the inflation rate, i_t is the nominal interest rate, (y_w, y_r) are structural parameters, u_t^d represents exogenous (real) variables, and the superscript e denotes expected values.

These two relationships can be derived from explicit optimal behaviour of representative firms and households (see e.g. McCallum and Nelson, 1999; Clarida *et al.*, 1999; Woodford, 2003, ch. 4). Different microeconomic assumptions may yield slight variations and specifications; yet the above format is fairly general and representative of the key features of the theory, which can be summarized as follows.

The *AS* function is the rate of production that profit-maximizing firms are ready to offer in the given time unit t upon employing their optimal inputs of physical and human capital, given the production function that relates output with these inputs. The standard properties of the production function are those of constant returns to scale and decreasing marginal productivity of factors (e.g. the Cobb–Douglas function). It is convenient to add that labour is the more readily variable factor (it can be immediately adjusted *vis-à-vis* current market conditions), whereas existing capital is the fixed factor (e.g. existing capital takes one period of time to wear out, new capital takes one period of time to become operative).

The thrust of the *AS* function is that firms produce exactly y_t^*, independently of nominal variables such as money wages or the GPL (the function is 'vertical' in output-price space), unless in the current period there arises a forecast error about the GPL. This is a feature quite sensitive to the underlying microeconomic assumptions, but the general common theme is that this phenomenon arises in relation to *'nominal rigidities'* in the economy. For instance, at time $t - 1$ work contracts may pre-set the money wage rate, or firms (if they are price-makers) may pre-set their sale prices, for the entire period t, on the basis of the forecast of the GPL in that period. Given the GPL at time $t - 1$, this amounts to forecasting the inflation rate. Then, if during period t the inflation rate π_t turns out to be higher (lower) than π_t^e, firms will find it profitable to expand (contract) production above (below) y_t^*. Note that this flexibility in production is possible to the extent that at least one factor (in our case labour) is also flexible.

The *AD* function is the amount of output that the economy can absorb in the same time period t. This amount may consist of consumption as well as investment in new physical capital. The formulation of *AD* focuses on the common variable that, according to modern theories of consumption and investment, regulates both expenditures – namely, the expected real interest rate $(i_t - \pi_{t+1}^e)$. In fact, the sign of the coefficient y_r indicates that when $(i_t - \pi_{t+1}^e)$ increases *AD* decreases because firms wish to invest less and households wish to consume less to save more. The exogenous variables u_t^d may capture real determinants of consumption or investment, such as future expected incomes or Friedman's permanent income or future expected profits.

The economy is 'on the trend', that is to say it produces its potential output in each period of time, when all markets clear and all agents' plans are realized and mutually consistent. In other words, points in time on the trend correspond to the economy being in general equilibrium, and

$$y_t^s = y_t^d = y_t^*, \tag{4.3}$$
$$\pi_t^e = \pi_t$$

As is clear from this definition, and from the *AS–AD* equations, being on trend implies that expected values of variables match actual values, in particular the inflation rate. Consequently, it should also hold that $\pi_{t+1} = \pi_{t+1}^e$. It is then convenient to assume that potential output is constant (the trend growth rate of output is nil) except for exogenous shocks u_t^s to the determinants of the production function, $y_t^* = y^* + u_t^s$, whereas the trend growth rate of the GPL is also constant but may be non-zero, $\pi_t = \pi^*$ all t.[3]

At this point, the *AD–AS* functions can be rewritten in a way that highlights our analytical problem, i.e. *fluctuations around the trend* or *output (and inflation) gaps*.

First, note that from the equilibrium condition (4.3) it follows that *AD* should satisfy:

$$y_t^* = -y_r(i_t - \pi^*) + u_t^d$$

Clearly, the *AD–AS* equilibrium at potential output and constant inflation rate implies a unique value of the real interest rate:

$$r_t^* = \frac{1}{y_r}(u_t^d - (y^* + u_t^s))$$

This may be called the *'natural interest rate'* (Woodford, 2003, in homage to Knut Wicksell, 1898, who first introduced this notion), which is constant unless there are exogenous shocks to either *AD* (u_t^d) or *AS* (u_t^s).

The modern interpretation of this 'natural' value of the real interest rate is that it is part of the real determinants of the general equilibrium of the economy, and that it therefore provides (or should provide) the reference value, or the 'anchor', for the nominal interest rate i_t at any point in time t. In nominal terms, this requirement can be written as $i_t^* = r_t^* + \pi^*$, which is called the *'neutral interest rate'* or NAIRI (non-accelerating-inflation rate of interest) (e.g. Blinder, 1998). In fact, suppose that $i_t \neq i_t^*$: it is easy to see that *AD* in period t deviates from y_t^* by the amount:

$$\hat{y}_t^d \equiv y_t^d - y^* = -y_r(i_t - i_t^*) \tag{4.4}$$

As a result, we have a 'gap equation' for *AD*.

Now we can turn to the supply side of the economy. Whenever $\hat{y}_t^d \neq 0$, for the economy to produce less (more) output than potential, $\hat{y}_t^s = \hat{y}_t^d$, equation (4.1) says that the current inflation rate should fall (rise) with respect to π^* by the amount:

$$\hat{\pi}_t \equiv \pi_t - \pi^* = \frac{1}{y_w}\hat{y}_t^s \tag{4.5}$$

Thus, we also have a 'gap equation' for inflation, which is the inverted *AS* function. Remember that this representation embeds the assumption that all agents expect the inflation rate to be at its trend value π^*, so that inflation gaps are in fact unanticipated and generate forecast errors.

3 Money and the Nominal Interest Rate

In the previous section it was stressed that a key role in determining fluctuations is played by nominal rigidities. These, in general, arise by combining transactions denominated in money units with sluggish indexation of these money denominations *vis-à-vis* the actual evolution of the GPL. Hence the notion of nominal rigidity implies the existence of a *monetary economy*, where all transactions take place by means of fiat money issued by the central bank. One of the permanent achievements of the 'Keynesian Revolution' in modern macroeconomics is that a monetary economy is not just a 'barter economy' with 'the veil of money' (Hahn, 1982). A consistent representation of a monetary economy should start with money being rationally understood and managed by individual agents. As a consequence, the presence of money should change agents' decisions and market allocations with respect to an economy with no need for money. In the previous section we took a first step in this direction by showing the implications of goods and production factors being denominated in money units. In this section we shall examine the implications of agents' direct management of money.

3.1 The demand for money and the *LM* equation

The Keynesian legacy to modern monetary macroeconomics lies in the general proposition that money serves two fundamental purposes in the economy: *means of payment* and *store of value*. Yet it is seldom clarified that these two functions are not separable; they cannot be analysed or modelled as if they were independent. If agents benefit from *using* money as a means of payment for their *current* transactions, they must also rely on *holding* money as a store of value for their *future* transactions. On this latter dimension, in a developed monetary economy, fiat (paper) money competes with other stores of value, namely interest-bearing financial assets. On the other hand, financial assets in general cannot be used as means of payment: they must be converted into money, or 'liquidated', and this is usually a costly operation. Hence money retains a comparative advantage *vis-à-vis* financial assets in terms of *liquidity*. As a result, money and financial assets are substitutes, but not perfect substitutes, in households' portfolios.

The demand for money, as a relationship between the propensity to use money as a store of value and the interest rate on other assets, can be, and has been, articulated in a variety of approaches and models. A quite general distinction may be drawn between models where the interest rate is certain and those where it is uncertain.

Under certainty, the demand for money arises from the comparison between the opportunity cost of money (forgone interest) and the liquidity cost of assets (typically, fixed costs of conversion). The classical references here are the Baumol (1952) and Tobin (1956) 'inventory models', or alternatively the 'money in the utility function' approach inspired by Patinkin (1965) that has recently been applied extensively (see Walsh, 2003, ch. 2).

Under uncertainty, the actual return to an interest-bearing asset when the asset will be liquidated is not known with certainty ex ante. If i_t is the fixed nominal interest rate paid by a corporate bond issued in period t, and p_{bt} is its market price, then the actual return rate one period later will be

$$\tilde{i}_{t+1} = \frac{i_t}{p_{bt}} + \hat{p}_{bt+1}$$

where $\hat{p}_{bt+1}$ is the rate of change of the market price, which is the typical source of uncertainty over $\tilde{i}_{t+1}$. Therefore, in this context, the opportunity cost of money is given by the *expected* return to risky assets, while the liquidity cost of assets is given by *prospective capital losses*. This approach has led to the inclusion of money in portfolio analysis, as first put forward by Hicks (1935) and then fully developed by Tobin (1969).

In spite of the substantial differences across the various approaches, the resulting specifications of the demand for money boil down to a remarkably simple common core, which, in logs, reads as follows:

$$m_t^d = p_t + m_y y_t - m_i i_t + u_t^m \tag{4.6}$$

That is to say, the demand for money is exactly proportional to (or 'homogeneous of degree 1' with) the GPL, positively related to the real value of transactions (i.e., output), and negatively related to the nominal interest rate on bonds. The variables in u_t^m and the parameters m_y and m_i reflect the different assumptions underlying the different models (e.g. Goodhart, 1989). For instance, in a simple inventory model under certainty u_t^m is proportional to the fixed liquidation costs and $m_y = m_i = 0.5$. Under uncertainty, u_t^m is related to total financial wealth, and m_i is weighted by the degree of risk aversion and the variance of the return to bonds, indicating that high risk and high risk aversion reduce the elasticity of money demand to the interest rate (or that risky assets are poorer substitutes for money). As a result, a higher interest rate is needed to induce a shift from money to bonds.

Equation (4.6) can be used to make the relationship between the interest rate and money explicit. If m_t is the stock of money available in the economy in period t, monetary equilibrium requires that $m_t = m_t^d$. As a result, we obtain the Hicksian *LM* equation, which indicates the value of i_t for which the money stock m_t satisfies the demand m_t^d, i.e.

$$i_t = \frac{m_y}{m_i} y_t - \frac{1}{m_i}(m_t - p_t) + \frac{1}{m_i} u_t^m \tag{4.7}$$

As is clear from this equation, all the determinants of money demand, together with the *real value* of the stock of money in the economy ($m_t - p_t$), influence the interest rate and all interest-sensitive expenditures.

3.2 The *LM* equation and inflation

It is convenient to immediately recast the demand for money and the *LM* equation in our macroeconomic framework. In the first place, we may wish to see how much money the economy demands on the trend. Given the potential output y^* and the NAIRI i^*, equation (4.6) gives us the answer for a constant GPL. If on the trend the GPL grows at the constant rate π^*, we should first understand how inflation affects money demand. This is quite simple to see. Starting on trend in any period, the first difference of equation (4.6) indicates by how much money demand may change in the next period, i.e.

$$\mu_t^d \equiv m_t^d - m_{t-1}^d = \pi_t^* + m_y \hat{y}_t - m_i \hat{i}_t + \hat{u}_t^m \qquad (4.8)$$

Hence, on the trend ($\hat{y}_t$, $\hat{i}_t$, $\hat{u}_t^m = 0$), money demand *grows one-to-one with the inflation rate as a direct consequence of the increasing value of transactions.* Consequently, *monetary equilibrium requires an equivalent growth rate of the money stock,* $\mu^* = \pi^*$.

This condition is important: for instance, it guarantees that the interest rate coincides with the NAIRI. In fact, we can use the *LM* equation (4.7) to examine the consequences for i_t of the economy being off the trend. Actually, what we need is an *LM* 'gap equation' that indicates how i_t may deviate from i^*, i.e.

$$\hat{i}_t = \frac{m_y}{m_i} \hat{y}_t - \frac{1}{m_i}(\hat{\mu}_t - \hat{\pi}_t) + \frac{1}{m_i} \hat{u}_t^m \qquad (4.9)$$

where $\hat{\mu}_t \equiv \mu_t - \mu^*$. Therefore, apart from exogenous money demand shocks $\hat{u}_t^m$, *the interest rate may deviate from the NAIRI in response to output gaps, inflation gaps or too fast (or slow) money growth.*

The reader can check that, as argued above, as long as output and inflation are on the trend ($\hat{y}_t = 0$, $\hat{\pi}_t = 0$), and $\hat{u}_t^m = 0$, $\hat{\mu}_t = 0$ indeed guarantees that $i_t = i^*$. Otherwise, excessive or insufficient μ_t with respect to μ^* makes i_t increase or decrease with respect to i^*. On the other hand, if $\hat{\mu}_t = 0$, i_t may still increase or decrease as a result of a rise or fall in the demand for transaction balances (in real, $\hat{y}_t$, and/or nominal, $\hat{\pi}_t$, terms), or because of exogenous shocks $\hat{u}_t^m$.

The positive relation between interest rate gaps and inflation gaps is interesting and corresponds to the so-called '*real balance effect*' in an inflationary context. To see this point more clearly suppose that all variables are at their trend values ($\hat{y}_t = 0$, $\hat{u}_t^m = 0$, $\hat{\mu}_t = 0$) except excess inflation ($\hat{\pi}_t > 0$). In this situation the trend money growth rate μ^* is no longer commensurate to actual inflation, the real value of money balances falls, the economy develops excess money demand and the interest rate increases.

4   Alternative Monetary Regimes: Exogenous vs Endogenous Money

We now have all of the elements for a complete system of *AD*, *AS*, *LM* equations 'in gaps' that describes how the economy may deviate from the trend. Imposing the condition that the goods market clears in each period, $\hat{y}_t^d = \hat{y}_t^s$, and including possible changes in exogenous variables, we obtain:

$$\hat{y}_t = -\gamma_i \hat{i}_t + \hat{u}_t^d \tag{4.10}$$

$$\hat{\pi}_t = \frac{1}{\gamma_w}(\hat{y}_t - \hat{u}_t^s) \tag{4.11}$$

(a) $\hat{i}_t = \dfrac{m_y}{m_i}\hat{y}_t - \dfrac{1}{m_i}(\hat{\mu}_t - \hat{\pi}_t) + \dfrac{1}{m_i}\hat{u}_t^m$ \hspace{1cm} (4.12)

(b) $\hat{\mu}_t = \hat{\pi}_t + m_y\hat{y}_t - m_i\hat{i}_t + \hat{u}_t^m$

The system consists of three equations, the last two being alternative specifications of the *LM* relationship. These reflect the alternative choice between two monetary policy instruments to which there correspond two different monetary regimes. In case (a), the economy is said to be in a *regime of exogenous money*: the central bank controls μ_t and lets i_t be determined by the market. In case (b), the economy is in a *regime of endogenous money*: the instrument is i_t and the determination of μ_t is left to the market. The two regimes will be discussed below.

Given the set of trend variables (y^*, π^*, i^*, μ^*) and any of the shocks ($\hat{u}_t^d$, $\hat{u}_t^s$, $\hat{u}_t^m$), the system allows for determination of three endogenous 'gap' variables ($\hat{y}_t$, $\hat{\pi}_t$, $\hat{i}_t$ or $\hat{\mu}_t$), This ensures that the system is determinate. Moreover, for ($\hat{u}_t^d$, $\hat{u}_t^s$, $\hat{u}_t^m$) = 0, it admits of a configuration consistent with the economy being on the trend, namely ($\hat{y}_t$, $\hat{\pi}_t$, $\hat{i}_t$, $\hat{\mu}_t$) = 0. It also highlights two main classes of phenomena that may shift the economy off the trend:

- *real shocks*, either from the *AD* side ($\hat{u}_t^d$) or from the *AS* side ($\hat{u}_t^s$)
- *monetary shocks*, either from the demand side ($\hat{u}_t^m$) or from the supply side ($\hat{\mu}_t$, $\hat{i}_t$)

The point on which we focus in this section is the role of monetary policy within this picture. The two main messages of today's 'consensus view' are as follows. First, *do not disturb the economy with undue money supply shocks*. For the economy to remain on the trend, the money stock should grow at the trend inflation rate, otherwise the interest rate deviates from the NAIRI and feeds off-trend movements of *AD* and *AS*. Second, in the presence of other exogenous shocks, monetary policy should *implement a suitable stabilization policy driving the economy back on trend*.

Both recommendations require accurate understanding of how monetary policy works and can be implemented, which is beyond our scope here. It suffices here to consider the preliminary and fundamental issue concerning the choice of policy instrument: money growth rate or interest rate.

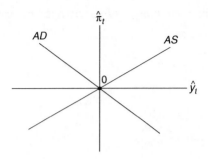

Figure 4.1   The *AD* and *AS* 'gap functions'

4.1   Exogenous money

This term indicates that the central bank has direct control of (and adopts as its instrument) the process of money growth μ_t; consequently, the interest rate is the dependent variable in the *LM* equation, i.e. it is determined endogenously by the monetary equilibrium conditions, the other variables in the equation being given. Typically, the central banks that opt for this regime (e.g. the former Bundesbank in Germany, and now, in part, the European Central Bank in the Euro area) announce a target for the money growth rate and operate accordingly. Our model, as explained above, also indicates what this target should be as long as the economy is on the trend. The proportionality between the growth rate of the money stock and the inflation rate along the general equilibrium path of the economy was (re)established in the post-Keynes era by Friedman (1968) and his Monetarist school. He spelt it out in his well-known slogan of the 'k% growth rule', which can therefore be called the 'Friedman rule'. This view had a strong influence on the theory and practice of monetary policy for the subsequent two or three decades.

It may be added that the Monetarists were also convinced that there was no particular need for the central bank to intervene actively to stabilize the economy even in the presence of exogenous shocks. Their idea was that the real part of the system (equations (4.10) and (4.11)) is inherently resilient to shocks, even though the money growth rate is just kept in line with its trend value. A preliminary check of this claim can be done upon noting that, in the exogenous money regime, the *LM* equation (4.12)(a) can be substituted for $\hat{i}_t$ into the *AD* equation. As a result, as long as $\hat{\mu}_t = 0$, *AD* is *decreasing with respect to* $\hat{\pi}_t$ (e.g. $\hat{\pi}_t < 0$ *ceteris paribus* lowers the interest rate which stimulates *AD*, as in Figure 4.1). This is equivalent to the textbook *AD* equation decreasing with the GPL. Since the *AS* function *is increasing with* $\hat{\pi}_t$, elementary market stability analysis suggests that the system is stable.

In order to gain a better assessment of the Monetarist approach it may be useful to see the model at work by means of simulations. To this end, our system must be enriched with a proper dynamic structure of 'leads and lags'.

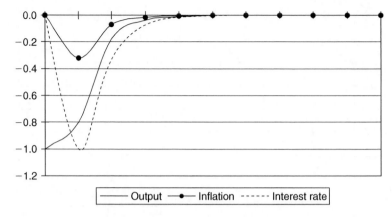

Figure 4.2 Simulation of 1% exogenous fall in aggregate demand

The simplest, yet sufficient, modification consists of adding a lagged output gap term to the right-hand side of the *AD* equation(4.6). As a matter of fact, there is ample evidence that output gaps display some autocorrelation or 'inertia' (e.g. Sims, 1992). The trend inflation rate is fixed at $\pi^* = 2\%$, so that $\mu^* = 2\%$.[4]

Now let us look at Figure 4.2, the simulation of a 1% exogenous fall in *AD* with the money growth rate left unchanged. After the initial *AD* shock reduces output and inflation, the interest rate falls spontaneously and progressively drives the system back to trend. Essentially, the real balance effect is at work here: monetary policy remains passive, but as long as inflation is below its trend value, the trend money growth corresponds to an expansionary impulse that increases real money balances with the effect of reducing the interest rate below the NAIRI.

It is worth stressing that the model, as well as the simulation, are based on the assumption that all agents' inflation expectations are anchored to the belief that the inflation rate will eventually return to its trend value. This belief is in fact supported by the system, so that it can also be described as a 'rational expectation'.

Perhaps the best known argument of Monetarism is that 'activist monetary policy', that is to say on–off deviations from the Friedman rule, have only temporary effects on output (and employment) at the cost of creating cyclical swings in the economy. Figure 4.3 illustrates this point by simulating an on–off 1% spike in the money growth rate. After the initial fall in the interest rate and increase of output, inflation starts accelerating. With money growth back to the trend value, monetary policy has a restrictive effect. The underlying mechanism is again the real balance effect, with reversed sign.

The idea that monetary policy should be anchored to a fixed rule, rather than being left to the 'discretion' of the central banker under contingent

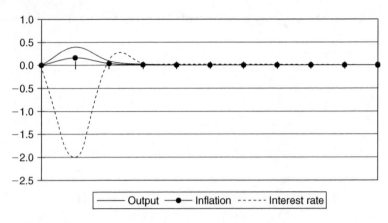

Figure 4.3   Simulation of 1% temporary increase in the money growth rate

circumstances is a permanent legacy of Monetarism. The milestone papers by Kydland and Prescott (1977) and Barro and Gordon (1983) showed that even a benevolent central banker promising 'to do the best for the economy in any contingent situation' (e.g. push output above trend if there is unemployment) may end up with an inflation rate higher than the historical trend with no permanent increase in output and employment. Suppose that a central banker, having learned that on–off monetary impulses have only transitory effects, sets out to raise output by means of a *permanent* increase in the money growth rate (an 'inflationary bias'). With the help of the rational expectations hypothesis (which was still undeveloped during the early stages of Monetarism) it is possible to show that this would be an inconsistent policy with respect to monetary equilibrium. In fact, if the new money growth rate is μ', then monetary equilibrium, that is $\hat{i}_t = 0$ for all future t, implies a new inflation rate $\pi' = \mu'$. Anticipating this result, rational agents will immediately revise their expected inflation rate in nominal contracts nullifying any real effect of the policy change. The reader can easily check that, upon substituting μ' into the *LM* equation (a), this yields $\hat{i}_t = 0$ for $y_t = y^*$ (the previous potential output) and $\pi_t = \pi'$ (the new, higher, inflation rate).

This result is important because it suggests that the trend inflation rate depends on the central bank's ability to set a *credible* inflation target for the economy. 'Credible' means that if the announced target is π^*, agents have reasons to believe in this target: they adopt it in their forecasts as shown in the various steps of the model, and their expectations are in fact fulfilled. On paper, therefore, the trend inflation rate is an entirely *conventional* variable in the hands of the central bank, meaning that there is no apparent reason why it should be greater than zero. In practice, however, there are various reasons why the historical inflation rates in almost all countries, and the target inflation rates of all major central banks, cannot be, and are not, zero. Thus, if the trend inflation rate contains some structural components (the long-run growth rate of world commodity prices, say) then a central bank that tries to maintain too low an inflation rate would make a mistake (by creating a 'deflationary bias') that would jeopardize the system's stability.

4.2 Endogenous money

Endogenous money means that the central bank has direct control of (and adopts as an instrument) the nominal interest rate i_t, so that the money growth rate is the dependent variable of the *LM* function. More precisely, once i_t is set, the central bank must be ready to inject into the system any amount of money that is consistent with money demand according to equation (4.12)(b). If the exogenous money regime is closely related with Monetarism and the 'Friedman rule', the endogenous money regime is the hallmark of New Keynesianism and the 'Taylor rule' (Taylor, 1993)[5]. This is, however, a rule in a different sense than Friedman's, in that it does not fix a determinate value of the control variable irrevocably but indicates how the central bank *changes the control variable in relation to changes in specified conditions in the economy*. Hence a better term is that of a 'reaction function' which makes monetary policy transparent and predictable, though not predetermined (Blinder, 1998).

The basic specification of the Taylor rule can easily be translated into our framework as follows:

$$\hat{i}_t = \gamma\hat{y}_t + \delta\hat{\pi}_t \tag{4.13}$$

That is to say, the central bank commits itself to setting the nominal interest above or below the NAIRI if output and/or inflation are above or below their respective trend values. The parameters γ and δ are related to the central bank's policy weights assigned to output *vis-à-vis* inflation stabilization. These weights may also be obtained by assuming (or imposing) that the central bank minimizes a loss function defined over output and inflation gaps (Clarida *et al.*, 1999).

Much of the scholarly work subsequent to Taylor's 'discovery' of how the US Federal Reserve engineers its control of the interest rate has focused on three issues: whether the empirical evidence extends over time and in other countries; whether reaction functions such as the Taylor rule have stability properties similar to those of the Friedman rule; and whether the Taylor rule can be designed so as to maximize welfare in the face of macroeconomic shocks (Clarida *et al.*, 1999; Woodford, 2003). Here we shall consider the second issue in the context of our macro model.

This issue is typically addressed by combining a Taylor rule with an output gap and an inflation gap equation: in our case, equations (4.10), (4.11) and (4.13). We can now repeat the same preliminary stability check as in the case of the exogenous money regime: let us use equation (4.13) to substitute for

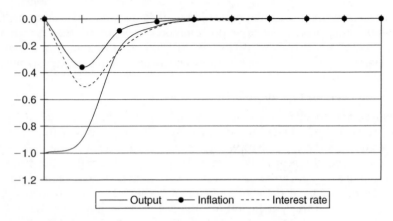

Figure 4.4   Simulation of 1% exogenous fall in aggregate demand

$\hat{i}_t$ in equation (4.10) to obtain the relationship between $\hat{y}_t$ and $\hat{\pi}_t$. It is immediately seen that, as long as $\delta > 0$, $\hat{y}_t$ remains decreasing with respect to $\hat{\pi}_t$
as it was in the exogenous money regime. The important conclusion is that,
like the exogenous money regime, the endogenous money regime is consistent with stability *provided that the interest-rate reaction function is responsive to
inflation gaps* (note that from this point of view the responsiveness to output
gaps is not necessary).[6]

To see this point more clearly, we can simulate the new system and examine how it reacts to the same negative *AD* shock that we imparted to the
exogenous money system above. The structural parameters of the *AD* and *AS*
functions are the same. The policy weights of the Taylor rule have been set
equal to those found in Taylor's original paper, namely $\gamma = 0.5$ and $\delta = 1.5$. As
can be seen from Figure 4.4, the qualitative dynamic pattern of the economy
is in fact analogous to the exogenous money regime.

It is also worth drawing attention to the fact that, contrary to the Friedman
rule, *the Taylor rule implies an active monetary policy*. In fact, the Taylor rule
commits the central bank to intervening in the face of macroeconomic shocks
whereas, as seen above, the Friedman rule does not. Indeed, in the endogenous money system the nominal interest rate provides the single link between
the monetary and the real sides of the economy, and if the central bank does
not intervene by manipulating $\hat{i}_t$, the system will not adjust spontaneously
to shocks. This, it should be stressed, is an extreme characterization of the
endogenous money system due to the structure of the *AD–AS–TR* system,
where the interest rate, in the absence of active monetary policy, would
be totally unrelated to changes in inflation or output. This is not the case
with the *LM* function thanks to the real balance effect. As a matter of fact,
it is a long-standing argument of Old and New Keynesians (e.g. Greenwald
and Stiglitz, 1987, 1993) that the real balance effect is *empirically* weak and

negligible. This fact may provide an additional argument in favour of the direct control of the interest rate by the central bank. Yet, from a conceptual point of view, it does not seem desirable that the non-policy linkages between the interest rate and other macro variables are completely hidden from view.

At this point, an important methodological issue should be stressed. The bare *AD–AS–TR* framework may transmit the faulty idea that the central bank can set the interest rate at will, with no connection at all to money demand and supply. This is certainly not the case, and a correct and complete representation of the endogenous money regime *should include the endogenous LM equation* (4.12)(b). Hence we end up with the *four* equations system that I reproduce here for the reader's convenience:

$$\hat{y}_t = -y_i\hat{i}_t + \hat{u}_t^d$$

$$\hat{\pi}_t = \frac{1}{y_w}(\hat{y}_t - \hat{u}_t^s)$$

$$\hat{i}_t = \gamma\hat{y}_t + \delta\hat{\pi}_t$$

$$\hat{\mu}_t = \hat{\pi}_t + m_y\hat{y}_t - m_i\hat{i}_t + \hat{u}_t^m$$

This format of the system highlights that controlling the interest rate by means of the Taylor rule implies an endogenous evolution of the money stock determined by the inflation gap, the output gap and the Taylor rule itself. Thus, explicit consideration of the endogenous money growth process may convey interesting insights. Consider, for instance, the following two examples.

First, let us consider again the case of a negative *AD* shock. As can be understood from the equation for $\hat{\mu}_t$, this variable results from two opposite tendencies: the negative *AD* shock tends to reduce money demand both in nominal and real terms, while the subsequent decrease in the interest rate tends to raise it. The overall outcome cannot be predicted a priori as it depends on the magnitude of the relevant parameters. Figure 4.5 shows the path of the money growth rate underlying the Taylor-rule-driven adjustment process to the negative 1% *AD* shock in Figure 4.4. The deflationary shock causes a net deceleration of the money growth rate even though the central bank lowers the interest rate. This seemingly odd result is due to the fact that the simulated Taylor rule yields a relatively small cut in the interest rate (compare Figures 4.4 and 4.2) which is not sufficient to overcome the negative effect of the deflationary shock on money demand (indeed, the Taylor rule is engineered to close the output and inflation gaps, not to control the money growth rate). Therefore, it is interesting to note that the sign of the change in the money growth rate may not give the right information about the actual stance of monetary policy.

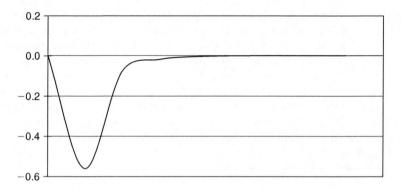

Figure 4.5   Path of the money growth rate after a 1% fall in aggregate demand under the Taylor rule

A second example, which to some extent vindicates the informational role of the (endogenous) money growth rate, relates to the Wicksellian view of the New Keynesian model popularized by Woodford (2003). As recalled above, the model yields results that are reminiscent of Wicksell's theory of 'cumulative processes'. The economy is in a steady state as long as the market interest rate equates the NAIRI (the market real rate equates to the natural rate). As the market rate lies above (below) the NAIRI the economy is set on a path of excess deflation (inflation). The Taylor rule provides a means of 'endogenizing' the market rate in a way that ensures convergence to stable GPL (inflation), consistently with Wicksell's prescription that the central bank should raise (lower) the market rate in the face of inflation (deflation) (e.g. Wicksell, 1898, p. 102). However, unlike his modern followers, Wicksell was well aware that the natural interest rate may be highly variable and hardly observable. It was certainly not a good candidate as a target variable in Wicksell's view. The (quite likely) misalignment of the market interest rate with the NAIRI is the key to Wicksellian business cycles boosted by low interest rates and over-lending and over-investment in excess of planned saving. This class of phenomena is now regarded with growing interest as the seed of financial crises that challenge the new 'art and science' of monetary policy encapsulated in the Taylor rule (e.g. Borio and Lowe, 2002; Leijonhufvud, 2008). Our four-equations system is flexible enough to introduce students to this up-to-date field of discussion.

A Wicksellian cycle can easily be obtained in our system by imparting a shock directly to the interest rate gap on the left-hand side of the Taylor rule. Consider the case where the natural interest rate rises (an improvement in production technology allows for a higher real return to capital). Given the general belief in the target inflation rate π^*, the NAIRI rises as much as the natural rate. Suppose that, by contrast, the central bank fails to adjust the interest rate, that is, $\hat{i}_t < 0$. The ensuing business cycle is depicted in Figure 4.6(a).[7]

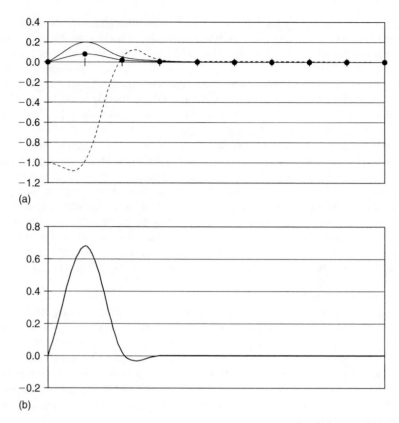

Figure 4.6 (a) Simulation of −1% interest-rate gap under the Taylor rule; (b) path of the money growth rate

The Taylor rule appears to be resilient to this type of shock, driving the interest rate, output and inflation back on trend, not (necessarily) because the central bank tracks the NAIRI, but simply because it reacts to the output and inflation gaps generated by the interest-rate gap. This is in fact the prevailing opinion in the profession, a corollary of which is that the central bank need have no explicit target among financial variables in addition to its output and inflation targets (e.g. Bernanke and Gertler, 2001).

The challenge to this view comes from the so-called 'missing inflation puzzle', i.e. the recurrent fact that 'financial imbalances [i.e. over-investment] can and do build up in periods of disinflation or in a low inflation environment' (Borio and Lowe, 2002, p. 1). Indeed, even loosely 'realistic' parameters in our oversimplified simulation yield disproportionately small inflationary effects of the initial interest rate gap. These may in practice be too small for the central bank to react to. Thus, the Taylor rule alone may not be sufficient to tame Wicksellian cycles, which may over time evolve into the cumulative processes studied by the great Swedish economist. Supporters of this view point out the necessity of monitoring other indicators of 'financial imbalances'. Among these, the same study by Borio and Lowe indicates rapid growth of credit as a clear leader of subsequent instability. In the present model, as a first approximation, this variable can be captured by $\hat{\mu}_t$, the growth of money that the supply side of the money market is ready to grant to the economy as long as the central bank pegs the interest rate (more on the banking sector in the next paragraph). Panel (b) of Figure 4.6 gives a quantitative idea of the sizeable acceleration of the growth of endogenous money that is associated with the initial interest rate gap in panel a). In the basic *IS–AS–TR* model, changes in the money growth rate are ignored on the presumption that they have no impact on the real economy, which responds only to the interest rate, and have no impact on the interest rate, which is determined only by the central bank. To the extent that these presumptions cannot be taken at face value, tracking the evolution of the money growth rate may still find a place in the conduct of monetary policy (see also Friedman, 2003).[8]

4.3   Which monetary regime?

Another teaching advantage of the monetary framework presented here is that it allows for an integrated, comparative analysis of the exogenous and endogenous money regimes, neither of which is posited as an article of faith. On the one hand, this analysis helps establish the principle that the two regimes are alternative, in the sense that they cannot be adopted simultaneously[9]. It is also clear that, on the other hand, both alternatives are rooted in the concept of monetary equilibrium that has been explained in the previous paragraphs.

First of all, comparison between the *LM* equation (4.12)(a) with the Friedman rule, and equation (4.13) with the Taylor rule reveals that *the two regimes yield an interest rate equation which is formally identical* (apart from money demand shocks, on which see below). It is no surprise, then, that the two regimes have the analogous stability properties that we found above. Students can therefore understand that there is no fundamental theoretical difference between the two regimes, and the choice between them is essentially on operational grounds in consideration of the structural features of the economy and the way in which these impinge upon the conduct of monetary policy.

The classic reference in this perspective is still Poole's (1970) analysis, which showed that the exogenous money regime is preferable (in terms of stability) to the extent that the demand for goods is more volatile than the demand for money (e.g. the variance of $\hat{u}_t^m$ is smaller than the variance of $\hat{u}_t^d$), whereas the endogenous money regime is preferable in the opposite case. At this juncture, students may notice a natural connection with issues arising from the financial dimension of money demand (another topic under threat of extinction at the principles level). As a matter of fact, the main force driving major central banks away from quantitative control of money and towards the (overt) direct control of the interest rate has been the dramatic increase in the volatility of money demand with respect to AD volatility that has occurred in all major industrialized countries over the last few decades, mostly as a consequence of financial innovations (Moore, 1988, Goodhart, 1988). Note that equation (b) contains the money demand disturbance $\hat{u}_t^m$, which is notably absent from the Taylor rule. What happens in the endogenous money regime? If money demand shocks are not explicitly included in the Taylor rule, they have to be accommodated by way of money market operations (see Walsh, 2003, ch. 9). If , say, $\hat{u}_t^m > 0$ and $\hat{i}_t = 0$, the supply side of the money market (through its different articulations) must be ready to inject more money at the current interest rate. This explains why these disturbances are the main source of difficulty for the central bank (and for central bank watchers) when it comes to using the money growth rate as a precise signal of monetary policy[10].

Another key topic, the role of the banking sector, falls into place here. Our framework (like all standard textbook treatments) is kept at a level that does not accommodate this sector explicitly, and this represents a critical simplification *for both monetary regimes*. As a matter of fact, in developed systems the central bank has no direct relations with the non-bank private sector. Also, the real-world monetary variables most relevant to the non-bank private sector – bank deposits and their close substitutes, and corporate bond rates as to the interest rate – are not directly controllable by the central bank. The 'transmission mechanism' between these variables and their counterparts within the reach of the central bank – bank reserves and inter-bank interest rates, respectively – goes through the banking sector. Therefore, the matching process between money demand and money supply, whether it takes place in one regime or the other, is intermediated by the banking sector. The old Monetarist presumption that this fact could be safely ignored (as in Friedman's well-known metaphor of money being dropped onto the public from a helicopter) or that it could be tamed by the mechanics of the 'money multiplier', has in the long run proved to be untenable. Contrary to that presumption, and vindicating Keynesian criticisms, developments in the banking sector and its increasing sophistication have dramatically weakened and blurred the transmission mechanism between 'high powered money' and the final money stock in the hands of the public that underpinned the Monetarist theory and practice of the exogenous money regime.

On the other hand, the New Keynesian theory and practice of the endogenous money regime is no less crucially dependent upon very delicate, and perhaps transient, transmission mechanisms; the demand for and supply of bank reserves in the first place, and the term structure of interest rates in the second place (Romer, 2000; Walsh, 2003, ch. 9). Therefore, the ideal extension of the basic model of *either monetary regime* at a more advanced level should include the inter-bank market as the true money market where monetary policy is conducted.

5   Conclusions

Ongoing developments in macroeconomics and in the theory and practice of monetary policy render increasingly flimsy, obsolete and awkward the teaching of the traditional *LM* apparatus as a means of determining the interest rate and providing a link between the monetary and real sides of the economy. On the other hand, although replacement of the *LM* schedule with the Taylor rule may make these tasks more immediately intelligible and tangible, it conveys the wrong ideas that the central bank has no other means to conduct monetary policy, that it can set the interest rate at will with no connection to money market equilibrium, and that there is no other non-policy relationship between the interest rate and output and inflation. This chapter has put forward a macroeconomic framework of New Keynesian inspiration which shows how to overcome the drawbacks of both the old *LM* equation and the new *TR* approach, by amending the *LM* block rather than suppressing it.

The model consists of *AD*, *AS* and *LM* functions that are consistently re-expressed in terms of output gaps and inflation gaps, and shows that once the *LM* apparatus has been properly re-worked in this way, it has no faults and fits the general framework perfectly. Indeed, it may be used to explain that the central bank can choose between controlling the money growth rate or the nominal interest rate, and that the latter choice may be represented by the Taylor rule. By showing that the two policy regimes are formally equivalent and have analogous stability properties, the model clarifies that the central bank's choice is mainly dictated by considerations of operational efficiency, as is very well-known from the literature on central banking.

The present teaching framework presents additional advantages in that it allows a smoother transition towards more advanced notions in money and finance:

- It makes clear that controlling the interest rate implies a path of the money growth rate dictated by the underlying money market equilibrium, providing a better and wider perspective for monetary policy evaluation;
- It creates an opportunity to (re)introduce the financial dimensions of money demand (money-bond substitutability, financial innovations, stability) and therefore the relationship between monetary policy and asset markets;
- It allows consistent extensions of the model to include the role of the banking sector and of the inter-bank market as the actual place where monetary policy is conducted.

Notes

1. Indeed, Woodford (2003) argues that the *IS–AS–TR* model can be conceived as being totally independent of the existence of money.

2. It may be added that, over the short time horizon appropriate to the observed frequency and amplitude of fluctuations, the assumption that the autonomous determinants of the growth trend of output are substantially invariant, so that they can be taken as exogenously given, may be accepted as realistic. Or to put it differently, there is not sufficient evidence that the determinants of growth change with the frequency and amplitude necessary to fit those of the actual business cycles in major industrial economies (Mankiw, 1989). More problematic is the objection that fluctuations themselves may react back onto the determinants of growth (e.g. a slump may shift the economy onto a lower growth path). This possibility is simply ruled out by the way in which the *efficient level of output* – i.e. the level of output that lies on the trend at each point in time – is obtained in the model (see below).

3. It should be stressed that modern theory distinguishes different types of general (real) equilibrium, and different levels of potential output, depending on the working of factor as well as goods markets. If all markets are perfectly competitive and with no 'frictions', or more generally if they obey the Walrasian paradigm, then potential output takes the highest possible level corresponding to Pareto efficient allocations in the economy. If any market deviates from perfect competition (e.g. firms or workers have some degree of monopoly power in the goods or labour markets), the economy will suffer a loss of potential output failing to achieve Pareto efficiency. Generally speaking, these inefficiencies fall under the rubric of '*real rigidities*'. Of particular importance in this connection is the idea of a 'natural rate of unemployment' (or else 'structural unemployment'), introduced into modern macroeconomics by Friedman (1968) and Phelps (1968, 1970). These imperfections notwithstanding, potential output, being the result of optimal responses by agents to the given market conditions and signals, remains the best possible outcome for the economy, and corresponds to the general equilibrium of markets, under the given conditions and constraints.

4. The other parameters of the model have been set with reference to broad empirical regularities of developed countries, namely, an autocorrelation coefficient of 0.3, an *AD* elasticity to interest rate gaps $y_r = 0.2$, an *AS* elasticity to inflation gaps $y_w = 2.0$ (remember that $y_w = \alpha/(1-\alpha)$); this is, according to the underlying Cobb–Douglas production function, the labour to capital income ratio which is roughly of that order of magnitude), and finally the income and interest elasticities of money demand $m_y = m_r = 0.5$ (these values are taken from the Baumol–Tobin inventory model; actually, there has never been general agreement on estimated money demand functions, except on the claims that neither of the two parameters exceed unity and that the interest elasticity is no greater than the income elasticity – see Goodhart, 1989).

5. Endogenous money comes from a long-standing tradition in monetary theory that was well entrenched in Old Keynesianism as well (see Tobin, 1970; Kaldor, 1982; Moore, 1988). Meanwhile, on the opposite front, the New Classical real business cycle theorists, denying any real effect of monetary variables, are ready to subscribe to the view that the co-movements between output and money aggregates are the result of the latter being driven by the former rather than the other way round (see e.g. King and Plosser, 1984).

6. If the reaction function places a zero weight on the output gap, then we are in a pure 'inflation targeting' regime (see e.g. Svensson, 1997).

7. Note that the Wicksellian cycle also has a Keynesian counterpart in that output fluctuates too.

8. This conclusion might mitigate the fierce criticism directed towards the ECB's 'two-handed' monetary policy of interest rate control with money growth monitoring.
9. As a relevant example, the European Central Bank has been criticized since its inception because it claims that its policy is based on 'the two pillars' of controlling the money growth rate and controlling interest rates (e.g. ECB, 1999). Since these two pillars cannot stand together, critics argue that the ECB's monetary policy is in fact opaque and unaccountable. See e.g. Wyplosz (2006).
10. Of course, this may be a counter argument to those who argue in favour of monitoring the money growth rate as an indicator of financial imbalances, as explained in section 4.2.

References

Allsopp, C. and Vines, D. (2000), 'The Assessment: Macroeconomic Policy', *Oxford Review of Economic Policy*, 16, 1–32.

Barro, R. J. and Gordon, D. B. (1983), 'A Positive Theory of Monetary Policy in a Natural-Rate Model', *Journal of Political Economy*, 91, 589–610.

Baumol, W. (1952), 'The Transactions Demand for Cash', *Quarterly Journal of Economics*, 67, 545–56.

Bernanke, B. and Gertler, M. (2001), 'Should Central Banks Respond to Movements in Asset Prices?', *American Economic Review*, Papers and Proceedings of the American Economic Association, 91, 253–7.

Blanchard, O. J. (2000), 'What Do We Know about Macroeconomics that Fisher and Wicksell Did Not Know?', *Quarterly Journal of Economics*, 115, 1375–409.

Blinder, A. (1998), *Central Banking in Theory and Practice*, Cambridge, MA: MIT Press.

Borio C. and Lowe, P. (2002), 'Asset Prices, Financial and Monetary Stability: Exploring the Nexus', BIS Working Papers, no. 114.

Carlin, W. and Soskice, D. (2004), 'The 3-Equation New Keynesian Model: A Graphical Exposition', Discussion Paper Series, CEPR, no. 4588.

Clarida, R., Galí, J. and Gertler, M. (1999), 'The Science of Monetary Policy: A New Keynesian Perspective', *Journal of Economic Literature*, 37, 1661–707.

European Central Bank (1999), *Monthly Bulletin*, no. 1.

Friedman, B. M. (2003), 'The *LM* Curve: A Not-so-fond Farewell', NBER Working Paper Series, no. 10123.

Friedman, M. (1968), 'The Role of Monetary Policy', *American Economic Review*, 58, 1–17.

Goodfriend, M. and King, R. G. (1997), 'The New Neoclassical Synthesis and the Role of Monetary Policy', in Bernanke, B. S. and Rotemberg, J. J. (eds.), *NBER Macroeconomics Annual*, Cambridge, MA: MIT Press.

Goodhart, C. A. E. (1988), 'The Conduct of Monetary Policy', *Economic Journal*, 98, 330–65.

Goodhart, C. A. E. (1989), *Money, Information and Uncertainty*, 2nd edn. London: Macmillan.

Greenwald, B. and Stiglitz, J. E. (1987), 'Keynesian, New Keynesian and New Classical Economics', Oxford Economic Papers, 31, 119–33.

Greenwald, B. C. and Stiglitz, J. E. (1993), 'New and Old Keynesians', *Journal of Economic Perspectives*, 7, 23–44.

Hahn, F. H. (1982), *Money and Inflation*, Oxford: Blackwell.

Hicks, J. R. (1935), 'A Suggestion for Simplifying Monetary Theory', in *Critical Essays in Monetary Theory*, Oxford: Clarendon Press, 1965.

Kaldor, N. (1982), *The Scourge of Monetarism*, Oxford: Oxford University Press.

Keynes, J. M. (1937), 'The General Theory of Employment', *Quarterly Journal of Economics*, 14, 109–23.

King, R. G. and Plosser, C. I. (1984), 'Money, Credit and Prices in a Real Business Cycle', *American Economic Review*, 74, 363–80.

Kydland, F. E. and Prescott, E. C. (1977), 'Rules Rather Than Discretion: The Inconsistency of Optimal Plans', *Journal of Political Economy*, 85, 473–91.

Leijonhufvud, A. (1983), 'What Was the Matter With *IS–LM*?', in J. P. Fitoussi (ed.), *Modern Macroeconomic Theory*, Oxford: Blackwell.

Leijonhufvud, A. (2008), 'Keynes and the Crisis', CEPR *Policy Insight*, no. 23.

Lucas, R. E. (1977), 'Understanding Business Cycles', *Journal of Monetary Economics,* in Brunner, K. and Meltzer, L. H. (eds), *Stabilization of the Domestic and International Economy*, Amsterdam: North Holland.

Mankiw, G. N. (1989), 'Real Business Cycles: A New Keynesian Perspective', *Journal of Economic Perspectives*, 3, 79–90.

McCallum, B. T. and Nelson, E. (1999), 'An Optimizing IS-*LM* Specification for Monetary Policy and Business Cycle Analysis', *Journal of Money, Credit and Banking*, 31, 296–316.

Moore, B. (1988), *Horizontalists and Verticalists*, Cambridge: Cambridge University Press.

Patinkin, D. (1965), *Money, Interest and Prices: An Integration of Money and Value Theory*, 2nd edn, New York: Harper & Row.

Phelps, E. S. (1968), 'Money Wage Dynamics and Labour Market Equilibrium', *Journal of Political Economy*, 76, 678–711.

Phelps, E. S. (ed.) (1970), *Microeconomic Foundations of Employment and Inflation Theories*, New York: Norton.

Poole, W. (1970), 'Optimal Choice of Monetary Policy Instruments in a Simple Stochastic Macro Model', *Quarterly Journal of Economics*, 84, 197–216.

Romer, D. (2000), 'Keynesian Macroeconomics Without the *LM* Curve', *Journal of Economic Perspectives*, 14, 149–69.

Sims, C. (1992), 'Interpreting the Macroeconomic Time Series Facts: The Effects of Monetary Policy', *European Economic Review*, 36, 975–1000.

Svensson, L. E. O. (1997), 'Inflation Forecast Targeting. Implementing and Monitoring Inflation Targets', *European Economic Review*, 41, 1111–47.

Taylor, J. B. (1993), 'Discretion Versus Policy Rules in Theory and Practice', *Carnegie-Rochester Conference Series on Public Policy*, 39, 195–214.

Taylor, J. B. (2000), 'Teaching Macro at the Principles Level', *American Economic Review*, Papers and Proceedings of the American Economic Association, 90, 90–4.

Tobin, J. (1956), 'The Interest Elasticity of the Transactions Demand for Cash', *Review of Economics and Statistics*, 38, 241–7.

Tobin, J. (1969), 'A General Equilibrium Approach to Monetary Theory', *Journal of Money Credit and Banking*, 1, 15–29.

Tobin, J. (1970), 'Money and Income: Post Hoc Ergo Propter Hoc?', *Quarterly Journal of Economics*, 84, 301–17.

Walsh, C. E. (2003), *Monetary Theory and Policy*, 2nd edn, Cambridge, MA: MIT Press.

Wicksell, K. (1898), *Interest and Prices*, London: Macmillan, 1936.

Woodford, M. (2003), *Interest and Prices*, Princeton: Princeton University Press.

Wyplosz, C. (2006), 'European Monetary Union: The Dark Sides of a Major Success', *Economic Policy*, April, 207–61.

5
The New Consensus in Macroeconomics: A Critical Appraisal

Philip Arestis[1]

1 Introduction

A conference was held under the aegis of the UK's 'Government Economic Service', 30 November 2005, under the title 'Is There a New Consensus in Macroeconomics?', and a book emerged from that conference (Arestis, 2007a). The conference concluded that there is now a new macroeconomic consensus in the sense that there is today a level of agreement among economists on macro issues not seen since the late 1960s/early 1970s.[2] This does not imply, of course, that there is complete agreement, with no detractors and opponents, or that the consensus will be permanent. Neither does it mean that the new consensus is above board without much criticism in place. On the contrary, one of the aims of this chapter is to do just that, namely to appraise it critically.

It would be interesting to discuss at this early stage how the New Consensus Macroeconomics (NCM) has come about. This exercise is very important for it is the case that this model has replaced the *IS–LM* model. The latter has been taught over the years as the main framework of macroeconomics for both teaching and policy analysis. There is, thus, an urgent need to explain the move from the *IS–LM* macroeconomics teaching, which does not reflect current research in the area, to the NCM that is very much the current trend. Our view on the birth of NCM is that it has come about in view of the fact that, after the collapse of the Grand Neoclassical Synthesis in the 1970s,[3] macroeconomists never took much notice of the reconstruction of New Classical macroeconomics with rational expectations. By contrast, New Keynesian macroeconomics was transformed into what we now label as New Consensus Macroeconomics. The latter has managed to encapsulate those early developments of macroeconomics in the 1970s, including rational expectation, but with assumptions that were also acceptable to the old Neoclassical Synthesis proponents. Galí and Gertler (2007) suggest that the New Keynesian paradigm, which arose in the 1980s, provided sound microfoundations along with the concurrent development of the real business cycle approach that promoted the explicit optimization behaviour aspect. Those developments along with macroeconomic features that previous paradigms lacked, such as the long-run vertical Phillips curve, resulted in the NCM.

The policy implications of the NCM paradigm are particularly important for this development aspect of macroeconomics. Price stability can be achieved through monetary policy since inflation is a monetary phenomenon; as such it can only be controlled through changes in the rate of interest. Goodfriend (2007) argues that this particular set of propositions, amongst many other, have been backed by actual monetary policy experience in the US, and other countries around the globe, following the abandonment of money supply rules in the early 1980s.[4] Academic contributions also helped the foundations of the NCM on both theoretical and empirical grounds; e.g. 'The Taylor Rule became the most common way to model monetary policy' (Goodfriend, 2007, p. 59; see also, Orphanides, 2007). In fact, for Goodfriend (2007), 'One reason the Federal Reserve began to talk openly about interest rate policy in 1994 was that academic economists had begun to do so. Indeed, thinking about monetary policy as interest rate policy is one of the hallmarks of the new consensus that has made possible increasingly fruitful interaction between academics and central bankers' (p. 59).

The discussion and assessment of the New Consensus in Macroeconomics (NCM) in this chapter is in the context of an open economy. As such, it draws on Arestis (2007b), a contribution to the conference referred to above. This exercise is important for two reasons. The first is that the reader is made aware of the current state of macroeconomics, a different one from the old *IS–LM* macroeconomic model. At the same time, though, it is very important to appraise this new way of thinking about macroeconomics. And as we show below, the 'new' way of doing macroeconomics is not without its problems. Ultimately, the chapter alerts instructors to some of the shortcomings of and questions that remain about the New Consensus. These are issues that can and should be raised in the classroom if the teaching of the consensus view is to be used as a vehicle for critical thinking about the economy, rather than an apologia for current policy practices.

We begin in section 2, after this introduction, with the open economy aspect of the NCM, which enables some attention to be given to the exchange rate channel of the transmission mechanism of monetary policy in addition to the aggregate demand channel and the inflation expectations channel. In the context of this extended model of NCM its policy implications are examined in the same section. We critically appraise NCM and its policy implications in section 3, while section 4, the final section, summarizes and concludes.

2   An Open Economy New Consensus Macroeconomics and Policy Implications

We discuss an open economy NCM model first, followed by its policy implications. It is worth noting at the outset that the NCM is a framework in which there is no role for 'money and banking', and there is only a single rate of interest.[5] Two of the key assumptions made are worth emphasizing: the first is that price stability is the primary objective of monetary policy; and the second is that inflation is a monetary phenomenon and as such it can only be controlled by monetary policy means, this being the rate of interest under the control of the central bank. This should be undertaken through interest rate manipulation. Monetary policy is thereby upgraded but at the same time fiscal policy is downgraded. This raises the issue of whether deflation can be tackled through changes in interest rates since the latter cannot fall below zero. These and many other aspects of the NCM framework are further highlighted and discussed in what follows in this section.

2.1   The open economy NCM model

Drawing on Arestis (2007b; see also Angeriz and Arestis, 2007b), we utilize the following six-equation model for this purpose:

$$Y_t^g = a_0 + a_1 Y_{t-1}^g + a_2 E_t(Y_{t+1}^g) + a_3[R_t - E_t(p_{t+1})] + a_4(rer)_t + s_1 \tag{5.1}$$

$$p_t = b_1 Y_t^g + b_2 p_{t-1} + b_3 E_t(p_{t+1}) + b_4[E_t(p_{wt+1}) - E_t \Delta(er)_t] + s_2 \tag{5.2}$$

$$R_t = (1 - c_3)[RR^* + E_t(p_{t+1}) + c_1 Y_{t-1}^g + c_2(p_{t-1} - p^T)] + c_3 R_{t-1} + s_3 \tag{5.3}$$

$$rer_t = d_0 + d_1[[(R_t - E_t(p_{t+1})] - [(R_{wt}) - E(p_{wt+1})]] + d_2(CA)_t$$
$$+ d_3 E(rer)_{t+1} + s_4 \tag{5.4}$$

$$(CA)_t = e_0 + e_1(rer)_t + e_2 Y_t^g + e_3 Y_{wt}^g + s_5 \tag{5.5}$$

$$er_t = rer_t + P_{wt} - P_t \tag{5.6}$$

with $b_2 + b_3 + b_4 = 1$, thereby implying a vertical Phillips curve. Furthermore, a_0 is a constant that could reflect, *inter alia*, the fiscal stance; Y^g is the domestic output gap and Y_w^g is world output gap; R is nominal rate of interest (and R_w is the world nominal interest rate); p is rate of inflation (and p^w is the world inflation rate); p^T is inflation rate target; RR^* is the 'equilibrium' real rate of interest, e.g. the rate of interest consistent with zero output gap, which implies from equation (5.2) a constant rate of inflation; (*rer*) stands for the real exchange rate, and (*er*) for the nominal exchange rate, defined as in equation (5.6) and expressed as foreign currency units per domestic currency unit; P_w and P (in logarithms) are world and domestic price levels respectively; CA is the current account of the balance of payments, and s_i (with $i = 1, 2, 3, 4, 5$)

represents stochastic shocks, and E_t refers to expectations held at time t. The change in the nominal exchange rate appearing in equation (5.2) can be derived from equation (5.6) as $\Delta er = \Delta rer + p_{wt} - p_t$.

Equation (5.1) is the aggregate demand equation with the current output gap determined by past and expected future output gap, the real rate of interest and the real exchange rate (through effects of demand for exports and imports). It is important to also note that what monetary policy is thought to influence via this relationship, therefore, is the output gap, namely the difference between actual output from trend output. The latter is the output that prevails when prices are perfectly flexible without any cyclical distortions in place; it is, thus, a long-run variable, determined by the supply side of the economy. Equation (5.1) resembles the traditional *IS* function, but they differ substantially. The original *IS* curve represents equilibrium in the goods market and is used to derive the aggregate demand (*AD*) side of the *AD–AS* (aggregate supply) framework. The NCM *IS* curve emanates from intertemporal optimization of a utility function that reflects optimal consumption smoothing. It is, thus, a forward-looking expectational *IS* relationship. There are both lagged adjustment and forward looking elements.

Equation (5.2) is a Phillips curve with inflation based on current output gap, past and future inflation, expected changes in the nominal exchange rate, and expected world prices (and the latter pointing towards imported inflation). The model allows for sticky prices, the lagged price level in this relationship, and full price flexibility in the long run. The real exchange rate affects the demand for imports and exports, and thereby the level of demand and economic activity. The term $E_t(p_{t+1})$ in equation (5.2) captures the forward looking property of inflation. It actually implies that the success of a central bank to contain inflation depends not only on its current policy stance but also on what economic agents perceive that stance to be in the future. Consequently, the term $E_t(p_{t+1})$ can be seen to reflect central bank credibility. If a central bank can credibly signal its intention to achieve and maintain low inflation, then expectations of inflation will be lowered and this term indicates that it may be possible to reduce current inflation at a significantly lower cost in terms of output than otherwise. In this way monetary policy operates through the expectations channel. This forward looking Phillips curve, though, could produce credibility problems, known as the 'inflation bias' and the 'stabilization bias'. The first is the well-known bias, which can come about in view of imperfect competition. The 'stabilization bias' is due to lack of central bank reputation and credibility and thereby inability to influence inflation expectations. As has just been argued, under the circumstances of lack of reputation and credibility, the central bank loses the ability to affect inflation expectations through the expectations channel (see Galí and Gertler, 2007, for more details).

Equation (5.3) is a monetary policy rule, where the nominal interest rate is based on expected inflation, output gap, deviation of inflation from target (or 'inflation gap'), and the 'equilibrium' real rate of interest. The lagged interest rate (often ignored in the literature) represents interest rate 'smoothing' undertaken by the monetary authorities. Equation (5.3), the operating rule, implies that 'policy' becomes a systematic adjustment to economic developments in a predictable manner. Inflation above the target leads to higher interest rates to contain inflation, whereas inflation below the target requires lower interest rates to stimulate the economy and increase inflation. In the tradition of Taylor rules (Taylor, 1993, 1999, 2001), the exchange rate is assumed to play no role in the setting of interest rates (except in so far as changes in the exchange rate have an effect on the rate of inflation which clearly would feed into the interest rate rule). The monetary policy rule in equation 3 embodies the notion of an equilibrium rate of interest, labelled as RR^*. Equation (5.3) indicates that when inflation is on target and the output gap is zero, the actual real rate set by monetary policy rule is equal to this equilibrium rate. This equilibrium rate has often been seen as akin to the Wicksellian 'natural rate of interest' equating savings and investment at full employment.

Equation (5.4) determines the exchange rate as a function of the real interest rate differentials, current account position, and expectations of future exchange rates (through domestic factors such as risk premiums, domestic public debt, the degree of credibility of the inflation target, etc.). Equation (5.5) determines the current account position as a function of the real exchange rate, domestic and world output gaps; and equation (5.6) expresses the nominal exchange rate in terms of the real exchange rate. There are six equations and six unknowns: output, interest rate, inflation, real exchange rate, current account, and nominal exchange rate defined as in (5.6). Exchange rate considerations are postulated (as in equation 5.3) not to play any direct role in the setting of interest rates by the central bank. There may be indirect effects in so far as changes in the exchange rate influence expectations of future inflation.

2.2   NCM policy implications

The major economic policy implication of the NCM is that monetary policy has been upgraded in the form of interest rate policy, where a major objective of policy is 'maintaining price stability' (King, 2005, p. 2).[6] This policy is undertaken through inflation targeting (IT). Fiscal policy, by contrast, should only be concerned with possibly broadly balancing government expenditure and taxation, effectively downgrading its importance as an active instrument of economic policy. This is an assumption based on the usual arguments of crowding out of government deficits and thus the ineffectiveness of fiscal policy (see, however, Arestis and Sawyer, 2003, for a critique and a different view).

An important assumption that permits monetary policy to have the effect that it is assigned by the NCM, is the existence of temporary nominal rigidities. So that, the central bank by manipulating the nominal rate of interest is able to influence real interest rates and hence real spending in the short run. A further important aspect of IT is the role of 'expected inflation' embedded in equation (5.3). The inflation target itself and the forecasts of the central bank are thought of as providing a strong steer to the perception of expected inflation. Given the lags in the transmission mechanism of the rate of interest to inflation, and the imperfect control of inflation, inflation forecasts become the intermediate target of monetary policy in this framework where the ultimate target is the actual inflation rate (Svensson, 1997, 1999). Under these circumstances, 'The central bank's forecast becomes an explicit intermediate target. Inflation targeting can then be viewed as a monetary policy framework under which policy decisions are guided by expected future inflation relative to an announced target' (Agénor, 2002, p. 151). Furthermore, the target and forecasts add an element of transparency seen as a paramount ingredient of IT. Consequently, inflation forecasting is a key element of IT. It is, indeed, argued that it represents a synthesis of simple monetary rules and discretionary monetary policy, and as such it constitutes an improvement over targeting monetary aggregates and weaker versions of IT (Woodford, 2007).

The emphasis, however, on inflation forecast IT entails serious problems. Some of these problems relate to the format IT may take (Woodford, 2007). If it were to be implemented as a monetary standard, it would be too rigid. On the other hand if it were to resemble flexible IT, credibility might suffer substantially. Woodford (2007) suggests that in the real world successful inflation forecast IT central banks use neither. They are more concerned with the IT criterion but also with the output stabilization criterion as in the case of the central bank of Norway. Another problem with the inflation forecast IT is due to the large margins of error in forecasting inflation, which can damage the reputation and credibility of central banks. Utilizing a probabilistic approach under these circumstances (the so-called 'fan chart' of the Bank of England in the UK) to present inflation forecasts can alleviate potentially the reputation and credibility problems. The central bank by signalling the uncertainty inherent in economic forecasts can contain the potential damage to its reputation and credibility. But there is still the problem of how interest rate projections are undertaken. The two types already used by central banks, constant interest rate projections or projections based on market expectations, are problematic as Woodford (2007) highlights. The main problem common to both approaches to projections is that the nominal interest rate will remain fixed in the future regardless of how inflation evolves in the first case, or that it is exogenously fixed again unaffected by inflation in the second case. Either projection cannot be sustained. Woodford (2007) suggests that a way forward would be the adoption of a forecast IT approach, which would also be concerned with output stabilization. But even in this approach the problems just alluded to would still be there.

There can be a self-justifying element though to inflation forecasting in so far as inflation expectations build on forecasts, which then influence actual inflation. The centrality of inflation forecasts in the conduct of this type of monetary policy represents a major challenge to countries that pursue IT. Indeed, there is the question of the ability of a central bank to control inflation. Oil prices, exchange rate gyrations, wages and taxes, can have a large impact on inflation, and a central bank has no control over these factors. To the extent that the source of inflation is any of these factors, IT policy would be problematic. Negative supply shocks are associated with rising inflation and falling output. A central bank pursuing IT would have to try to contain inflation, thereby deepening the recession. Galí and Gertler (2007) argue that under these conditions the impact of monetary policy on inflation would be stronger the more credible the central bank is; the fall in output, though, would be the same regardless of the degree of central bank credibility.

3   Assessing the Theoretical Foundations of the NCM

We assess the theoretical and policy dimensions of the NCM in this section. The empirical aspects are discussed in a separate section that follows in section 4.

3.1   Price stability is not enough

The vigorous focus on price stability by the NCM raises the issue of whether such an objective is enough by itself. White (2006) suggests that achieving price stability in the short run might not be sufficient to avoid serious macroeconomic downturns in the medium term. History is replete with examples of periods of relative absence of inflationary pressures followed by major economic and financial crises. We may cite only but a few instances to make the point. Perhaps the best case in this context is that of the US in the 1920s and 1930s. Most of the 1920s in the US were characterized by price stability with tendencies of deflation in the same decade. All that turned into the 1930s Great Depression in the US. Massive decreases in output and employment, cumulative deflation along with financial distress, were the main characteristics. A more recent example is Japan. The 1980s was a decade of price stability, characterized by healthy investment rates with the financial sector enjoying technological innovation and deregulation. That, however, did not prevent the problems in Japan ever since the early 1990s. The South East Asia crisis in the late 1990s is still another recent example. After the effects of the oil price and debt crisis came to an end by the early 1980s, inflation in these countries was stable. However, that was not enough to prevent the deep crisis in the summer of 1997, causing countries in the area to experience high costs in terms of GDP, thereby triggering rising unemployment, which in most countries continues to be high even nowadays. Even more recently, the collapse of stock markets in the US and elsewhere in March 2001 had been preceded by price stability, along with a sharp increase in private investment associated with advances in productivity of the 'New Economy'. Here again, price stability was not sufficient to ensure high and sustained growth in economic activity. Not to mention the credit crunch of August 2007 after a period of 'non-inflationary consistently expansionary' era (NICE in the words of the Governor of the Bank of England, King, 2003, p. 3). Indeed, from a Minskyan perspective it may have been the cause.

The inevitable conclusion of this sub-section is that price stability does not necessarily guarantee benefits to the relevant economies. Consequently, the objective of price stability might have to be applied more flexibly, with a longer-term time span, which would allow more emphasis on output stabilization. We would suggest that price stability should be pursued in tandem with other objectives, especially so with output stabilization.

3.2 The separation of real and monetary factors

The points just made about the desirability of low inflation are closely linked with the view that there is a separation of real and monetary factors in the economy. The assignment can then be made: monetary policy to the nominal side of the economy, and specifically to inflation, and supply side policies to address the real side of the economy (and often, though not an intrinsic part of IT, labour market policies to address problems of unemployment). The supply side of the economy is often represented in terms of an unchanging supply side equilibrium. For example, the 'natural rate of unemployment' or the 'non-accelerating inflation rate of unemployment' (NAIRU) is used to summarize the supply-side equilibrium; with the estimates provided of the 'natural rate' or the NAIRU being often presented as a single (and hence implicitly unchanging) number. In the six equations above, the supply-side equilibrium is represented as a zero output gap. A less extreme view would be that the supply-side equilibrium may change over time but not in response to the demand side of the economy. Changes in labour market institutions and laws, for example, would be predicted to lead to changes in the supply-side equilibrium. In the context of IT, the significant question is whether interest rates through their effect on the level of aggregate demand have any lasting impact on the supply side of the economy. Even worse for the IT case under the circumstances of a changing NAIRU, say due to productivity increases, and to the extent that the central bank fails to account for it, inflation would worsen since the accompanying increase in RR^* is not compensated by an equivalent increase in R (see equation (5.3)). In the real world the central bank does not directly observe RR^*, of course. Only inferences about its level can be gauged.

3.3   The causes of inflation

This New Consensus focuses on the role of monetary policy (in the form of interest rates) to control demand inflation, and not cost inflation, as is evident from equation (5.2). As Gordon (1997) remarked (though not in the context of this New Consensus), 'in the long run inflation is always and everywhere an excess nominal GDP phenomenon. Supply shocks will come and go. What remains to sustain long-run inflation is steady growth of nominal GDP in excess of the growth of natural or potential real output' (p. 17). The position taken by IT supporters on cost inflation is that it should either be accommodated, or that supply shocks come and go – and on average are zero and do not affect the rate of inflation (see, for example, Clarida *et al.*, 1999). The significance of the IT on this score is that it strongly suggests that inflation can be tamed through interest rate policy (using demand deflation). In addition, there is an equilibrium rate (or 'natural rate'), which is feasible, and can balance aggregate demand and aggregate supply and lead to a zero gap between actual and capacity output.

In the context of the working of monetary policy, this view of inflation – namely that it is caused by demand factors–raises two issues. The first is that if inflation is a 'demand phenomenon', and not a cost phenomenon, as reflected in the Phillips curve of equation (5.2), then the question arises as to whether monetary policy is the most effective (or least ineffective) way of influencing aggregate demand. This touches on the relevant empirical evidence, and we tackle this issue in section 4 where we conclude that it does not support the IT contentions. Second, there is the question of whether the possibility of sustained cost–push and other non-demand related inflation could be as lightly dismissed, as the New Consensus appears to do. The version of the Phillips curve which appears as equation (5.2) is a (heavily) reduced form that does not explicitly consider wages, material costs and imported prices. A sustained money wage push makes no appearance in equation (5.2) and it would appear that there is no explicit representation of such pressures. An increase in, for example, wage aspirations on the part of workers or pressure for higher profit margins are not incorporated, though it could be argued that they would be reflected in the stochastic term.

This may be acceptable if pressures for higher wages and profit margins varied in a stochastic fashion over time (and averaged to zero). But even a sequence of time periods in which wage or profit margin pressures were positive, reflected in positive stochastic terms in equation (5.2), would have long lasting effects as one period's inflation feeds through to subsequent periods' inflation (through the lagged inflation term in equation (5.2)). Similarly if expectations on inflation were to rise (for whatever reason), then inflation would rise according to equation (5.2), and subsequent inflation would also be higher than otherwise. In the event of a sustained increase in inflation (due to cost pressures, as would seem to have been the case during the 1970s), this could only be met, in this framework, by raising interest rates and grinding down inflation by low demand and high unemployment.

3.4 Insufficient attention paid to the exchange rate

A further problem with the NCM analysis has to do with the exchange rate, which may not be given sufficient attention. It is actually clear from equation (5.3) that the NCM framework does not consider exchange rate considerations to play any direct role in the setting of interest rates. And yet the interest rate parity theorem indicates that the difference between the domestic interest rate and the foreign interest rate will be equal to the (expected) rate of change of the exchange rate. A relatively high (low) domestic interest rate would then be associated with expectations of a depreciating (appreciating) currency. Although the uncovered interest rate parity result often appears not to hold empirically, it could still be expected that there is some relationship between domestic interest rates, relative to international rates, and movements in the exchange rate. Changes in domestic interest rates, relative to international interest rates and for given expectations, would affect the exchange rate, which can have significant effects on the real part of the economy. Furthermore, there may be indirect effects in so far as changes in the exchange rate influence expectations on future inflation. The exchange rate, therefore, could be an important channel through which the effects of interest rates may operate. It transmits part of the effects of changes in the policy instrument, and also the effects of various foreign shocks.

Given this potentially critical role of the exchange rate in the transmission process of monetary policy, excessive fluctuations in interest rates may lead to a relatively high degree of output volatility (Agénor, 2002). The adoption of IT, it is argued, leads to a more stable currency since it signals a clear commitment to price stability in a freely floating exchange rate system (see Cobham, 2006). This, of course, does not mean that monitoring exchange rate developments should not be undertaken. Indeed, weighting them into decisions on setting monetary policy instruments is common practice. Still, the monolithic domestic focus on inflation targeting, however, entails the real danger of 'a combination of internal price stability and exchange rate instability' (Goodhart, 2005, p. 301). This occurrence is very real in view of the desire, especially by policy-makers, to uphold domestic price stability at any cost. There is also the related argument, which relates particularly to the developing countries that have adopted the IT strategy, that the strategy has been accompanied by relatively high interest rates and has led to over-valued exchange rates; this has been rather severe to a number of these countries.

3.5 The nominal anchor

An important criticism is that the adoption of a nominal anchor, such as an inflation target, does not leave much room for manoeuvre for output stabilization. As discussed above, this is viewed by most, though not all, proponents as possible in the short run (but not an issue in the long run since output returns to its equilibrium level; and this only if the central bank gets the interest rate 'right' equal to the equilibrium real interest rate). It is true, though, that there are supporters of IT who argue quite conspicuously that monetary policy should concentrate on both output and price fluctuations. It is shown (Svensson, 1997; Rudebusch and Svensson, 1999) that it is optimal to respond to the determinants of the target variable, current inflation and the output gap, rather than to the target itself. This is so, since both inflation and output gap determine future inflation. More recently, Svensson (2003) argues for 'a commitment to minimize a loss function over forecasts of the target variables' (p. 451). The loss function contains forecasts for both inflation and output gap as target variables.

There is an important related issue, namely the desirability of low inflation within the context of the IT framework. It is generally assumed within the IT framework that lower inflation is always more desirable than higher inflation, and that lower inflation can be achieved without any loss of output (as embedded in the framework of equations above). This should be judged against evidence provided by Ghosh and Phillips (1998), where a large panel set that covers IMF countries over the period 1960–96 is utilized, to conclude that

> there are two important nonlinearities in the inflation-growth relationship. At very low inflation rates (around 2–3 per cent a year, or lower), inflation and growth are positively correlated. Otherwise, inflation and growth are negatively correlated, but the relationship is convex, so that the decline in growth associated with an increase from 10 per cent to 20 per cent inflation is much larger than that associated with moving from 40 per cent to 50 per cent inflation. (p. 674)

However, the point at which the nonlinearity changes from positive to negative is thought to deserve a great deal more research. The IT argument should also be judged in terms of statements like 'there is an optimal rate of inflation, greater than zero. So ruthless pursuit of price stability harms economic growth and well-being. Research even questions whether targeting price stability reduces the trade-off between inflation and unemployment' (Stiglitz, 2003; see also Akerlof *et al.*, 1996).

3.6   Asset pricing

The standard argument in terms of asset price control is that asset price inflation (the percentage yearly change in equity prices, house prices or land prices) is out of the realm of central banks, as it reflects market forces and any control is widely regarded as infringing with the principles of the free market economy, or, indeed, it is the result of 'irrational exuberance'. Bernanke and Gertler (2000) argue that trying to stabilize asset prices is problematic, essentially because it is uncertain whether a given change in asset values results from fundamental or non-fundamental factors or both. In this thesis, proactive monetary policy would require the authorities to outperform market participants. Inflation targeting in this view is what is important, where policy should not respond to changes in asset prices. Clews (2002) argues along similar lines, and concludes that asset price movements 'rarely give simple unequivocal messages for policy on their own' so that they are 'unlikely to be suitable as intermediate targets for a policy whose main aim is to control inflation' (p. 185). Greenspan (2002a) argues that the size of the change in the rate of interest to prick a bubble may be substantial and harmful to the real economy. Another argument against asset pricing would be that asset price bubbles develop in some assets (e.g. recently housing) but not others (e.g. share prices in the recent bubble) and using interest rates would affect all asset prices. At the same time, however, this may show up the limitations of the one instrument policy, that of manipulating the rate of interest, when there are other instruments such as various reserve requirements.

Yet the experience of many countries shows that successful control of CPI-inflation does not guarantee low asset price inflation. In the examples mentioned in sub-section 3.1 above, inflation may have been stable over the periods examined, but asset prices certainly were not. IT central banks are, therefore, too narrowly focused on consumer prices, ignoring in the process the impact of rapidly changing asset prices. When asset price inflation gets out of control bubbles are built and while they grow they generate a lot of euphoria. But bubbles have ultimately burst with devastating consequences not only for the investors in the stock markets, but also for the economy as a whole. The experience of the last 20 years shows that the adverse consequences of the burst of a bubble hit not only weak economies, but also strong economies such as the US and Japan. Monetary policy should, therefore, target asset prices in addition to inflation (Dupor, 2002; Cecchetti *et al.*, 2000). Goodhart's (2001) suggestion, based on Alchian and Klein (1973), and in contrast to Bernanke and Gertler (2000), that central banks should consider housing prices and, to a lesser extent, stock market prices in their policy decisions, is very pertinent. Arestis and Karakitsos (2005) argue along similar lines but suggest that targeting wealth may be a better variable for which to opt. A wealth target would not impede the free functioning of the financial system as it deals with the consequences of the rise and fall of asset prices on the economy. It is not a target for asset prices, equities or houses, which requires the authorities to outperform market participants. A wealth target will also help control liquidity, which is at the heart of the current crisis and results from securitization, without interfering with the financial engineering of banks.

4   Assessing the Empirical Aspects of Inflation Targeting

We discuss two types of empirical evidence concerning the impact of interest rate changes, the main policy instrument of NCM economic policy. We first draw on evidence that is based on macroeconometric models, and utilize previous work in which we reported a range of evidence. This is followed by evidence that emanates from the application of single equation techniques.

4.1   Empirical evidence based on macroeconometric models

Arestis and Sawyer (2004a) attempted to gauge quantitatively the strength of interest rate changes through reporting the results of dynamic simulations carried out by others in the case of three macroeconometric models currently used in official economic policy-making. These are the macroeconometric models of the European Central Bank, the Bank of England and the USA Federal Reserve System (Bank of England, 1999, 2000; Van Els *et al.*, 2001; Angeloni *et al.*, 2002). The conclusions we draw from this exercise are along the following lines. The effects of interest rate changes on the rate of inflation are rather modest. A 1 percentage point change in interest rates is predicted to lead to a cumulative fall in the price level of 0.41 per cent in one case and 0.76 per cent in the other, after five years. The rate of inflation declines by a maximum of 0.21 percentage points. However, when interest rates have an effect on aggregate demand this comes through from substantial changes in the rate of investment. This means that interest rate variations can have long-lasting effects, in that the effects on investment will lead to changes in the size of the capital stock.

It is clear from this brief excursion of the potential impact of interest rate changes that there is very little support of its most important tenet. Changes in the rate of interest are not expected to have the impact assigned to them by the theoretical propositions of the IT model. We next look at the evidence based on the application of single equation techniques.

4.2   Empirical evidence based on single equation techniques

A number of studies have reviewed the empirical work undertaken on IT, when single equation econometric techniques are employed. A reasonably comprehensive review of the early empirical literature on IT (Neumann and von Hagen, 2002) concludes that the evidence supports the contention that IT matters. Those countries which adopted IT managed to reduce inflation to low levels and to curb inflation and interest rate volatility. Indeed, 'Of all IT countries it is the United Kingdom that has performed best even though its target rate of inflation is higher than the inflation targets of most other countries' (Neumann and von Hagen, 2002, p. 144). The evidence, however, is marred by an important weakness (Neumann and von Hagen, 2002): this is that the empirical studies reviewed fail to produce *convincing* evidence that IT improves inflation performance. After all the environment of the 1990s was in general terms a stable economic environment, 'a period friendly to price stability' (Neumann and von Hagen, 2002, p. 129). So that IT may have had little impact over what any sensible strategy could have achieved; indeed, non-IT countries also went through the same experience as IT countries (Cecchetti and Ehrmann, 2000).

Ball and Sheridan (2003) measure the effects of IT on macroeconomic performance in the case of 20 OECD countries, seven of which adopted IT in the 1990s. They conclude that they are unable to find any evidence that IT improves economic performance as measured by the behaviour of inflation, output and interest rates. Not that better performance was not evident for the IT countries. Clearly, inflation fell in these countries and became more stable; and output growth stabilized during the IT period as compared with the pre-IT period. But then the same experience was evident for countries that did not adopt IT. Consequently, better performance must have been due to something other than IT.

A related recent study by Bodkin and Neder (2003), examines IT in the case of Canada for the periods 1980–1989 and 1990–1999 (the IT period). Their results, based on graphical analysis, clearly indicate that inflation over the IT period did fall, but at a significant cost of unemployment and output–a result which leads the authors to the conclusion that a great deal of doubt is cast 'on the theoretical notion of the supposed long-run neutrality of money', an important, if not the most important, ingredient of the theoretical IT framework. They also, suggest that the 'deleterious real effects (higher unemployment and ... lower growth) during the decade under study suggests that some small amount of inflation (say in the range of 3 to 5 per cent) may well be beneficial for a modern economy' (p. 355).

More recently, a number of contributions have attempted to examine empirically the IT experience around the world, using what is known as intervention analysis to structural time-series models. Angeriz and Arestis (2006) show in the case of 10 IT countries that when countries are successful in terms of this framework they had already managed to tame inflation. Angeriz and Arestis (2007b, 2008a) in the case of developed countries, Angeriz and Arestis (2008b) in the case of developing countries, and Angeriz and Arestis (2007a) in the case of 'lite' countries, confirm the results of Angeriz and Arestis (2006) but they go on two steps further. The first is that they test whether the implementation of IT reduced inflation at the point of intervention; the results of these studies provide a negative answer. The second is the extent to which subsequent to the IT implementation, the framework succeeded in locking-in inflation at low levels; by contrast to the previous result, this time they are positive. But then non-IT countries were also successful in this latter regard. The low inflation experience of the last 20 years or so is not due to IT but something else. We speculate that it is probably globalization that has been responsible for the low levels of inflation the world has experienced over the recent past.

5   Summary and Conclusions

This contribution has attempted to highlight the main characteristics of what has come to be known as the New Consensus in Macroeconomics. This 'new' way of conducting macroeconomic analysis has replaced the *IS–LM* model, which used to be the standard teaching tool for many years if not decades. The acronym Consensus is very interesting for it pinpoints that a rare level of agreement among economists of the traditional persuasion on macro issues has been achieved. Such a consensus has not been witnessed since the late 1960s/early 1970s when the first consensus was in place, the Neoclassical Synthesis.

NCM has been generally analysed under the assumption of a closed economy. This chapter has dealt with the open economy NCM where the role of the exchange rate provides an additional channel of monetary policy. Not only has this chapter attempted to clarify the main features of the NCM but it has also focused on its main policy implications. We have also discussed a number of issues that are associated with the empirical work undertaken on IT.

In so doing, the chapter has raised a number of issues with both the NCM's theoretical foundations and its monetary policy prescriptions, which centre on the IT framework.[7] On both accounts, we find that a number of problems and weaknesses are present, suggesting that a great deal more research is necessary to tackle the issues raised in this chapter. The overall evidence on IT is that it has gone hand-in-hand with low inflation, but there is still the question of causation. The available evidence suggests that a central bank does not need to pursue an IT strategy to achieve this and other objectives. Non-IT central banks have done as well, if not better in some cases. As suggested in the Introduction, it is important that this and the various other issues raised in this chapter find their way into modern macroeconomics education. To state the case bluntly, it is important that the teaching of the consensus view be used as a vehicle for critical thinking about the economy, and not simply an apologia for current policy practices.

Notes

1. Helpful comments by the editors are gratefully acknowledged, without implicating them in terms of any remaining errors and/or omissions.
2. The NCM framework, and its implications for monetary policy, was suggested initially by Goodfriend and King (1997) and Clarida *et al.* (1999). For an extensive theoretical treatment see Woodford (2003).
3. See Galí and Gertler (2007) for a summary of the reasons for the collapse of Neoclassical Economics.
4. Goodfriend (2007) refers to a number of examples: notably New Zealand and Canada were the first countries to adopt the economic policy implications of the

NCM framework in the early 1990s. The UK and Canada followed similar initiatives shortly afterwards in 1992, with many other countries adopting similar policies since that period (with the developing and emerging world following suit by the end of the 1990s decade; indeed, the IMF in the case of Brazil in 1999 strongly recommended the adoption of NCM type of economic policies).

5. There is of course the role of money as a unit of account. However, in view of real money balances being a negligible component of total wealth there are no wealth effects of money on spending. Although monetary policy is central in NCM, money plays no role other than being a unit of account (Galí and Gertler, 2007, pp. 28–9).

6. King (2005) also argues that 'Far from being ineffective, a monetary policy aimed at price stability has proved to be the key to successful management of aggregate demand' (p. 2).

7. We have also discussed elsewhere (for example, Arestis and Sawyer, 2004b) the problematic nature of both NCM and IT.

References

Agénor, P. (2002), 'Monetary Policy Under Flexible Exchange Rates: An Introduction to Inflation Targeting', in Loayza, N. and Soto, N. (eds), *Inflation Targeting: Design, Performance, Challenges*, Central Bank of Chile: Santiago, Chile.

Akerlof, G.A., Dickens, W.T. and Perry, G.L. (1996), 'The Macroeconomics of Low Inflation', *Brookings Papers on Economic Activity*, 1, 1–76.

Alchian, A.A. and Klein, B. (1973), 'On a Correct Measure of Inflation', *Journal of Money, Credit and Banking*, 5(1), 173–91.

Angeloni, I., Kashyap, A., Mojon, B., Terlizzese, D. (2002), 'Monetary Transmission in the Euro Area: Where Do We Stand', *European Central Bank Working Paper Series*, no. 114.

Angeriz, A. and Arestis, P. (2006), 'Has Inflation Targeting Had Any Impact on Inflation?', *Journal of Post Keynesian Economics*, 28(4), 559–71.

Angeriz, A. and Arestis, P. (2007a), 'Assessing the Performance of "Inflation Targeting Lite" Countries', *World Economy*, 30(11), 1621–45.

Angeriz, A. and Arestis, P. (2007b), 'Monetary Policy in the UK', *Cambridge Journal of Economics*, 31(6), 863–84.

Angeriz, A. and Arestis, P. (2008a), 'Assessing Inflation Targeting Through Intervention Analysis', *Oxford Economic Papers*, 60(2), 293–317.

Angeriz, A. and Arestis, P. (2008b), 'An Empirical Investigation of Inflation Targeting in Emerging Economies', mimeo, Cambridge Centre for Economic and Public Policy, University of Cambridge.

Arestis, P. (ed.) (2007a), *Is There a New Consensus in Macroeconomics?*, Basingstoke: Palgrave Macmillan.

Arestis, P. (2007b), 'What is the New Consensus in Macroeconomics?', in Arestis, P. (2007a) ch. 2.

Arestis, P. and Karakitsos, E. (2005), 'On the US Post-"New Economy" Bubble: Should Asset Prices be Controlled?', in P. Arestis, M. Baddeley and J. McCombie (eds.), *The 'New' Monetary Policy: Implications and Relevance*, Cheltenham: Edward Elgar.

Arestis, P. and Sawyer, M. (2003), 'Reinstating Fiscal Policy', *Journal of Post Keynesian Economics*, 26(1), 3–25.

Arestis, P. and Sawyer, M. (2004a), 'Can Monetary Policy Affect the Real Economy?', *European Review of Economics and Finance*, 3(3), 9–32.

Arestis, P. and Sawyer, M. (2004b), *Re-examining Monetary and Fiscal Policies in the Twenty-First Century*, Cheltenham: Edward Elgar.

Ball, L. and Sheridan, N. (2003), 'Does Inflation Targeting Matter?', *NBER Working Paper Series*, no. 9577, Cambridge, MA: National Bureau of Economic Research.

Bank of England (1999), *Economic Models at the Bank of England*, London: Bank of England.

Bank of England (2000), *Economic Models at the Bank of England*, London: Bank of England (September Update).

Bernanke, B. and Gertler, M. (2000), 'Monetary Policy and Asset Price Volatility', *NBER Working Paper No. 7559*, Cambridge, MA: National Bureau of Economic Research.

Bodkin, R.G. and Neder, A.E. (2003), 'Monetary Policy Targeting in Argentina and Canada in the 1990s: A Comparison, Some Contrasts, and a Tentative Evaluation', *Eastern Economic Journal*, 29(3), 339–58.

Cecchetti, S.G., Genberg, H., Lipsky, J., and Wadhwani, S.B. (2000), *Asset Prices and Central Bank Policy, Geneva Reports on the World Economy*, no. 2, Geneva and London: International Centre for Monetary and Banking Studies and Centre for Economic Policy Research.

Cecchetti, S.G. and Ehrmann, M. (2000), 'Does Inflation Targeting Increase Output Volatility? An International Comparison of Policymakers' Preferences and Outcomes', *Working Paper 69*, Central Bank of Chile: Santiago.

Clarida, R., Galí, J., and Gertler, M. (1999), 'The Science of Monetary Policy: A New Keynesian Perspective', *Journal of Economic Literature*, 37(4), 1661–707.

Clews, R. (2002), 'Asset Prices and Inflation', *Bank of England Quarterly Bulletin*, Summer, 178–85.

Cobham, D. (2006), 'The Overvaluation of Sterling Since 1996: How the Policy Makers Responded and Why', *Economic Journal*, 116(512), F185–F207.

Dupor, W. (2002), 'Nominal Price Versus Asset Price Stabilisation', mimeo, University of Pennsylvania.

Galí, J. and Gertler, M. (2007), 'Macroeconomic Modelling for Monetary Policy Evaluation', *Journal of Economic Perspectives*, 21(4), 25–45.

Ghosh, A. and Phillips, S. (1998), 'Warning: Inflation May be Harmful to Your Growth', *IMF Staff Papers*, 45(4), 672–710.

Goodfriend, M. (2007), 'How the World Achieved Consensus on Monetary Policy', *Journal of Economic Perspectives*, 21(4), 47–68.

Goodfriend, M. and King, R.G. (1997), 'The New Neoclassical Synthesis and the Role of Monetary Policy', in Bernanke, B.S. and Rotemberg, J.J. (eds), *NBER Macroeconomics Annual: 1997*, Cambridge, MA: MIT Press.

Goodhart, C.A.E. (2001), 'What Weight Should Be Given to Asset Prices in the Measurement of Inflation', *Economic Journal*, 111(472), F335–F356.

Goodhart, C.A.E. (2005), 'Safeguarding Good Policy Practice', in Reflections on Monetary Policy 25 Years after October 1979, *Federal Reserve Bank of St Louis Review*, 87(2), Part 2, 298–302.

Gordon, R.J. (1997), 'The Time-Varying NAIRU and its Implications for Economic Policy', *Journal of Economic Perspectives*, 11(1), 11–32.

Greenspan, A. (2002a), 'Economic Volatility', Speech given to a Symposium Sponsored by the Federal Reserve Bank of Kansas City: Jackson Hole, Wyoming.

King, M. (2003), 'Speech to East Midlands Development Agency/Bank of England Dinner', Leicester, 14 October. Obtainable from the following website: http://www.bankofengland.co.uk/publications/speeches/2003/speech204.pdf

King, M. (2005), 'Monetary Policy: Practice Ahead of Theory', *Mais Lecture*, Cass Business School, City University, London.

Neumann, M.J.M. and von Hagen, J. (2002), 'Does Inflation Targeting Matter?', *Federal Reserve Bank of St. Louis Review*, 84(4), 127–48.

Orphanides, A. (2007), 'Taylor Rules', in Blum, L. and Durlauf, S. (eds), *The New Palgrave: A Dictionary of Economics*, Basingstoke: Palgrave Macmillan.

Rudebusch, G.D. and Svensson, L.E.O. (1999), 'Policy Rules for Inflation Targeting', in Taylor, J.B. (ed.), *Monetary Policy Rules*, Chicago: Chicago University Press.

Stiglitz, J. (2003), 'Too Important for Bankers: Central Banks' Ruthless Pursuit of Price Stability Holds Back Economic Growth and Boosts Unemployment', *The Guardian*, 10 June.

Svensson, L.E.O. (1997), 'Inflation Forecast Targeting: Implementing and Monitoring Inflation Targets', *European Economic Review*, 41(6), 1111–46.

Svensson, L.E.O. (1999), 'Inflation Targeting as a Monetary Policy Rule', *Journal of Monetary Economics*, 43(3), 607–54.

Svensson, L.E.O. (2003), 'What is Wrong with Taylor Rules? Using Judgement in Monetary Policy through Targeting Rules', *Journal of Economic Literature*, 41(2), 426–77.

Taylor, J.B. (1993), 'Discretion Versus Policy Rules in Practice', *Carnegie-Rochester Conference Series on Public Policy*, December, 195–214.

Taylor, J.B. (1999), 'A Historical Analysis of Monetary Policy Rules', in Taylor, J.B. (ed.), *Monetary Policy Rules*, Chicago: Chicago University Press.

Taylor, J.B. (2001), 'The Role of the Exchange Rate in Monetary-Policy Rules', *American Economic Review*, 91(2), 263–7.

Van Els, P., Locarno, A., Morgan, J. and Villetelle, J.-P. (2001), 'Monetary Policy Transmission in the Euro Area: What Do Aggregate and National Structural Models Tell Us?', *European Central Bank Working Paper Series*, no. 94.

White, W.R. (2006), 'Is Price Stability Enough?', BIS Working Papers No. 205, Basel, Switzerland: Bank for International Settlements.

Woodford, M. (2003), *Interest and Prices: Foundations of a Theory of Monetary Policy*, Princeton: Princeton University Press.

Woodford, M. (2007), 'The Case for Forecast Targeting as a Monetary Policy Strategy', *Journal of Economic Perspectives*, 21(4), 3–24.

6
Complexity and Macro Pedagogy: The Complexity Vision as a Bridge between Graduate and Undergraduate Macro

David Colander and Casey Rothschild

1 Introduction

The macro economy is complex; everyone knows that. Complex systems are difficult to analyse and manage; everyone knows that too. The best approach to teaching and describing the complex macro economy is something we know much less well. Currently, in teaching macro to both graduate and undergraduate students, we don't stress just how complex the economy really is. The argument in this chapter is that we should emphasize that complexity to frame the macro question.[1] Having done that, we can get on with what we do, and much of the structure of both the graduate and undergraduate macro can be taught as it currently is. But instead of seeing the approaches at the two levels as substitutes for one another, complexity helps to frame them as what they really are: complementary approaches to addressing a challenging set of questions.

The standard academic approach employed today at the graduate level is to downplay the complexity and to de-emphasize the interactions among agents that make the macro economy so complex. Given their assumptions, the graduate models are intellectually satisfying and internally consistent. They may even help to shed light on certain key macro questions such as the need for policy consistency, and the importance of expectations. However, in teaching these models to graduate students, instructors generally don't emphasize the complexity of the economy that the models assume away. Similarly, they don't explain to students why, because of the assumptions necessary to make the models tractable, these models are not particularly useful for addressing short run real-world macro policy concerns. This means that students come out of graduate macro with little understanding of how the models relate to policy in practice. As one graduate student noted: 'Monetary and fiscal policy are not abstract enough to be a question that would be answered in a macro course' (Colander, 2007, p. 46.)

The standard academic approach employed today at the undergraduate level is also to downplay the complexity, but in a quite different way. Specifically, since short run stabilization policies are the very issues that are important to most undergraduates, undergraduate macro pedagogy has focused on those. It presents a set of seemingly formal models that are, at best, a hodgepodge of rough-and-ready models that are only loosely grounded in theory. Because the complexity of the economy isn't emphasized, and the enormous limitations of the models aren't noted, undergraduate students are led to believe they are learning a scientifically based macro theory, when in fact, they aren't. This means that when students move on to graduate work, the first thing many graduate macro professors tell them is that everything they learned in undergraduate theory is wrong.

In our view, the lack of connection between the formal graduate teaching and the rough-and-ready teaching of macro at the undergraduate level has been detrimental to pedagogy at both levels. We believe that a connection can be made by bringing a vision of the macro economy as a complex system to the fore of both graduate and undergraduate instruction. Once one does that, both approaches can be seen as reasonable ways of dealing with that complexity, albeit with different aims in mind.

Our argument can be viewed as an alternative to Krugman's (2000) argument that 'thinking about micro-foundation is a productive enterprise' – as is typically done at the graduate level – but that we should not allow simple *ad hoc* undergraduate models to be 'driven out of circulation'. His argument is pragmatic: he views the graduate-level approach as better in principle but much more complicated and not 'demonstrably better' descriptively or prescriptively in practice. Our argument is stronger; while we agree with these practical considerations, we go further and argue that in many cases the microfoundations approach is demonstrably *worse* for describing the world and for prescribing policy. We also question the conventional wisdom that graduate models are even *theoretically* more sound. As Kirman (1989) and others have noted, the aggregation problems identified by Sonnenschein (1972) and Debreu (1974) undermine the structural integrity of what typically passes for microfoundations in these models, suggesting that this approach and *ad hoc* undergraduate approach have equally (un-) firm theoretical foundations. Furthermore, in intrinsically complex systems like the macro economy, it is not clear that models built from the micro-level up – *however* firm their foundations – are theoretically more satisfactory than models built around 'high-level' emergent macro-properties. (Employing macro models without describing microfoundations is common in science. For example, understanding the physics of gases can proceed quite nicely without focusing on the 'microfoundations'. While it is certainly nice to know that the macro-properties from gases can 'ultimately' be derived from the interactions of the many gas molecules, it is not clear that thinking in terms of the individual particles is theoretically any 'better' than using macro-properties like pressure and temperature to model the physics and chemistry of these gases.) In short, rather than viewing undergraduate macro models as pedagogically necessary but intrinsically inferior to their graduate counterparts, our argument is that they should be viewed as an alternative, complementary approach, which, if they are not presented as something other than what they are, are equally justifiable (or unjustifiable) from a theoretical perspective.

2   The Graduate DSGE Model

At the graduate level, macro theory is presented to students as a dynamic stochastic general equilibrium (DSGE) system. This framework nicely captures some of the intertemporal dimensions of individuals' and policy-makers' decisions, but it has limitations. Specifically, to make the model tractable, the framework requires making strong simplifying assumptions, such as positing a single representative agent or an (often implicit) Walrasian auctioneer who solves all the inter-agent coordination problems. In our view, there is nothing wrong with presenting stylized but tractable DSGE models to graduate students: it reflects where the profession is in our understanding of those aspects of macro that we can tackle with a top-down modelling approach. It also provides a common formal language for exploring this frontier. One might reasonably even hope that by successively enriching an abstract model that is tractable enough to permit full analytic understanding, we will eventually gain insight into many or even most key macroeconomic issues.[2]

The problem with this top-down approach is that the simplifying assumptions with which it buys tractability make it unsuitable for addressing certain sets of questions – at least for now. In so far as it is precisely inter-agent interactions and coordination problems that ultimately underlie the macroeconomics with which most policy-makers are concerned, the DSGE approach involves abstracting away from the essence of most actual policy problems.[3] If interactions and coordination failures drive short-run macroeconomic fluctuations, the DSGE approach is not, and will likely never be, particularly helpful for informing the standard macro policy responses, such as countercyclical monetary and fiscal policy, which are central to real-world policy discussions. Graduate macro has responded to the unsuitability of these models by either avoiding policy discussions entirely or else by focusing on those few aspects of policy (capital taxation, aspects of social insurance) that *can* be addressed in a DSGE framework. This typically means that countercyclical policies are almost never discussed; if anything, only the *long-run* consequences of fiscal and monetary policies receive any attention.

Were graduate instructors clear in their teaching of graduate students that DSGE models are currently only useful in helping to address a small subset of macro issues (and that the failure of the industry-standard models to address short-run policy issues fruitfully doesn't make those issues any less important), we would have no problem with what is taught in graduate macro. We can accept the argument that emphasizing DSGE models and downplaying policy is perfectly appropriate at the graduate level – just as it can be natural to teach string theory and de-emphasize specific applications to physics PhDs. But the students should have a sense that that is what is being done. Currently, they too often don't.

3   The Undergraduate *IS/LM* Model

While the DSGE model may be appropriate for graduate macro, it is clearly inappropriate for undergraduates. Their eyes would glaze over long before one reached the point where one could teach them what a Bellman equation is – and why they should be concerned about it. It would be like teaching Chinese to them, in Latin.

Ultimately, the typical undergraduate economics student is not going to be a macro theorist any more than the typical introductory physics student will end up being a string theorist (well ... perhaps a bit more). Undergraduate economics students want and need to cultivate a practical working knowledge of *policy*. They need an engineering approach, not a scientific one. The macro theory taught in undergraduate intermediate macro courses reflects this, having evolved into a mishmash of supposed microfoundations, rough-and-ready semi-developed policy models (such as *IS–LM* and *AS–AD*), and equilibrium growth models that let the policy discussion move beyond a focus on short-run stabilization.

In our view, there is nothing wrong with presenting this mishmash to undergraduate students: it reflects where the profession is in our understanding of these aspects of macro policy, crucial aspects such as how to respond in the short run to the fluctuations and coordination failures that plague complex systems. One cannot expect much more than a mishmash when dealing practically with a system as complex as the macro economy. Further, the mishmash successfully captures the models that policy-makers have in mind when they think about policy, so it is precisely what undergraduate courses should be teaching.

Were undergraduates first presented with a complexity frame of the macro economy, and the undergraduate models were presented for what they are – a mishmash of empirical regularities and reasonable conjectures, and not as *macro theory*, we would have no problem with it. In fact, we believe that undergraduate students would better *understand* the models, were these models explicitly presented as a set of engineering models – models developed to deal practically with the difficult dynamic problems that can develop in complex systems, rather than as a set of scientifically grounded models that rely on rigorous micro foundations.

4   The Complexity Frame

What allows both graduate and undergraduate models to make sense and fit together is the complexity frame for the economy. Thus, helping students to envision the aggregate economy's fundamental complexity can and should play a central role in teaching students macro theory and macro policy. The macro economy should be framed as a complex system we will likely never be fully able to control, predict, and analyse. Thus, the role of theory is limited, and the role of engineering models is limited; the two approaches complement one another.

The complexity frame allows almost all of 'standard' intermediate macro to stay at the core of undergraduate macro. As well it should: as Robert Solow (1984) and James Tobin (1980) noted, it is the shared intuition of macro policy economists, or, in James Tobin's words, this 'simple apparatus is [our] trained intuition ... when we confront questions of policy and analysis' (Tobin, 1982). Moving to a complexity frame is not difficult; it simply involves a pedagogical shift away from presenting the standard undergraduate material as if it has scientific microfoundations. (Indeed, if macro theorizing has taught us anything in the past 40 years, it is that the intermediate undergraduate macro models are decidedly lacking in formal microfoundations.)

Similarly, only after appreciating the incredibly difficult task of understanding complex dynamic systems such as the economy can graduate students fully appreciate why previous work has made the simplifications it has. If students are bothered by the representative agent model, try solving for an equilibrium in a two-person model. If students are bothered by single model consistency assumptions, try formally solving a dynamic optimization problem with multiple models. Shifting to the complexity frame explicitly acknowledges these trade-offs, and, once presented with them, graduate students can understand and admire the simplifications made by previous researchers. They can want to acquire the technical skills to be able to further develop the model.

This shift highlights a more practical reason to teach within the complexity frame: within this frame, the analytic apparatus of undergraduate macro theory – poor microfoundations and all – is entirely consistent with modern developments in macro theory. It is consistent within this frame because it explicitly distinguishes engineering models (models useful for policy, but not fully grounded in theory) from scientific models (models grounded in theory, but because of the simplifications necessary to make them tractable, not necessarily useful for policy).

5 An Example

An example of how the complexity frame can usefully frame the policy questions can be seen by contrasting how the Fed's response to the 2007 sub-prime mortgage crisis would be presented in the standard undergraduate macro theory text, and how it would be presented in a complexity framed text. In the standard approach, the sub-prime mortgage crisis is simply presented as a potential cause of a recession – either as a sudden increase in the demand for money, and corresponding decrease in the supply of loanable funds, or as an expected sudden decrease in aggregate demand. Thus, it is not unlike any other shift factor of aggregate demand. In the standard presentation the Fed reacts to that crisis by expanding the money supply, shifting the interest rate down, and thereby shifting the aggregate demand curve out.

That explanation is good as far as it goes, but it fails to illuminate the nature of the *crisis*, as perceived by the Fed. To see how, consider how this explanation would operate within the standard Taylor rule, which is frequently presented in the texts as guiding Fed policy. The Taylor rule would have the Fed setting the Fed funds rate at 2% plus inflation, (of about 3.5%) plus two adjustment factors – one for inflation (which was higher than desired by about 2%) and the second adjustment for potential output (while it was at the time about the level that was desired, they were worried that it was going to decrease). That would suggest a Fed Funds rate of about 6% to 7%. At the beginning of the crisis the Fed Funds rate was about 4.5%, so the presumption that a student would take from the texts is that it should be expected to rise. It did not rise; instead the Fed lowered the Fed Funds rate to 2.25%. The current textbook framework cannot provide a good story as to why. The complexity framework can.

In the complexity framework, there is not only the linear policy adjustment that the normal textbook model focuses on; there is also a non-linear systemic adjustment problem that the Fed is always keeping in the back of its mind. The fear in 2007 was of a systemic breakdown, which would undermine the entire economy. It was not fear of edging into a recession that the Fed was worried about; it was fear of winding up in a full depression because of a breakdown of the entire financial system. Were that breakdown to occur the economy would shift to an entirely different equilibrium, and the standard model would not hold. Thus, they did everything they could to prevent the economy from moving into that alternative equilibrium.

Our recent experiences advising undergraduate students in the Boston Fed Challenge competition in November 2007 is illustrative: our team was the only team in its group to suggest rate cuts. Though, in retrospect, the cuts may well have helped keep the economy from falling into the financial crisis it did, the team failed to advance beyond the first round, in part because their arguments didn't comport with the recommendations of the Taylor rule, and were therefore considered theoretically poorly grounded. We view this as strongly indicative of a failure of the standard *sans*-complexity undergraduate approach to account for the Fed's actual behaviour – and hence the need to shift towards a complexity framework. (It is worth noting that the graduate approach – with its no-Ponzi conditions and no-trade theorems – cannot even begin to address the crisis in the first place, and certainly not the Fed's response to it.)

We envision that instructors teaching within the complexity framework would present the standard rules such as the Taylor rule as operating in standard times, but would also present to students that the Fed is always vigilant (or should always be vigilant) for signs that the economy is moving outside the standard times, and shifting to a completely different equilibrium. Illustrations of how complex systems can exhibit tipping points could be used, complemented by historical examples of catastrophic macroeconomic collapses.

6   A Return to Classical Economics

In many ways, our proposed 'new' approach to undergraduate pedagogy in macro theory reflects a return to the Classical approach to macro. Classical macro economists (that is, the majority of macro economists before the 1940s, and, yes, this includes Keynes) saw the macro economy as far more complicated than the average economist of subsequent vintage. They saw it as beyond full analytic understanding, and thus did not try formally to model it. They saw the aggregate economy as a complex system, and they saw macro policy as an engineering, not a scientific, problem. They either didn't theorize about it, recognizing its complexity, or they theorized about it using heuristic models without micro foundations, something A. C. Pigou (1920) called realistic theorizing.

That classical approach to teaching macro faded in the 1950s, as it was replaced with what – for want of a better term – can be called the neoclassical/neo-Keynesian synthesis. This shift reflected a belief within the profession that macro economists had figured out how to surmount the problems of analysing the complex macro economy and could now treat and study the economy and offer policy advice scientifically. In this new synthesis, the multiplier model and *IS–LM* models were presented as simplifications of larger multi-sector aggregate macro econometric models that were taught in graduate programmes and were used by government and business. These models blended science and engineering, statics and dynamics, and made it seem as if the macro economy could be captured by a set of solvable static equations. These models were closely tied to macro econometric models, and undergraduate macro texts of the time were simply simpler versions of macro graduate texts. Students then, unlike now, could move almost seamlessly from undergraduate to graduate work, and graduates could easily teach undergraduate courses in macro.

Within these models, distinctions were often made between Keynesians and Classicals; they were presented as differing in the degree of wage and price flexibility they assumed, and in their assumptions about the elasticities of demand for money functions. The result was a teachable set of models that conveyed a sense of a controllable macro economy, except in special circumstances. Going into a recession? – run a deficit and expand the money supply. Have inflation? – run a surplus and cut the money supply. Have both inflation and unemployment? – struggle with the Phillips curve trade-off.

There were, of course, many variations – debates about identification of variables, and the nature of reduced form equations, for example – and for a while the monetarist–Keynesian debate was part of standard textbooks. But that debate was quickly subsumed into the model; monetarists were presented as believing the *LM* curve was inelastic and Keynesians were presented as believing the *LM* curve was elastic. Dynamics, where much of the debate actually centered, were left to sidebars. The presentation did justice to neither side, but it captured some of the debate and was easy for students to learn.

In the 1970s, that synthesis approach came under fire, and it rapidly ceased to be viewed as scientific or well founded. The fixed wages and prices models were abandoned by macroeconomists as both theoretically and empirically unjustified. Microfoundations, rational expectations, the Lucas Critique, and real business cycle analysis all became central to graduate macro. Theoretical debates moved from discussions of slopes of *IS* and *LM* curves to more diverse issues as the New Classical/New Keynesian macroeconomic debate replaced the neoclassical/neo-Keynesian debate. The evolving debate was marked by a significant change in the nature of macroeconomic theorizing; it emphasized a much more technical analysis of intertemporal agent choice, and de-emphasized the multi-market equilibrium analysis that underlay *IS–LM* analysis. These debates ultimately evolved into the DSGE synthesis, which is essentially the real business cycle model with some added institutional rigidities. This DSGE synthesis is what is generally taught in graduate macro today.

While graduate macro theorizing and teaching changed fundamentally over the past decades, undergraduate macro did not; it has remained tied to the *IS–LM* presentations, in part because the other was too hard to present to undergraduate students. While *IS–LM* analysis remained and even expanded (there are three *IS–LM* graphs in Ackley's book – the top selling book in the 1960s; there are more than 28 in Mankiw) the careful analysis of the foundations of *IS–LM* analysis disappeared, since the *IS–LM* model was no longer being related to a multi-sector general equilibrium model, but instead was being used as a heuristic model to discuss policy. Determination of elasticities of the curves was de-emphasized, replaced with reduced-form relationships that captured empirical regularities in the macro economy. This has led to pedagogical debates about issues such as whether the *LM* curve should be abandoned, and whether the aggregate supply/aggregate demand model should be presented in output/inflation space rather than output/price space.

These debates highlight the different way in which the *IS–LM* and the *AS–AD* models are now presented compared to how they were presented when they actually were seen as being connected to scientific theory. Today, these models are presented more as rough-and-ready policy models rather than as a carefully derived summary of a well-specified general equilibrium model. They have, in a sense, come nearly full circle and returned to their Classical roots. But the circle has not quite been completed: modern undergraduate macro texts have not made a full break with the past and still carry some of the vestiges of a time when they were viewed as scientific. Intermediate macro is consequently very difficult to teach, both for young professors whose training emphasizes DSGE modelling, and for older professors whose training is in the multi-market equilibrium approach. It is easy to understand how it arose, but the current approach satisfies no one.

Explicitly severing the standard undergraduate models from their scientific past by viewing them as engineering approaches to a complex system – by teaching them within the complexity frame – completes its return to its Classical roots. This is valuable in its own right. The complexity frame is also a unifying worldview: within it, the *IS–LM* undergraduate standard and the graduate-level DSGE standard are two complementary ways of gaining some understanding of a complex system we do not, and may never, fully understand.

The approach taught to undergraduates is deeply practical and policy centred, as it well should be: we don't have time to worry much about deep theoretical foundations (or even internal consistency) when we need to respond, post-haste, to a credit crunch. Lacking strong foundations, it is inherently error prone, however: we might end up *thinking* that a model is useful when it turns out not to apply at all. The Phillips curve and the experience of the 1970s is a natural example here. On the other hand, the DSGE standard is well founded, scientific, and potentially more progressive. It involves idealizing to a world we *can* fully understand in the hope that understanding this simplified world will help us better understand our own. It can provide insight, for example, into *why* our engineering models didn't work as well as we originally expected – the Lucas Critique being a natural example. The concern with it, of course, is that it is not yet of much more practical use to policy-makers than string theory is for helping mousetrap engineers.

The complexity frame does not involve an enormous change in the way intermediate macro is presented. Indeed, macro pedagogy can be taught in pretty much the same way as the current standard (Blanchard–Mankiw) approach. It differs only in how those models are framed; it returns to the earlier Classical vision that sees the macro economy as involving so many complex interactions of heterogeneous agents that a full model of it is impossible to construct, at least at this point. Once that frame has been presented to students, they can get on with learning the standard material as engineering relationships that have developed over time as useful – but ulti- mately heuristic – ways of dealing with the macro economy. That approach also permits a discussion of 'modern' insights, such as time-inconsistency and Ricardian equivalency problems with policy, right alongside the stan- dard presentation. Thus, it allows us to present a modern approach to macro, while maintaining much of the standard intermediate macro apparatus.

Even though moving to a complexity frame represents a relatively minor pedagogical shift, the benefits of presenting undergraduate material in this way are likely to be substantial. In addition to the intellectual benefits of a more honest presentation of difficult material, the shift will have non- trivial practical benefits: by reconnecting intermediate undergraduate macro with graduate macro, it makes macro more easily teachable, both by older professors (for whom the DSGE model is often thought of as technical gob- bledygook) and recent grads (for whom the *IS–LM* model is often thought of as simply gobbledygook).

7 Conclusion

The economy is complex, and, as such, is inherently difficult to under- stand. The profession's current approach to teaching undergraduate macro economics compounds this difficulty: it presents heuristic practical models as if they were well-founded scientific theories, even though nobody really believes the theories any longer. Admitting up-front that we don't 'get' the economy – and using the complexity vision to explain why not – will go a long way towards resolving this problem and improving undergraduate macroeconomic pedagogy.

It will also go some way towards bridging the yawning divide between graduate and undergraduate pedagogy. The vestiges of a more scientific past in the current approach to undergraduate macro make it come across as a substitute to modern scientific macro – a particularly poor substitute in light of the intellectual coherence and the mathematical elegance of DSGE mod- els. We are arguing here that they should not be viewed as substitutes at all. Thanks to DSGE we know more than we used to about the economy. Not much more, though, and certainly not much more about the practi- cal responses to short-run macroeconomic fluctuations that are, and should continue to be, the bread and butter of undergraduate macro. Teaching at *both* levels should reflect our lack of understanding – groping to gain small footholds in a complex system that is inherently difficult to understand.

The two approaches represent two distinct approaches to gaining such a foothold: DSGE offers deeper insights into a currently limited set of ques- tions – an approach appropriate for graduate instruction. The 'tools' of undergraduate macro, *IS–LM*, *AS–AD* and so forth, deliberately spurn deep insight – a perfectly appropriate approach given its goal of helping to guide policy-makers as they deal with real, practical, and pressing macroeconomic concerns in a complex world. A pedagogical emphasis on the complex nature of the economy highlights this complementary nature of the two approaches and better reflects our modern, self-consciously imperfect, understanding of the macro economy.

Notes

1. Elsewhere Colander (2006) has called this complexity frame a post-Walrasian approach. The term used is unimportant.
2. Views on the potential long-run usefulness of the DSGE approach vary widely. Robert Solow would see it as close to useless; Robert Lucas would see it as highly useful. In this chapter we do not discuss such issues. Our concern here is simply pedagogical – How can one justify the current graduate approach to macro to students?
3. These issues are discussed in more depth in Colander (2006) and Colander *et al.* (2008).

References

Colander, D. (ed.) (2006), *Post Walrasian Macroeconomics*, Cambridge: Cambridge University Press.

Colander, D. (2007), *The Making of an Economist Redux*, Princeton: Princeton University Press.

Colander, D., Howitt, P., Kirman, A., Leijonhufvud, A., and Mehrling, P. (2008), 'Beyond DSGE Models', *American Economic Review*, May.

Debreu, G. (1974), 'Excess Demand Functions', *Journal of Mathematical Economics*, March (1974).

Kirman, A. (1989), 'The Intrinsic Limits of Modern Economic Theory: The Emperor has no Clothes', *Economic Journal*, 99(395) Supplement: Conference Papers.

Krugman, P. (2000), 'How Complicated Does the Model Have to Be?', *Oxford Review of Economic Policy*, 16(4).

Pigou, A.C. (1920), *The Economics of Welfare*, London: Macmillan.

Solow, R. (1984), 'Mr. Hicks and the Classics', *Oxford Economics Papers*, 36, Supplement.

Sonnenschein, H. (1972), 'Market Excess Demand Functions', *Econometrica*, 40(3).

Tobin, J. (1980), *Asset Accumulation and Economic Activity*, Oxford: Basil Blackwell.

Tobin, J. (1982), 'Money and Finance in the Macroeconomic Process', *Journal of Money, Credit and Banking*, 14(2).

Part II
An Endogenous-Money Theory Amendment of the New Consensus Macroeconomic Model

7
Teaching Macroeconomics When the Endogeneity of Money is Taken Seriously

Malcolm Sawyer[1]

1 Introduction

The purpose of this chapter is to consider the implications of treating money as endogenously created within the banking system rather than the more traditional use of the assumption of exogenous money (that is money created by an external agency such as the central bank) for the teaching of macroeconomic analysis and how that teaching could be approached. The underlying view on which this chapter is based is that macroeconomic analysis based on endogenous money has to be substantially different from one based on exogenous money, and the differences are much more fundamental than merely shifting from an assumption that the stock of money is given to the one that the (policy) rate of interest is given (cf. Romer, 2000). With the endogenous money approach, in contrast with the exogenous approach, 'money matters' for the level of economic activity and for the evolution of the economy over time[2]. Expenditure can only take place if it is backed by purchasing power, and expenditure has to be financed through the possession of money, which can come from provision of loans by the banks. The level and composition of expenditure clearly determines what is produced and sold. The decisions on loans by banks influence the number of investment plans that can be financed and which can take place, and thereby the size and character of the capital stock, and hence on the development of the supply side of the economy. Endogenous money does however mean that inflation cannot be viewed as a 'monetary phenomenon' if that is interpreted as saying that (the growth of) money *causes* inflation and a full macroeconomic analysis would require analysis of inflation and its interaction with the monetary sector. In the context of a single chapter it is not possible to provide a full macroeconomic analysis based on endogenous money but, rather, we seek to highlight the central role of endogenous money in developing a macro-economic analysis.

This chapter seeks to address a range of macro-economic issues which arise from treating money as endogenous (sometimes in comparison with money treated as exogenous), the implications of those issues for the teaching of macroeconomics, and the ways in which key elements of endogenous money can be presented to students. In the next section we indicate five key features of endogenous money as it pertains to macroeconomic analysis as the background for the rest of the chapter. Section 3 considers the appropriate measures of money and of the interest rate for use in the context of endogenous money. Endogenous money is created through the loan processes of the banking system, (money destroyed when loans are repaid) and the next section discusses the presentation of the banking system and the conditions on which loans are provided. The central bank also has a crucial role to play in terms of the ways in which it provides base money to the banking system, and particularly the conditions (i.e. rate of interest) on which it does so, and this is discussed in section 5. The way in which aggregate demand is presented is considered in section 6, within which there is discussion of the roles of fiscal policy and monetary policy. Section 7 argues that not only the *LM* curve but also the demand for money is largely redundant and can be dropped from macroeconomic analysis. There are some brief remarks on inflation in the context of endogenous money in section 8. The final section provides some concluding remarks.

2   The Nature and Role of Endogenous Money

The ways in which endogenous money is envisaged will clearly impact on the way in which it is analysed in a macroeconomic setting. There are, in our view, five keys features of endogenous money, which reflect conditions in a modern industrialized economy and which are central to the workings of such an economy. These are:

(i) Money is largely created by the banking system, and it comes into existence through the loan process and disappears with the repayment of loans. The creation of money is then intrinsically linked with spending since a loan has a cost: a person taking out a loan intends to use that loan for expenditure purposes and a bank deposit is created in the process.

(ii) Endogenous money does not constitute net worth since it involves credits and debts, assets and liabilities, for example a loan is an asset for the bank and a liability for the borrower, a bank deposit is an asset for holder but a liability for the bank.

(iii) The endogeneity of money arises at the interface between banks and the non-bank public, and at the interface between banks and the central bank. In terms of the provision of loans and the creation of money, there are then two margins of endogeneity, namely banks provide loans to the non-bank public, and the central bank provides reserves to the banks. There is a third element of endogeneity, namely the repayment of loans by the non-bank public and the destruction of money.[3]

(iv) The stock of money in existence is essentially determined by a willingness to hold money, generally referred to as the demand for money, which depends on factors such as the levels of expenditure and output, the spectrum of interest rates. As such the stock of money is akin to a residual in the sense that it follows on from the determination of variables such as levels of expenditure and income, and the stock of money does not feed back to influence the economy.

(v) Monetary policy is identified with the setting of a key policy interest rate by the central bank, and the central bank is willing to supply (through open market operations etc.) whatever base money is required by the banking system (at the set policy interest rate). The central bank operates as the 'lender of last resort'.

3 The Definition(s) of Money and Interest Rate

The view which has permeated the presentation of the exogenous money view is that 'The term *M* may represent M1, M2, or some other measure of money. For the purpose of developing the theoretical model, which measure of money *M* refers to doesn't matter' (Abel and Bernanke, 2005, p. 252). And 'in modern economies, the money supply is determined by the central bank—in the United States, the Federal Reserve System' (Abel and Bernanke, 2005, p. 251). The endogenous money approach would firmly reject the latter statement, and that approach would also identify the key measure of money with M1, that is the form of money which is widely used as a medium of exchange and a means of payment. In one sense which measure of money is used does not matter in the endogenous money approach since that approach can be presented and understood without any reference to the size of the stock of money (which is essentially a residual which has no causal impact on the economy).

When consideration is being given to the creation and destruction of money and to the role of the central bank, then the way in which money is measured does matter, and different measures of money need to be distinguished. Three measures of money can be usefully distinguished for the purposes of macroeconomic analysis, namely 'base money' M0, the form of money provided by the central bank, narrow money or what may be termed transactions money M1, and broad money such as M2, M3 or M4. The first of those is clearly relevant for the operation of the central bank, though the assumption is made that the central bank supplies M0 on request, albeit at a price, to the banking system. The second (M1) is central to the key function of money highlighted by the endogenous money approach that money is the means of payment, and expenditure cannot occur unless there is prior possession of spending power, namely money. The third (such as M2) takes something of a back seat. Broad money (other than the component of it which is part of narrow money) is not directly used as a means of payment. For the individual broad money deposit can be quickly converted into a narrow money deposit but that may not be the case in the aggregate. A shift from broad money to narrow money may trigger responses from the banks as their portfolio of liabilities changes. In what follows, when the term money is used without further qualification, it will be akin to M1.

Money is generally said to have three functions: means of payment (or a medium of exchange), store of wealth (or store of value) and unit of account. Money serves as a generally accepted medium of exchange but we prefer to talk of means of payment as this indicates the legal tender nature of money and that it is used for payment of taxes, settlement of debts which are not immediately related to exchange. In the endogenous money approach the key function of money is that it is the means of payment.

In the endogenous money approach a number of interest rates need to be distinguished: how many depends on the complexity of the analysis. The starting point would be the policy interest rate set by the central bank (this policy rate varies between countries and would be the Federal funds rate in the US and the bank rate in the UK and the 'repo' rate in the Eurozone). The rate of interest on loans is set by the banking system, often seen as a 'mark-up' over the policy interest rate, where the 'mark-up' can depend on a variety of factors including the degree of monopoly in the banking sector as well as risk and liquidity considerations by the banks. The rate of interest on (government) bonds would be relevant when fiscal policy is considered, and the rate of interest on bank deposits when savings decisions are being discussed.

Thus in the presentation of the endogenous money approach there should not be reference to 'the' rate of interest but rather a number of interest rates need to be distinguished and the relationship between them discussed (e.g. the rate of interest on loans may be a simple mark-up on the policy rate of interest).

4   Banks' Behaviour and Loan Creation

It is useful to start from a highly simplified version of the balance sheet of a bank in order to consider the conditions under which loans are provided and it also helps to underpin some of the key features of endogenous money discussed in section 2. Such a simplified balance sheet is given in Figure 7.1.

This balance sheet is simplified in two particular respects. First, the assets of the bank only include loans and reserves and the bank's ownership of other

Assets	Liabilities
Loans	Deposits
Reserves	

Figure 7.1   Simplified balance sheet of a bank

financial assets such as government bonds and their ownership of buildings, land etc., is ignored. Second, the two sides of the balance sheet are assumed to be equal, and hence the net worth of the bank is taken to be zero.

The bank deposits, which appear in the balance sheet of banks, are part of the stock of money and form a means of payment, and the transfer of those deposits between economic agents is the major way by which payments are made. When loans increase then there must be some corresponding changes in reserves and in deposits. But conversely an increase in deposits (and that is in the amount of money) would go along with some corresponding changes in loans and reserves. Since Figure 7.1 represents a balance sheet, the expansion on one side must be accompanied by an expansion on the other side. For endogenous money, the expansion of the balance sheet generally comes from an expansion of loans. Further, the central bank is willing to provide base money to the banks (to form part of reserves) at a price, which they set.

Since for individuals and firms wanting to take out loans there are costs involved (notably the rate of interest to be paid on the loan), there is presumed to be some purpose in taking out the loan, generally to acquire the finance to undertake expenditure. Thus the financing of expenditure is closely linked with the creation of loans. The immediate effect of expansion of the loans outstanding is to generate an increase in bank deposits, and thereby in the stock of money. At the immediate stage that a loan is taken out and spent, it creates a deposit in the bank account of the person to whom payment is made. In turn it can be expected that the person receiving the deposit (created by the loan) will spend it and pass it on to someone else. The newly created deposit thereby circulates through the economy as it is spent and received.

When a person receives the bank deposit, they have a number of options on what to do with the bank deposit. They can spend it on goods and services, and then it is passed on to someone else. They can seek to acquire a financial asset, and again the bank deposit is passed on to someone else, in this case as payment for a financial asset. A further option for someone who has an outstanding loan is to pay off part of the loan. In the case of someone with an overdraft this would in effect operate automatically – as the deposit is received it serves to reduce the amount of the overdraft. In other words, loans can be created and can be paid off and extinguished: bank deposits are created, and then destroyed. The bank deposits created by the initial loan remain in existence so long as people are willing to hold them and to spend them. Once the bank deposit reaches someone who uses it to pay off a loan then the bank deposit disappears.

The banks will meet the demand for loans, provided that they think it will be profitable to do so. The profitability for banks of loans will depend on the interest rate, which is charged for loans and the risk of default on the loans. The rate of interest on loans is closely related to the rate of interest charged by the central bank, with the loan interest rate a mark-up over the central bank interest rate. The rate of interest charged by the central bank is the rate of interest which banks would have to pay the central bank if the banks sought to borrow reserves from the central bank.

The derivation of a supply of loans function in any rigorous way appears to be not possible. Individual banks are treated as price-makers, and the difficulties of deriving a supply curve for a price-maker is well known. The supply function for loans is further complicated in that the providers of loans differentiate between customers, based on their creditworthiness, in terms of the rate of interest charged and the amount which they are willing to provide.

However, what may be described as a supply relationship between the amount of loans and the rate of interest on loans can be readily derived, and will be horizontal in the short run, where the short run can be given a precise meaning. The nature of the quantity–price relationship for loans is not unique to loans but rather is a feature of services produced to order and of goods which can be supplied from stock. The producer sets the price at which they will trade: the price is set according to the objectives of the firm and its perception of the expected demand and cost condition, which it faces. On any particular day the actual demand which presents itself to the producer will in general deviate, positively or negatively, from the expected level. But the producer is not in a position to know what the actual demand is until the day is over but then it is too late to make any adjustment to the price. Thus having set the price, the producer will meet the demand, and this will give the appearance of a horizontal quantity–price relationship. The producer would not adjust the price until their perception of the expected demand changed or their cost conditions changed significantly: for example, a run of daily demand above the expected level could lead to a revision of the expected level of demand. The short-run is then clearly the period of time over which perceptions of expected demand and of cost conditions remain unchanged. In the case of loans, the cost conditions for banks will include the price at which they can secure funds and this will be closely related to the policy interest rate of the central bank. Thus it could be expected that while the policy rate remains unchanged the supply of loans relationship remains unchanged and horizontal (with respect to the interest rate on loans) but that the rate of interest on loans will change when the policy interest rate changes.

The consideration of the relationship between the rate of interest on loans and the volume of loans outside of the short run as defined above is complex and requires the precise specification of the nature of the period being considered. For example, a relationship could be mapped out for a substantial period of time based on a series of short-run periods which differed in terms of the central bank policy interest along with a given specification of central bank behaviour. Another example would be that a relationship could be mapped out based on a given central bank interest rate and shifting demand for loans (as perceived by the banks).

5 Central Bank: Its Role and Interest Rate Setting

The central bank acts as the 'lender of last resort': i.e. the central bank will provide reserves to the bank system (at a price) and subject to banks being able to provide collateral for the loans from the central bank. The central bank stands ready to supply base money as and when required. Thus, it is argued, banks can expand their balance sheets, provided that the public wish to take out loans (at the price charged by the banks) and the public are prepared to hold the deposits which are generated. When this expansion requires that more reserves may be required by the banking system, these will be augmented by the central bank.

The analysis of endogenous money can proceed on the basis of treating the policy interest rate as given and work through the consequences of the chosen policy rate. This can be seen as analogous with the treatment of the stock of money as given in the exogenous money *IS–LM* approach. In macroeconomic analysis at the text book level this has been the usual approach with regard to government policies, e.g. treat government expenditure as a given and analyse the consequences of a particular level (or change in) government expenditure. However, in the context of endogenous money, there has been much discussion on how the policy interest rate is set and to which macroeconomic variables it responds. The use of Taylor's rule (named after Taylor, 1993):

$$i_p = r^* + \pi + \alpha_1(\pi - \pi^T) + \alpha_2(y - y^*) \tag{7.1}$$

where i_p is the policy interest rate in nominal terms, r^* the 'equilibrium' real policy interest rate (which is taken to be the nominal interest rate minus expected inflation), π the rate of inflation, π^T the target rate of inflation, y output and y^* some 'equilibrium' level of output, α_1, α_2 the adjustment parameters (taken as positive and often given values of 0.5), is the prime example of this.

But Taylor's rule is more than just a possible closure based on the way in which the central bank operates. It serves as an adjustment process by which aggregate demand adjusts to supply, and specifically the economy is guided towards y*. When the real rate $(i_p - \pi)$ is equal to r^*, then $\pi = \pi^T$ and $y = y^*$ are required. A positive output gap (and a presumed inflationary situation) would lead to the interest rate being raised, which is presumed to lower demand, thereby reducing the output gap. It also assumes the existence of an 'equilibrium' interest rate r^* which equates demand and supply, or alternatively expressed the interest rate equates investment and savings at y*.

The alternative, and in my view preferable way, is to consider the effects of different levels of the policy interest rate, and the effects which they would have on demand, as indicated in the next section. This permits discussion of alternative objectives for and influences on monetary policy, e.g. whether exchange rate or asset price considerations play a role.

6   Aggregate Demand and Interest Rates

In the analysis of the level of aggregate demand in the short run the policy rate of interest is taken as given, which would also mean that the rate of interest on loans is given. In that context, the level of aggregate demand is approached through the *IS* curve. It has been implicit in previous discussion and will be explicit in the next section that the *LM* curve has no role to play in short-run macroeconomic analysis.

In the context of an open economy, the equality between leakages and injections provides an equation such as:

$$I(r_l, E) + G + X(Y, Y_w, e) = S(Y) + T + M(Y, Y_w, e) \qquad (7.2)$$

where S is savings, I private investment, G government expenditure and T taxation, X exports and M imports, e the real exchange rate and E the state of expectations and confidence. The relevant rate of interest here would be the rate on loans, and it is the real rate of interest that is used, and implicitly the rate of inflation and inflationary expectations are assumed to have no effects on real variables.

The equality between leakages and injections also means that the withdrawals from the circular flow of income fund the injections into the circular flow. This is an equilibrium condition. An increase in one component of injections (say investment) would increase the level of expenditure and output, and the level of output would increase up to the stage where the equality between leakages and injections is restored. This is the familiar Keynesian multiplier story. However, whilst in equilibrium leakages fund injections, in the exogenous money analysis it is not possible to explain how an intended increase in injections is financed. In a monetary economy, expenditure can only occur if backed by purchasing power, i.e. money. With endogenous money the financing of injections is readily resolved. Banks provide loans which enable the injections to be financed. But banks also possess the power to cut off an expansion if loans are not forthcoming. A fuller treatment would consider the ways in which willingness of banks to provide loans and credit rationing could constrain the level of demand (notably investment expenditure).

The *IS* curve would then be of the form:

$$Y = F(r_l, E, G, T, e, Y_w) \qquad (7.3)$$

From such a formulation, as may be expected, many comparative static exercises can be undertaken. Specifically the effects of fiscal policy and of monetary policy can be examined and, indeed, compared. This could be extended also to consider changes in credit conditions, for example an increase in the mark-up applied by banks in the setting of the rate of interest on loans.

The *IS* relationship (or equivalent) can be derived in a number of ways. The traditional Keynesian approach can be followed. An alternative would be the forward-looking optimization approach, which lies behind the 'new consensus in macroeconomics' approach.

The level of output given by equation (7.3) would clearly be the demand-determined level of output. The effects of a range of variables, including fiscal policy and monetary policy, on the level of output can be examined from equation (7.3). How would the level of output (and employment) which is indicated by equation (7.3) compare with any notion of a supply-side equilibrium such as the 'natural rate of unemployment', zero output gap? As it stands there is no reason why the level of output from (7.3) would correspond with a supply-side equilibrium. Further, in the endogenous money approach there is no market mechanism which would draw the two together. In the exogenous money approach appeal to real balance effect has been the route but since a feature of endogenous money is its zero net worth property there is not a corresponding real balance effect. Within the New Consensus in macroeconomics approach, the postulated adjustment process is in effect monetary policy taking the form of Taylor's rule (equation 1 above). By assumption when the real rate of interest is equal to r^* then the output gap would be zero (which is assumed to be consistent with constant inflation). An alternative adjustment process would come from fiscal policy. The significant point here is the lack of an automatic market-based mechanism to reconcile the demand side and the supply side.

7 The Demand for Money and the *LM* Curve: Relics of the Past

The *LM* arm of the *IS–LM* approach would be derived from the equality between the demand for money and the supply of money. The *LM* approach could be seen as firmly based on two postulates. First, the supply of money can be taken as a given as a constant set by the central bank, though some have postulated a supply of money as a function of 'the' rate of interest and then remarked that such an assumption makes no essential difference[4]. The level of the supply of money would be viewed as the key indicator of monetary policy. Second, the demand for money is viewed as a stable function of a small range of variables, with specific focus on the level of nominal income and a rate of interest. There has been much ink spilt over whether the demand for money is indeed a stable function. The issue of the stability of the demand for money is not central to our argument here, but rather whether it is even necessary to discuss the demand for money.

The traditional demand for money has two components – the transactions demand, and the portfolio (or speculative) demand (the precautionary demand may be noted but then largely absorbed into the transactions demand). The transactions demand is linked with income and expenditure. As an aside we may mention the terminology here – when money is held in connection with transactions, the reason for holding money is one of convenience and the intention is to get rid (spend) the money. Money is held in order to get rid of it, and the holding of money does not generate any 'utility'.

Godley (1999, pp. 397–8) argues that 'even the term "demand" for money strains language, for it badly described a situation where people aim to keep their holdings within some normal range but where the sums they end up with are determined in large part by impulse purchases, windfalls and other unexpected events'. An individual holds money and may do so willingly but the holding of money is designed to be temporary. The money is held in order to dispose of it. It cannot be inferred from the observation that an individual holds money that he or she has a demand for that money, in the usual sense of the term 'demand'. The receipt of money may have been unanticipated, and the holding is temporary until the individual has time and opportunity to use the money.

The transactions demand for money arises from money's role as a means of payment. But it is not a demand in the traditional sense as money is held temporarily as an intermediate step between receipt as income and disbursement as expenditure. It should be referred to as average transactions holdings. As such the level of the stock of money held is not of any great significance.

The demand for money can be seen as essentially a residual in the sense that a range of factors (such as income) influence the stock demand for money. Further, the stock of money is seen as determined (over the long haul) by the demand for money. But neither the demand for money nor the stock of money feed back to influence any other variables in the economy (see Arestis and Sawyer, 2003). The contrast with exogenous money is stark: the well-known helicopter story told by Friedman (1969) portrayed the exogenous injection of money (dropped from the helicopter) as initially leaving those picking up the dollar bills as better off, leading them to increase spending, bidding up output and prices etc. In the endogenous money approach, money does not constitute net worth and the notion of 'excess money' is denied. This suggests that considering the demand for money within macroeconomics teaching is not needed, as it does not contribute to any understanding of the macroeconomic process. In so far as the stock of money has some informational content, this should be interpreted in terms of credit creation and loans.

The portfolio demand for money generally presents money and bonds as the alternative ways of holding (financial) wealth and hence it is the rate of interest on bonds (and also prospective capital gains and losses) along with a presumed zero (or constant) interest rate on money which enter the demand for money. The portfolio demand for money is a demand for broad interest bearing money, and as such does not need to be considered in short-run macroeconomic analysis.

Re-writing equation (7.2) above as:

$$S(Y) - I(r_l, E) + T - G + X(Y, Y_w, e) - M(Y, Y_w, e) = 0 \qquad (7.4)$$

serves as a reminder that the net financial flows from each sector (private, government, foreign) sum to zero. One sector's inflow is another sector's outflow. Further, the outflow from a sector represents a rise in the liabilities of that sector and the inflow into a sector a rise in the assets of that sector. The financial assets, which a sector acquires, can take a variety of forms, e.g. cash, bank deposits, bonds, equity, and the liabilities similarly. The financial assets which economic agents in a sector own will reflect their willingness to acquire and to hold those assets, which may be described as their demand for those assets. This points in the direction of complementing the short-term macroeconomic analysis with a consistent stock-flow approach along the lines developed by Godley and Lavoie (2007).

8 Inflation

One of the key propositions arising from endogenous money is that 'inflation is *not* too much money chasing too few goods', and the proposition often ascribed to Friedman that inflation is always and everywhere a monetary phenomenon only holds in the sense that rising prices generate a rising stock of money. The traditional causation running from exogenous money to inflation is rejected by the endogenous money perspective, and it is more a matter that inflation involves changes in the stock of money, though it is not clear cut whether inflation precedes changes in money in time or vice versa. The treatment of inflation requires some discussion as to how inflation brings about a rising stock of money. This can be illustrated in a number of ways. The one which I tend to use relates to a situation where costs are rising. Firms have to spend out more to acquire the inputs required for production. In order to do so, the firms have to acquire the finance to pay for the inputs, and may do so by making greater use of their overdraft facilities (and by arranging further loans from the banks). Loans are thereby increased, and the stock of money rises. From the individual firm's perspective, with rising costs they aim to charge higher prices, resulting in (they hope) higher money profits (and perhaps retaining the same mark-up of price over average costs). The higher revenues will enable them to pay off some of the loans, and in effect provides ex post funding for the higher input costs. This may suggest that the stock of money begins rising as loans are taken out to finance higher expenditure on costs, and may well precede in time the rise in prices.

Endogenous money is compatible with a variety of theories of inflation – it could be said with any theory of inflation other than 'money causes inflation'. The New Consensus in macroeconomics tends to use a Phillips curve approach to inflation, whereas Post Keynesian writers are more likely to use a conflict approach (for further discussion see Arestis and Sawyer, 2006, 2007). The key feature of the endogenous money approach is that inflation is not a monetary phenomenon in the sense of money causing inflation, though the stock of money would be expected to grow alongside price inflation. The creation of money in the endogenous money approach provides a clear guide to how the stock of money and prices can move together.

9 Concluding Remarks

The teaching of macroeconomics when money is treated as endogenous rather than exogenous requires attention to be paid to the process by which loans are provided by banks and the mechanisms by which money is created and destroyed. Since loans are costly they are taken out for the purpose of spending them which leads into a close linkage between the banking sector and expenditure. The conditions which banks set for loans to be provided determines what expenditure can take place (and which not). Endogenous money overcomes the puzzle which is present with exogenous money as to how a move from one equilibrium to another can be financed. The analysis of aggregate demand can be based on the familiar *IS* curve, which enables the effects of fiscal and monetary policy to be analysed and compared. The policy instrument of the central bank is identified with the policy interest rate (though policies such as reserve ratio requirements would be compatible with the endogenous money approach). The endogeneity of money comes from the provision of loans by the banking system, which thereby creates bank deposits that are part of money, and also from the actions of the central bank, which provides base money in response to the requirements of the banking system.

Endogenous money is compatible with a range of inflationary mechanisms (e.g. demand-pull, cost-push) since money would be created through the banking system as part of the inflationary process, which enables the inflation to proceed. Attention needs to be paid to the relationship between the demand side and the supply side in that within the endogenous money context there is an absence of market mechanisms, which ensure compatibility between the level of demand and a supply-side equilibrium.

Notes

1. I am grateful to Giuseppe Fontana and Mark Setterfield for their comments and guidance on an earlier draft, and to Philip Arestis and Peter Howells for extensive discussions on the subject matter of this chapter.
2. The New Consensus in macroeconomics which treats money as endogenous excludes the impact of money and credit on the evolution of the economy. This is in contrast with the post Keynesian approach which would. For some discussion on the differences of the two approaches where monetary policy is concerned see Arestis and Sawyer (2007).

3. 'The endogeneity [of money] can be seen at three levels. First, there is endogeneity at the junction between the firm and the private bank. When firms worthy of credit ask for a loan, banks create one ... Secondly, there is endogeneity at the junction between the household and the bank. When households take a portfolio decision with respect to their wealth, the money which they desire to keep has already been created when banks make loans. Their residual demand for money is necessarily accommodated by the commercial banks ... Thirdly, there is endogeneity at the juncture between the commercial bank and the central bank. The latter must provide the high-powered money that the former requires' (Lavoie, 1992, p. 170). For extensive exploration of the implications of this endogeneity see Lavoie (2003).
4. An example is provided in the following: 'In summary, the potential size of the money supply depends in the final analysis on the volume of bank reserves. Since the volume of these reserves is almost entirely dependent on US Federal-Reserve-Treasury action, the money supply is often treated as a "policy variable," i.e. fixed unless changed by central direction. As we have seen, the ratio between the actual and the potential money supply may fluctuate under the impact of changing interest rates and varying degrees of uncertainty. Consequently, to treat the supply of money as a policy variable is not entirely satisfactory' (p. 115). 'Let us consider the possibility that rising interest rates cause banks to activate excess reserves and thereby increase the money supply' (p.137). Then from a model in which demand for money does not depend on rate of interest, they conclude 'our present assumption produces an *LM* curve that takes on a shape similar to that attained when we assumed the existence of a speculative demand on the part of the public.' (Dernburg and McDougall, 1963, p. 139).

References

Abel, A.B. and Bernanke, B.S. (2005), *Macroeconomics*, 5th edn, London: Pearson.

Arestis, P. and Sawyer, M. (2003), 'Does the stock of money have any significance?', *Banca Nazionale del Lavoro*, 56(225), 113–36.

Arestis, P. and Sawyer, M. (2006), 'Aggregate demand, conflict and capacity in the inflationary process', *Cambridge Journal of Economics*, 29(6), 959–74.

Arestis, P. and Sawyer, M. (2007), 'The nature and role of monetary policy when money is endogenous', *Cambridge Journal of Economics*, 30(6), 847–60.

Dernburg, T.F. and McDougall, D.M. (1963), *Macro-economics*, London: McGraw-Hill.

Friedman, M. (1969), 'The quantity theory of money: a restatement', in M. Friedman, *The Optimum Quantity of Money and other essays*, London: Macmillan, 51–68.

Godley, W. (1999), 'Money and credit in a Keynesian model of income determination', *Cambridge Journal of Economics*, 23, 393–411.

Godley, W. and Lavoie, M. (2007), *Monetary Economics: An Integrated Approach to Credit, Money, Income, Production, and Wealth*, Basingstoke: Palgrave Macmillan.

Lavoie, M. (1992), *Foundations of Post-Keynesian Economic Analysis*, Aldershot: Edward Elgar.

Lavoie, M. (2003), 'A primer on endogenous credit money', in Rochon, L.P. and Rossi, S. (eds), *Modern Theories of Money*, Cheltenham: Edward Elgar.

Romer, D. (2000), 'Keynesian macroeconomics without the LM curve', *Journal of Economic Perspectives*, 14(2), 149–69.

Taylor, J.B. (1993), 'Discretion versus policy rules in practice', *Carnegie-Rochester Conference Series on Public Policy*, North Holland, 39, 159–214.

8
A Simple (and Teachable) Macroeconomic Model with Endogenous Money

Giuseppe Fontana and Mark Setterfield

1 Introduction

According to Romer (2000), the *IS–LM* framework has outlived its usefulness as the basic model for teaching undergraduate students about short-run macroeconomic fluctuations. This is because central banks no longer use monetary aggregates as the instrument of monetary policy (as per the assumptions of the *IS–LM* model), but instead conduct policy by manipulating interest rates (see also Blinder 1997; Taylor 1997; Walsh 2002). Romer's solution to this problem involves replacing the *LM* curve with an *MP* (monetary policy) curve that describes how central banks manipulate interest rates in response to macroeconomic outcomes such as variations in inflation and/or the level of real economic activity. The result is what has come to be known as the 'New Consensus' model, in which the central bank varies the interest rate in order to anchor the rate of inflation at its chosen target value, while real activity is governed by a natural rate of unemployment or NAIRU.[1] Simple and teachable variants of this model have already been developed by, for example, Taylor (2000), Carlin and Soskice (2005), and Jones (2008).

Building on the work of Fontana (2006), the ambition of this chapter is to present a simple and teachable macroeconomic model that transcends *both* the *IS–LM* and New Consensus frameworks. We agree with Romer (2000) and others that a simple appeal to realism reveals obvious flaws with the continued use of the *IS–LM* framework, and that this demands that we reform the teaching of undergraduate macroeconomics. Experience teaches us that the central bank is the modern institution setting the price, rather than the quantity, of liquidity in the economy. The Fed in the US, the ECB in Europe, and the Bank of England in the UK, to mention just some of the world's major central banks, meet monthly in order to set the short-run interest rate used by commercial banks and other financial institutions for determining all other interest rates in the economy. Without doubt, the learning process of students can be enhanced by references to this real-world experience.

However, there is a crude empiricist bent to the New Consensus approach, according to which central banks manipulate interest rates (rather than monetary aggregates) because 'that's what central banks do', and the quantity of money in circulation (if it is mentioned at all) is treated as a residual by-product of central bank behaviour. We seek to replace this crude empiricism with a sounder analysis of the money supply process that leads students towards explicit consideration of the role of commercial banks, firms and consumers, together with the role played by the central bank, in an endogenous money system. An important pedagogical advantage of this approach is that it enhances students' appreciation of how economists base their arguments and policy conclusions on sound economic models, rather than casual observation.

Our model also differs from the New Consensus in two other important (and related) respects. First, it draws attention to the potential importance of the monetary processes described above for outcomes in both the goods and labour markets, even in the long run. In this way, it replaces the Classical hierarchy of the New Consensus – in which labour market outcomes (summarized by the NAIRU) dictate equilibrium output in the goods market, and money plays a strictly secondary role that involves no lasting impact on real variables – with a Keynesian hierarchy, according to which monetary and financial processes impinge upon aggregate demand formation and hence the determination of equilibrium output in the goods market, which in turn dictates events in the labour market. Second, it is capable of producing both Classical and Keynesian dynamics in the goods and labour markets that give rise to supply-constrained and demand-constrained equilibria, respectively. It therefore constitutes a more general model of economic activity than the New Consensus model, which describes only Classical dynamics in the goods and labour markets, together with the associated supply-constrained equilibria in each market.

The remainder of the chapter is organized as follows. In section 2, we describe the workings of the monetary sector (including the conduct of monetary policy by the central bank) in a manner consistent with the workings of an endogenous money supply process. Section 3 demonstrates the derivation of a conventional aggregate demand curve (in price–output space), and section 4 completes the model by describing pricing, production and the labour market. In section 5, the complete model is summarized and its workings are demonstrated using comparative static exercises. Finally, section 6 concludes, contrasting the model developed in this chapter with both the *IS–LM* and New Consensus frameworks, and drawing particular attention to some of the most pedagogically appealing features of the model.

2 Endogenous Money and the Conduct of Macroeconomic Policy

As intimated earlier, the *IS–LM* framework describes a world in which the quantity of money in circulation is exogenously manipulated by the central bank through its open market operations. But as noted by Romer (2000) and others, this does not describe central bank behaviour as we actually observe it. Central banks are concerned with the manipulation of interest rates rather than monetary aggregates in the conduct of their monetary policies.

In this section, we account for this behaviour by developing a simple model of endogenous money, in which any creditworthy demand for loans from the non-bank private sector elicits a supply response from commercial banks that results in an endogenous variation of the money supply – a process that is accommodated by the central bank albeit at a price (the overnight interest rate) of its own making.[2]

Firms and consumers (the non-bank private sector) demand bank loans in order to finance the purchase of inputs for the production process or of durable goods, respectively. Commercial banks, meanwhile, are institutions in the business of making loans. Commercial banks, therefore, fully accommodate all demands for loans made by creditworthy borrowers. The interest rate charged on these loans – the bank loans rate, r_L – is set by commercial banks as a mark-up (m) over the real short-run interest rate (i) set by the central bank.[3] Formally:

$$r_L = (1 + m)i \tag{8.1}$$

The behaviour of commercial banks in the bank loans market can thus be summarized by saying that commercial banks are price-makers and quantity-takers. Meanwhile, as the loans taken out by households and firms are spent, they accrue as receipts elsewhere in the non-bank private sector, and these receipts are, in turn, deposited into accounts at commercial banks. In this way, loans create deposits. Of course, these deposits are liabilities of the commercial banks. The liquidity of these deposits is thus a concern for commercial banks. In order to meet any expected demand from the non-bank private sector for cash withdrawals, commercial banks will therefore demand monetary reserves from the central bank in proportion to their deposits. At this point, it is important to note that one of the major functions of the central bank is to safeguard the economic system from financial crises. Thus, as the ultimate supplier of liquidity, the central bank will fully accommodate commercial banks' demands for monetary reserves, albeit at a price of its own making. This price is the real short-run (overnight) interest rate. Note, then, that not only is the quantity of credit endogenously determined by the demand for loans, but so, too, is the quantity of monetary reserves or high powered money endogenously determined, by the derived demand for liquidity of

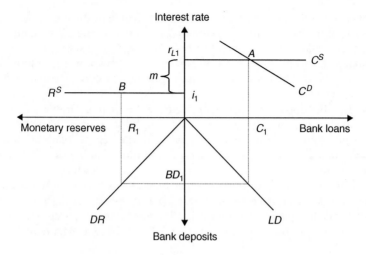

Figure 8.1 The endogenous money supply process

commercial banks. The central bank may be the sole legal issuer of high powered or base money, but is has no effective control over even this narrow component of the total money supply, which is instead endogenously determined by the processes governing the demand for and supply of credit in the private sector.

Having thus accommodated the liquidity needs of commercial banks, the behaviour of the central bank completes our description of the endogenous money supply process. The four-panel diagram in Figure 8.1 illustrates the sequence of events that characterizes this process.[4] The diagram should be read clockwise starting from the upper right panel.

The upper right panel shows the credit market, where firms and consumers on one hand and commercial banks on the other express the demand for and supply of bank loans, respectively. The supply curve of bank loans is represented by a perfectly elastic schedule at a bank loans rate (r_{L1}) that is determined as a fixed mark-up (m) over the specific short-term real interest rate (i_1) that has been set by the central bank. The demand for bank credit (i.e., loans), C^D, is a decreasing function of the bank loans rate and, together with the supply of bank credit (C^S), determines (at equilibrium point A) the total volume of credit created (C_1).

The two lower panels of Figure 8.1 describe two of the main insights of endogenous money theory, namely, that: (a) bank loans create bank deposits (as captured by the Loans–Deposits or *LD* schedule); and (b) bank deposits give rise to the demand for monetary reserves (as captured by the Deposits–Reserves or *DR* schedule). The credit market equilibrium at point A thus determines, via the *LD* schedule, the supply of new bank deposits (BD_1) in the lower right panel and hence (via the *DR* schedule in the lower left panel) commercial banks' demand for reserves (R_1). Note that the *LD* schedule represents the balance sheet constraint of commercial banks and, for the sake of making the graphical exposition feasible, it is drawn on the assumption that banks hold their liabilities (such as time or demand deposits) in fixed proportions.

Finally, the upper left panel of Figure 8.1 describes the workings of the market for monetary reserves. The supply of reserves is represented by the horizontal line R^S, which shows how the central bank accommodates the demand for monetary reserves by commercial banks at its quoted short-term real interest rate, i_1. Ultimately, the market for monetary reserves clears when the supply of monetary reserves adjusts to equate the demand for reserves (R_1) that was generated by the new supply of bank deposits (BD_1) in the lower left panel of Figure 8.1. Monetary reserve market clearing is illustrated at equilibrium point *B* in the upper left panel of Figure 8.1.

3   Deriving the Aggregate Demand Curve

Having described the endogenous money supply process, we now extend our analysis by showing how this process is related to the shape of the aggregate demand (*AD*) schedule, which is conventionally drawn in price (*P*) – output (*Y*) space. In order to accomplish this, we begin by writing:

$$AD = ND + cD$$

and

$$D = f(r_L), \quad f' < 0$$

where *ND* denotes components of aggregate demand that are not debt-financed by loans from commercial banks (such as consumption expenditures funded from current income, or government spending), *D* denotes planned or desired debt-financed spending by households and firms, and *c* is the proportion of households and business loan applications that are deemed creditworthy by banks. Note, then, that *cD* captures the *actual* (rather than planned or desired) debt-financed spending by the non-bank private sector, and also that:

$$C^D \equiv cD$$

In other words, the demand for bank loans schedule (C^D) in the upper right panel of Figure 8.1 is identical to the actual debt-financed spending (*cD*) by households and firms. This of course makes sense since, as was assumed earlier, households and firms are motivated to borrow from banks by their desire to spend on goods and services. Finally, note that it follows from the equations for *AD* and *D* introduced above that:

$$AD = ND + cf(r_L) \qquad (8.2)$$

Equation (8.2) is consistent with the notion that an increase in the bank loans rate (r_L), by raising the cost of borrowing for households and firms and thus reducing their willingness and/or ability to borrow, will reduce the total expenditures that households and firms undertake, and thus reduce the aggregate demand for goods and services.

Our analysis also requires one further equation, linking the value of the short-run interest rate to conditions in the goods market. Hence we write:

$$i = g(P), \quad g' > 0 \qquad (8.3)$$

Equation (8.3) is a monetary policy rule describing the operation of the central bank's monetary policy (which, in keeping with the theory of endogenous money developed in the previous section, involves manipulation of the short-run interest rate). In general, monetary policy rules describe the response of real short-run interest rates to changes in the state of the economy.[5] Of course, there are, in principle, many types of monetary policy rules. The central bank could target a single economic variable (such as inflation), or a combination of variables (such as output, employment and inflation). In many contemporary industrialized economies, central banks have been assigned the specific task of meeting an inflation objective, and doing so through changes in the real short-run interest rate. In view of this, equation (8.3) has been formulated to represent the simplest type of monetary policy rule consistent with the practice of 'inflation targeting' described above, in which the real short-run interest rate changes in response to variations in the price level.[6]

In the *IS–LM* model, an increase in the general price level, *P*, will automatically reduce the aggregate quantity demanded via the real balance or Pigou effect. Given an exogenously determined stock of money *M*, an increase in *P* will reduce the real purchasing power of *M* (the value of 'real balances', (M/P)), and hence the aggregate quantity demanded.[7] But in the endogenous money environment discussed in the previous section, the Pigou effect is weakened and may disappear altogether. Hence, if an increase in *P* results in an equal proportional increase in the demand for loans by households and firms, and if this is accommodated by an equivalent increase in the supply of loans by commercial banks, then *M* will automatically increase with *P* leaving real balances (M/P) unchanged. In this scenario, thanks to the endogeneity of the money supply, there is no Pigou effect, so that an increase in prices leaves the aggregate quantity demanded unchanged.

It may therefore appear that, since there is no real balance or Pigou effect, the *AD* curve is vertical in price–output space. However, this need not be so. Indeed, equations (8.1)–(8.3) above have been deliberately contrived to show how a conventional, 'downward sloping' *AD* curve can arise in an endogenous money environment.[8] The important thing to remember is that, as derived from equations (8.1)–(8.3), the shape of the *AD* curve is a *policy construct*, depending critically on the operation of the monetary policy rule described in equation (8.3). In other words, the *AD* curve describes how the central bank sets, via changes in the short-run interest rate (i), the level of output (Y) for any general price level (P) in the economy.

To begin with, assume that the general price level (P) increases. According to the monetary policy rule in equation (8.3), this will trigger an increase in the short-run interest rate (i) set by the central bank. Bearing in mind that the bank loans rate (r_L) is set, by commercial banks, as a constant mark-up (m) over the short-run interest rate, an increase in i will result in an increase in r_L, as in equation (8.1). This means that the cost of borrowing is now higher for both households and firms in the non-bank private sector – with adverse consequences for aggregate demand. First, the cost of borrowing to finance investment is now higher so that *ceteris paribus*, for a given expected rate of return, the demand for investment goods will now be lower. A similar story can be told about the demand for consumption goods. An increase in the short-run interest rate and hence in the bank loans rate means that it is more expensive to borrow money from commercial banks in order to buy durable goods like homes and new cars. This will decrease the willingness and/or ability of households to borrow so that, *ceteris paribus*, consumption expenditures will decline. Since both consumption and investment are components of aggregate demand, the upshot of these developments is that an increase in r_L will be associated with a reduction in the aggregate quantity demanded – as per the inverse relationship between *AD* and r_L in equation (8.2).

In summary, by combining the relationships in equations (8.1)–(8.3), a downward sloping aggregate demand curve is easily derived. An increase in the price level triggers an increase in the short-run interest rate by the central bank, which is passed on by commercial banks in the form of a higher bank loans rate. This negatively affects the demand for investment and consumption goods, and hence the aggregate quantity demanded. In short – and thanks to the operation of the monetary policy rule in (8.3) – an increase in the price level (P) gives rise to a reduction in the aggregate quantity demanded (Y). The resulting negatively sloped aggregate demand schedule is illustrated in Figure 8.2 below, together with the structural relations from which it is derived (equations (8.1)–(8.3)). Figure 8.2 shows how an increase in prices from P_1 to P_2 will raise the short-run interest rate set by the central bank (from i_1 to i_2 – see the upper left panel) and hence the bank loans rate (from r_{L1} to r_{L2} – see the lower left panel). The lower right panel of Figure 8.2 then shows that this will reduce the aggregate quantity demanded from Y_1 to Y_2

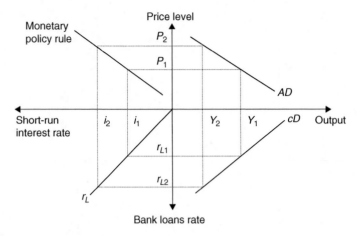

Figure 8.2 A conventional (downward-sloping) aggregate demand schedule

(note that, for the sake of simplicity, the *ND* component of aggregate demand is assumed to equal zero in Figure 8.2).

4 Completing the Model: Pricing, Production and the Labour Market

So far, our model consists of a monetary sector describing an endogenous money supply process, and an aggregate demand curve. In this section, we complete our model by introducing theories of pricing and production that give rise to an aggregate supply (*AS*) relationship (which, in tandem with the aggregate demand relationship in equation (8.2), completes our description of the goods market), and by discussing the labour market.

4.1 Pricing, production and aggregate supply

We begin with a description of pricing in the goods market that mirrors our description of the pricing behaviour of commercial banks. Specifically, we posit that firms set prices (*P*) as a fixed mark-up (*n*) over the average cost of labour, namely the nominal wage (*W*) multiplied by the number of workers employed (*N*) divided by total output (*Y*). Note that we take the nominal wage (*W*) as given, since once negotiations between workers and firms are concluded, *W* is fixed for the entire length of the employment contract. The pricing behaviour of firms can be written as:

$$P = (1+n)\frac{WN}{Y}$$

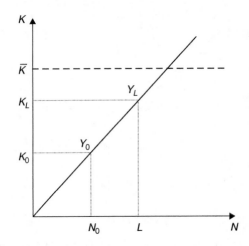

Figure 8.3   The aggregate production function

or

$$P = (1 + n)Wa \qquad (8.4)$$

where $a = (N/Y)$ denotes the labour/output ratio, i.e. the labour required to produce one unit of output. We treat a, together with the corresponding capital/output ratio, $v = (K/Y)$, as fixed in the short run. This means that, given the current state of technology, it takes a specific amount of labour combined with a specific amount of capital to produce any given level of output. The resulting fixed coefficient production function is depicted in Figure 8.3 which illustrates both the quantity of capital (K_0) and level of employment (N_0) necessary to produce an arbitrarily chosen level of output (Y_0). Note that Figure 8.3 also illustrates the level of output that can be produced (Y_L) if the entire labour force (L) is employed (together with the quantity of capital, K_L, necessary to facilitate this level of production).[9] This draws attention to an important supply constraint on the level of output, since Y_L denotes the *maximum* level of output that the economy can produce. Obviously, the actual level of output, Y, cannot exceed this maximum value.

The description of pricing and production above gives rise to the aggregate supply (*AS*) schedule depicted in Figure 8.4. This schedule is horizontal, capturing the substance of equation (8.4), which suggests that firms are price-makers and quantity-takers. They are willing to accommodate any demand for their output at price level P_0, which is associated with the given nominal wage W_0.[10] The schedule ends at Y_L since, as demonstrated above, this is the maximum level of output that can be produced regardless of the price level.

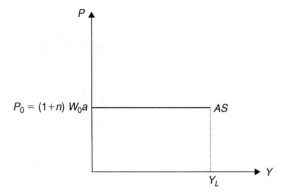

Figure 8.4 The aggregate supply schedule

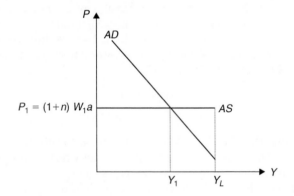

Figure 8.5 The goods market

It is now a simple matter to combine the aggregate supply schedule in Figure 8.4 with the aggregate demand schedule in Figure 8.2 to illustrate equilibrium outcomes in the goods market. This task is performed in Figure 8.5, in which it is assumed that the nominal wage takes the value W_1, and hence the price level is P_1. Figure 8.5 also illustrates the equilibrium level of output, Y_1, associated with the aggregate demand (AD) curve and the aggregate supply (AS) curve.

4.2 The labour market

It is conventional to derive labour market outcomes from the interaction of labour demand and labour supply schedules. Note, however, that in the model developed above, two important labour market outcomes have already been determined.

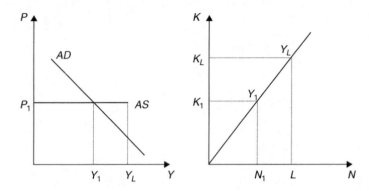

Figure 8.6   Equilibrium output and employment

First, given the exogenously determined value of the nominal wage, W_1, and the associated price level, (P_1) (see Figure 8.5), it follows that the value of the real wage (w) is given as $w_1 = W_1/P_1$. Indeed, it follows from equation (8.4) that, *regardless* of the value of the nominal wage and associated price level, the value of the real wage is always given by:

$$w = \frac{W}{P} = \frac{1}{(1+n)a}$$

This means that the pricing decisions of firms (specifically, the value of the mark-up, n) and features of the production process (the labour/output ratio, a) are the ultimate determinants of the real wage: once workers sign their labour contracts, the amount of goods and services that can be bought by workers, i.e. their real wage, is determined (given the value of a) by the value of n set by firms.

Second, the equilibrium level of employment follows from the interaction of the equilibrium level of output (Y_1) determined in Figure 8.5, and the production function depicted in Figure 8.3. This is illustrated in Figure 8.6, which shows how the equilibrium level of output (Y_1) implies both a capital requirement (K_1) and a labour requirement (N_1) in the production function. This labour requirement (N_1) is the equilibrium level of employment.

The preceding analysis thus confirms that the monetary sector impinges upon the formation of the aggregate demand curve, and hence the determination of the equilibrium level of output (Y_1) in the goods market, which in turn determines the equilibrium level of employment (N_1) in the labour market. This means that in our model, the Classical hierarchy of the New Consensus view, according to which labour market outcomes determine goods market outcomes (and monetary factors are of secondary importance), is replaced by a Keynesian hierarchy, where monetary factors influence goods market outcomes which, in turn, determine labour market outcomes.

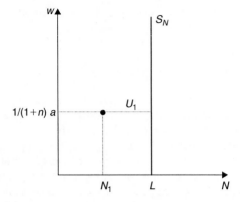

Figure 8.7 The labour market

The consequences for the labour market of this Keynesian hierarchy are illustrated in Figure 8.7, which shows a vertical labour supply schedule (S_N), corresponding to the labour supply function:

$$S_N = L \qquad (8.5)$$

where S_N denotes the supply of labour. According to equation (8.5), the supply of labour, which is based on the active labour force at any point in time, is invariant with respect to the value of the real wage (w). This labour supply function provides a good first approximation of real-world labour supply functions, which are known to be highly inelastic with respect to the real wage.[11] Figure 8.7 also depicts the equilibrium real wage ($w = 1/(1+n)a$) and level of employment (N_1) derived above. Finally, it shows that the difference between (L) and (N_1) gives rise to an equilibrium level of unemployment (U_1):[12]

$$U_1 = L - N_1$$

As is clear from Figure 8.7, the quantity of labour supplied at the real wage w, namely L, exceeds the quantity of labour demanded by firms, which is given by the equilibrium level of employment (N_1) determined in Figure 8.6. In other words, there are too many workers chasing too few jobs. However, the roots of unemployment (U_1) lie in the aggregate demand and supply curves in the goods market. It is in fact the equilibrium level of output (Y_1) in the goods market, which determines the equilibrium level of employment (N_1) and hence the equilibrium level of unemployment (U_1) in the labour market. This means that U_1, rather than being the outcome of the *individual choices* of workers in the labour market, is the result of a *macroeconomic constraint* on the behaviour of workers emanating from the behaviour of the central bank, commercial banks, households and firms on one hand (the *AD* side of the goods market), and the pricing decisions of firms (the *AS* side of the goods market) on the other.

5   Some Comparative Static Exercises

Our complete model now consists of a monetary sector, a goods market and a labour market, as summarized by Figures 8.1, 8.6 and 8.7. This model suggests that the monetary sector influences the formation of aggregate demand, since both the bank loans rate (r_L) and the propensity of commercial banks to deem household and business borrowers creditworthy affect the willingness and ability of households and firms to borrow, and thus execute debt-financed expenditures. Aggregate demand, meanwhile, affects goods market outcomes, which in turn affect labour market outcomes. Figure 8.8 illustrates the structure of the resulting endogenous money model.

Note also that in our model, there is no automatic reversion in the 'long run' away from the general equilibrium depicted in Figures 8.1, 8.6 and 8.7 towards an equilibrium based on a NAIRU determined independently of monetary conditions and aggregate demand. Instead, the model always generates a Keynesian hierarchy, according to which monetary conditions affect real outcomes in the goods market, which in turn affect outcomes in the labour market. Figure 8.8 must therefore be read strictly from left to right.

The workings of the model can be understood in greater detail by referring to the specific outcomes illustrated in Figures 8.1, 8.6 and 8.7. We begin in Figure 8.6 with the establishment of the price level (P_1) (and corresponding *AS* schedule), which are based on the given nominal wage W_1 (as in Figure 8.5). This gives rise to the short-run interest rate (i_1) derived from the monetary policy schedule in Figure 8.1, which in turn establishes the bank loans rate (r_{L1}) in the upper right panel of the same figure. Referring now to the foundations of our aggregate demand relation in equation (8.2), we can see that given the bank loans rate (r_{L1}), the non-bank private sector will formulate planned or desired debt-financed spending plans of size $D_1 = f(r_{L1})$,

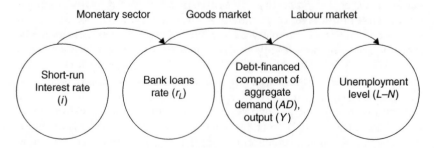

Figure 8.8   The structure of our endogenous money model

which will translate into *actual* debt-financed spending of size $cD_1 = cf(r_{L1})$ following decisions by commercial banks regarding the creditworthiness of loan applicants. These borrowing and lending decisions by the bank and non-bank private sector will now have two consequences. First, in the upper right hand panel of Figure 8.1, the demand for and supply of bank credit will coincide at $C_1 = cD_1$. This will give rise to bank deposits to the value of BD_1 (in the lower right panel of Figure 8.1), and hence a quantity of reserves created by the central bank of size R_1 (in the lower left panel of Figure 8.1). This completes our analysis of the endogenous money supply process.

Second, the determination of actual debt-financed spending $cD_1 = cf(r_{L1})$ described above will give rise to an aggregate quantity demanded in the goods market of size $AD_1 = ND + cD_1 = Y_1$, which is illustrated by the intersection of the AD and AS schedules in Figure 8.6 at P_1 and Y_1. The equilibrium level of output (Y_1) will, in turn, give rise to the labour requirement (and hence equilibrium level of employment) N_1 in the production function, as also shown in Figure 8.6. Finally, Figure 8.7 shows how, given the current size of the labour force, L, the equilibrium level of unemployment is determined by the equilibrium level of employment as $U_1 = N_1 - L$ at the equilibrium real wage $w = 1/(1 + n)a$.

5.1 The Credit Crunch of 2007–2008 and the Policy-Makers' Response

Our model can be used to illustrate the credit crunch of 2007–2008 and the difficult task faced by central banks and policy-makers more generally in avoiding a global recession. In plain English, a credit crunch is a sudden reduction in the availability of bank loans and/or a sudden increase in the cost of obtaining a loan from commercial banks. In terms of our endogenous money supply process, this means that a credit crunch is measured by a reduction in the parameter c (see equation (8.2)) and/or an increase in the mark-up (m) and hence, *ceteris paribus*, an increase in the bank loans rate (r_L) (see equation (8.1)). There is a number of reasons why banks may suddenly make borrowing more difficult or increase the costs of borrowing. One of the factors most frequently accredited for the credit crunch in 2007–2008 was the collapse of America's (sub-prime) mortgage market, which led to a global financial crisis. As a result, liquidity became scarce in international markets, and banks suddenly reduced the availability of loans.

The effects of the credit crunch are represented in Figures 8.9(a), 8.9(b), 8.9(c) below. The global financial crisis of 2007–2008 caused banks to adopt a more precautionary lending behaviour, which led banks to cut the proportion of household and corporate loan applications that were deemed creditworthy. In terms of equation (8.2) this means that banks cut the value of the parameter c. The upper right panel of Figure 8.9(a) shows that the actual demand for loans (C^D) shifts to the left. The new equilibrium point in the

158

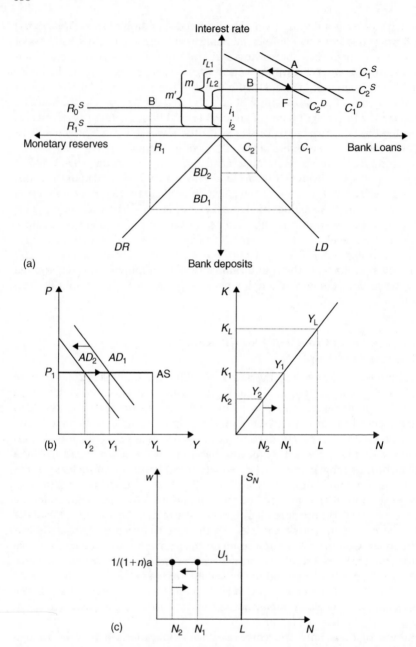

Figure 8.9 (a) The 2007–2008 credit crunch and the endogenous money supply process; (b) the effects of the 2007–2008 credit crunch on equilibrium output and employment; (c) the effects of the 2007–2008 credit crunch in the labour market

credit market is then at point B, and the total volume of credit created is now C_2, which in turn determines, via the LD schedule, the supply of new bank deposits (BD_2) (see lower right panel of Figure 8.9(a)).[13] These financial developments negatively affect the actual debt-financed spending by households and firms, namely the cD component of AD in equation (8.2). In terms of Figure 8.9(b), this means that the aggregate demand curve (AD) shifts to the left. As a result of this shift, the equilibrium level of output now decreases from Y_1 to Y_2. Figure 8.9(b) also shows that for the new lower level of output Y_2, the capital and labour requirements are K_2 and N_2, respectively. The consequences of these changes in the monetary sector and the goods market are shows in Figure 8.9(c): the equilibrium level of unemployment now rises from $(L–N_1)$ to $(L–N_2)$. In short, as a result of the credit crunch, the economy experiences a lower level of output and a higher level of unemployment. This is in fact what happened in 2007 and 2008, when most countries experienced slowdowns in economic activity and increases in unemployment.

How should monetary and fiscal authorities react to these events? Figure 8.9(a) shows the reaction of the monetary authorities and some of its drawbacks. The central bank may try to offset the negative real effects of the credit crunch through a more accommodating monetary policy, i.e., by reducing the short-run interest rate from i_1 to i_2. This means that, *ceteris paribus*, the new bank loans rate is (r_{L2}). We will return to the *ceteris paribus* condition shortly, but for the time being let us focus on the outcome of the new, more accommodating monetary policy. The new supply of bank loans is now C_2^S, and the new equilibrium point in the credit market is at point F, at the intersection of C_2^S and C_2^D. Therefore, as a result of monetary policy, the total volume of credit created is now back to the pre-credit crunch level C_1, as is the supply of new bank deposits (BD_1). Figure 8.9(b) shows that the aggregate demand curve (AD) shifts to the right, back to its original level. This is caused by the stimulus to debt-financed expenditures (cD) that results from the reduction in the bank loan rate to r_{L2}. As a result, the aggregate equilibrium level of output is again Y_1, with the equilibrium level of unemployment equal to $(L–N_1)$. If our analysis were to stop here, we could conclude that the central bank has succeeded in offsetting completely the negative effects of the credit crunch. At the time of writing this chapter (summer 2008), however, we know that this did not happen. How, then, can we use our model to explain the apparent failure of a more accommodating monetary policy strategy?

In order to answer this question, we need to understand that while the central bank can certainly reduce the short-run interest rate from i_1 to i_2, this does not mean that it will necessarily succeed in reducing the bank loan rate from r_{L1} to r_{L2}. We have said that a credit crunch is: (1) a sudden reduction in the availability of bank loans *and/or* (2) a sudden increase in the cost of obtaining a loan from commercial banks. The analysis above has focused exclusively on the first feature of a credit crunch, and maintained all other economic factors fixed. This is the meaning of our *ceteris paribus* condition. But what happens if we allow for the second feature of a credit crunch, namely a sudden increase in the cost of obtaining a bank loan? In terms of equation (8.1), this means that banks raise their mark-up (m) over the short-run interest rate (i) set by the central bank. The upper panels of Figure 8.9(a) show that, even with the new short-run interest rate i_2, the bank loan rate will remain at r_{L1} if the mark-up rises to m', which is higher than m. In other words, we have now assumed that commercial banks respond to the reduction of i with an offsetting increase in m. If this is the case, the equilibrium point in the credit market remains at point B, at the intersection of C_1^S and C_2^D. As discussed above, this point is associated with the low equilibrium level of output Y_2, and the high equilibrium level of unemployment ($L-N_2$). Figure 8.9(a) also illustrates a further problem for the central bank. The effectiveness of its monetary policy strategy is greatly reduced as the short-run interest rate (i) approaches the zero lower bound. In other words, the more the central bank cuts the short-run interest rate now, the less it can do so in future. In short, an accommodative monetary policy is not necessarily successful in offsetting a credit crunch, especially when, in the face of liquidity shortages in global financial markets, banks raise their mark-up over the short-run interest rate.

However, policy-makers have an alternative tool to smooth or eliminate altogether the negative effects of a credit crunch. They can try to affect the components of aggregate demand that are *not* debt-financed by loans from commercial banks. For instance, the fiscal authorities of a country can increase government spending or reduce taxes in order to boost the *ND* component of aggregate demand (*AD*) (see equation (8.2)). This is in fact what the US Congress did early in 2008, when it passed the so-called Economic Stimulus Act. This Act offered tax rebates for low- and middle-income taxpayers and tax incentives for business investments. The potential beneficial effects of the Economic Stimulus Act can be analysed through our model. In particular, Figure 8.9(b) shows how a shift leftward of the *AD* curve caused by a credit crunch is offset by a shift rightward of the same curve due to an increase in the *ND* component of aggregate demand. In this way, the fiscal authorities can bring the economy back to the pre-credit crunch level of output Y_1, and to the equilibrium level of unemployment ($L-N_1$). Of course, tax rebates and tax incentives are a net loss of income for the government. For this reason, policy-makers may be reluctant to use them in order to stimulate the economy, except for a very short period of time.

5.2   How to Solve Unemployment: Stabilizing Effects (the Classical View) vs Destabilizing Effects (the Keynesian View) of Wage Flexibility

Our model allows us to explore a very thorny theoretical issue in macroeconomics, which has quite important practical implications for the well-being of individuals and the prosperity of our society: what, if anything, should policy-makers do to alleviate the problem of unemployment? In order to answer this question, we begin by adding to our analysis of the labour market in Section 4.2 one further equation:

$$W = h(L - N), \quad h' < 0 \tag{8.6}$$

Equation (8.6) tells us that when the labour supply of workers exceeds the quantity of labour demanded by firms, the nominal wage (W) will drop. Figures 8.10(a), 8.10(b), and 8.10(c) show the seemingly positive effects on unemployment of such reductions in the nominal wage.

Figure 8.10(c) shows that our economy is suffering from a level of unemployment (U_1) equal to the difference between the fixed labour supply (L) and the quantity of labour demanded (N_1), which is determined in the goods market (see Figure 8.6). According to Equation (8.6), in these circumstances the nominal wage (W) drops. As it does, via equation (8.4), the price level (P) will also fall. These changes affect both the aggregate supply curve and the aggregate quantity of goods demanded.

Figures 8.10(a) shows that the reduction in the nominal wage from W_1 to W_2 shifts the aggregate supply curve downward. Importantly, the curve will keep shifting downward as long as there is unemployment in the labour market. Figure 8.10(b) confirms that as the AS curve moves downward along the AD_1 curve, the level of output and the level of employment increase. This is because as the price level drops from P_1 to P_2, the central bank reduces the short-run interest rate (i) which lowers the bank loans rate (r_L). This, in turn, increases the debt-financed (ND) component of aggregate demand (AD). The new equilibrium is at point B, where the level of output is equal to Y_L. Figure 8.10(b) shows that this level of output is associated with the capital and labour requirements K_L and L, respectively. Finally, Figure 8.10(c) confirms that with Y_L level of output, the quantity of labour demanded is equal to the labour supply (L), i.e. there is full employment in the economy.

Our simple model thus shows how wage flexibility can be the means by which the economy is able to achieve full use of all available workers in the labour market. Going back to our initial question, then, what is the role of policy-makers in alleviating unemployment? According to the analysis above, policy-makers must make sure that the nominal wage (W) and the price level (P) are perfectly flexible, such that they can stabilize the economy when, for whatever reason, it happens to move away from full employment. This is in fact the general thrust of all modern policies promoting wage flexibility in the labour market. Strong trade unions or minimum wage laws, which are seen to obstruct free movement of the nominal wage in response to shocks to the labour market, are in this view the enemies of employment. This stabilizing role of wage and price flexibility was first discussed by such

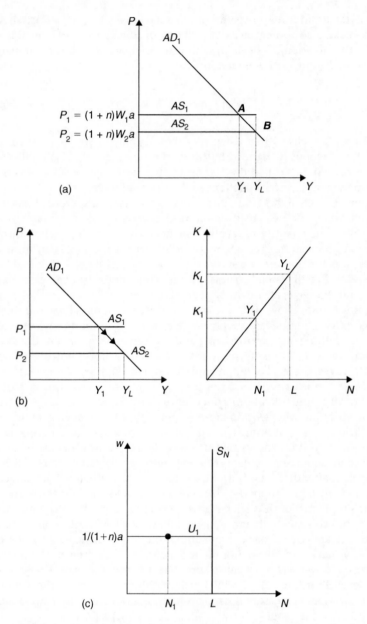

Figure 8.10 (a) The classical view and the (stabilizing) effects of wage flexibility in the goods market; (b) the classical view of equilibrium output and employment; (c) the classical view and the effects of wage flexibility in the labour market

founders of economics as Adam Smith and David Ricardo, and for this reason it is often labelled the Classical view of the economy.

But our model also allows us to explore a different view of the economy which, in contrast to the Classical view, stresses the destabilizing role of wage flexibility in the economy. This is the view of another great master of our discipline, John Maynard Keynes. According to Keynes, wage flexibility is likely to increase rather than decrease unemployment.[14] How did Keynes arrive at a view so completely opposed to that of Smith and Ricardo? Our model helps to explain both Keynes's view and his accompanying policy solution to unemployment.

As in the previous case, Figure 8.11(c) shows that our economy is suffering from an initial level of unemployment (U_1) equal to the difference between the fixed labour supply (L) and the quantity of labour demanded (N_1). According to Equation (8.6), in these circumstances the nominal wage (W) drops and, as it does, the price level (P) declines via equation (8.4). Now, let us see what happens to the AD and AS curves. We begin with an analysis of the aggregate supply curve. As the nominal wage falls from W_1 to W_2, the AS curve shifts downwards. In Figure 8.11(a), the new AS_2 curve intersects the AD_1 curve at point B, where the level of output is equal to Y_L.

However, as the price level drops from P_1 to P_2, there is a second mechanism at work on aggregate demand. When the price level declines, the real value of debts (namely the ratio of households' and firms' liabilities over the price level) rises, and this negatively affects the consumption and investment plans of households and firms, respectively.[15] In other words, by virtue of this mechanism, households and firms are less inclined to borrow money from banks, hence the debt-financed (cD) component of AD falls, shifting the AD curve left to AD_2 in Figure 8.11(a).[16]

Keynes believed that in a falling-wage environment, the second mechanism (which shifts the AD curve) dominates the first mechanism (which causes movement along the AD curve). This is reflected in Figure 8.11(a), which shows the economy now in equilibrium at point C, where it experiences a *lower* level of output (Y_2) than we began with. In effect, the AD curve is now upward sloping (a fall in P results in a fall in Y), as captured by the dashed schedule labelled AD' in Figure 8.11(a).

Figures 8.11(b) and (c) show the effects of these developments in the goods and labour markets respectively . The equilibrium level of output (Y_2) is associated with the capital and labour requirements K_2 and N_2, respectively. Figure 8.11(c) shows that the level of unemployment has now increased from $(L-N_1)$ to $(L-N_2)$ – in other words, the economy has moved *further away* from full employment as a result of a cut in nominal wages.

Our model thus shows that wage flexibility can destabilize the economy: the more wages are downwardly flexible, the more unemployment is created, *ceteris paribus*. What, in these circumstances, can policy-makers do to reduce unemployment? According to the Keynesian analysis presented above,

164

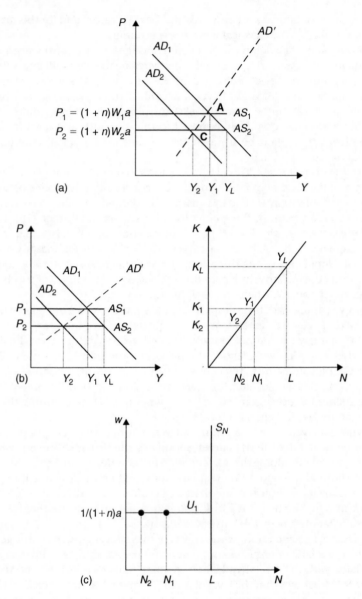

Figure 8.11 (a) The Keynesian view and the (destabilizing) effects of wage flexibility in the goods market; (b) the Keynesian view of equilibrium output and employment; (c) the Keynesian view and the effects of wage flexibility in the labour market

policy-makers must stimulate debt and non-debt financed components of the *AD* function. For instance, they may offer tax incentives for business investments, which should raise the debt financed (*cD*) component of *AD*. Similarly, policy-makers may raise the non-debt financed (*ND*) component of *AD* by increasing government spending or by offering tax rebates for low- and middle-income taxpayers, just as the US Congress did in early 2008 when it passed the Economic Stimulus Act.

In summary, there is no unique solution to the problem of unemployment. According to the Classical view, wage and price flexibility is a stabilizing mechanism that allows the achievement of full employment. In this case, the focus of the analysis and its policy implications is the effects of changes in the aggregate supply curve. By contrast, according to the Keynesian view, wage and price flexibility is a destabilizing mechanism, which increases rather than decreases the level of unemployment. In this second case, the focus of the analysis and its policy implications is the effects of changes in the aggregate demand curve. Which of these two cases – the Classical view or the Keynesian view – is more relevant for explaining unemployment in any given country depends on historical circumstances, and hence on the relative importance of demand-side or supply-side considerations in the specific circumstances considered.

6 Conclusion

In this chapter, we have developed a simple, short-run macroeconomic model that transcends shortcomings of both the *IS–LM* and New Consensus frameworks. Our model improves on *IS–LM* analysis by incorporating an endogenous rather than exogenous money supply, and by positing that the instrument of monetary policy is the interest rate. At the same time, it improves on the New Consensus framework by providing an explicit model of the endogenous money creation process that draws attention to the roles of commercial banks and the non-bank private sector, as well as the central bank, in the monetary process. Our model also rests on a Keynesian rather than Classical hierarchy of markets, and can therefore generate both Keynesian *and* Classical macro adjustment dynamics, making it more general than the New Consensus model.

The pedagogical values of our approach are several. First, our model of the money creation process complements an important general message that undergraduate teaching seeks to impart to students: that economic discourse is conducted in terms of explicit analytical models of economic processes. Our analysis of the money supply process also shows that it is possible to add realism and rigour to the teaching of undergraduate macro *without* sacrificing the simplicity that is a virtue of both *IS–LM* and New Consensus teaching models. Second, the Keynesian hierarchy of markets embodied in our model shows how modern monetary theory can be de-coupled from the innate Classicism of the New Consensus. Moreover, as intimated above, the ability of our model to encompass both Classical (supply-constrained) and Keynesian (demand-constrained) macroeconomic equilibria makes it a more general model of short-run macro-activity than the New Consensus. It is therefore a better vehicle for introducing students to the variety of opinions about the operation of the economy that characterize macroeconomic debate.

Notes

1. The long-run rate of interest is governed by a similar (Wicksellian) natural rate.
2. See, for example, Moore (1988).
3. In reality, both central and commercial banks set *nominal* rather than *real* interest rates in the first instance. But given that in the short run the rate of inflation displays inertia (or stickiness), changes in nominal interest rates will translate into changes in real interest rates. We therefore assume, for simplicity, that both central and commercial banks exercise direct control over real interest rates.
4. This four-panel diagram is derived from Fontana (2003, 2004), and is drawn on the assumption that the state of long-run expectations of all agents involved in the money supply process is given and constant. The result is what has been labelled a single period analysis of endogenous money. The authors are indebted to Dow (1996, 1997), Howells (1995), Lavoie (1996), and Palley (1994, 1996) for useful insights and similar diagrammatic representations of endogenous money theory.
5. Strictly speaking, what we have described here are 'activist' monetary policy rules. It is also possible to identify 'benchmark' monetary policy rules, in which the short-run interest rate is set in such way that it is either invariant to, or else responds only infrequently to, changes in the state of the economy. See, for example, Rochon and Setterfield (2007).
6. Equation (8.3) is consistent with a literal interpretation of the objective of 'price stability', as a result of which the central bank responds (by varying the short-run interest rate) whenever prices change (see, for example, Feldstein, 1997). In reality, however, most advocates of inflation targeting – including academic economists and central bankers – associate 'price stability' with low (0–3%) rather than zero rates of inflation (see, for example, Mishkin, 2001). Our use of equation (8.3) therefore involves some loss of realism. We regard this as worthwhile because, as will be demonstrated below, it allows us to derive a conventional *AD* schedule in price–output space, rather than the 'dynamic' *AD* schedule (in inflation–output space) associated with New Consensus models (see, for example, Taylor, 2000). This, in turn, facilitates more straightforward comparison and contrast between the results of our model and those of earlier, exogenous money models such as the *IS–LM* framework.
7. Strictly speaking, the Pigou effect operates only on the 'outside money' component of *M*. This detail is overlooked in the analysis above for the sake of simplicity. It could easily be re-introduced by regarding the total money supply *M* as a fixed proportion, *b*, of the quantity of high powered or base (i.e. outside) money created by the central bank (*B*) – so that $M = bB$. This expression can be interpreted as the conventional monetary base multiplier equation in an exogenous money (e.g., *IS–LM*) environment, or re-written as $B = (1/b)M$ to capture the endogeneity of the

monetary base to 'inside' (i.e. credit money) components of the money supply created by commercial banks and their customers.

8. It is important to note that in the analysis that follows, the inverse relationship that is derived between the price level and the aggregate quantity demanded is a strictly *partial equilibrium* result. It depends critically on the assumption that other things (specifically, the variable *ND* in equation (8.2)) remain equal, whereas in fact, they may not. For example, a reduction in prices may be associated with a redistribution of income that depresses consumption expenditures, or with debt-deflation effects that negatively impact both consumption and investment spending. In this case, even if the central bank lowers interest rates (via equations (8.3) and (8.1)) and thus stimulates aggregate demand (via $f' < 0$ in equation (8.2)) as in the analysis above, the *total* effect of a drop in the price level on the aggregate quantity demanded may be negative rather than positive. In this case, the *AD* schedule will be upward sloping. See section 4.2 below and Palley (1996, chapter 4) for further analysis.

9. Note that $K_L < \overline{K}$ in Figure 8.3, where $\overline{K}$ denotes the total available capital stock. In other words, we assume that the level of economic activity – as measured by *Y* and *N* – is never constrained by a shortage of capital.

10. Recall that both *a* and *n* are fixed.

11. See, for example, Blundell and McCurdy (1999). Indeed, labour supply schedules are often found to be 'backward bending' – that is to say, the quantity of labour supplied diminishes as the real wage rises.

12. Note that U_1 is an equilibrium outcome even though the quantity of labour demanded (N_1) is not equal to the quantity of labour supplied (*L*), since the real wage is determined by the pricing decision (specifically, the value of *n*) and the structure of production (specifically, the value of *a*), *not* by the demand for and supply of labour. Hence there is no automatic tendency for $N_1 \neq L$ to cause change in the real wage which could, in principle, change the equilibrium levels of employment and hence unemployment depicted in Figure 8.7.

13. In order to simplify our figures, here and in what follows, we leave it to the reader to trace out the consequences for the quantity of monetary reserves that will be supplied by the central bank.

14. See chapter XIX, entitled '*Changes in money wages*' in Keynes's magnum opus *The General Theory of Employment, Interest and Money* (1936).

15. Of course, creditors will gain from an increase in the real debt burden, and this may boost their spending. But since creditor households are typically wealthy and have a low marginal propensity to consume, the net effect on aggregate demand of an increase in the real debt burden will be negative.

16. Note that if the initial fall in *W* is accompanied by an increase in *n*, so that *P* does not fall as far as P_2, the value of the real wage will fall. This redistribution of income away from workers can further reduce aggregate demand, which would result in the *AD* curve shifting still further to the left than is depicted in Figure 8.11(a).

References

Blinder, A. S. (1997), 'What Central Bankers Could Learn from Academics – and Vice Versa', *Journal of Economic Perspectives*, 11, 3–19.

Blundell, R. and T. McCurdy (1999), 'Labor supply: a review of alternative approaches', in O. Ashenfelter and D. Card (eds), *Handbook of Labor Economics*, 3A, Amsterdam: North Holland, 1599–695.

Carlin, W. and Soskice, D. (2005), *Macroeconomics Imperfections, Institutions, and Policies*, Oxford: Oxford University Press.

Dow, S. C. (1996) 'Horizontalism: A Critique', *Cambridge Journal of Economics*, 20(4), 497–508.

Dow, S. C. (1997) 'Endogenous money', in G. C. Harcourt and P. A. Riach (eds) (1997) *A 'Second Edition' of the General Theory*, London: Routledge, 61–78.

Feldstein, M. (1997), 'Capital income taxes and the benefits of price stability', NBER Working Paper, no. 6200, September.

Fontana, G. (2003), 'Post Keynesian Approaches to Endogenous Money: A Time Framework Explanation', *Review of Political Economy*, 15, 291–314.

Fontana, G. (2004), 'Rethinking Endogenous Money: A Constructive Interpretation of the Debate Between Horizontalists and Structuralists', *Metroeconomica*, 55, 367–85.

Fontana, G. (2006), 'Telling better stories in macroeconomic textbooks: monetary policy, endogenous money and aggregate demand', in Setterfield, M. (ed.) *Complexity, Endogenous Money and Macroeconomic Theory: Essays in Honour of Basil J. Moore*, Cheltenham: Edward Elgar, 353–67.

Howells, P. G. A. (1995) 'Endogenous Money', *International Papers in Political Economy*, 2(2), 1–41.

Jones, C. I. (2008), *Macroeconomics*, London: Norton.

Lavoie, M. (1996) 'Horizontalism, Structuralism, Liquidity Preference and the Principle of Increasing Risk', *Scottish Journal of Political Economy*, 43(3), 275–300.

Mishkin, F. S. (2001), 'Issues in inflation targeting', in *Price Stability and the Long-Run target for Monetary Policy*, Ottawa: Bank of Canada.

Moore, B. J. (1988), *Horizontalists and Verticalists: The Macroeconomics of Credit Money*, Cambridge: Cambridge University Press.

Palley, T. I. (1994), 'Competing Views of the Money Supply Process: Theory and Evidence', *Metroeconomica*, 45(1), 67–88.

Palley T. I. (1996), 'Accommodationism, Structuralism and Superstructuralism', *Journal of Post Keynesian Economics*, 18(4), 585–94.

Palley, T. (1996), *Post Keynesian Economics: Debt, Distribution and the Macro Economy*, London: Macmillan.

Rochon, L. P. and M. Setterfield (2007), 'Interest Rates, Income Distribution and Monetary Policy Dominance: Post-Keynesians and the "Fair Rate" of Interest', *Journal of Post Keynesian Economics*, 30, 13–42.

Romer, D. (2000), 'Keynesian Macroeconomics Without the *LM* Curve', *Journal of Economic Perspectives*, 14, 149–69.

Taylor, J. B. (1997), 'A Core of Practical Macroeconomics', *American Economic Review*, 87(2), 233–35.

Taylor, J. B. (2000), 'Teaching Macroeconomics at the Principles Level', *American Economic Review*, 90 (2), 90–4.

Walsh, C. E. (2002), 'Teaching Inflation Targeting: An Analysis for Intermediate Macro', *Journal of Economic Education*, 33, 330–46.

9
Money and Banking
in a Realistic Macro Model

Peter Howells

1 Introduction

In the last few years there has been a long overdue recognition that the treatment of money in mainstream macroeconomics has been fundamentally erroneous. In the real world, the money supply is not exogenously determined by administrative decisions of central banks and monetary 'shocks' do not take the form of a disequilibrium between supply and demand working their way out through real balance effects. In practice, central banks set a nominal rate of interest at which they are willing to make reserves available to the banking system and what happens to the money supply is the outcome of a complex interaction between banks and non-bank agents involving the (income-related) demand for credit and the (portfolio-related) demand for monetary assets. This process cannot be captured by an *LM* curve, derived from a fixed money supply.

Attempts to develop a 'macroeconomics without an *LM* curve' are now various–starting, implicitly, with Clarida *et al.* (1999) and more explicitly with Romer (2000). Walsh (2002) took the task forward by developing a framework which avoided the pitfalls of *LM* and also facilitated a discussion of inflation targeting – reflecting the contemporary trend in policy design. More recently we have seen a new framework for the teaching of monetary economics developed by Bofinger, Mayer and Wollmershäuser [BMW] (2006) and by Carlin and Soskice [CS](2005) who have since incorporated it in an intermediate level textbook (2006) (see also the chapter by Carlin and Soskice in this volume).

As part of a larger picture, these developments are often presented as part of the New Consensus macroeconomics (NCM), the idea of 'consensus' originating, presumably, in its combining the ability of monetary policy to influence real variables (after Keynes) in the short run with the neutrality of money (after the 'classics') in the long run. As a representation of the fundamental ideas of Keynes, this 'consensus' is unlikely to appeal to many Keynesian scholars who would question the long-run independence of output and monetary policy (see for example Fontana and Palacio-Vera, 2005; Arestis and Sawyer, 2005; Lavoie, 2006; and the chapters in this book by Arestis, Sawyer and Lavoie). However, the recognition that the money supply is endogenously determined and that the role of central banks is limited to setting a short-term rate of interest should be a matter of at least limited satisfaction in Post Keynesian circles.

In this chapter, in section 2, we review the latest suggestions for dispensing with the *LM* curve, focusing primarily on the (quite similar) BMW (2006) and CS (2005 and 2006) approaches. The novelty, however, lies in section 3 with the further development of these models in such a way that incorporates the behaviour of the banking sector. In section 4 we 'test' the legitimacy of this development by showing how the effects of a shock emerging from the macro part of the model can be traced through the banking sector where it produces perfectly sensible outcomes. The same section also provides a test of the model (reversing direction) by showing how the effect of a recent disturbance originating in the banking sector, the alarm over sub-prime lending, can be incorporated in the banking sector of the model and followed through to the macro part where again they show sensible results. Section 5 concludes.

2   Dispensing with the *LM* Curve

Criticisms of the *LM* curve, and attempts to provide something better, are not new. Firstly, the *IS/LM* model as a whole has attracted criticisms for many years. For example, Hicks (1980) himself drew attention to the problems of combining a stock equilibrium (the *LM* curve) with a flow equilibrium (the *IS* curve) as well as the model's contradictory demand for a real and nominal interest rate while Moggridge (1976) warned students that the model downplayed dramatically Keynes's emphasis upon uncertainty – as regards the returns from capital spending and the demand for money – by incorporating them into apparently stable *IS* and *LM* functions respectively. Its survival as the centrepiece of intermediate macroeconomics for so long is testimony to its versatility: it captures a very large number of simultaneous relationships in a very compact way. There are few aspects of macroeconomic policy that cannot be explored using the model. Ironically, the way in which central banks actually behave is one of these.

As regards the *LM* curve specifically, its assumption of a fixed money supply was never going to be acceptable to economists who felt that the money supply was to any degree endogenously determined. Leaving aside the more distant monetary controversies such as the debate over the 'Great Inflation' of fifteenth century Europe[1] and the issues between the 'bullionist' and 'banking' schools in nineteenth-century Britain, both of which involve views on the endogeneity/exogeneity of money, it has been the so-called Post Keynesian school that has been most vociferous in its rejection of the central bank's willingness/ability to determine the path of any monetary aggregate, even the monetary base. In these circles, therefore, there has been an implicit rejection of the *LM* curve since Davidson and Weintraub (1973) and an increasingly explicit rejection as the project gathered momentum through Kaldor (1982), Rousseas (1986), Moore (1988), Palley (1991) and many others.[2]

In spite of this, attempts to construct a tractable model, for teaching purposes, which incorporates an endogenous money supply have not hitherto been successful. In fact, diagrammatic representations of an endogenous money supply have verged on the chaotic. For the most part, this is the result of starting from the same interest–money space that is used to represent a fixed money supply and a downward sloping money demand curve from which the *LM* curve was derived. It is understandable that critics wished to confront the orthodoxy as directly and simply as possible and therefore the temptation to turn the money supply curve through 90 degrees and claim that the money supply was completely elastic at the rate of interest of the central bank's choosing (now represented by the intercept on the vertical axis), was irresistible. Indeed, it lay behind the title of Basil Moore's treatise published in 1988.[3] Unfortunately, however intuitively appealing, it was misleading. That framework was intended to show the behaviour of stock demand and supply, while the endogeneity of money was concerned with *flows*. Even worse, there was confusion as to whether this was a money supply or credit supply curve. Be that as it may, the idea that turning the (stock) money supply curve through ninety degrees could yield a useful comparison with the orthodox view caught on.

What all this shows is that the initial decision to tell the story of endogenous money supply creation within an orthodox framework led to a good deal of confusion. As we shall see in the rest of this section, a more satisfactory approach was to start from a completely different position.

From a monetary point of view the weaknesses of the *IS–LM* model are well-known. Amongst other things, it postulates:

- The money supply is fixed exogenously by the central bank.
- The policy instrument is the monetary base.
- In the absence of policy intervention the money supply is fixed.
- Policy interventions are transmitted to the real economy through a series of portfolio adjustments.
- The rate of interest is determined by the interaction of the demand for money and the exogenously determined supply.

All of these are so patently misleading as to make *IS–LM* a thoroughly unsuitable pedagogic device for students who are alert to what actually happens as widely reported by the media (and on increasingly helpful central bank websites). And as the enthusiasm for 'transparency' in monetary policy increases so the enquiring student becomes more and more confused. If interest rates are market-determined, what is the MPC (and the FOMC) doing? If the transmission of policy effects relies upon the quantity of money why do central banks make no mention of the money stock? If 'loose' monetary conditions (in the *IS–LM* model) lead to a fall in interest rates, why does the financial press predict a rise in interest rates when the consensus is that monetary policy is too slack? If stocks of money (and credit) can change only at the deliberate behest of the authorities, why is the relentless *growth* of consumer debt a recurrent theme in the media?

Furthermore, things get worse when *IS–LM* is combined with an *AD–AS* framework which links aggregate demand to output and the *price level*, when current debates in macroeconomics require a link between demand, output and the rate of inflation. This can be done, of course, by introducing a dynamic aggregate demand curve but only at the cost of some extraordinarily complex (and uninteresting) dynamics – and all of this to maintain the fiction that the DAD curve shifts if, and only if, the policy-maker adjusts the rate of growth of the money stock.

It might be thought that one could solve the problem by turning the *LM* curve through 90 degrees and drawing it horizontal, on the grounds that when the central bank sets the interest rate, the money supply is effectively perfectly elastic. Changes in the policy rate can then be shown by upward (or downward) shifts of the horizontal *LM* curve. But the problem with this is that we have the wrong rate of interest on the vertical axis. In the *IS–LM* diagram the interest rate must be a rate which represents the return on non-money assets. Whatever we use, it can not be the policy rate. In 2000, David Romer courageously suggested dispensing with the *LM* curve altogether. By way of alternative, he proposed an *IS–MP–IA*[4] model, central to which is the replacement of the *LM* curve with a rate of interest imposed by the central bank, represented by a horizontal line, designated appropriately the *M*(onetary) *P*(olicy) curve. Further developments allowed him to re-introduce the *IS* curve and to derive an aggregate demand curve in output/*inflation* space.[5]

Given its simplicity and its avoidance of the basic defects of the *LM* curve, it is perhaps surprising that the Romer model was not more widely adopted. By comparison with later developments, the model says little about the supply side of the economy and there is little detail about the basis of policy decisions (or 'monetary rules'). Both may be seen as drawbacks but only in comparison with subsequent developments. For monetary specialists, however, what was more discouraging was the account that Romer gave of the way in which the policy rate was set. Firstly, Romer presents the decision to use the interest rate as a *choice*, to which the alternative could presumably still be direct control of the monetary base. In a section on 'The Money Market' Romer gives an explanation of how the central bank imposes its chosen rate 'by injecting or draining high-powered money' (p.162). In so far as the focus is on high-powered (rather than broader measures of) money, this is correct. But when it comes to explaining how operations on the monetary base influence the policy rate, we switch to changes in the quantity of broad money and real balance effects. A change in reserves causes a change in broad money and by 'the standard experiment of the central bank increasing the money supply when the money market is in equilibrium ... the supply of real balances now exceeds the demand' (p. 163). This description is a long way from the reality recognized by economists working with central banks. This is, by contrast, that central banks have little choice but to set a rate of interest and that they do this by adjusting the price at which they re-finance past borrowings of reserves and banks then convert that cost of reserves to a market rate of interest (relevant to the *IS* curve, for example) by a variable mark-up. It also understates the extent to which Woodford and other members of the 'new consensus' have moved in recognizing the hegemony of the interest rate instrument:

> It is often supposed that the key to understanding the effects of monetary policy on inflation must always be the quantity theory of money... It may then be concluded that what matters about *any* monetary policy is the implied path of the money supply... From such a perspective, it might seem that a clearer understanding of the consequences of a central bank's actions would be facilitated by an explicit focus on what evolution of the money supply the bank intends to bring about – that is by monetary targeting... The present study aims to show that the basic premise of such a criticism is incorrect. One of the primary goals ... of this book is the development of a theoretical framework in which the consequences of alternative interest-rate rules can be analyzed, *which does not require that they first be translated into equivalent rules for the evolution of the money supply.* (Woodford, 2003, p.48. Second emphasis added)[6]

Since Romer, Bofinger, Mayer and Wollmerhäuser (BMW) (2006) have develo-ped a more comprehensive framework 'for teaching monetary economics' – more comprehensive in the sense that it is more explicit about the supply side and introduces monetary policy rules (e.g. after Taylor), and central bank credibility. More interesting in many ways are the attempts to 'apply' these models, in the sense of incorporating them into mainstream macro teaching. As we have noted already, there are precious few such but Carlin and Soskice (2006) is a notable example.

The CS book is doubly interesting since it represents one of the first attempts to introduce a more realistic treatment of money into a mainstream textbook. This requires the treatment to provide not just a sensible framework for the discussion of money and policy but also to be consistent with the mod-elling of the external sector and economic growth and a wide range of topics covered later in the book. It is also interesting because it starts from a pos-ition which embraces more wholeheartedly the essence of the new consensus.

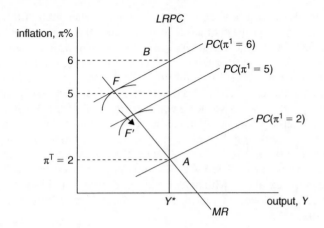

Figure 9.1 Responding to an inflation shock

There is no reference to central banks controlling stocks of narrow (or broad) money with a view to targeting interest rates. In this sense the 'rejection' of the *LM* curve is more complete than it is in Romer. In Carlin and Soskice, the interest rate is set as part of a Taylor-*type* rule, and in so far as a mechanism for setting such a rate is required it is consistent with the Woodford (2003) view expressed above.

The basic model in Carlin and Soskice is developed in pages 81–7. It consists of three equations and is described as the *IS–PC–MR* model. As with Romer (and BMW), the *IS* curve remains but Romer's 'inflation adjustment' is replaced by an 'inertia-augmented Phillips curve'. 'Inertia-augmented' is preferred to the more usual 'expectations-augmented' since the latter relies for its upward slope on expectational errors which CS regard as implausible. The inertia derives from a combination of Calvo pricing and monopolistic competition (so everyone 'knows' what the rate of inflation is but institutional realities prevent it from being incorporated everywhere instantaneously. Finally, 'monetary policy' is modelled more explicitly as a 'monetary rule'. (Notice that it is a *monetary policy* rule and not an *interest rate* rule at this stage).

The starting point is Figure 9.1 in which the central bank is assumed to have an inflation target of 2 per cent. Initially, the economy is in equilibrium at *A*, with inflation running at that level. Output is at its 'natural' level (on a long-run vertical Phillips curve) so there is no output gap to put positive (or negative) pressure on inflation. An inflation shock is introduced which moves the economy to *B* at which inflation is 6 per cent. In order to return to target, the central bank raises the real interest rate[7] and pushes output below its natural level and we move down the short-run Phillips curve (drawn for

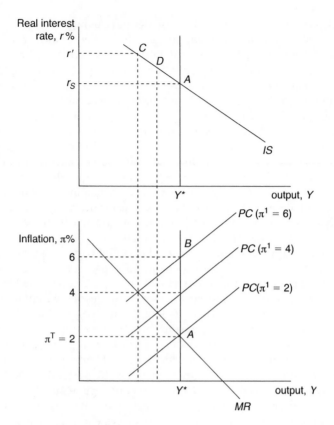

Figure 9.2 Introducing the *IS* curve

$\pi^1 = 6$) to the point labelled *F*. Notice that *F* is selected because the central bank is at a point tangential to the best available indifference curve at that combination of output and inflation. The indifference curve represents the output/inflation trade-off (the degree of inflation aversion) for that particular central bank. (A more inflation-averse central bank would have a different indifference map and would move the economy to a point on *PC* ($\pi^1 = 6$) to the left of *F*).[8] As the inflation rate falls to 5 per cent, the short-run *PC* shifts down to ($\pi^1 = 5$). The central bank can then lower the real interest rate, allowing output to rise, so the economy moves to *F'* and by this process (described as following a monetary rule) the central bank steers the economy back to equilibrium at *A*.

The next step is to introduce the *IS* curve and the real rate of interest. This is done in the upper part of Figure 9.2. To begin with the economy is in equilibrium, shown in both panels by the point *A*. Notice that in the upper panel, this includes a real rate of interest identified as r_s (a 'stabilizing' rate of interest which maintains a zero output gap). In the lower part, we then have a replay of Figure 9.1. There is an inflation shock which takes the economy from equilibrium at A to a rate of inflation of 6 per cent (at B). In Figure 9.2a, the central bank now raises the real rate of interest (to r') which has the effect of moving us up the IS curve to C at which the level of output is reduced. (In the lower panel we move down the PC $\pi^1 = 6$ curve to a point at which the reduction in demand pressure lowers inflation to 4 per cent). As inertia is overcome, contracts embrace 4 per cent and the Phillips curve shifts down to PC ($\pi^1 = 4$), the real rate is reduced allowing some expansion of output. We are now at point D on the IS curve but since we are still to the left of Y^* inflation continues to fall. This allows a further reduction in the real interest rate when inflation comes back to target at 2 per cent.

The dynamics are essentially the same as Romer. There is an *implicit* aggregate demand curve (the MR curve), with inflation on the vertical axis, which is *made* downward sloping by virtue of the central bank's reaction to inflation. But in Carlin and Soskice the dynamics are spelt out in more detail and the reaction function of the central bank (here the 'monetary rule') is clearer and if we are interested in the banking sector, this detail is welcome. The big difference comes, however, when we look at later pages where Carlin and Soskice discuss 'How the MR relates to the LM curve' (pp. 92–3). The first point they make is that the choice of model (MR or LM) must depend upon the nature of the monetary regime. 'If the central bank is using an *interest-rate based monetary rule* ... the correct model is the 3-equation model with the MR. This is often called an inflation-targeting regime' (p.92).[9] Of course, they recognize that there is at any time a stock of monetary assets in existence and that these must be held by the non-bank private sector (since that is how money is defined). In that sense there is a permanent equilibrium between the demand for money and its supply. In an inflation targeting model one can *imagine* an LM curve if one so chooses: 'it goes through the intersection of the IS curve and the interest rate set by the central bank but *it plays no role in fixing the position of the economy in terms of output, inflation or the interest rate*' (p.93. Emphasis added). In a footnote they add: 'in a world in which the central bank sets the interest rate, the causality goes from $i \rightarrow L \rightarrow M \rightarrow H$ (where "L" is the demand for money) whereas in the traditional LM model the causality is reversed from: $H \rightarrow M \rightarrow i$, where H is high powered money'.[10]

In Figures 9.1 and 9.2, we have a scheme which incorporates many of the features of a mainstream macro model wherein the Phillips curve is vertical in the long run but monetary policy can cause deviations from the equilibrium level of output because the realities of price-setting ensure a continuous lagged adjustment to the current rate of inflation. Furthermore, it incorporates much of the emerging consensus about modern monetary regimes and the way in which monetary policy is conducted. For example, the central bank sets interest rates and the money supply is endogenously determined.

The rate of interest for this purpose is whatever rate is relevant to the central bank's refinancing of bank reserves (a very short-term repo rate in most regimes) and while it is only the nominal rate that the central bank can control directly, this rate is set and revised at short intervals in order to produce the real rate required to adjust or maintain the rate of inflation.

3 Introducing the Monetary Sector

We commented earlier that dissatisfaction with the incorporation of money into simple macromodels has a long history. This dissatisfaction was founded in most cases in the unrealistic nature of bank behaviour which they assumed. Consequently, many of the attempts, pre-Romer, to devise a more realistic approach started by looking at the banking sector. Most of these were unsuccessful because they still tried to analyse the monetary consequences of bank decisions within the conventional framework of interest–money space.

We begin with a summary of the system we are trying to model. In a paraphrase of Goodhart (2002):

- The central bank determines the short-term interest rate in the light of whatever reaction function it is following.
- The official rate determines interbank rates on which banks mark up the cost of loans.
- At such rates, the private sector determines the volume of borrowing from the banking system.
- Given the banks' balance sheet identity, the additional borrowing must be matched by a corresponding willingness to hold the resulting deposits. This will involve quite complex changes in the *structure* of interest rates (on deposits, loan and other assets).
- Step 4 determines the money stock and its components as well as the desired level of reserves.
- In order to sustain the level of interest rates, the central bank engages in repo deals to satisfy banks' requirement for reserves.

Figure 9.3, based on Palley (1994, 1996) and Fontana (2003, 2006),[11] embraces these requirements in four quadrants.

In QI the central bank sets an official rate of interest, r_0:

$$r_0 = \overline{r_0} \tag{9.1}$$

This official rate determines the level of interbank rates on which banks determine their loan rates by a series of risk-related mark-ups. We make two simplifications. The first is that interbank rates are conventionally related to the official rate so that the mark-ups are effectively mark-ups on the official

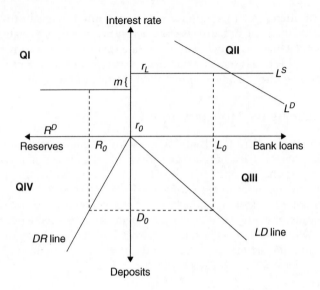

Figure 9.3   The monetary sector

rate. The second is that we can represent the range of mark-ups by a single, weighted average, rate. This is shown as m:

$$r_L = r_0 + m \tag{9.2}$$

In QII banks supply whatever volume of new loans is demanded by credit-worthy clients at the loan rate r_L. Notice that the loan supply curve, L^S, denotes flows, consistent with what we have said about the flow of funds being positive at the going rate of interest. This is further confirmed by the downward-sloping loan demand curve, L^D, showing that the effect of a change in the official rate is to alter the *rate of growth* of money and credit. At r_0, loans are expanding at the demand-determined rate L_0:

$$L^S = L^D \tag{9.3}$$

$$L^D = f(\underset{+}{\Delta \ln P}, \underset{+}{\Delta \ln Y}, \underset{-}{r_L}) \tag{9.4}$$

that is, the demand for loans is a positive function of inflation and the growth of output (the 'state of trade' in Post Keynesian terminology) and a negative function of the loan rate.

QIII represents the banks' balance sheet constraint (so the $L=D$ line passes through the origin at 45°). In practice, of course, 'deposits' has to be understood to include the bank's net worth while 'loans' includes holdings of money market investments, securities etc. At r_0 the growth of loans is creating deposits at the rate D_0:

$$L^S = L^D = L_0 = D_0 \tag{9.5}$$

The DR line in QIV shows the demand for reserves. The angle to the deposits axis is determined by the reserve ratio. In most developed banking systems this angle will be very narrow, but we have exaggerated it for the purpose of clarity:

$$DR = \frac{R}{D}(D) \tag{9.6}$$

In a system, like the UK, where reserve ratios are prudential rather than mandatory, the *DR* line will rotate with changes in banks' desire for liquidity. Even in a mandatory system, the curve may rotate provided that we understand it to represent total (i.e. required + excess) reserves. Thus one of the model's strengths is that it can show changes in banks' liquidity preferences either induced by changes in central bank operating procedures (as in the UK in April 2006),[12] or as an autonomous response to changed market conditions (see section 5).

Finally, in QI again we see the central bank's willingness to allow the expansion of reserves at whatever rate (here R0) is required by the banking system, given developments in QII–QIV:

$$R_0 = \frac{R}{D}(D_0) \tag{9.7}$$

$$R_S = R_D \tag{9.8}$$

How do we combine this with the analysis of Carlin and Soskice (or BMW) in Figure 9.2? The key lies in QI. Recall that the rate of interest in QI is the official rate, r_0, (usually a repo rate) plus a mark-up, m, set by commercial banks. We have already agreed that r_0 can be reasonably interpreted as a real rate of interest. This is what is required by the *IS* curve.[13] All that we have done in QI is add a mark-up in order to convert r_0 into a loan rate, r_L. Since the *IS* curve represents an equilibrium between investment and saving, there should be no objection to showing changes in equilibrium output to be dependent upon changes in the loan rate. This is directly relevant to investment spending and while one may object that the rate paid to savers is different, this objection could be made to any single rate of interest on the vertical axis. We are bound at accept that *any* single rate is a proxy for a spread term.[14] In Figure 9.4, therefore, we show (in QI–QIV) a banking system in flow equilibrium (loans and deposits are expanding at a rate which

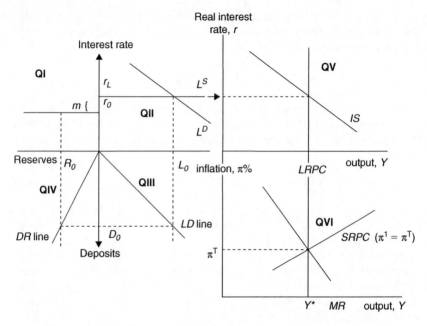

Figure 9.4 The monetary sector and *IS–PC–MR*

satisfies all agents at the current level of interest rates and banks can find the appropriate supply of reserves to support this expansion. This sounds like a reasonable description of how the banking/monetary sector behaves in normal circumstances. At the same time, the rate of interest set by the central bank is consistent with its inflation target. Output is at its 'natural rate', Y^*, (the output gap is zero).

Joining up six quadrants to show a static equilibrium is all very well, however. The more interesting question is whether, if we introduce a shock at some point, the model traces out a plausible set of adjustments in the banking system (QI–QIV) *and* in the real economy (QV–QVI). In the next section we look firstly at how a shock in the real economy reacts upon the banking sector and then (in reverse) at how a disturbance in the banking sector affects the real economy.

4 Introducing Some Disturbances

For our first illustration we begin with a disturbance in the real sector since this allows us to use the case already featured in Figure 9.2: there is an inflationary shock which doubles the rate of inflation from the target of 2% to 4%. This requires the central bank to raise the rate of interest, reducing the level of demand and output, until the rate of inflation begins to fall, when

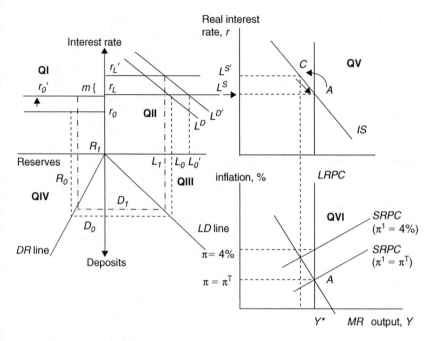

Figure 9.5 Responding to inflation

the central bank can begin to reduce the rate of interest until inflation and output return to their target levels.

The implications for the banking sector can be seen in Figure 9.5.

We begin with the official rate at r_0 (QI) giving a loan rate of r_L (QII). New lending, dependent on nominal output, is forthcoming at L_0, giving a monetary expansion of D_0 (QIII) which is accommodated by the central bank (QI). When the inflationary shock arrives, it causes an increase in *nominal* income which pushes the loan demand curve out to $L^{D'}$. Without policy intervention, loans and deposits would grow more rapidly (at L_0' and D_0' – the latter not shown) and would support the higher inflation rate. However, an inflation targeting central bank will raise the policy rate (from r_0 to r_0') in Figure 9.5. With a constant mark-up, market rates increase by the same amount (from r_L to r_L'). The demand for new loans is reduced (to L_1), the rate of monetary expansion is reduced and banks requirement for new reserves also falls.[15] (At r_L the connections are shown by dotted lines; at r_L' they are shown by dash/dot lines).

In the real economy (QV) the rise in interest rate reduces the level of output (from A to C). As inflation begins to fall (QVI) two things happen. The central bank begins to lower the official rate (to return eventually to r_0 in QI) and market rates begin a return towards r_L – the loan curve shifts downward (in QII). Also, the loan demand curve shifts to the left, reflecting the reduction in nominal income. Eventually, the intersection of L^S and L^D converges on its original position and monetary conditions return to those consistent with Y^* and π^T. This seems a reasonable representation of how we think the monetary system performs under an inflationary shock followed by a deflationary policy. Initially, loans and deposits expand more rapidly as a result of the inflationary pressure. When the central bank raises the policy rate, there is a tightening of monetary conditions involving the rate of expansion of loans and deposits and the level of interest rates.

We turn our attention now to a shock of a different kind. This originates in the banking system itself and we take the recent case of a so-called 'credit-crunch' induced by anxieties over sub-prime lending. If we are to judge the model's ability to represent these developments successfully we need to be clear on the main features of this episode. The following paragraph describes the key events as they developed from mid-August until October 2007.

Banks have built up a substantial portfolio of lending to so-called 'sub-prime' borrowers. In some cases these loans had been securitized and sold on to various types of 'special vehicles' and hedge funds, in some cases lending to these SPVs and hedge funds themselves. A downturn in the US housing market calls the value of some of this lending into question. However, compared with housing market recessions in the past, there are two novel problems. The first is that the securitization obscures the ownership of the loans and thus the *distribution* of the associated risk; the second is that the *extent* of the risk is unknown because many of the collateralized debt obligations (CDOs) are never traded.

The results, which we shall try to represent in the model, are:

- The market for CDOs collapses.
- Banks cannot securitize further loans.
- Banks become nervous about their own liquidity position.
- They are unwilling to lend to each other since they don't know the risk exposure of the counterparty.
- The market rate (i.e. LIBOR, FIBOR, Fed Funds) premium over the official rate jumps by as much as 100 basis points.
- Central banks become concerned about likely effects on the real economy.
- Central banks reduce the official rate and widen the range of securities that they are prepared to accept from banks in exchange for liquidity.

Figure 9.6 shows this dramatic change in monetary conditions as well as the possible effects on the real economy that caused such anxiety.

Our starting point is in QII, where, in contrast to their willingness to lend on demand at the official rate plus the conventional mark-up, banks are now

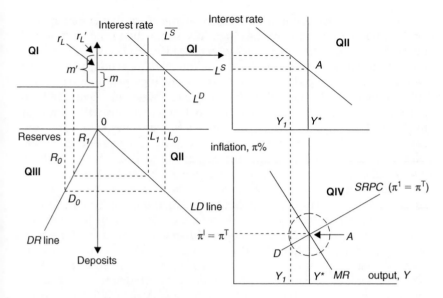

Figure 9.6 The credit crunch

restricting their lending to $\overline{L^S}$. Far from loans being available on demand, banks are effectively rationing credit. This is because, hitherto, they have been accustomed to securitizing a fraction of their new lending. For simplicity in the diagram, we shall suppose that total lending is shown by the distance $0 - L_0$ of which the securitized fraction is shown by $L_1 - L_0$. Now that the market for securitized loans has collapsed, all lending must be taken on to the asset side of the balance sheet in the form of conventional loans and we know that banks are willing to hold only $0 - L_1$ in this form. In practice, the rate of interest charged by banks is a mark-up on LIBOR. Conventionally, the relationship between LIBOR and the official rate was so stable that it made no difference whether we based the mark-up on the official rate (as in Figures 9.4, 9.5, 9.6) or on LIBOR. However, in the new circumstances, the conventional relationship between LIBOR and the official rate is broken (the spread has widened) so that when we express the mark-up in relation to the official rate it is now m'. The cost of loans has risen to r'.

With credit and money now growing more slowly, banks' need for additional reserves is reduced and in the diagram we show this at R_1. However, it would be a simple task also to show banks reacting to the crisis by wishing to increase their liquidity. In such a case, we would rotate the *DR* line clockwise. If we rotated by the critical amount we could show banks wanting to acquire additional reserves at the original rate (R_0) – thereby increasing their reserve ratios.

As regards the real economy, we can show the effect that commentators (and central banks) have been fearing. This is that the restricted flow and increased cost of credit is deflationary. In the case of the UK, spread between the official rate and 3-month LIBOR (the interbank rate from which most bank products are priced) widened under the credit crunch from its normal 10 basis points to 100 bp, within the space of two weeks in August 2007. To put this in context, that is in monetary policy terms, this was equivalent to the Bank of England raising the policy rate four times within fourteen days. In Figure 9.6, it threatens to push us up the *IS* curve and down the *SRPC* (π^T) curve (to *D*) increasing the output gap to $Y^*\text{-}Y_1$. Notice that the policy maker is now on an inferior indifference curve and will seek to move the economy to the preferred point which is at *A*. In order to do this, s/he seeks to move the loan market back to its original position where the flow of new credit is restored to L_0 and the cost comes down to the level *intended by policy*. Different central banks adopted different expedients to begin with although, eventually, they all reduced the policy rate and broadened the range of securities that they would accept as collateral for lending. In April 2008, the Bank of England created a minor stir by offering to swap treasury bills for mortgage-backed securities (but only those rated 'AAA'). The relaxing of collateral requirements and the cuts in official rates could be seen as a way of trying to revive the mortgage-backed securities market. This in turn was meant to restore banks' confidence in lending to each other and thus to bring LIBORs back to their conventional spread over official rates and, in the meantime, to lower the whole structure of interest rates. In the diagram (QII), this amounts to trying to reduce m' to m; r'_L to r_L; and above all, the gap $L_1 - L_0$.

5   Conclusion

For many years, simple models of the macroeconomy and of the role of monetary policy within it have been based on the fundamentally incorrect principle that the money supply is exogenously determined and that the policy instrument available to the central bank is the monetary base. From this stemmed the adoption of the *IS–LM* model wherein policy was shown by shifts of the *LM* curve and explained by reference to real balance effects. Policy makers themselves, and their advisers, have known for years that this is quite misleading.

Fortunately, the last few years have seen the emergence of a widespread consensus about monetary policy works and the desire to represent this accurately within a reasonably simple model has led to the replacement of the *LM* curve by various devices all of which recognize that the rate of interest is a policy instrument set by the central bank.

Starting from this position, we have shown in this chapter how the setting of that rate of interest affects not just the macroeconomy (the subject of the

IS–PC–MR model) but also the banking or monetary sector. Using a simple four-quadrant diagram we have shown how monetary policy works in normal circumstances and where the central bank needs to respond to inflationary shocks. We have also shown that it can capture the current situation where bank lending is inhibited by fears of default in the sub-prime market and where policy-makers fear for the effects of this credit squeeze on the real economy.

Notes

1. For a summary of *very* early allusions to money's exogeneity/endogeity see Arestis and Howells (2002).
2. How it was that the *LM* curve survived for so long in the face of this academic onslaught and the repeated statements of central bankers that the money supply is endogenous should yield an interesting research topic for future students of the philosophy of social science.
3. B. J. Moore (1988) *Horizontalists and Verticalists: The Macroeconomics of Credit Money* (Cambridge: Cambridge University Press).
4. Standing for $I = S$/Monetary Policy/Inflation Adjustment.
5. The term 'aggregate demand' needs to be interpreted with some care. The *AD* curve in Romer is derived from, and is totally contingent upon, the reaction of the central bank to (e.g.) inflation. It is not an alternative route to what is conventionally described as an *AD* curve which is derived from fundamental, structural, features of the economy.
6. If a topical illustration of the independent supremacy of the rate of interest were needed, it can be found in the behaviour of central banks in the face of the sub-prime lending crisis (discussed further below). On 11/12 August 2007, the *Financial Times* reported 'Central banks have been forced to inject massive doses of liquidity in excess of $100bn into overnight lending markets, in an effort to ensure that the interest rates they set are reflected in real-time borrowing ... The Fed is protecting an interest rate of 5.25 per cent, the ECB a rate of 4 per cent and the BoJ an overnight target of 0.5 per cent' (p. 3).
7. Carlin and Soskice (p.84) make the same point as Romer, that the central bank strictly speaking sets the *nominal* interest rate but does so with a view to achieving a *real* interest rate. Since it reviews the setting of this rate at regular, short, intervals, and the behaviour of inflation is a major factor in the decision, it is reasonable to see it as setting a real rate.
8. *If* the central bank's inflation target is symmetrical (undershoots are just as unwelcome as overshoots) the indifference curves in Figure 9.1 are segments of a series of complete concentric circles centred on *A*. This is the case for the Bank of England but not for the ECB where the target is described as 'below, but close to, 2 per cent'. Furthermore, if the central bank's loss function gives equal weight to inflation and output, the rings will be perfect circles. If the central bank puts more weight on inflation, the rings will be ellipsoid (stretched) in the horizontal plane. Hence greater inflation aversion on the part of the central bank would create a tangent 'further down' the *PC*.
9. There are echoes here of the point made by Chick (1983, ch. 12) where she argues that the reversal of causality in the savings–investment nexus proposed by Keynes

should not be seen as the triumph of correct theory over error but as a change in theory which was required by state of evolution of the banking system.

10. In other words, the model assumes a permanent equilibrium between the demand for and supply of money. This has its antecedent in the 'flow of funds' approach to the analysis of money supply determination which was popular in the UK in the 1970s and 1980s. The flow of funds identity explained the change in *money supply* in terms of the sum of additional *bank lending*. This was based upon the banks' balance sheet identity in which loans must equal deposits but it side-stepped the issue that the deposits newly-created by loans had to be willingly held. As Cuthbertson (1985, p. 173) commented at the time, 'There is an implicit demand for money in the model but only *in equilibrium*.' (Emphasis in original). The same issue was briefly controversial in the Post Keynesian literature where it was a cornerstone of monetary analysis that 'loans create deposits'. The debate between Goodhart (1989, 1991), Moore (1991a, 1991b, 1997) and Howells (1995, 1997) explored the question of why the preferences of deficit units for loans should coincide with the portfolio preferences of money holders. Consequently, Post Keynesian economists would recognize (and endorse) the $i \rightarrow L \rightarrow M \rightarrow H$ sequence in CS immediately, except that they would view 'L' as the demand for *loans* rather than the demand for money.

11. See also Chapter 8 by Fontana and Setterfield in this volume.

12. See Bank of England, *The Framework for the Bank of England's Operations in the Sterling Money Markets* (the 'Red Book'), February 2007.

13. As we noted above, it was a widespread criticism of the *IS–LM* model that while the behaviour summarized in the *IS* curve required a real rate, the relationships in the *LM* curve depended upon a nominal rate.

14. Although the *LM* curve was traditionally drawn for a single rate of interest (usually the bond rate), this was strictly correct only if money's own rate was zero. Strictly, the rate should have been a spread term incorporating the rate on money and the rate on non-money substitutes.

15. In QII the tightening of monetary policy has reduced the flow of new loans below the level prior to the inflationary shock ($L_1 < L_0$). There is no significance in this, other than that it can be clearly seen. The tightening may have been less, reducing the flow of new loans only to its original level at L_0. The point is that the tightening takes us up to L'_S. In practice, the scale of the monetary tightening will depend upon the central bank's degree of inflation aversion.

References

Arestis, P. and Howells, P. G. A. (2002), 'The 1520–1640 "Great Inflation": an early case of controversy in money', *Journal of Post Keynesian Economics*, 24(2).

Arestis, P. and Sawyer, M. C. (2005), ' Can Monetary Policy Affect the Real Economy?', Levy Economics Institute Working Paper no. 355.

Bofinger, P., Mayer, E. and Wollmerhäuser, T. (2006), 'The BMW Model: a new framework for teaching monetary economics', *Journal of Economic Education*, 37(1), 98–117.

Carlin, W. and Soskice, D. (2005), 'The 3-Equation New Keynesian Model – a graphical exposition', *Contributions to Macroeconomics*, 5(1), 1–27.

Carlin, W. and Soskice, D. (2006), *Macroeconomics: Imperfections, Institutions and Policies*, Oxford: Oxford University Press.

Chick, V. (1983), 'The evolution of the banking system and the theory of saving, investment and interest', in Arestis, P. and Dow, S. C. (eds), *On Money. Method and Keynes*, London: Macmillan.

Clarida, R., Galí, J. and Gertler, M. (1999), 'The science of monetary policy: a new Keynesian perspective', *Journal of Economic Literature*, 37, 1661–707.

Cuthbertson, K. (1985), *The Supply and Demand for Money*, Oxford: Blackwell.

Davidson, P. and Weintraub, S. (1973), 'Money as Cause and Effect', *Economic Journal*, 83, (332) 1117–32.

Fontana, G. (2003), 'Post Keynesian Approaches to Endogenous Money: a time framework explanation', *Review of Political Economy*, 15(3), 291–314.

Fontana, G. (2006), 'Telling better stories in macroeconomic textbooks: monetary policy, endogenous money and aggregate demand', in Setterfield, M. (ed.), *Complexity, Endogenous Money and Macroeconomic Theory: Essays in Honour of Basil J Moore*, Cheltenham: Edward Elgar.

Fontana, G. and Palacio-Vera, A. (2005), 'Are Long-run Price Stability and Short-run Output Stabilization All that Monetary Policy Can Aim For?', Levy Economics Institute Working Paper no. 430.

Goodhart, C. A. E. (1989), 'Has Moore become too horizontal?', *Journal of Post Keynesian Economics*, 12(1), 29–34.

Goodhart, C. A. E. (1991), 'Is the concept of an equilibrium demand for money meaningful?', *Journal of Post Keynesian Economics*, 14(1), 134–36.

Goodhart, C. A. E. (2002), 'The endogeneity of money', in Arestis, P., Desai, M. and Dow, S. C. (eds), *Money, Macroeconomics and Keynes: Essays in Honour of Victoria Chick*, vol. 1, London: Routledge.

Hicks, J. R. (1980), 'IS–LM: An explanation', *Journal of Post Keynesian Economics*, 3(2), 139–54.

Howells, P. G. A. (1995), 'The Demand for Endogenous Money', *Journal of Post Keynesian Economics*, 18(1), Fall, 89–106.

Howells, P. G. A. (1997), 'The Demand for Endogenous Money: A Rejoinder', *Journal of Post Keynesian Economics*, 19(3), 429–35.

Kaldor, N. (1982), *The Scourge of Monetarism*, Oxford: Oxford University Press.

Lavoie, M. (2006), 'A Post-Keynesian Amendment to the New Consensus on Monetary Policy', *Metroeconomica*, 57(2), 165–92.

Moggridge, D. (1976), *Keynes*, London: Fontana.

Moore, B. J. (1988), *Horizontalists and Verticalists*, Cambridge: Cambridge University Press.

Moore, B. J. (1991a), 'Money supply endogeneity', *Journal of Post Keynesian Economics*, 13(3), 404–13.

Moore, B. J. (1991b), 'Has the demand for money been mislaid?', *Journal of Post Keynesian Economics*, 14(1), 125–33.

Moore, B. J. (1997), 'Reconciliation of the supply and demand for endogenous money', *Journal of Post Keynesian Economics*, 19(3) pp.423–28.

Palley, T. (1991), 'The Endogenous Money Supply: Consensus and Disagreement', *Journal of Post Keynesian Economics*, 13, 397–403.

Palley, T. I. (1994), 'Competing Views of the Money Supply Process: Theory and Evidence', *Metroeconomica*, 45(1), 67–88.

Palley, T. I. (1996), 'Accommodationism, structuralism and superstructuralism', *Journal of Post Keynesian Economics*, 18(4), 585–94.

Romer, D. (2000), 'Keynesian Macroeconomics without the LM curve', *Journal of Economic Perspectives*, 2(14), 149–69.

Rousseas, S. (1986), *Post Keynesian Monetary Economics*, New York: M. E. Sharpe.

Walsh, C. E. (2002) 'Teaching Inflation Targeting: an analysis for intermediate macro', *Journal of Economic Education* 33 (Fall), 333–46.

Woodford, M. (2003), *Interest and Prices: Foundations of a Theory of Monetary Policy*, Princeton: Princeton University Press.

Part III
Financial Fragility, Liquidity Preference, Unemployment Hysteresis and Other Amendments

10
Taming the New Consensus: Hysteresis and Some Other Post Keynesian Amendments

Marc Lavoie[1]

1 Introduction

Not so long ago, most economists believed that central banks ought to set money supply targets, implementing these targets by controlling the supply of base money. The New Consensus among central bankers and economists active in the field of monetary economics is now that central banks ought to set target nominal interest rates, thus controlling real interest rates and influencing output and inflation rates. Still, in the 1960s and 1970s, those academics who argued that central banks could not control the supply of money and had to implement monetary policy through interest rate targeting were ridiculed. Their views were considered sterile and *dépassées*.

Part of the New Consensus is now the eclectic view that money supply control is preferable when the real side in macroeconomics is more volatile than the monetary side, while interest rate targeting is better when the monetary side – the demand for money – is more volatile. Authors of all stripes rely on Poole (1970) for this insight. Whether they agree or disagree with Monetarism, the argument of these authors comes down to asserting that if we could just go back to a world where financial innovations would vanish or be predicted, with no changes in moods about liquidity and no changes in money multipliers and the velocity of money (however defined), then monetary targeting and Monetarism could be brought back (Fontana and Palacio-Vera, 2004). This would make life much easier for teachers, because, in the meantime, in macroeconomic textbooks, the description of interest rate targeting in the chapter devoted to the central bank is quite incompatible with the description of the money multiplier, based on reserve control, which is usually found in the previous chapter devoted to the banking system.

In reality, the volatility of the *LM* curve (the monetary side) relative to the *IS* curve (the real side) has nothing to do with the revival of interest rate targeting. Monetary targeting was never an alternative because central banks cannot directly control monetary aggregates, be they money deposits or the monetary base. In other words, Poole's choices do not exist: the monetary base is not a quantity that can be controlled (Bindseil, 2004). The reason, in a nutshell, is that central banks must operate on a day-to-day basis, indeed on an hour-per-hour basis. Their interventions in monetary markets are tied to the daily operations of the settlement system and the overnight market – the market where banks trade their daily settlement balances. The size of these balances, deficits and surpluses, are uncorrelated with economic activity or the money supply; rather they reflect the random fluctuations in payment flows – inflows and outflows – between the various financial institutions, generated by their clients and the government. The role of the central bank within the payment and settlement system is to iron out the huge fluctuations in liquidity, through open market operations, repos, shifts of government deposits, or advances to the banking system. In standard economics language, central bankers are forced, through their daily operations, to supply monetary base on demand. Their daily role is essentially defensive (Fullwiler, 2003).

While central bankers have always been aware of these microeconomic constraints arising from the payment system, in the 1970s they were forced into the money-targeting experiment by the incredible pressures exercised by prestigious ivory-tower economists, led by Milton Friedman, whose influence grew exponentially following his presentation of the NAIRU concept to explain the apparent shifts in the Phillips curve. The New Consensus has dispensed with monetary targets and even the *LM* curve, but it has kept the crucial NAIRU concept and its vertical Phillips curve.

In the midst of the monetarist craze, Post Keynesian economists kept arguing that interest-rate targeting was the instrument through which central banks could implement monetary policy (Kaldor, 1982, p. 25). These views were long out of fashion, but these then-heterodox views are now being vindicated. Central banks throughout the world have shown that monetary implementation was possible in a world devoid of any compulsory reserves, as in Canada, Sweden, or Australia. Post Keynesian economists have also always questioned the relevance of the NAIRU or other similar concepts. While the NAIRU is still the kingpin of macro textbooks, a large minority of economists now also question its real-world relevance (Fuller and Geide-Stevenson, 2003), and hence the present chapter aims at representing amendments to the New Consensus that could convey this more critical stance about the NAIRU. Since, as Cambridge economist D.H. Robertson often remarked, 'economic ideas move in circles: stand in one place long enough, and you will see discarded ideas come round again' (Cramp, 1971, p. 62), non-NAIRU models may soon be the new fad in economics. That is why they are being presented here!

The rest of the chapter is organized as follows. In section 2, a simple New Consensus model is being presented. Section 3 presents a first amendment, by examining what happens when the Phillips curve incorporates a flat segment. Section 4 returns to the simple New Consensus model, but this time by considering growth rates, thus introducing hysteresis in unemployment rates. Section 5 adds a complication to this growth representation, by introducing hysteresis in growth rates. Finally, section 6 introduces a feature which has turned out to be important over the recent past – the possibility that changes in market interest rates diverge from changes in the interest rate set by central banks.

Thus, briefly put, the aim of the chapter is to present a critique and extension of the basic New Consensus model, hoping that this will help students look beyond the increasingly sophisticated variants of this basic New Consensus model that they are likely to encounter in their later studies.

2 The Basic New Consensus Model

The basic New Consensus model is well-known and is being presented in several chapters of the present book, so there is no need to dwell on it. In the basic version we assume away growth, and consider the following three equations:

$$u = a - bf \qquad\qquad IS \qquad\qquad (10.1)$$

$$\Delta\pi = \gamma(u - u_n)_{-1} + \varepsilon \qquad PC \qquad\qquad (10.2)$$

$$f = f_0 + \alpha(\pi - \pi^{\mathrm{T}}) \qquad RF \qquad\qquad (10.3)$$

The first equation is the *IS* equation. It says that the rate of capacity utilization u is inversely related to the real rate of interest, f, set by the central bank.[2] The second equation – called either the supply equation or the Phillips curve equation (PC) – claims that the inflation rate π *increases* whenever the rate of capacity utilization is higher than some rate, which we will call the normal rate u_n. This is the accelerationist hypothesis associated with a vertical Phillips curve. Here the Phillips curve in the output–inflation space is vertical at the normal rate of utilization u_n, which we assume to correspond to the NAIRU in the unemployment–inflation space. Note that we assume that high rates of utilization have an inflationary impact, but with a lag, as signalled by the -1 subscript on the $(u - u_n)$ term in equation (10.2). Supply-side effects that raise the inflation rate temporarily, such as increases in oil prices or improvements in the bargaining power of labour, are represented by a positive ε parameter.

Finally, there is the central bank reaction function, *RF*. The federal funds (real) rate f, the rate set by the central bank, is assumed to be a linear function of some neutral interest rate f_0 (more about which will be said later) and of the discrepancy between the actual inflation rate and the target inflation rate π^{T}. In a more complete model, as is the case in the famous Taylor rule, the interest rate set by the central bank would also depend on the discrepancy between the actual rate and the normal rate of capacity utilization.

If we put together equations (10.1) and (10.3), we obtain equation (10.4), which is the so-called aggregate demand curve, which, in this model, links the inflation rate to the level of capacity utilization:

$$\pi = \pi^T + (a - bf_0 - u)/b\alpha_1 \qquad AD \qquad (10.4)$$

The standard results of the New Consensus are pictured in Figure 10.1. We start by assuming that in the baseline case the economy was at its normal rate of capacity utilization u_n and at the target inflation rate π^T, at point A on both the AD_1 and the IS_1 curves. The interest rate as set by the central bank is f_1, as can be seen with the help of the MP curve, the monetary policy curve, which here is a simple flat line since we assumed away the influence of the rate of capacity utilization on the interest rate set by the central bank (the real interest rate only depends on the inflation rate relative to the target). The vertical Phillips curve associated with equation (10.2) is represented by the vertical line that arises from u_n. If the economy is on the right of u_n, inflation rates will tend to rise; if the economy is on the left of u_n, inflation rates will tend to fall; only if rates of utilization are at u_n will the inflation rate remain steady.

Assume now an increase in one of the components of aggregate demand, for instance an increase in public spending or an increase in consumption due to a rise in the propensity to consume. The constant a term in equation (10.1) rises and the IS curve gets shifted out to the right (from IS_1 to IS_2). As a result the aggregate demand curve also gets shifted out to the right (from AD_1 to AD_2), and the economy, for a moment stands at points B on both the AD_2 and IS_2 curves, on the IA curve. This horizontal line, sometimes called the inflation-adjustment curve, reflects the lagged impact of high rates of utilization on inflation rates, as identified in equation (10.2). When rates of utilization first exceed the normal rate of utilization, inflation does not bulge, which is why the economy moves horizontally to point B. But this is a temporary situation, because the higher-than-normal rates of utilization will induce faster inflation in the following periods. As a result the IA curve shifts up, and the economy moves leftward along the IS_2 and AD_2 curves as the inflation rate keeps crawling up, under the action of equation (10.2). This happens as long as the actual rate of capacity utilization exceeds its normal level. The dynamics of the model come to a rest at points C on the IS_2 and AD_2 curves. In the steady state, the actual rate of capacity utilization is at its normal level. Equivalently, one could say that the rate of unemployment is equal to its NAIRU value.

But now the central bank faces a problem: we assumed that the monetary authorities would react to a discrepancy between the actual and the target inflation rates, but still, despite this, the economy comes to rest at an inflation rate which is higher than the target: the inflation rate is π_2 in Figure 10.1. How is this possible? The answer can be found in equation (10.4). The actual inflation rate will be equal to the target rate in the steady state only if the

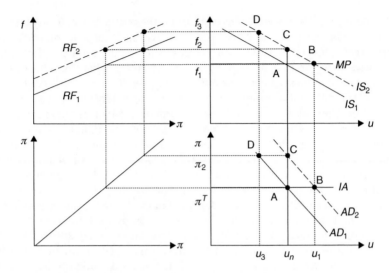

Figure 10.1 The basic four-quadrant New Consensus model

term inside the parentheses is equal to zero. Thus when the inflation rate becomes steady, i.e., when $u = u_n$, for the actual inflation rate to equal the target rate, the following equation must be fulfilled:

$$a - bf_0 - u_n = 0$$

that is

$$f_0 = f_n = (a - u_n)/b \qquad (10.5)$$

The particular value of f_0 given by equation (10.5), which we call f_n, is the so-called natural rate of interest, associated with Knut Wicksell. When the economy is brought back to its normal rate of capacity utilization, the realized interest rate will necessarily be the natural rate of interest. So even if the central bank does not know what the natural rate of interest is, it will finally hit it, moving along its reaction function, as the economy is gradually brought back to its normal rate of capacity utilization. In the present case, the increase in aggregate demand – the increase in the value taken by a – leads to an increase in the value of the natural rate of interest, as can be seen in equation (10.5). In Figure 10.1, the increase in public spending or in the propensity to consume has driven up the natural rate of interest, from f_1 to f_2, and this is the interest rate that the central bank will end up setting in its attempt to stabilize inflation rates.

However, as is clear from Figure 10.1, unless the central bank already knows what the new natural rate of interest is, it will be unable to hit its inflation target. This explains why central banks have put so much effort into econometric research, in attempting to identify and predict the value of the natural rate of interest. So far these efforts have been unsuccessful, as different authors and different techniques end up predicting wildly different estimates (Orphanides and Williams, 2002; Weber, Lemke and Worms, 2008). In addition, the estimates have such large confidence intervals, that, for all practical purposes, they are totally useless for central bankers that need to act in a timely manner. In the present case, having realized that its inflation target is off, the central bank would need to modify upwards the value of f_0, i.e., its estimate of the natural rate of interest, thus shifting its reaction function from RF_1 to RF_2. With a properly identified natural interest rate, i.e., by setting $f_0 = f_n$, the central bank would manage to bring back the economy to point A on the aggregate demand curve, as the latter would shift from AD_2 to AD_1, as a result of the shift in the central bank reaction function. The IS curve however would remain at IS_2, with the economy initially entering a recession, at point D and interest rate f_3, so that the inflation rate could be reduced. Eventually the economy would settle at point C on the IS_2 curve, so that the interest rate in the new steady state at the target inflation rate would still be at interest rate f_2.

Besides the problem of identifying the correct natural rate of interest, the main lesson to draw from the basic New Consensus model is that an increase in public spending and a reduction in the propensity to save both lead to an increase in the natural rate of interest and hence in the interest rate found in the new steady state. The New Consensus is thus old wine in a new bottle, being perfectly compatible with the old loanable funds story. This theory, found once more in many introductory or intermediate macroeconomics, asserts that interest rates are determined by productivity and thrift, i.e. by the demand for and the supply of loanable funds. A fall in thrift – for instance a fall in the propensity of households to save out of disposable income, as would be the case here – leads to an increase in interest rates.

Furthermore, in the New Consensus model, the actions being pursued by the monetary authorities have no impact on real output (or the rate of unemployment). They only have an impact on the inflation rate. In other words, the choice of a lower inflation target will have no negative impact on the real economy.

3   First Post Keynesian Amendment: A Horizontal Phillips Curve Segment[3]

Figure 10.1 assumed that there was a unique NAIRU, corresponding to what we called the normal rate of capacity utilization, which some authors, such as Emery and Chang (1997) or McElhattan (1978), also call the NAICU (the non-accelerating inflation capacity utilization) or the SICUR (the stable inflation capacity utilization rate). But what if there is a multiplicity of NAICU? What if there is a whole range of rates of capacity utilization such that the inflation rate remains constant? In other words, what if the NAICU is a wide band rather than a thin line?

There is now a substantial amount of empirical evidence that this is indeed the case. Several authors are now claiming that the Phillips curve has a middle segment which is flat (Eisner, 1996; Filardo, 1998; Barnes and Olivei, 2003; Kim, 2007). In other words, for rates of unemployment or for rates of capacity utilization that are neither too large nor too low, the rate of inflation tends to remain where it is, unless subjected to supply-side shocks (non-negative values of the ε parameter). How can that be?

Two reasons have been advanced. The first reason, which central bankers enjoy suggesting, is based on the credibility of the monetary authorities. With inflation targeting, the inflation target becomes a benchmark, which economic agents take into account when making wage and price decisions. As a result, as long as the fluctuations in the real economy are not too large, the inflation target of the central bank will act as an attractor. The second reason, mostly suggested by Post Keynesian authors, is linked to inertia and the shape of the cost curves of firms. According to Post Keynesians, marginal cost curves in most industries are essentially flat, or even slightly downward-sloping, up to full capacity (Lavoie, 1992, ch. 3). But most firms operate below capacity. An increase in rates of capacity utilization does not generate upward price pressures or upward inflation pressures, as it does within the standard neoclassical model with upward-sloping marginal cost curves and demand-led inflation. Within this Post Keynesian model of the firm, inertia will keep wage and price inflation where they are, within a fairly large range of rates of utilization (Hein, 2002; Kim, 2007). Thus, within this range, changes in real interest rates, while having an impact on rates of capacity utilization, will have little impact, if any, on inflation rates (Arestis and Sawyer, 2004).

Formally, equation (10.2) of our amended New Consensus model can be rewritten in the following way:

$$\Delta \pi = +\gamma_1(u - u_n) + \varepsilon \quad \text{if } u > u_{nh}$$
$$\Delta \pi = +\gamma_2(u - u_n) + \varepsilon \quad \text{if } u < u_{nl}$$
$$\Delta \pi = +\varepsilon \qquad\qquad\quad \text{if } u_{nl} \leq u \leq u_{nh} \qquad (10.\,2\text{B})$$

The short-run Phillips curve which corresponds to this empirical reality and the description of equation (10.2B) is shown in Figure 10.2. We may call it the *PUP* curve, or the prices-utilization possibilities curve, since the curve looks like a puppy. The flat Phillips curve area is found between u_{nl} and u_{nh}, which are the lower and the upper limits of the flat zone. Within this area the Phillips

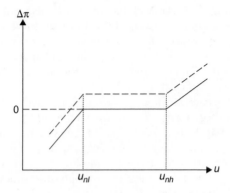

Figure 10.2   The *PUP*: the flat Phillips curve segment

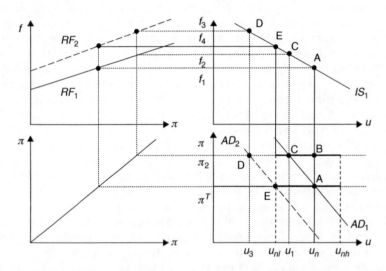

Figure 10.3   The New Consensus model amended with a flat Phillips curve segment

curve is horizontal. The rate of inflation will not change unless there is a supply-side shock, represented by the ε parameter in equation (10.2B). If such a shock arises, for instance if oil and gasoline prices rise, there will be a vertical upward shift of the horizontal Phillips curve, now shown as a dotted line.

The consequences of such a reality for the New Consensus model are illustrated with the help of Figure 10.3. The flat area of the Phillips curve is shown with the horizontal heavy lines of the south-east quadrant. Suppose that the economy was initially at the target rate of inflation π^T and at the rate of utilization u_n. The economy is at point A on both the aggregate demand curve AD_1 and the IS_1 curve. Assume now that the economy is subjected to some adverse supply-side inflation shock ($\varepsilon > 0$), again an increase in oil and gasoline prices, that brings the country from point A to point B. The entire flat portion of the Phillips curve is being vertically pushed up, as can be seen from the two heavy horizontal lines, with the inflation rate moving from π^T to π_2. The central bank may decide to do nothing, waiting for another supply shock – a favourable one this time ($\varepsilon < 0$) – hoping that this favourable shock will counterbalance the initial shock, thus bringing the economy back to point A and inflation rate π^T, hoping for instance that oil and gasoline prices will fall relative to other prices, as happened in the mid 1980s and 1990s.

But suppose that the central bank loses patience or does not believe that relative oil and gasoline prices will fall relative to other prices, thus acting to bring back the inflation rate towards its target π^T. In order to do so, the central bank will raise interest rates, say to f_2, moving along its reaction function RF_1, in an attempt to slow down the economy and eventually reduce inflation rates, as it had done in our example of section 2. But this won't do. The economy will run into a recession, moving to point C on the IS_1 and AD_1 curves, with rates of capacity utilization falling to u_1, but the rate of inflation will stay where it is, at π_2, because the economy is still on the flat portion of the Phillips curve. The central bank will thus believe that it has made an incorrect assessment of the natural rate of interest, and thus, as discussed in the example of section 2, it will revise upwards the value of f_0, thus shifting upwards its reaction function. To achieve its target inflation rate π^T, the central bank will need to shift its reaction function to RF_2, thus shifting down the aggregate demand curve to AD_2. By so doing, the central bank needs to raise interest rates momentarily to f_3, thus bringing down economic activity to a rate of utilization u_3, at point D on the IS_1 and AD_2 curves. As the economy is now out of the flat Phillips curve area, inflation rates will indeed fall, as New Consensus analysis tells us. Eventually the economy will reach point E, at the target inflation rate π^T, with a rate of utilization u_{nl} and a real interest rate equal to f_4.

There are many lessons that can be drawn from this analysis that incorporates a flat Phillips curve segment. First, we see that the decision of the central bank bureaucrats to reduce the inflation rate back to its target level does have implications for the real economy. In contrast to the New Consensus model that was presented in section 2, the anti-inflation policy does lead to higher real rates of interest in the long run, and it also leads to lower economic activity – here lower rates of capacity utilization. An identical result would have been achieved without a supply shock, if, for instance, the central bank had decided to lower the inflation target, as many central banks did in the late 1980s and early 1990s. The decision to have lower inflation rates would also have required higher real interest rates and lower economic activity, both in the short run – during the transition to the new inflation rate – and in the long run, once the inflation target has been achieved. Thus, with a flat Phillips curve segment, a feature which seems to be supported by empirical research, monetary policy does have an impact on the real economy, something which is denied by central bankers and New Consensus authors.

Keen students may object that some countries have had high rates of capacity utilization and low rates of unemployment over the last few years, and hence they may question whether the present model correctly represents reality. First, it should be noted that the model can work in reverse gear. If the economy is mainly subjected to favourable supply shocks, for instance falling oil and gasoline prices relative to general prices, or falling relative import prices, due to relative decreases in the prices of commodities or because of cheap imports coming from emerging nations such as China or India, the flat portion of the Phillips curve will tend to shift down. If central banks attempt to keep the inflation rate around the inflation target π^T, they will now lower interest rates and shift their reaction function downwards, thus bringing the rate of capacity utilization towards u_{nh} in Figure 10.2.[4] Secondly, even without favourable supply-side shocks, if central bankers are brave enough to test the waters, by lowering real rates to push up rates of capacity utilization, they will manage to increase the level of economic activity without generating higher inflation as long as the achieved rates of capacity utilization remain within the flat portion of the Phillips curve. It is said that this is what Allan Greenspan did for the United States in the late 1990s. The boom in the United States had a positive impact on economic activity in the entire world economy.

What is interesting here is that several different configurations are possible. In other words, there is not a unique equilibrium, as in the standard New Consensus model. There is a multiplicity of possible equilibria, that depend on the estimates of the central bank. Obviously, the 'equilibrium' of the economy is something which is highly arbitrary. It depends on the central bank assessment of u_n – the NAICU as assessed by the monetary authorities. With the flat Phillips curve, any rate of utilization between u_{nl} and u_{nh} keeps inflation at a constant rate. Thus, if central bankers are overly prudent, as the European Central Bank has often been accused of having been, the economy will run close to u_{nl}, and average rates of unemployment will be high; by contrast, if central bankers are more audacious, as Allan Greenspan is said to have been in the late 1990s, the economy can run with constant inflation at high rates of utilization, close to u_{nh}, and with low average rates of unemployment.

4 Second Post Keynesian Amendment: Unemployment Hysteresis[5]

So far capital accumulation has been omitted. Estimates of Phillips curves were initially based on unemployment rates, but many estimates are based on rates of capacity utilization, as in the previous sections, but also on growth rates of real output (Goodhart, 2003). One reason for this is unemployment hysteresis, an hypothesis put forward by both New Keynesian and Post Keynesian economists, and for which there is considerable empirical evidence (McDonald, 1995; Stanley, 2004; Mitchell and Muysken, 2008). Hysteresis is a term taken from physics. In economics, it means that we cannot know the final position of a variable without knowing what happened during the transition towards this final or long-run equilibrium. By contrast, in most economic models, the equilibrium can be defined without knowing the dynamics of the transition that would lead the economy to this equilibrium.

Within the context of the traditional Phillips curve, hysteresis implies that changes in wage and price inflation depend essentially on the *change* in the unemployment rate, rather than its *level*, a claim that, surprisingly, could already be found more than 40 years ago in Bowen and Berry (1963). The main justification for this is that employed workers have little reason to fear the possibility of losing their job as long as the rate of unemployment is not rising. But the faster unemployment is rising the more threatened workers feel, and the more likely they are to waive real wage objectives, thus giving rise to falling inflation. Formally, this implies that we have:

$$\Delta \pi = -\gamma(\Delta U) + \varepsilon \qquad (10.2C)$$

where U is the rate of unemployment and where $\gamma > 0$.[6]

But what is the relationship with growth rates? In a model where labour employment is roughly proportional to real output, the growth rate of employment, noted e, is given by:

$$e = g - \lambda \qquad (10.6)$$

where g is the growth rate of real output, while λ is the growth rate of technical progress as measured by labour productivity.

A traditional concept in economics is the concept of the natural rate of growth, which we denote by g_n. This natural rate of growth is the sum of the growth rate of the labour force, which we denote by n, and the growth rate of technical progress, so that:

$$g_n = n + \lambda \qquad (10.7)$$

Putting equations (10.6) and (10.7) together, and remembering that the change in the rate of unemployment is approximately equal to the difference between the rate of growth of the labour force and that of employment, we get:

$$\Delta U = n - e = g_n - g \qquad (10.8)$$

The change in the rate of unemployment is thus also equal to the difference between the natural and the actual rate of growth of the economy. On that basis, we can rewrite the basic New Consensus model of section 2 in terms of growth rates, in a way which is very analogous. We have:

$$g = a - bf \qquad\qquad IS \qquad\qquad (10.1B)$$

$$\Delta\pi = \gamma(g - g_n) + \varepsilon \qquad PC \qquad\qquad (10.2D)$$

$$f = f_0 + \alpha_1(\pi - \pi^T) \qquad RF \qquad\qquad (10.3)$$

In equations (10.1B), (10.2D) and (10.3), the actual and natural growth rates g and g_n play the role that u and u_n were playing in the initial basic model given by equations (10.1), (10.2) and (10.3).[7] The actual output growth is said to depend negatively on real interest rates; changes in inflation are caused by changes in the rate of unemployment; and real interest rates are set on the basis of the difference between actual and target inflation. The graphical representation of our new model is thus exactly similar to that of Figure 10.1. We get the same results. Following any temporary or permanent shock, the growth rate of real output will be brought back to the natural rate of growth. If the monetary authorities assess correctly the natural rate of interest, the target inflation rate will be achieved. Thus, in analogy with the model of Figure 10.1, the actions being pursued by the monetary authorities have no impact on the natural rate of growth, they only have an impact on the inflation rate.

However, there is one difference. In the model of Figure 10.1, the choice of a lower inflation target would have had no effect on the rate of utilization and the rate of unemployment. Here, by contrast, there is unemployment hysteresis. The choice of a lower inflation target would force the appearance of a sequence of periods during which the actual growth rate of real output, g, is smaller than the natural rate of growth of the economy, g_n, as would occur in Figure 10.1 when the economy moves to point D and then from D to A. As a result, as can be read off equation (10.8), the rate of unemployment would be rising during a number of periods. Once the economy is back to point A, where the target inflation rate is achieved with $g = g_n$, the rate of unemployment U is constant, but it is higher than it was before the decision to have a lower inflation target. Thus, within this framework, there is also no unique NAIRU, although long-run growth is supply-led, being determined by the natural rate of growth (Taylor, 2000, p. 91).

5   Third Post Keynesian Amendment: Unemployment and Growth Hysteresis[8]

Post Keynesians however make a further argument. They believe that if the concept of a natural growth rate is to be of any assistance, it is determined by the path taken by the actual growth rate. The most likely candidate for endogenous changes in the natural rate of growth induced by high growth rates of demand is the rate of technical progress. This argument was made by Joan Robinson in her magnum opus:

> But at the same time technical progress is being speeded up to keep up with accumulation. The rate of technical progress is not a natural phenomenon that falls like the gentle rain from heaven. When there is an economic motive for raising output per man the entrepreneurs seek out inventions and improvements. Even more important than speeding up discoveries is the speeding up of the rate at which innovations are diffused. When entrepreneurs find themselves in a situation where potential markets are expanding but labour hard to find, they have every motive to increase productivity. (Robinson 1956, p. 96)

And it was also a point made by Nicholas Kaldor in a lecture in 1954:

> The stronger the urge to expand ... the greater are the stresses and strains to which the economy becomes exposed; and the greater are the incentives to overcome physical limitations on production by the introduction of new techniques. Technical progress is therefore likely to be greatest in those societies where the desired rate of expansion of productive capacity ... tends to exceed most the expansion of the labour force (which, as we have seen, is itself stimulated, though only up to certain limits, by the growth in production). (Kaldor, 1960, p. 237)

These arguments go beyond theory. In a study based on a sample of fifteen developed countries over the post-war period, León-Ledesma and Thirlwall (2002) have shown that the natural rate of growth is endogenous to the rate of growth of output demand. They show that the natural rate of growth rises in booms, and falls in recessions. As they say, 'growth creates its own resources in the form of increased labour force availability and higher productivity of the labour force' (2002, p. 452). Thus this study, as well as that of Perrotini and Tlatelpa (2003) for the three North American countries (Mexico, Canada, and the United States), provide empirical support for this third Post Keynesian amendment to the New Consensus model. They show that the long-run equilibrium is not only supply-led, but also demand-led.

Formally, we can assume that there is an increase in the rate of growth of productivity as long as the natural rate of growth does not catch up with the actual rate of accumulation (the rate of productivity growth will decline as long as the natural rate of growth exceeds the actual rate), which we can write as:

$$\Delta g_n = \phi(g - g_n) \tag{10.9}$$

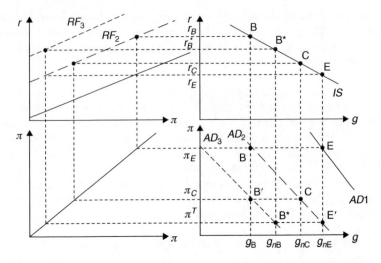

Figure 10.4 Impact of reducing the inflation target in the new consensus model amended with an endogenous natural rate of growth

Thus, in the world described by equations (10.1B), (10.2D), (10.3) of the model presented in the previous section, with the addition of equation (10.9), the decision to reduce the target inflation rate is likely to bring about not only a higher rate of unemployment but also a permanently lower growth rate of the economy. Intuitively, this can be seen in the following way. The central bank decides to reduce the target inflation rate. This is equivalent to an upward shift in the central bank reaction function. The central bank needs to raise the real interest rate to reduce economic activity and bring down inflation. The reduced growth rate in GDP however reduces the natural rate of growth of the economy, as assumed in equation (10.9). This, in turn, leads to an increase in the natural rate of interest, as can be seen from equation (10.10), which puts together equations (10.1B) and (10.3):

$$f_0 = f_n = (a - g_n)/b \qquad (10.10)$$

Thus, unless the central bank is aware of this change in the natural rate of growth and in the natural rate of interest, it will be unable to achieve its new target inflation rate. As was the case in the example of section 2, the central bank will be forced to get into a new round of interest rate hikes, revising its estimate of the natural rate of interest, until finally the new target is achieved, but at a rate of output growth that is much lower than the one the economy was enjoying before the reduction in the target rate of inflation.

Figure 10.4 illustrates this third Post Keynesian amendment. Assume that initially the economy is at point E, growing at the rate g_{nE}, with a rate of inflation π_E and an interest rate at r_E. The relevant curves are *IS*, AD_1 and RF_1. Suppose now that the central bank is unhappy about this steady-state inflation rate, and decides to target a lower inflation rate, given by B^T, as shown in the second quadrant of Figure 10.4.

To the new inflation target corresponds a new reaction function, given by RF_2, inducing the central bank to set a higher real rate of interest, r_B. This brings the economy from point E to point B on the new aggregate demand curve AD_2, with a lower growth rate at g_B, thus inducing an economic slowdown in an effort to force down the inflation rate. If the natural rate of growth were to remain constant at g_{nE}, as assumed by New Consensus authors, the economy would slide along the AD_2 aggregate demand curve, eventually reaching point E', with the target rate of inflation B^T being achieved at this growth rate g_{nE}.

However, the tight monetary policy induces a reduction in the natural rate of growth, and as a result, the economy will reach instead a new long-run equilibrium at point C, with a natural rate of growth g_{nC}, a real interest rate r_C, and an inflation rate π_C. The monetary authorities would thus realize that further, tougher, action is needed, and that more restrictive monetary policies need to be imposed to finally reach the new inflation target. In other words, the monetary authorities need to revise upwards their assessment of the natural rate of interest. A second round of high real interest rates would need to be administered, initially bringing the economy to point B', and so reducing further the natural rate of growth. The central bank reaction function would have to move as far up as RF_3, shifting in the aggregate demand curve to AD_3. Moving down along this new aggregate demand curve, the economy would eventually end up in its new equilibrium, given by point B* in Figure 10.4, with the lower inflation target π^T being achieved. At this point, the natural real rate of interest would stand at r_B^* – a higher rate than the initial natural rate r_E. The growth rate of demand and the natural rate of growth would be equal at g_{nB} – a smaller rate than the initial growth rate g_{nE}.

The implications of this Post Keynesian amendment can also be illustrated with the help of Figure 10.5. As is obvious from equation (10.9), the economy will stop moving only when $g = g_n$, that is when the actual growth rate and the natural growth rate are equal. This implies that any point on the 45 degree line of Figure 10.4 is a potential long-run equilibrium. The 45-degree line is an equilibrium locus. There is a continuum of equilibria.

Initially the economy stood at point E in Figure 10.5. With the new inflation target, a recession is being orchestrated, with the economy being pushed to point B, away from the 45-degree line. As the economy moves down the aggregate demand curve of Figure 10.4, it goes back towards the equilibrium locus, first at point C. But since point C still corresponds to an inflation rate higher than the new inflation target, a new round of interest rate hikes will be required, pushing the economy to point B'. Eventually the reduced economic activity will be successful in reducing inflation rates enough, and the

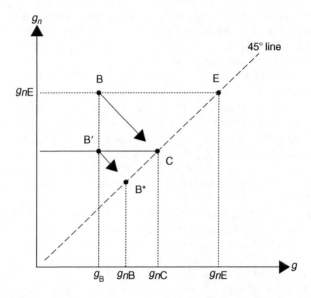

Figure 10.5   Hysteresis in growth rates: a continuum of equilibria

economy will achieve the new long-run equilibrium, given by point B*, on the 45-degree line.[9]

The implications of this amendment to the New Consensus are of course much more dramatic than the previous ones, and perhaps have not yet been emphasized enough. The costs in terms of output or capital (K) lost are growing exponentially and are not limited to the transitional phase. Beyond hysteresis of the rate of unemployment, what we have is hysteresis in the rate of growth of the economy.

Figure 10.6 summarizes all this by illustrating the implications of a reduction in the target inflation rate in: (a) the standard New Consensus case;[10] (b) unemployment hysteresis; (c) growth hysteresis. In contrast to New Consensus authors, Post–Keynesians fear that monetary policies designed to restrain demand have a negative impact on actual long-run economic activity (Fontana and Palacio-Vera, 2007). The argument above has raised serious questions about the advisability of such restrictive policies.

6   Fourth Post Keynesian Amendment: Taking Liquidity Preference into Account[11]

So far we have completely set aside an important issue. We did not care to differentiate the short-term interest rate under the control of the central bank – the overnight rate in most countries, also called the federal funds rate

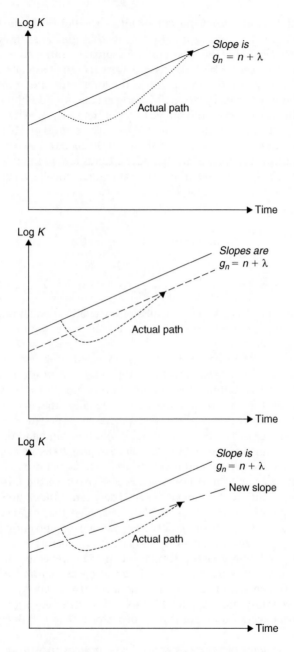

Figure 10.6 Three views of the long-run impact of restrictive monetary policies

in the United States – from the rate of interest which is of concern to the private economy. Economists usually assume that this rate is the long-term rate of interest. But what long-term rate? Presumably, entrepreneurs or home buyers are not concerned with the riskless Treasury long-term rate of interest. Rather, what they are concerned with is the long-term rate of interest that is relevant to most private actors, the mortgage rate for households and, for instance, the Baa graded corporate yield for entrepreneurs. What we should really have been saying is that economic activity depends on this long-term risky market interest rate, which we shall call the *market rate* and denote by r, and that this rate depends on the federal funds rate f, the term spread ρ and the risk spread τ. A more appropriate amended model, starting from the basic model of section 2, would thus be:

$$u = a - br \qquad IS \qquad (10.1C)$$

$$\Delta\pi = \gamma(u - u_n) + \varepsilon \qquad PC \qquad (10.2)$$

$$f = f_0 + \alpha(\pi - \pi^{\mathrm{T}}) \qquad RF \qquad (10.3)$$

$$r = f + \rho + \tau \qquad TM \qquad (10.11)$$

where equation (10.11) is the transmission mechanism equation, *TM*, that links the federal funds rate to the market rate that is relevant to the private sector (both in real terms).[12]

Figure 10.1 needs to be a bit more complicated now. We need to dispatch the 45-degree quadrant, and introduce the transmission mechanism equation *TM*. The reaction function equation is moved to the south-west quadrant, while the transmission mechanism equation makes its appearance in the fourth quadrant – the north-west quadrant – as drawn in Figure 10.7.

What difference does this make? It helps to understand and picture what has been occurring on financial markets since August 2007. Several observers of the financial scene have described the recent financial turmoil as a 'Minsky moment'. Hyman Minsky (1986) is a Post Keynesian economist who paid considerable attention to financial markets, debt ratios, stock-flow relations, and liquidity preference.[13] In particular, he argued that capitalism inherently brings about fragile financial structures, as bankers and borrowers forget about past crises, taking ever risky positions that eventually generate defaults, insolvencies, and falling asset prices, as seems to be the case since 2007. In a nutshell, his view, as argued by Joan Robinson, was that *tranquillity breeds instability*. Had he known about the New Consensus, Minsky would have been most certainly quite appalled by its simple three-equation apparatus that ignores payment flows arising from debt stocks as well as fluctuations in asset prices.

But how can *some* of Minsky's concerns be dealt with within the model of Figure 10.7? Assume that the economy starts off from point A, shown in all quadrants of the Figure. In a 'Minsky moment', the risk spread τ rises

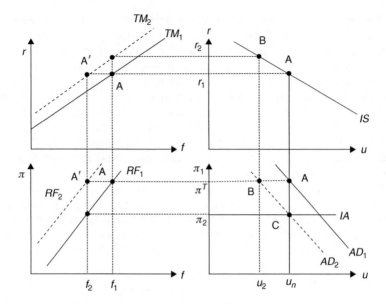

Figure 10.7 The four-quadrant New Consensus model upgraded with liquidity preference

considerably.[14] As there is a rush towards liquidity and riskless assets, the prices of risky assets fall, and hence the interest rates on these assets rise. This is represented in Figure 10.7 by an upward shift of the transmission mechanism curve, from TM_1 to TM_2. Thus, even if the financial crisis does not have a direct impact on the real economy – meaning here that the a coefficient in the *IS* equation remains put, there will be consequences for the real economy because market rates will rise from r_1 to r_2. If the central bank does not modify its reaction function, the aggregate demand curve will get shifted downwards from AD_1 to AD_2 and economic activity will fall to u_2, with the economy moving from point A to point B. Then, as inflation rates start to fall, as a result of the rates of capacity utilization being below their normal levels, nominal and real federal funds rates will be brought down by the central bank, moving along the RF_1 reaction function.

If the monetary authorities react in the normal way, without taking into account the turmoil in the financial markets and the higher risk premia, the economy will be brought back to the normal rate of capacity utilization, but at a steady rate of inflation that will be below the target, at point C. In other words, the risk premium in financial markets acts like a negative shock on the aggregate demand curve, just like a real negative shock would. If this financial shock is large enough it could even bring about negative inflation, and hence debt-deflation as argued by Minsky.

The higher risk premium requires the central bank to modify its assessment of the natural rate of interest, f_0, in a counter-intuitive way, since it must reduce the federal funds rate when long-term market interest rates are rising. The monetary authorities must shift their reaction function, to RF_2, and reduce the federal funds rate to f_2 in order to keep inflation on target at π^T and avoid a reduction in economic activity (thus keeping market interest rates at r_1). If they do so, and assuming the financial turmoil does not have further effects, the central bank could succeed in keeping the economy at the normal rate of utilization, thus keeping the economy at points A in the north-east and south-east quadrants, which correspond to points A' of the north-west and south-west quadrants.

The central bank may not claim, as it sometimes does, that long-term market rates are a proper proxy for the natural interest rate and a guide to help setting the federal funds rate. In the present case, if the central bank were to raise its estimate of the natural rate of interest, in an effort to follow the apparent increase in long-term market rates, it would only make matters worse.

7 Conclusion

The purpose of the present chapter was to show how easily the New Consensus model can be amended in ways that substantially alter its main results. New Consensus authors are certainly on the right track when they model interest rate targeting – a requirement of macro models long made by Post Keynesian authors. But as pointed out by Pollin (2003, p. 293), their hypothesis of a unique stable equilibrium is unwarranted and leads to overly simplistic policy prescriptions. Things are much more complicated once hysteresis effects are introduced in an amended New Consensus model. The addition of liquidity preference effects also enriches the model, showing that the life of central bankers in setting interest rates is far from being simple, irrespective of their role as lender of last resort, even if they only assign to themselves the task of keeping inflation rates stable. Whether this ought to be their main task is another issue, discussed by others.[15]

Notes

1. Many thanks for the timely and pertinent comments of Louis-Philippe Rochon. Grateful thanks also to Giuseppe Fontana and Mark Setterfield, who strongly encouraged me to make substantial changes, thus inducing me to simplify the analysis.
2. The rate of capacity utilization is the ratio $u = Y/Y_{fc}$, where Y is output and Y_{fc} is output if all productive capacities were fully used (full-capacity output). Thus, in general, firms have spare capacity and could produce more.
3. This section draws implications from a critique of the New Consensus that can be found in Kriesler and Lavoie (2007).
4. We leave it as an exercise to draw such a situation with the help of a modified Figure 10.3.

5. This section is mainly inspired by Lavoie (2006), which was first presented at the University of Burgundy in 2002. See also Lavoie (1992, pp. 405–7).
6. The standard view would say that: $\Delta\pi = -\gamma(U) + \varepsilon$
7. To introduce capital accumulation, an alternative to the suggested amended model would be to keep equations (10.1), (10.2), and (10.3) as they are, while adding the following equation:

$$g = g_n + \mu(u - u_n)$$

in which case the efforts of the central bank to bring back the economy to its normal level of capacity utilization would also bring back the actual growth rate to its natural level.
8. This section is mainly inspired by Lavoie (2006), where more details and graphs can be found. See also Dutt (2006) for a similar approach, and also Cornwall (1977).
9. In reality, a second case is also possible (Lavoie, 2006). But lower inflation targets still induce lower growth rates in the long run.
10. In the event that there is growth, but no hysteresis.
11. This section is inspired by Villieu (2004, p. 299) and the presentation of Barbera and Weise (2008). See also their chapter in this book.
12. There is another issue, which will be set aside, but that warrants careful attention: there is evidence that economic agents react just as much to nominal interest rates as they do to real rates. For instance, the investment decisions of firms are known to be influenced by their cash flow, but the cash flow depends on nominal interest rates not real ones, as Mark Setterfield has reminded me. Similarly, as pointed out by Haight (2007–8), mortgage loans to households are usually granted on the basis of various measures of cash flow expenditures on housing relative to current income, and thus are based on nominal interest rates and not real rates (unless expected future housing price increases are taken into account – a cause of the sub-prime crisis). Doing justice to this issue would require more than an amendment to the New Consensus model. This point, however, may help to explain why Seccareccia (2008) finds that *real* interest rates set by the Bank of Canada are generally inversely related to inflation. Raising nominal interest rates when inflation is rising may be enough.
13. The contribution of Minsky is explained in more detail in the chapter of Wray and Tymoigne for this book.
14. As Stiglitz and Greenwald (2003, p. 200) point out: 'The links ... between T-bills and lending rates are weak. They may move in tandem "normally"; but it is when matters are *not* normal – when the economy is facing a crisis or an episode of inflation – that macro-economic policy becomes important. It is just at those times that the usual relationships break down'.
15. See in particular the special issue of the *Journal of Post Keynesian Economics*, edited by Rochon (2007).

References

Arestis, P. and Sawyer, M. (2004), 'Can Monetary Policy Affect the Real Economy?', *European Review of Economics and Finance*, 3(2), 9–32.
Barnes, M. L. and Olivei, G. P. (2003), 'Inside and Outside Bounds: Estimates of the Phillips Curve', *New England Economic Review*, 3–18.

Barbera, R. J. and Weise, C. L. (2008), 'A Minsky/Wicksell Modified Taylor Rule', presentation made at the 17th Minsky Conference, Levy Economics Institute of Bard College, 18 April.

Bindseil, U. (2004), *Monetary Policy Implementation: Theory, Past and Present*, Oxford; Oxford University Press.

Bowen, W. G. and Berry, R. A. (1963), 'Unemployment and Movements of the Money Wage Level', *Review of Economics and Statistics*, 45(2), May, 163–72.

Cornwall, J. (1977), *Modern Capitalism: its Growth and Transformation*, London: Martin Robertson.

Cramp, A. B. (1971), 'Monetary Policy: Strong or Weak', in Kaldor, N. (ed.), *Conflict in Policy Objectives*, Oxford: Basil Blackwell, 62–74.

Dutt, A. K. (2006), 'Aggregate Demand, Aggregate Supply and Economic Growth', *International Review of Applied Economics*, 20(3), July, 319–36.

Eisner, R. (1996), 'The Retreat from Full Employment', in Arestis, P. (ed.), *Employment, Economic Growth and the Tyranny of the Market: Essays in Honour of Paul Davidson, Volume Two*, Cheltenham: Edward Elgar, 106–30.

Emery, K. M. and Chang, C. P. (1997), 'Is There a Stable Relationship Between Capacity Utilization and Inflation?', *Federal Reserve Bank of Dallas Economic Review*, 1, 14–20.

Filardo, A. J. (1998), 'New Evidence on the Output Cost of Fighting Inflation', *Federal Reserve Bank of Kansas City Quarterly Review*, 83(3), 33–61.

Fontana, G. and Palacio-Vera, A. (2004), 'Monetary policy uncovered: Theory and practice', *International Review of Applied Economics*, 18(1), 25–41.

Fontana, G. and Palacio-Vera, A. (2007), 'Are Long-run Price Stability and Short-run Output Stabilization all that Monetary Policy Can Aim for?', *Metroeconomica*, 57(2), 269–98.

Fuller, D. and Geide-Stevenson, D. (2003), 'Consensus among economists: revisited', *Journal of Economic Education*, 34(4), 369–87.

Fullwiler, S. T. (2003), 'Timeliness and the Fed's Daily Tactics', *Journal of Economic Issues*, 37(4), 851–80.

Goodhart, C. (2003), 'What is the Monetary Policy Committee Attempting to Achieve?', in *Macroeconomics, Monetary Policy and Financial Stability: A Festschrift in Honour of Charles Freedman*, Ottawa: Bank of Canada, 153–69.

Haight, A. D. (2007–8), 'A Keynesian Angle for the Taylor Rule: Mortgage Rates, Monthly Payment Illusion, and the Scarecrow Effect of Inflation', *Journal of Post Keynesian Economics*, 30(2), Winter, 259–78.

Hein, E. (2002), 'Monetary Policy and Wage Bargaining in the EMU: Restrictive ECB Policies, High Unemployment, Nominal Wage Restraint and Inflation Above the Target', *Banca del Lavoro Quarterly Review*, 222, September, 299–337.

Kaldor, N. (1960), 'Characteristics of Economic Development', in *Essays on Economic Stability and Growth*, London: Duckworth, 232–42.

Kaldor, N. (1982), *The Scourge of Monetarism*, Oxford: Oxford University Press.

Kim, J. H. (2007), *Three Essays on Effective Demand, Economic Growth and Inflation*, PhD. Dissertation, Department of Economics, University of Ottawa.

Kriesler, P. and Lavoie, M. (2007), 'The New View on Monetary Policy: The New Consensus and its Post-Keynesian Critique', *Review of Political Economy*, 19(3), July, 387–404.

Lavoie, M. (1992), *Foundations of Post-Keynesian Economic Analysis*, Aldershot: Edward Elgar.

Lavoie, M. (2006), 'A Post-Keynesian Amendment to the New Consensus on Monetary Policy', *Metroeconomica*, 57(2), 165–92.

León-Ledesma, M. A. and Thirlwall, A. P. (2002), 'The Endogeneity of the Natural Rate of Growth', *Cambridge Journal of Economics*, 26(4), July, 441–59.

McDonald, L. M. (1995), 'Models of the Range of Equilibria', in Cross, R. (ed.), *The Natural Rate of Unemployment: Reflections on 25 Years of the Hypothesis*, Cambridge: Cambridge University Press, 101–52.

McElhattan, R. (1978), 'Estimating a Stable-Inflation Capacity-Utilization Rate', *Federal reserve Bank of San Francisco Economic Review*, 78, Fall, 20–30.

Minsky, H. P. (1986), *Stabilizing an Unstable Economy*, New Haven: Yale University Press. Reprinted in 2008, New York: McGraw-Hill.

Mitchell, W. and J. Muysken (2008), *Full Employment Abandoned: Shifting Sands and Policy Failures*, Cheltenham : Edward Elgar.

Orphanides, A. and Williams, J. C. (2002), 'Robust Monetary Rules with Unknown Natural Rates', *Brookings Papers on Economic Activity*, 2, 63–145.

Perrotini, I. and Tlatelpa, H. Y. D. (2003), 'Crecimiento Endógeno y Demanda en las Economías de América del Norte', *Momento Económico*, 128, 10–15.

Pollin, J. P. (2003), 'Une Macroéconomie sans LM: Quelques Propositions Complémentaires', *Revue d' Economie Politique*, 113(3), 273–93.

Poole, W. (1970), 'Optimal Choice of Monetary Policy Instruments in a Simple Stochastic Macro Model', *Quarterly Journal of Economics*, 84, 197–216.

Robinson, J. (1956), *The Accumulation of Capital*, London: Macmillan.

Rochon, L. P. (2007), 'The State of Post Keynesian Interest Rate Policy: Where are We and Where are We Going?', *Journal of Post Keynesian Economics*, 30(1), Fall, 3–12.

Seccareccia, M. (2008), 'In Search of the Will-o'-the-wisp: Central Banking and the Natural Rate of Interest', Paper presented at the 10th International Post Keynesian Conference in Kansas City, Missouri, USA., 29 June–2 July.

Stanley, T. D. (2004), 'Does Unemployment Hysteresis Falsify the Natural Rate Hypothesis? A meta-regression analysis', *Journal of Economic Surveys*, 18(4), 589–612.

Stiglitz, J. E. and Greenwald, B. (2003), *Towards a New Paradigm in Monetary Economics*, Cambridge: Cambridge University Press.

Taylor, J. B. (2000), 'Teaching Modern Macroeconomics at the Principles Level', *American Economic Review*, 90(2), May, 90–4.

Villieu, P. (2004), 'Une Macroéconomie sans LM: Un Modèle de Synthèse pour l'Analyse des Politiques Conjoncturelles', *Revue d' Economie Politique*, 114(3), 289–322.

Weber, A. A., Lemke, W. and Worms, A. (2008), 'How Useful is the Concept of the Natural Real Rate of Interest for Monetary Policy?', *Cambridge Journal of Economics*, 32(1), 49–63.

11
Minsky Meets Wicksell: Using the Wicksellian Model to Understand the Twenty-First Century Business Cycle

Charles L. Weise and Robert J. Barbera

The recent turmoil in US financial markets presents undergraduate macroeconomics instructors with an opportunity to link dry textbook presentations to exciting and important real world events. Speculative excess and panic in financial markets, vulnerability of the banking system, widening credit spreads, the Fed's difficulty in managing long-term risky interest rates, and its use of unconventional open market operations are topics that have been discussed extensively in the financial press. Unfortunately, the *IS–LM* model that is still the centerpiece of most Intermediate Macroeconomics and Money and Banking textbooks is not well-suited for an analysis of such topics. *IS–LM* takes the money supply rather than the interest rate as the target for monetary policy and makes no distinction between short and long, risk-free and risky interest rates. The Romer (2000) model, variants of which have appeared in some recent textbooks (e.g. Taylor, 2003; Frank and Bernanke, 2004; DeLong and Olney, 2006), rectifies the first of these problems but at great expense. By assuming that the Federal Reserve controls the *key* interest rate, the Romer model has monetary policy directly affecting investment, thereby abstracting entirely from the banking and financial sector. Thus a great virtue of the *IS–LM* framework, its depiction of monetary policy as a tool that acts through the financial system, is lost. On two counts we would submit that the loss is unacceptable. First, financial markets/banking system developments have played a central role in unfolding US and global macroeconomic developments over the past twenty years. Second, the ascendance of financial economics in the world of economic theory, over the past twenty years, is undeniable. This, in turn, argues for a larger – not smaller – place for banks and asset markets in an ideal intermediate macro framework.

This chapter demonstrates how a variant of the Wicksellian model in Weise (2007) can be used to help students understand recent events in financial markets and the macroeconomy. In the process, it introduces students to some of the insights of financial economics and some of the key arguments made by Hyman Minsky as to the centrality of finance in the generation of business cycles. Basic financial economy notions concerning yield curve and credit spread theories are key drivers in the model and thus render discussions of these concepts central rather than ancillary. We do not attempt a complete formalization of Minsky's theories (for a recent treatment see Bellofiore and Ferri, 2001); instead, we integrate one key Minskyan concept – the evolution of perceptions of risk over the business cycle as reflected in credit spreads – into the Wicksellian model and draw out the implications for the macroeconomy and the challenges facing the Federal Reserve. Echoing Weise (2007), the paper emphasizes financial market dynamics between Fed controlled overnight rates and the risky real rates that drive investment. In addition, by adding Minsky's insights about risk appetites, the model is able to explain periodic sharp shifts in Fed policy in a fashion that is missing from more traditional approaches.

1   A Minskyan Interpretation of Recent Financial Market Crises

Referring to the recession of 2001, Paul Krugman (2002) wrote 'this is not your father's recession – it's your grandfather's recession.' By this he meant that the 2001 recession (and by extension the recession of 2008) was not triggered by interest rate increases intended to reduce inflation as was typical of post-Great Depression recessions. Rather, today's recessions are driven by the kind of investment boom and bust cycle that produced repeated 'panics' in the nineteenth and early twentieth centuries. Seeking a way of understanding the current financial market crisis-cum-recession, a number of authors (e.g. Kregel, 2007; Leamer, 2007; Whalen, 2007; Wray, 2007) have argued for a reconsideration of the works of Hyman Minsky. As Barbera and Weise (2008) argue, the Federal Reserve's success in eliminating inflation as an important destabilizing influence in the US economy since the early 1980s has laid bare the financial sources of business cycles of the kind described by Minsky (1975) and elsewhere. Minsky's ideas are worth incorporating into undergraduate macroeconomics courses.

The core of Minsky's theory is the 'financial fragility hypothesis', according to which financial institutions' tolerance for taking risky positions in asset markets evolves over time, affecting firms' financing decisions and the level of investment. In Minsky's model, the level of investment by a firm is constrained by the net cash flow generated by its assets and liabilities and its ability or willingness to borrow to finance investment. Firms and prospective lenders adopt conventions that guide the optimal ratio of external (debt) financing to internal financing. These conventions reflect perceptions of risk or what Minsky refers to as the appropriate 'margin of safety'. When confidence is high, firms want to rely more heavily on external versus internal finance, and therefore increase purchases of capital goods. When confidence is low, firms want to reduce external finance and so reduce the pace of investment.

Minsky (1986) describes the typical phases of a finance-led business cycle. In the early stages of recovery from a recession, memories of previous financial calamity heighten the perception of risk by borrowers and lenders. Firms leave themselves a large 'margin of safety' by reducing debt and financing most of their investment internally. What external financing they do is in the form of 'hedge financing': the purchase of assets that generate sufficient income to cover interest payments and amortize the debt. As recovery persists and leads to expansion, perceptions of risk are reduced and firms begin to increase the amount of debt used to finance investment. In this phase borrowing takes the form of 'speculative financing', in which the income generated by the purchased assets is sufficient to cover interest payments alone. As the expansion endures, perceptions of risk fall further. A high level of leverage becomes the norm, the purchase of new assets being financed by 'ponzi borrowing', under which the firm's ability to make interest payments and pay down the debt is contingent on rising prices of its purchased assets. At some point during the expansion, some event will inevitably cause realized profits to fall short of expectations, causing firms to increase their perception of risk and pull back on investment. The result is a cumulative process in which profits fall, perceptions of risk increase, firms purge their balance sheets of debt, asset prices fall, and the economy sinks into a deep recession.

Minsky's template aptly characterizes the internet boom and bust of 1997–2001 and the housing market boom and bust of 2003–2008. The internet bubble of the 1990s began with real productivity-enhancing innovations that sparked a stock market and investment boom. These are shown in Figure 11.1. The boom accelerated as borrowers and speculators took advantage of new markets for exotic financial derivatives and money poured into hedge funds and other loosely regulated entities. Interest rate increases followed by a slowdown in growth in 2000 popped the bubble, causing stock markets to crash and non-residential investment to nosedive, and the economy fell into recession in early 2001. The housing market bubble emerged out of the ashes of the recession as the Fed maintained a low interest rate policy and savers, stung by losses in the stock market, searched for higher-yielding assets elsewhere. Rising housing prices attracted speculative and then ponzi borrowing in the form of innovative mortgage contracts such as no down payment mortgage loans, adjustable rate mortgages, and 2/28 adjustable rate loans with 'teaser' rates. The availability of cheap finance created a boom in housing construction as shown in Figure 11.2. As the housing boom began to cool off at the end of 2006, housing price increases failed to match expectations and borrowers who had counted on being able to re-finance on the basis of higher home values were unable to do so. Beginning in 2007, households and lenders sought to de-leverage their positions in the housing market,

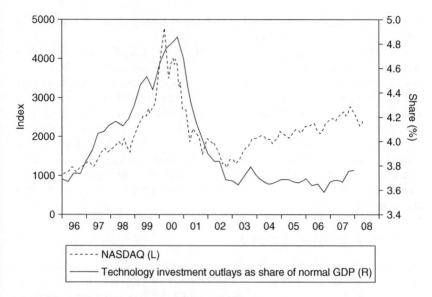

Figure 11.1   The 1990s technology boom and bust

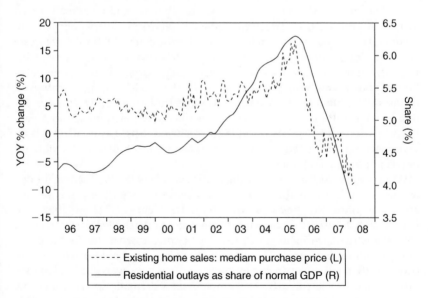

Figure 11.2   The 2000s housing boom and bust

resulting in a tightening of lending standards, foreclosures, a steep drop in residential investment, and another recession.

The housing boom and bust carried with it a Minskyan boom–bust cycle in other financial markets. The securitization of home mortgages during the boom period and the overly optimistic estimates of likely default rates provided a cheap form of financing for a number of speculative activities in the business sector. The proliferation of mortgage-backed securities, collateralized debt obligations, conduits, and structured investment vehicles facilitated an increase in leverage in the business sector as a whole. The collapse of the housing market called into question the value of mortgage-backed securities and led to a de-leveraging process that has pushed asset prices down and caused liquidity to dry up in certain sectors of the financial system, worsening the threat of recession.

2   Minsky Modifies Wicksell

Minsky's story of evolving attitudes toward risk and the consequent asset market imbalances and crashes can be taught in an undergraduate macroeconomics class using a version of Weise's (2007) Wicksellian macroeconomic model. The centerpiece of Minsky's financial instability hypothesis is that there is a consistent pattern to the perception of risk over the course of a business cycle. The original version of the Wicksellian model abstracted from considerations of risk. In this chapter we add a risk premium or credit spread as an additional wedge between the Federal Reserve's monetary policy instrument and the market interest rates relevant for the determination of aggregate demand. This model modification allows us to provide a much more realistic description of both the late 1990s technology boom and the more recent housing boom and bust. More importantly, the model does three things. It exposes the difficulties the Fed now faces as it tries to respond to the current financial crisis. It offers a rationale for the unconventional market interventions to which the Fed has resorted in recent months. Lastly, it reveals an asymmetry in recent Fed policy that may have contributed to the violence of recent asset market upheavals.

When we discuss the risk premium in the context of the Wicksellian model, we have in mind something like the difference between the yields on Baa corporate bonds and 10-year US Treasury notes. Figure 11.3 shows that, consistent with Minsky's theory, recessions (shown as shaded areas) tend to coincide with sharp increases in this credit spread while the credit spread plunges during recoveries. Importantly, the spread has a clear tendency to continue to shrink as expansion endures. At times, however, financial market turmoil not associated with recession generates dramatic spread widening. Spreads soared during the 1987 stock market crash, the Mexican peso crisis of 1994–95, and the collapse of Long Term Capital Management in 1998. In each of these cases the Federal Reserve responded with lower interest

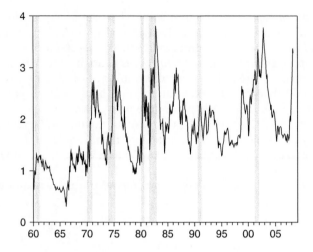

Figure 11.3   Credit spreads (BAA corporate bond rate minus 10-year Treasury rate), 1960–2008

Note: Shaded areas are NBER recession dates.

rates and expanded access to the discount window. Spreads tightened thereafter. Clearly monetary policy-makers are quite sensitive to major swings in spreads. Statements by Fed officials make it equally clear that these reactions are linked to concerns about risk assessments.

Our model makes an important distinction between perceptions of risk in our model and the state of expectations of consumers and investors. Perceptions of risk, represented by the risk premium, refers to the subjective probability assigned to adverse events: technically, in Minsky's theory, the probability that the cash flow generated by the firm's assets will be insufficient to make payments required by the firm's liabilities. More generally, the risk premium reflects considerations of liquidity preference, which is a concept inseparable from broader conceptions of financial risk. Thus sharp shifts in credit spreads at once reflect changing attitudes about risk and shifting sentiments about liquidity needs. In an uncertain environment, firms will seek to weight their asset holdings towards more liquid assets such as Treasury securities so that they are in a position to cover shortfalls in cash flow. During a crisis, the demand for safe securities relative to more risky securities rises as firms try to stay (or become) liquid, driving the risk premium up.

Whereas risk reflects in a sense the variance of asset returns, the state of expectations refers to the expected value of future returns on a firm's assets or the profitability of investment.[1] The risk premium as we define it enters into the cost of capital for the firm, while the state of expectations affects the demand for investment at a given cost of capital. Of course, during booms and busts the risk premium and state of expectations tend to move together: optimism about rates of return goes hand in hand with conviction that bad outcomes are only a remote possibility. But Minsky, insightfully, distinguishes between mean expectations and concerns about potential for disappointment. In Minsky's framework consumer and business expectations may well remain rational over the course of an expansion. But even amidst steady mean expectations, fear of disappointment recedes as an expansion matures – and as such risk appetites grow. Thus it is essential that we model these two concepts separately.

The Wicksellian model with credit risk consists of three equations:

$$\text{\textit{TS} curve:} \quad r_t = \omega(f_t - E_t\pi_{t+1} + \tau + \sigma) + (1 - \omega)r_t^* + \eta_t \tag{11.1}$$

$$\text{\textit{IS} curve:} \quad y_t = -\alpha(r_t - r_t^*) + u_t \tag{11.2}$$

$$\text{\textit{AS} curve:} \quad \pi_t = E_t\pi_{t+1} + \theta y_t + v_t \tag{11.3}$$

The *IS* and *AS* curves are consistent with widely-used linearized versions of the New Keynesian model. The *IS* curve says that the output gap (y_t) is negatively related to the deviation of the real long-term risky interest rate (r_t) from the Wicksellian natural rate of interest (r_t^*), defined as the real risky interest rate consistent with full employment in the absence of temporary demand shocks, plus a demand shock (u_t). The *AS* curve says that the inflation rate π_t is determined by expectations of future inflation, the output gap (y_t), and a price shock (v_t).

The term structure (*TS*) curve determines the real long-term risky interest rate (r_t). A complete derivation of this equation is provided in the Appendix. The *TS* curve embodies the expectations theory of the term structure of interest rates, according to which long-term rates are a weighted average of current and expected future short-term rates. The first term is the federal funds rate (f_t) adjusted for expected inflation ($E_t\pi_{t+1}$), the term premium (τ), and the average risk premium (σ). This is meant to represent the 'short end' of the yield curve. The second term represents the 'long end' end of the yield curve, which is anchored by the Wicksellian natural rate of interest (r_t^*). The real long-term risky interest rate is a weighted average of these two terms plus a stochastic risk premium shock (η_t). The coefficient ω may be interpreted as the length of time (expressed as a fraction of the term of the long-term bond) during which short-term rates are expected to depart from their long-run equilibrium values. As such, we can interpret ω as the 'persistence' of monetary policy decisions. In the Appendix, ω is defined as the length of the 'period' during which shocks occur and monetary policy decisions are made, expressed as a fraction of the term of the long-term bond.

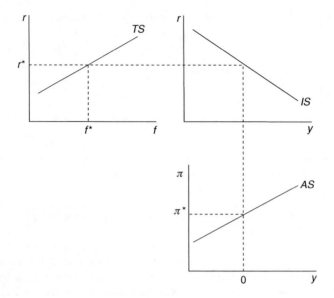

Figure 11.4 The Wicksellian (*TS–IS–AS*) model

The model can be presented in graphical form as in Figure 11.4. A similar graphical apparatus appears in Marc Lavoie's paper in this volume (Lavoie, 2009). As explained in Weise (2007), in equilibrium the federal funds rate is equal to its neutral rate $f_t^*(= r_t^* + \pi^* - \tau - \sigma)$. When the federal funds rate is at this level and there are no risk premium, demand, or price shocks, the real interest rate is equal to the Wicksellian natural rate, the output gap is zero, and inflation is at its long-run average or target rate (π^*). If the Federal Reserve reduces the federal funds rate, the real interest rate falls along the TS curve. The reduction in the real rate is less than one-for-one because the long end of the yield curve is anchored by the Wicksellian natural rate. The decline in the real interest rate increases output along the *IS* curve, which causes inflation to rise along the *AS* curve. If expectations are adaptive, deviations of inflation from the target level in one period may cause the *AS* and *TS* curves to shift in later periods, generating interesting dynamics. These are discussed in detail in Weise (2007) but are not considered here for reasons given below.

There are four types of shocks that can shift the curves in Figure 11.4. The first three are risk premium shocks (η_t), which shift the *TS* curve; price shocks (v_t), which shift the *AS* curve; and temporary spending shocks (u_t), which shift the *IS* curve. The fourth type of shock is a shock to the Wicksellian natural rate of interest. The natural rate of interest is generated by the process

$$r_t^* = r_{t-1}^* + z_t \tag{11.4}$$

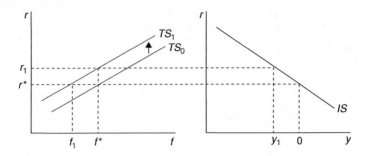

Figure 11.5 The effect of a risk premium shock (increase in η_t)

A non-zero realization of z_t is interpreted as a permanent spending shock that changes the long-run equilibrium interest rate consistent with full employment. For example, in the loanable funds model with output fixed at the full employment level, a decrease in savings or an increase in investment demand results in a higher equilibrium interest rate. Thus a non-zero realization of z_t shifts the *IS* curve, and because the *IS* curve is expected to remain in its new position for the indefinite future, the *TS* curve shifts as well.

The important events of the internet and housing boom and bust can be represented by shocks to the natural rate of interest and the risk premium. The story can be told without reference to the inflation rate, so we omit the aggregate supply component of the model in the analysis that follows.

Consider first a shock to the risk premium (η_t), shown in Figure 11.5. A rise in perceptions of risk in the financial sector causes borrowers and lenders to reassess the 'margin of safety' associated with debt finance. Perceiving a higher probability of bad outcomes on loans (an increase in the variance around expected future cash flows), lenders offer less favourable borrowing terms on loan contracts, including higher interest rates on loans subject to default risk. The *TS* curve shifts up and the real long-term risky interest rate rises for any given federal funds rate (from r^* to r_1). This stimulates a lower level of investment and output – the output gap falls from 0 to y_1 along the *IS* curve. If the Fed's objective is to stabilize the output gap around zero, the appropriate response is to reduce the federal funds rate one-for-one with the reduction in the risk premium. Likewise a tightening of credit spreads that lowers risky rates requires a higher federal funds rate. As we show below, the Federal Reserve seems to have failed to appreciate this implication of the model during the internet and housing bubble periods.

The effect of a positive shock to the Wicksellian natural rate of interest ($z_t > 0$) is shown in Figure 11.6. The *IS* curve shifts to the right such that the output gap is zero at the new higher natural rate r^{**}. If the real long-term interest rate stays at r^* the output gap rises to y_1'. Because the increase in expenditures is expected to be long-lasting, however, the expected future

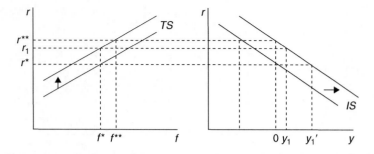

Figure 11.6 The effect of a natural interest rate shock (increase in z_t)

interest rate rises to r^{**} which pushes the current long-term interest rate up. But since the short end of the yield curve is held down by the Fed's choice of federal funds rate, the long rate rises less than one-for-one with the rise in the natural rate. Graphically, the *TS* curve shifts up part way towards r^{**}. If the federal funds rate stays at f^* the long-term interest rate rises to r_1, causing output to fall back to y_1 along the new *IS* curve. The difference between y_1' and y_1 is a measure of the 'crowding out' effect of spending shocks brought on by automatic changes in long-term interest rates. The net effect of the expenditures shock is to increase output. If the Fed wants to stabilize the output gap around zero it needs to increase the federal funds rate to the new neutral rate, f^{**}.

3 Booms and Crashes

The story of the internet bubble in the late 1990s and the housing boom and bust in recent years can be told in terms of shocks to expenditures and the risk premium. The canonical speculative boom begins to be formed after a period of steady growth. As memories of previous recessions and financial crises recede, borrowers' and lenders' tolerance for taking risky positions in asset markets increases: the risk premium (η_t) falls. At the same time, forces real and imagined contribute to a feeling of optimism about the profitability of new investment, stimulating an increase in investment expenditures and asset prices. The rise in asset prices stimulates a higher level of consumption. The increase in investment and consumption constitutes an increase in expenditures that is perceived as long-lived, so z_t takes a positive value.

Figure 11.7 shows the effects of these shocks. The positive expenditures shock shifts the *IS* curve to the right and pushes the *TS* curve up towards the dashed line shown in the *TS* graph. At the same time, however, the Minskyan shift in risk tolerance shifts the *TS* curve down. The net effect is a shift in the *TS* curve from TS_0 to TS_1. As a result, the interest rate, rather than increasing

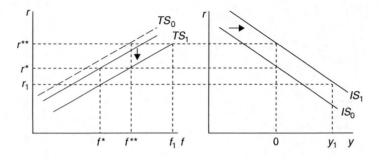

Figure 11.7   A Minskyan boom

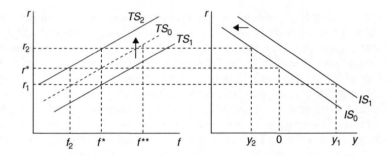

Figure 11.8   A Minskyan bust

as it would in the event of a pure expenditures shock, falls to r_1 while the output gap rises to y_1. The result is an economic boom fed by low borrowing costs.

The collapse of the bubble causes this process to reverse, as shown in Figure 11.8. We begin with interest rates at r_1 and output at y_1. A break in investors' psychology, perhaps brought about by concerns about inflation or an increase in interest rates, causes the new economy attitudes to disappear. Firms and households reduce expenditures, shifting the *IS* curve back to IS_0. At this point a 'soft landing' seems plausible: the output gap is moving toward zero on its own and a slight increase in interest rates driven by a reversal of the earlier reduction in credit spreads will finish the job. But in 2000 and again in 2007, attitudes toward risk swing violently in the direction of pessimism. As firms seek to reduce their leverage, prices of risky assets plummet and credit spreads widen dramatically. The *TS* curve shifts past its original level (TS_0) up to TS_2. Now if the federal funds rate remains at f^*, the real risky interest rate rises to r_2 and the economy falls into recession with an output gap of y_2.

4 The Complications for Monetary Policy

The Minskyan perspective exposes the complications the boom–bust cycle poses for monetary policy. Suppose that following the positive expenditures shock shown in Figure 11.7, the Fed considers a monetary policy response without accounting for the effect of the rising risk premium. Policy-makers operating in a conventional New Keynesian, rational expectations framework would interpret the expenditures shock as consumers' and investors' rational response to a revision of growth expectations. They would understand that the equilibrium real interest rate had risen to r^{**}. Their intuition would be confirmed when the yield on 10-year Treasuries rose. Counting on the stabilizing effect of the increase in the 10-year (risk-free) rate, they would calculate that a modest increase in the federal funds rate from f^* to f^{**} would be sufficient to restore the economy to full employment. Output would continue to rise, however, despite the Fed's attempts at tightening. Only a much more aggressive policy that accounts for the effect of rising risk appetites – increasing the federal funds rate to f_1 in Figure 11.7 – would be sufficient to keep the economy from overheating. Likewise, during the Minskyan bust in Figure 11.8, the Fed must ease dramatically by reducing the federal funds rate to f_2. If the Fed ignores the movement in credit spreads it will underreact, reducing the federal funds rate to f^*, and economic deterioration will accelerate.

This model can explain some recent puzzles in the Fed's conduct of monetary policy: the Fed's aggressive response to economic contraction in 2001 and 2007–08 and its failure more aggressively to combat the housing bubble in 2003–05. It is commonplace among economists and Fed watchers and in undergraduate economics courses to explain monetary policy decisions with reference to the Taylor (1993) rule. Taylor's original rule was

$$f_t = (r^* + \pi_{t,12}) + .5^*(\pi_{t,12} - 2) + .5^* y_t \tag{11.5}$$

where the real value of the neutral federal funds rate is assumed to equal 2, the inflation target is also equal to 2, $\pi_{t,12}$ is the inflation rate over the previous 12 months, and y_t is the output gap. In unemployment gap form with an Okun's coefficient of 2, the Taylor rule is

$$f_t = (2 + \pi_{t,12}) + .5^*(\pi_{t,12} - 2) - (u_t - u^*) \tag{11.6}$$

where u_t is the unemployment rate and u^* is the natural rate of unemployment. The model described above suggests modifying the Taylor rule by adjusting the neutral federal funds rate to changes in the Wicksellian natural rate of interest and shocks to the risk premium. That is, the Fed should follow a Taylor rule of the form:

$$f_t = (r_t^* - \tau - \sigma + \pi_{t,12}) + .5^*(\pi_{t,12} - 2) - (u_t - u^*) - \eta_t \tag{11.7}$$

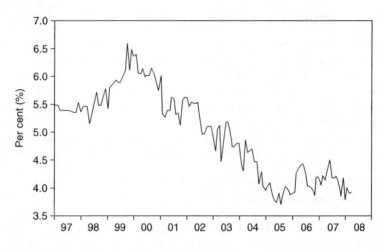

Figure 11.9   Estimated natural rate, 1997–2008

Note: Wicksellian natural rate: $r_t^* = 2*$10-year US Treasury TIPS yield − 5-year US Treasury TIPS yield +1.82.

as in the Appendix. Here the term $r_t^* - \tau - \sigma$ is the neutral real federal funds rate, which Taylor assumed to be equal to two and which we now take to vary with variation in the Wicksellian natural rate. The last term says that the Fed should offset shocks to the risk premium one-for-one with changes in the federal funds rate.

Operationalizing this Taylor rule requires estimates of r_t^*, τ, δ, and η_t. For τ and σ we use the average (over the period 1960–2008) values of the difference between the yields on 10-year US Treasury securities and the federal funds rate and the difference between the yields on Baa corporate bonds and 10-year US Treasuries, respectively. A simple back-of-the-envelope computation of the Wicksellian natural rate as perceived by participants in financial markets is the five-year forward rate implied by yields on five-year and 10-year US Treasury Inflation-Protected Securities (TIPS) plus the average risk premium on Baa corporate bonds. The risk premium shock η_t is the Baa-Treasury spread minus the average spread from 1960 to 2008.

Figures 11.9 and 11.10 show the evolution of our estimate of the Wicksellian natural rate and the risk premium shock for the period 1997–2008 (the period for which TIPS yields are available). Figure 11.9 shows an increase in the estimated natural rate of interest during the 'new economy' boom of the late 1990s followed by a substantial decline from 2000 to 2005. There is a slight increase during the housing boom of 2005–07 followed by another sharp drop beginning in the middle of 2007. In our model these movements are interpreted as fluctuations in the state of expectations among investors that produce shifts in the *IS* curve. Figure 11.10 shows a sharp increase in the

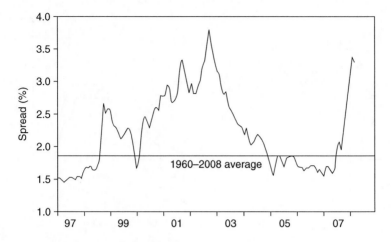

Figure 11.10   Risk premium, 1997–2008

Note: Baa corporate bond rate minus 10-year Treasury rate. Average risk premium, 1960–2008 = 1.82.

risk premium during the 1998 LTCM crisis, a return to 'normal' boom levels in 1999, and then an increase coinciding with the stock market crash of 2000 and the recession of 2001. The risk premium peaks in mid-2003, declining to near-1990s levels during the 2005–2007 housing boom. The financial crisis of 2007 brings about another sharp increase. In our model these movements are interpreted as changes in perceptions of risk that shift the *TS* curve.

Figure 11.11 compares the actual monthly federal funds rate with the rate predicted by two alternative versions of the Taylor rule described above. The first assumes that the Fed follows a conventional Taylor rule, ignoring risk premia while adjusting the neutral federal funds rate to changes in its estimate of the natural rate of interest. The second is the (Minskyan) Taylor rule recommended by our model, according to which the Fed adjusts the neutral federal funds rate one for one with shocks to the risk premium. The conventional Taylor rule cannot explain the Fed's aggressive interest rate reductions in 2001 to 2003 or in 2007–08. The Minskyan Taylor rule, by contrast, tracks the movements in the actual federal funds rate fairly well during these periods. The Minskyan Taylor rule prescribes a more aggressive tightening in 1998–2000 and 2003–05 than does the conventional Taylor rule. Neither rule, however, captures actual Fed policy during these periods. In both instances the Fed delayed raising the federal funds rate for several months after the Minskyan Taylor rule recommended a tightening, and then increased rates at a more modest pace than recommended by the rule. This analysis exposes an asymmetry in the Fed's response to changes in the risk premium: the Fed

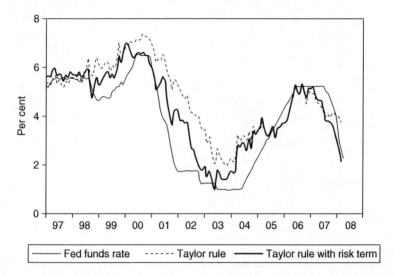

Figure 11.11   Federal funds rate and Taylor rule with and without response to risk premium shock, 2003–2008

Note: Taylor rule (no response to risk premium): $f_t^{TR} = (r_t^* + \pi_{t,12} - \tau - \sigma) + 0.5(\pi_{t,12} - \pi^*) - (u_t - u^*)$
Taylor rule (with response to risk premium): $f_t^{TR*} = (r_t^* + \pi_{t,12} - \tau - \sigma) + 0.5(\pi_{t,12} - \pi^*) - (u_t - u^*) - \eta_t$
$r_t^* =$ Wicksellian natural rate (2*10-year US Treasury TIPS yield – 5-year US Treasury TIPS yield + σ)
σ = average risk premium (Baa corporate bond rate minus 10-year Treasury rate, 1960–2008) = 1.82
$\pi_{t,12} =$ year over year core CPI inflation rate
τ = average term premium (10-year Treasury rate minus federal funds rate, 1960–2008) = 0.84
π* = target inflation rate = 2
u* = natural rate of unemployment = 5
$\eta_t =$ risk premium shock (Baa corporate bond rate minus 10-year Treasury rate)-σ

has acted aggressively to combat financial stress in periods of rising risk premia, but it has been slow to raise interest rates in response to signs of financial excess.

5   Unconventional Monetary Policy Actions

Sharp increases in the risk premium during financial crises have the potential to present the central bank with a familiar problem, that of a liquidity trap. In models that abstract from the risk premium, a liquidity trap is a rather exotic situation in which the real interest rate associated with full employment is so low that even a federal funds rate of zero cannot achieve it. In particular, if we ignore the risk premium a liquidity trap occurs when the real interest rate consistent with full employment is less than $\tau - E_t \pi_{t+1}$. For example, suppose that the term premium is 0.8 (the average over the 1960–2008 period) and inflation is expected to be 2.5 per cent, so that $\tau - E_t \pi_{t+1} = -1.7$ per cent. If a leftward shift in the *IS* curve creates a situation in which the real interest rate consistent with full employment is less than −1.7 per cent, the Fed will not be able to reduce the federal funds rate far enough to achieve full employment and the economy will be in a liquidity trap. A spike in the risk premium makes a liquidity trap much more likely. In ordinary times with a risk premium of 1.8 (the 1960–2008 average), a liquidity trap occurs if the real interest rate consistent with full employment falls below $\tau + \sigma - E_t \pi_{t+1} = 0.1$ per cent. In early 2008 the Baa ten-year Treasury spread rose to 3.4 per cent, raising the risk of a liquidity trap if the real interest rate consistent with full employment fell below 1.7 per cent.

Precisely this concern drove the Federal Reserve to introduce a number of new lending facilities in early 2008 that constitute a dramatic break from standard operating procedure. Using these facilities, namely the Term Auction Facility, the Term Securities Lending Facility, and the Primary Dealer Credit Facility, the Fed has rapidly replaced the Treasury securities on its balance sheet with agency debt (mortgage-backed securities). This manoeuvre is analogous to a central bank's using sterilized intervention to support its currency: the Fed lends reserves to the banking system taking agency debt as collateral, then offsets these purchases with sales of Treasury securities to prevent the aggregate level of reserves from rising, which would threaten its federal funds target. In the Minsky-adjusted Wicksellian model, the Fed is attempting to act directly on the risk premium in addition to lowering the federal funds rate. The Fed likewise attempts to affect the risk premium when it makes dramatic policy moves or statements. Of course, the literature on sterilized interventions suggests that the Fed's ability to manipulate the risk premium is severely limited because of the size of the market and the limited resources of the central bank. While the Minsky-adjusted Wicksellian model shows how the Fed's policies would work if successful, students can be made aware of the limitations in practice.

6 Conclusion

We have not attempted in this chapter to formalize some of the most important elements of Minskyan analysis. Wray and Tymoigne's paper in this volume (Wray and Tymoigne, 2008) present a more thorough analysis of Minsky's theories. We do not address Minsky's arguments concerning the endogeneity of attitudes toward risk. Minsky argued that there is a natural tendency for risk aversion to diminish as memories of previous financial calamity recede. Hence expansion sows the seeds of the financial crisis that brings it to an end. In modelling the risk premium as a stochastic variable we have done some violence to Minsky's theory in this respect. Another important point in Minsky's work is that increased leverage during expansions increases the financial sector's vulnerability to small disappointments of expectations. When growth in profits falls short of expectations in a highly leveraged economy, there can be a dramatic transition from boom to bust as firms seek to unwind their positions, driving down asset prices and reducing tolerance of risk. We have not attempted to model this non-linear process.

Nevertheless, the framework described here can be used to introduce undergraduate students to the complications that considerations of risk pose for macroeconomists and macroeconomic policy makers, opening the door for discussion of the finer points of Minskyan theory at an intuitive level. In doing so the framework can help students understand the important and exciting events occurring in the US economy today.

Appendix: derivation of the *TS* curve with credit risk

This appendix shows that the *TS* equation in the chapter is consistent with a standard New Keynesian, rational expectations macroeconomic model. Define ω^* to be the length of a period in months. According to the expectations theory of the term structure of interest rates modified to incorporate a term premium τ, in period t an n-month risk-free bond has a yield:

$$i_t = (\omega^*/n)[f_t + E_t \sum_{s=1}^{n/\omega^*-1} f_{t+s}] + \tau \tag{A1}$$

Let $\omega = \omega^*/n$. Then the yield becomes

$$i_t = \omega[f_t + E_t \sum_{s=1}^{1/\omega-1} f_{t+s}] + \tau \tag{A2}$$

Let $R_t = i_t - E_t \pi_{t+1}$ be the ex ante real rate of interest on the risk free bond. Substituting in the equation above, we have

$$R_t = \omega[(f_t - E_t \pi_{t+1}) + E_t \sum_{s=1}^{1/\omega-1} (f_{t+s} - \pi_{t+s+1})] + \tau \tag{A3}$$

The real risky long-term interest rate is

$$r_t = R_t + \sigma_t \tag{A4}$$

where $\sigma_t = \sigma + \eta_t$ is the risk premium, which gives us

$$r_t = \omega[(f_t - E_t \pi_{t+1}) + E_t \sum_{s=1}^{1/\omega-1} (f_{t+s} - \pi_{t+s+1})] + \tau + \sigma + \eta_t \tag{A5}$$

Suppose the Fed follows a Taylor rule of the form:

$$f_t = (r_t^* + E_t \pi_{t+1} - \tau - \sigma) + \gamma(\pi_t - \pi^*) + \delta y_t - \eta_t \tag{A6}$$

The rest of the economy is described by conventional New Keynesian *IS* and *AS* curves and an equation describing the evolution of the Wicksellian natural rate of interest:

$$y_t = -\alpha(r_t - r_t^*) + u_t \tag{A7}$$

$$\pi_t = E_t \pi_{t+1} + \theta y_t + v_t \tag{A8}$$

$$r_{t+1}^* = r_t^* + z_t \tag{A9}$$

We assume u_t, v_t, η_t, and z_t are mean zero i.i.d. shocks.

Now we compute the rational expectations equilibrium. Since the shocks are all i.i.d. and there are no lagged endogenous variables in any of the equations, the model is actually a static one. We guess that $E_t \pi_{t+1} = \pi^*$ and then verify that this guess is correct at the end. Substituting π^* for $E_t \pi_{t+1}$ in the equations above gives us:

$$y_t = -\alpha(r_t - r_t^*) + u_t \tag{A10}$$

$$\pi_t = \pi^* + \theta y_t + v_t \tag{A11}$$

$$r_t = \omega\left[(f_t - \pi^*) + E_t \sum_{s=1}^{1/\omega-1} (f_{t+s} - \pi^*)\right] + \tau + \sigma + \eta_t \tag{A12}$$

$$f_t = (r_t^* + \pi^* - \tau - \sigma) + \gamma(\pi_t - \pi^*) + \delta y_t - \eta_t \tag{A13}$$

Next update all the equations one period and take time t expectations. From the *AS* curve we know that $E_t y_{t+1} = 0$, so from the Taylor rule equation we have $E_t f_{t+s} = r_t^* + \pi^* - \tau - \sigma$. Substituting this into the term structure equation gives us:

$$r_t = \omega(f_t - \pi^*) + (1 - \omega)(r_t^* + \pi^* - \tau - \sigma) + \tau + \sigma + \eta_t \tag{A14}$$

and rearranging we have:

$$r_t = \omega(f_t - \pi^* + \tau + \sigma) + (1 - \omega)r_t^* + \eta_t \tag{A15}$$

which is the *TS* curve in the text.

We can verify that in fact $E_t \pi_{t+1} = \pi^*$ by substituting the Taylor rule equation into the *TS* curve to get:

$$r_t = r_t^* + \omega\gamma(\pi_t - \pi^*) + \omega\delta y_t - (1 - \omega)\eta_t \tag{A16}$$

Then substituting this into the *IS* curve gives:

$$y_t = -\alpha(\omega\gamma(\pi_t - \pi^*) + \omega\delta y_t - (1 - \omega)\eta_t + u_t \tag{A17}$$

$$y_t = \frac{-\alpha\omega\gamma}{1 - \omega\delta}(\pi_t - \pi^*) + \frac{\alpha(1 - \omega)}{1 - \omega\delta}\eta_t + \frac{1}{1 - \omega\delta}u_t \tag{A18}$$

Substituting this equation into the *AS* curve and rearranging gives us:

$$\pi_t - \pi^* = \frac{\alpha\theta(1 - \omega)}{1 - \omega\delta + \alpha\omega\gamma\theta}\eta_t + \frac{\theta}{1 - \omega\delta + \alpha\omega\gamma\theta}u_t + \frac{1 - \omega\beta\delta}{1 - \omega\delta + \alpha\omega\gamma\theta}v_t \tag{A19}$$

from which it follows that $E_t\pi_{t+1} = \pi^*$.

Note

1. Consider, for example, an asset that pays \$95 with probability one-half and \$105 with probability one-half. Its expected pay-off is \$100 and the variance of its pay-off is 25. An improvement in the state of expectations is an increase in the expected pay-off that does not affect the variance. For example, if the possible pay-offs rise to \$100 and \$110, the expected pay-off is now \$105 while the variance is unchanged. A decrease in risk is a decline in the variance that does not affect the mean. For example, if the possible pay-offs are \$99 and \$101, the expected pay-off is still \$100 while the variance has fallen to 1.

References

Barbera, Robert J. and Weise, Charles L. (2008), 'A Minsky/Wicksell Modified Taylor Rule', Paper presented at the 17th Annual Hyman P. Minsky Conference, April 17.

Bellofiore, Riccardo and Ferri, Piero (eds) (2001), *The Economic Legacy of Hyman Minsky* (Vols. 1 and 2), Edward Elgar.

DeLong, J. Bradford and Olney, Martha L. (2006), *Macroeconomics*, 2nd edn, Boston: McGraw-Hill Irwin.

Frank, Robert H. and Bernanke, Ben S. (2004), *Principles of Economics*, 2nd edn, Boston, MA: McGraw-Hill Irwin.

Kregel, Jan (2007), 'The natural instability of financial markets', Levy Economics Institute Working Paper no. 523 (December).

Krugman, Paul (2002), 'My economic plan', New York Times (4 October).

Lavoie, Marc (2009), 'Taming the New Consensus: Hysteresis and Some Other Post-Keynesian Amendments', in G. Fontana and M. Setterfield (eds), *Macroeconomic Theory and Macroeconomic Pedagogy*, Basingstoke: Palgrave Macmillan.

Leamer, Edward E. (2007), 'Housing is the business cycle', Federal Reserve Bank of Kansas City (October).

Minsky, Hyman P. (1975), *John Maynard Keynes*, New York: Columbia University Press.

Minsky, Hyman P. (1986), *Stabilizing an Unstable Economy*, Twentieth Century Fund Report, New Haven and London: Yale University Press.

Romer, David (2000), 'Keynesian macroeconomics without the LM curve', *Journal of Economic Perspectives*, 14, 2 (Spring), 149–69.

Taylor, John B. (1993), 'Discretion versus policy rules in practice', *Carnegie-Rochester Series on Public Policy* 39, 195–214.

Taylor, John B. (2003), *Principles of Macroeconomics*, 4th edn, Boston, MA: Houghton-Mifflin.

Weise, Charles L. (2007), 'A simple Wicksellian macroeconomic model', *B.E. Journal of Macroeconomics*: 7(1) (Topics), Article 11.

Whalen, Charles J. (2007), 'The U.S. credit crunch of 2007', Levy Economics Institute Public Policy Brief no. 92.

Wray, L. Randall (2007), 'Lessons from the subprime meltdown', Levy Economics Institute Working Paper no. 522 (December).

Wray, L. Randall and Tymoigne, Eric (2008), 'The Financial Theory of Investment', *Macroeconomic Theory and Macroeconomic Pedagogy*, Basingstoke: Palgrave Macmillan.

12
Macroeconomics Meets Hyman P. Minsky: The Financial Theory of Investment

L. Randall Wray and Eric Tymoigne

1 Introduction

In this chapter we will present a theory of the financing of investment in a modern capitalist economy. Our exposition will closely follow the approach developed by Hyman Minsky, arguably the most important contributor to our understanding of this topic. While Minsky began his research in the 1950s and continued to refine his theory until his death in 1996, his ideas are largely absent from undergraduate textbooks. In addition, his approach has been largely ignored by the mainstream of the profession even though the inclusion of some of his ideas in models similar to the New Consensus provides relevant insights (Lavoie, 2008; Weise and Barbera, 2008). This does not mean that his work was unknown, as it was long embraced by Post Keynesian economists and by Wall Street practitioners who recognized the real-world relevance of Minsky's arguments. Indeed, a few conventional economists – including some Nobel laureates (some of whom were personal friends of Minsky) – were influenced by his ideas. Still, as we prepare this chapter, there is little doubt that interest in his theory is at an all-time peak (e.g. Lahart, 2007; Chancellor, 2007; McCully, 2007). Indeed, the current financial crisis that began with a collapse of the sub-prime mortgage market in the US in 2007 provides a compelling reason to show how his approach provides students with a grounding in the workings of financial capitalism. Even if the spreading global financial crisis is successfully contained this time around, it is likely that analyses will incorporate a substantial dose of Minsky's ideas for many years to come.

It should be noted that what we present here is an alternative to the standard approach that was developed from the early 1970s, based on the 'efficient markets hypothesis'. We will not develop a detailed treatment of that theory here. Like all approaches derived from the old neoclassical theory, it relegates money and finance to the sidelines. As basic macroeconomics presented in the mainstream principles textbooks teaches, neoclassical theory presumes 'money neutrality' – the notion that at least in the long run, money only determines nominal prices. Various devices have been posited to allow money to have short run 'real' effects on relative prices, real output, levels of employment, or the composition of output. However, the market is continually striving to eliminate these non-neutralities as it seeks market clearing equilibria consistent with tastes and technologies. The primary barrier preventing market clearing is, of course, the government. The efficient markets hypothesis extends the analysis to alternative methods of financing activity. Whereas Milton Friedman had famously argued that good neoclassical analysis might as well assume that money is dropped from helicopters, orthodox finance theory tried to show that shedding that assumption would make little difference. Whether productive activity is financed by retained earnings, debt, or equity would, on the basis of 'rigorous' assumptions, be irrelevant for 'real' outcomes. As one orthodox (New Keynesian) economist puts it: 'prior to the introduction of informational asymmetries, the framework resembles a simple real business cycle model; financial structure is irrelevant' (Gertler, 1988, p. 581).

Minsky vehemently denied the relevance of such theory, at least for the modern capitalist economy with complex, expensive, and long-lived capital assets. In our kind of economy, money can never be neutral – not in the short run nor even in the long run. The method used to finance positions in assets is of critical importance both for theory as well as for real world outcomes. In particular, use of debt sets up a stream of obligations that must be fulfilled to maintain solvency. The problem is that at the time these commitments are made, neither party to the agreement can be sure that the contract for future payment will be fulfilled. Further, failure by one party to meet contractual payments can cause financial distress for the party expecting to receive payment. For this reason, one default can generate a snowball of defaults, as creditors holding bad debts fail to make good on their own debts. As defaults spread, the value of financial assets falls – since every financial asset represents a claim on an income stream or on cash expected from the sale of an underlying asset. As such, the value of each financial asset depends on the expected payments, which, if not forthcoming, causes asset values to fall.

Thus, if an unconstrained snowball of defaults affects asset prices generally, what Irving Fisher called a 'debt deflation' can take hold. Both Fisher and Minsky believed that such a process occurred during the 1930s, and that this is what made the 'Great Depression' so severe. It must be emphasized that mainstream theory rules out of existence such processes and argues in any case that deflation helps the economy by increasing real balances (and Friedman (1969) went as far as to argue that permanent deflation should be sought by central banks). As Goodhart and Tsomocos (2007) argue, 'rigorous' mainstream theory assumes that defaults never occur, meaning that deflation cannot generate a financial crisis when debtors find the real burden of debt rising because nominal prices and incomes are falling. However, Minsky and Fisher argued this is precisely what made the Great Depression so bad.

By ignoring default, mainstream economists such as Friedman can claim that financial crises are solely due to policy mistakes, not to any fundamental forces operating in modern economies. For this reason, Minsky argued that mainstream theory is irrelevant and even dangerous if it is applied to the world in which we actually live.

In the next section we present the investment theory of the business cycle developed by J.M. Keynes, and then examine Minsky's extension of that theory that added a financial theory of investment. This allowed Minsky to analyse the evolution of the modern capitalist economy over time. Indeed, the financial theory of investment plays a crucial role in Minsky's hypothesis that financially complex economies tend toward fragility – what is well-known as Minsky's financial instability hypothesis. In the subsequent section, we update Minsky's approach to finance with a more detailed examination of asset pricing and of the evolution of the banking sector. In the final section we briefly review the insights that such an approach can provide for analysis of the current global financial crisis.

2   The Investment Theory of the Cycle and Minsky's Financial Theory of Investment

Keynes's *General Theory* gave a central role to the investment decision in the determination of the aggregate level of effective demand, which in turn is the primary factor generating the equilibrium level of employment and output. As the undergraduate textbooks put it, investment is the *driving* variable that operates through a *multiplier* to establish total income. The size of the multiplier is rather mechanically calculated as the inverse of the marginal propensity to save, although more complicated expositions can take account of leakages to imports and taxes.[1] Hence, an increase of investment causes income and thus consumption to rise until saving rises to equality to the new level of investment. The level of investment is a function of the marginal efficiency of capital (essentially the discounted future profits) weighed against the market interest rate, which equilibrates the supply of and demand for money. When the marginal efficiency of capital is above 'the' market interest rate, investment is undertaken, raising income, output and employment through the spending multiplier. This proceeds until the marginal efficiency of capital falls, the interest rate rises, or some combination of the two eliminates the gap. As soon as the marginal efficiency of capital equals the interest rate, there is no advantage to investing so that the economy returns to equilibrium.

While such an exposition *can* be found in Keynes's book, this caricature does not come close to capturing Keynes's theory of investment. To really understand Keynes's theory, one must turn to chapter 17 of the *General Theory* – a rather complex exposition that is normally avoided by all but the most serious of his followers. In that chapter, the investment decision is incorporated within his liquidity preference theory of asset prices, or to put it another way, his theory of 'own rates'. He argued that 'for every durable commodity we have a rate of interest in terms of itself, – a wheat-rate of interest, a copper-rate of interest, a house-rate of interest, even a steel-plant-rate of interest' (Keynes, 1936, pp. 222–3). Each of these own rates can be stated in terms of money, which typically carries the 'greatest of the own-rates', hence, 'rules the roost' because money has special, peculiar, properties[2] (Keynes, 1936 p. 223; see also Kregel, 1997). The expected return on holding any asset measured in monetary terms is $q - c + l + a$, where q is the asset's expected yield, c is carrying costs, l is liquidity, and a is expected price appreciation (or depreciation). The total return is used to calculate a marginal efficiency for each asset, including money. The composition of returns varies by asset, with most of the return to illiquid assets such as capital consisting of $q - c$, while most of the return to holding liquid assets consists of the (subjectively evaluated) l. Finally, changing expectations differentially impact marginal efficiencies of different kinds of assets, depending on the composition of the returns. Increased confidence about future economic performance will raise the qs on capital assets while lowering the subjective values assigned to liquid positions (hence, the l falls), so the marginal efficiency of capital rises relative to that of assets that get much of their return from l. In that case, capital assets will be produced (investment rises, inducing the 'multiplier' impact) and the full range of asset prices adjusts. Thus, expectations about the future go into determining the equilibrium level of output and employment.

For example, if entrepreneurs expect that future demand for widgets will be higher, they might expect more profits in that line of business. This raises the marginal efficiency of widget-making machines, and if this exceeds the expected returns on all other assets that can be held, they will want to order the production of widget-making machines today. Production of the widget-making machines will provide wages to workers and revenues to those firms when the machines are sold. Workers in turn will spend their incomes, inducing a 'multiplier' impact on aggregate demand – leading to more employment. Some of the extra income generated will be spent on widgets, validating the expectations that led to the production of the widget-making machines. Of course, there will also be increased consumption of other kinds of output, that could raise profit expectations in other lines of business, inducing even more investment in other types of machines. Logically, investment, employment, output, and consumption can continue to grow through this process until there is no marginal efficiency of any type of machine that exceeds the expected return on liquid, financial, assets. Finally, we can see that the whole process of growth can be reversed if the expected returns of capital assets (the q less the c plus any a, as discussed above) fall *or* if the expected return to liquid assets (the l described above) rises.

Thus, we can see that his liquidity preference theory of asset prices is inextricably linked to the theory of the multiplier and thus the theory of effective

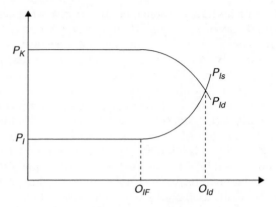

Figure 12.1   Determination of the level of investment

demand. Only if the marginal efficiency of *some* asset that can be produced using labour (plant, capital equipment, commercial and residential buildings, private infrastructure) exceeds the marginal efficiency on money will investment take place.[3] This then raises effective demand through the multiplier. The new equilibrium level of effective demand (and hence of employment, income and output) will be reached when all own rates are equal to the standard set by money's return.[4]

Minsky believed that Keynes's investment theory of the cycle is incomplete because it did not really analyse *how* investment is financed when the marginal efficiency of some capital asset exceeds the marginal efficiency of money. There seems to be an implicit assumption in the *General Theory* that the investment project *will* get funded. While Keynes did deal with this in a bit more detail in several publications after 1936, most of his effort went toward explaining why saving cannot be a source of finance. Hence, Minsky's most important contribution was to add the 'financial theory of investment' to Keynes's 'investment theory of the cycle'. Figure 12.1 provides a graphical illustration of Minsky's theory. The two key building blocks are the 'two price system', and the 'lender's and borrower's risk'. Following Keynes, Minsky distinguished between a price system for current output and one for asset prices. Current output prices can be taken as determined by 'cost plus mark-up', set at a level that will generate profits so long as the administered price can be maintained with adequate sales. Current output covers consumer goods and services, investment goods and services, exports, and even goods and services purchased by government.

In the case of investment goods, the current output price is effectively a supply price of capital – the price just sufficient to induce a supplier to provide new capital assets (P_I). However, this simplified analysis can be applied only to purchases of capital that can be financed out of internal funds (such as sales revenue from on-going operations). If external (borrowed) funds are needed, then the supply price of capital also includes explicit finance costs – most importantly the interest rate, but also all other fees and costs – that is, total supply price (P_{Is} in Figure 12.1) rises above the price administered by suppliers (P_I) due to 'lender's risk' that is covered by the finance costs of borrowed funds. In Figure 12.1, this is represented by an upward slope in the P_I-curve once investment is expected to require external funds. The quantity of investment goods that is expected to be purchased by using expected internal funds is given by the distance from the origin to O_{IF} while the external funds is equal to the distance from O_{IF} to O_{Id}.

There is a second price system for assets that can be held through time. Assets include capital assets, financial assets, and money – essentially anything that can be held through time as a store of nominal wealth. Except for money (the most liquid asset), these assets are expected to generate a stream of income and possibly capital gains.[5] Here, Minsky follows Keynes's treatment in chapter 17 described above. The important point is that the prospective income stream cannot be known with certainty, and thus depends on subjective expectations. By taking the price of old capital assets (P_K) as a point of reference, we obtain a demand price for new capital assets (P_{Id}) from this asset price system: how much would one pay for the asset, given expectations concerning the future net revenues that it can generate?

Again, however, this is too simplistic because it ignores the financing arrangements. Minsky argued that the price one is willing to pay depends on the amount of external finance required – greater borrowing exposes the buyer to higher risk of insolvency. This is why 'borrower's risk' must also be incorporated into demand prices. Unlike lender's risk, this 'cost' is solely subjectively determined and is not written into any contracts. One can think of it as a 'margin of safety': if one expects an asset to generate a stream of returns with a discounted value equal to $1 million, one would not be willing to pay more than $750,000 for the asset. The margin of safety provides a cushion ($250,000 in this case) to ensure that debt contracts created to finance the position in the asset can be serviced even if revenues turn out to be less than expected. That way, one will avoid bankruptcy unless the margin of safety proves to be too small. Obviously, there is no hard and fast rule governing the appropriate margin of safety because the borrower's risk cannot be calculated precisely for a future that is yet to unfold.

The quantity of investment goods purchased (O_{Id}) is determined where $P_{Id} = P_{Is}$, not when $P_K = P_I$.[6] The latter case is the explanation of investment developed by Tobin (1969). Tobin's q is the ratio of the market value of existing capital assets (P_K) to their replacement cost (P_I). If $q > 1$ it is cheaper for companies to buy new capital assets, i.e. to invest, rather than to buy existing capital assets (through mergers, acquisitions, or other means). If $q < 1$, investment declines as it is less costly to buy existing capital assets, so firms don't order new capital. However, Tobin's q assumes away the importance of uncertainty and funding structure for the determination of investment. Note that in Minsky's version, the demand price declines with level of investment demand, whereas the supply price increases with investment. This is due to Kalecki's principle of increasing risk, which states that, given expected internal funds and given conventions about the appropriate leverage-ratio, entrepreneurs and bankers assume that it is more and more risky to invest as the expected level of external funding increases. Thus, as the level of investment increases above O_{IF}, entrepreneurs become less willing to invest (the demand price declines as borrower's risk increases) and bankers become more and more stringent as external funding increases (the supply price increases as the lender's risk increases).

Investment can proceed only if the demand price (adjusted for borrower's risk) exceeds the supply price (adjusted for lender's risk) of capital assets. Because these prices include margins of safety, they are affected by expectations concerning unknowable outcomes. In the beginning of a recovery from a severe recession, margins are large as expectations are pessimistic; over time, if an expansion generates returns that exceed the projections these margins prove to be larger than necessary. This leads to a reduction in the perceived borrower's risk and lender's risk, which generates flatter P_{Id} and P_{Is} curves and so increases the demand for investment goods. This, in turn, means that, given the expected flow of internal funds, bankers and entrepreneurs expect and accept a higher proportion of external funding and greater investment. Thus, margins will be reduced to the degree that projects are generally successful.

Minsky created a famous taxonomy of financing profiles undertaken by investing firms: hedge (prospective income flows are expected to cover interest and principal with a safe margin); speculative (near-term income flows will cover only interest, although it is expected that finance costs will fall, that income flows will rise, or that assets can be sold at a higher price later – in which case revenues will be sufficient to cover principal); and Ponzi (near-term receipts are insufficient to cover interest payments so that debt increases because the Ponzi unit borrows to cover interest payments). Over the course of an expansion, financial stances evolve from largely hedge to include ever rising proportions of speculative and even Ponzi positions. Some Ponzi positions are undertaken voluntarily (due, for example, to expectations that debt can be refinanced at much more favourable terms, or that large capital gains can be realized from asset price appreciation), some are fraudulent (a 'pyramid' scheme is an example, in which a crook dupes ever larger numbers of suckers to provide the funds to pay the earliest participants), and some result from disappointment (revenues are lower than expected, or finance costs rise unexpectedly).

Attempts to raise leverage and to move to more speculative positions can be frustrated at least temporarily: if results turn out to be more favourable than expected, an investor attempting to engage in speculative finance could remain hedge because incomes realized are greater than were anticipated. This is because as aggregate investment rises, this has a multiplier impact on effective demand which can raise sales beyond what had been expected. Later, Minsky explicitly incorporated the Kaleckian result that in the truncated model, aggregate profits equal investment plus the government's deficit.[7] Thus, in an investment boom, profits would be increasing along with investment, helping to validate expectations and encouraging even more investment. This added strength to his proposition that the fundamental instability in the capitalist economy is upward – toward a speculative frenzy, as investment generates profits, which breeds more investment.

In addition, in the early 1960s, he had argued that impacts on private sector balance sheets would depend on the stance of the government's balance sheet (Minsky, 1963). A government-spending led expansion would allow the private sector to expand without creating fragile balance sheets – government deficits would add safe treasury debt to private portfolios even as it raised profits (through the expanded version of the Kalecki equation) and income and employment through the 'government spending multiplier'.[8] A robust expansion, however, would tend to cause revenues from progressive income taxes to grow faster than private sector income so that the government budget would 'improve' (move toward surplus) and the private sector balance would deteriorate (move toward deficit). Once he added the Kalecki equation to his exposition, he could also explain how this countercyclical movement of the budget would automatically stabilize profits – limiting both the upside in a boom (profits are squeezed by a declining budget deficit), and the downside in a slump (profits are boosted by growing budget deficits).

Further, with the Kalecki view of profits incorporated in his investment theory of the cycle, Minsky argued that investment is forthcoming today only if investment is expected in the future – since investment in the future will determine profits in the future (in the skeletal model). Because investment today produces profits to validate the decisions undertaken 'yesterday' to invest, expectations about 'tomorrow' affect ability to meet commitments that were made 'yesterday' when financing the existing capital assets. While this might sound complicated, it just means that firms need to obtain profits 'today' to satisfy the expectations they held in the past when they purchased capital. But profits 'today' will be lower if firms are not investing now (perhaps because they are pessimistic about the future). So to validate the decisions made in the past, we need investment today that in turn depends on expectations about 'tomorrow'. There is thus a complex temporal relation involved in Minsky's approach to investment that could be easily disturbed. By linking this to the 'two price' approach described above, Minsky made it clear that anything that lowers expected future profitability can push today's demand price of capital below the supply price, reducing investment and today's profits below the level necessary to validate past expectations on which demand prices were based when previous capital projects were undertaken. This also means that the margins of safety that had been included in borrower's and lender's risk can prove to be inadequate, leading to revisions of desired margins of safety going forward. As margins rise due to disappointments, the demand price of capital falls below its supply price (appropriately adjusted for lender's and borrower's risk), leading to less investment and through the multiplier to still lower output and employment. The economy can spiral ever downward into a deepening recession.

Minsky continually improved his approach to banking and finance, recognizing the futility of Fed attempts to control the money supply. This is because banks would try to avoid and evade constraints imposed by the Fed in order to obtain the profits available from providing finance to firms. He also expanded the analysis so that all entities were treated like banks – he argued that anyone can create money; the problem is to get it accepted (1986, p. 69) – acquiring assets by issuing liabilities. He argued that while the Fed had been created to act as lender of last resort, making business debt liquid (by lending against it), the Fed no longer discounted paper (1986, p. 47). Indeed, most reserves supplied by the Fed come through open market operations, which greatly restricts the Fed's ability to ensure safety and soundness of the system by deciding which collateral to accept, and by taking a close look at the balance sheets of borrowers. Instead, during the late 1970s through much of the 1980s the Fed had come to rely on Friedman's simplistic monetarist view that the primary role of the Fed is to 'control' the money supply and thereby the economy as a whole[9] – which it cannot do, as attempts to constrain reserves only induce innovative bank practices and encourage expansion of 'non-bank' sources of finance, ultimately requiring lender of last resort interventions and even bail-outs that validate riskier practices (1986, p. 94). Minsky believed that such interventions are necessary, but that they then encourage even more innovations that increase fragility. Together with countercyclical deficits to maintain demand, lender of last resort policy not only prevents deep recession, but also creates a chronic bias toward speculatory booms by market participants that believe government intervention will always bail them out.

3   Extending Minsky: Asset Prices and Finance

Asset prices play a crucial role in the determination of the investment level because the latter depends on a double arbitrage. On the one hand, following the logic of Keynes's chapter 17 presented above, it is assumed that capitalists make arbitrages among all types of assets (financial and capital assets) in order to get what is expected to be the greatest monetary return, given liquidity, maturity, and risk concerns. Contrary to the monetarist view, however, this does not mean that all assets are perfectly substitutable – the gross substitution axiom does not hold – because the logic of capitalism and uncertainty creates a preference for money and its close substitutes because they are liquid. Capitalism rewards economic activities that generate a high monetary return, and higher uncertainty lowers the qs and increase the ls as described earlier.[10] On the other hand, there is an arbitrage between old capital assets (i.e. existing capital equipment) and new capital assets (i.e. investment goods to be newly produced) and so those existing assets matter because low prices for existing assets can depress production of new assets.

The price of existing capital equipment is determined indirectly by the market quotation of shares and bonds of the owning firms and by the price at which mergers and acquisitions are settled. Aside from making a difference between marginal productivity-theory and liquidity-preference theory, one may classify the literature on asset pricing according to the assumed behaviours of individuals. This latter classification implies making a distinction among the rational, irrational and convention approaches to asset pricing. The first two of these are adopted by most analysts, while the third is more consistent with the views of Keynes and Minsky. Some authors would say that q, c, l and a are determined by 'rational' individuals who use the guidance of a priori fundamentals. This theory is closely associated with the efficient market theory and requires that informational problems exist (asymmetric information, lack of computational power or other problems) in order to explain the emergence of bubbles and of over-investment. Otherwise, according to the rational view, information is optimally used, and so asset prices are always at their fundamental value, and the level of investment is always at its optimal value: 'the primary role of the capital market is allocation of ownership of the economy's capital stock [. It is] ... a market in which prices provide accurate signals for resource allocation' (Fama, 1970, p. 383). The irrational approach argues that asset pricing is mostly done by individuals who show little concern for the existing a priori fundamentals. For some of the followers of this approach (the behavioural finance camp), this is a behavioural anomaly, but for others (e.g. J.K. Galbraith) it is a normal behaviour (albeit irrational). In any case, irrational behaviours are believed to generate waves of panics and bubbles, which lead to periods of over- and under-investment. The rational and irrational approaches have been used extensively in the mainstream literature (mostly in conjunction with the productivity-theory of asset pricing) and do provide some insights. But they miss some important points developed in chapter 12 of Keynes's *General Theory*.

As Keynes notes, asset pricing depends on 'a conventional valuation which is established as the outcome of the mass psychology of a large number of ignorant individuals' and 'this behaviour is not the outcome of a wrongheaded propensity' (Keynes, 1936, pp. 154–5). In this third theory of asset pricing, the convention theory, there are no a priori fundamentals toward which asset prices will tend inexorably. Individuals are ignorant, not because they do not know how to behave rationally, but because the future is not written in stone. It is fundamentally uncertain. In order to reduce ignorance about an unknowable future, fundamentals are created through social inter-actions in order to provide a vision of the future that justifies current decisions. This has two main implications. First, as in the irrational approach, there can be a self-fulfilling process in which the socially established fun-damental value tends toward existing asset prices – whatever prices are, individuals accept them as in some sense normal. Second, current decisions may lead to the concretization of the future contained in the convention – there may be a self-fulfilling process as the conventions cause individuals to behave in a manner such that the future unfolds as expected.

In conformity with Keynes, Minsky applied the convention approach (explicated in Keynes's chapter 12) to the liquidity-preference theory of asset price (from Keynes's chapter 17) and noted that conventional behaviours and liquidity preference go hand in hand in an uncertain world that rewards mon-etary accumulation. A rational approach to the liquidity-preference theory of asset prices (as in Tobin, 1958) applies only in a world without uncer-tainty; and an irrational approach to the same theory (Galbraith, 1961) may apply only during the periods of frenzy and panic. One may wonder what the convention approach to the liquidity-preference theory of asset prices looks like. Among the most recent authors, Wray (1992) and Orléan (1999) provide the foundation for such an approach to asset pricing. The market price of assets, as determined by q, c, l, and a, is compared to a normal price which provides an anchor for economic units. The normal price is socially determined through an imitation process that rests, not on following the pre-vious behaviour of individuals (irrational approach, cascade of information theory), but on anticipating the average opinion regarding the appropriate market price – as in Keynes's famous 'beauty contest'. Hence, the convention of a normal price provides an alternative to 'inherent' fundamentals in deter-mining expectations of price movements. If individuals in a market expect that structural changes have created an environment in which the 'normal price' should be much higher (as they did for NASDAQ stocks during the new economy boom of the late 1990s, or for real estate during the boom of the early 2000s), then a speculative boom can follow – justifying the expectations and fuelling more euphoria.

Aside from the theory of asset pricing, there have been developments in the financial system in the 1980s and 1990s that must be incorporated within the financial theory of investment. Minsky conceived his theory mostly in a compartmentalized financial system in which banks followed a commit-ment model to banking business. Within banks, there are two well-defined desks, the loan-officer desk (whose task is to judge the quality of the project proposed by potential borrowers and to attenuate the optimism of the lat-ter) and the position-making desk (whose task is to finance and to re-finance the positions in assets taken by the bank). In the commitment model, the point of the bank is to establish a long-term relationship with borrowers based on trust and recurring lending agreements, and to make money based on interest-rate spreads between deposit rates paid by banks and lending rates earned by them. This model has now been replaced by an originate-and-distribute banking model, and Minsky noted that today there are 'banks without loan officers (Minsky, 1981, p. 15). Here, banks only originate loans that are then packaged and sold, as discussed in the next section. Most of the profit-making activities have been shifted toward the position-making desk. Indeed, banks now make most of their profits from fees obtained from selling and servicing structured financial instruments (mortgage-backed securities, collateralized debt obligations, etc.) rather than from interest-rate spreads. Banks no longer look for a long-term individualized relationship with recurring borrowers; the relation is impersonal and judged in minutes through a credit-scoring method (Kregel, 2008).

This new banking model adds two additional novelties to the dynamics of the margins of safety. First, the development of financial fragility proceeds at an accelerated pace because banks and credit-rating agencies have an incentive to overestimate creditworthiness in order to stimulate the distribution of structured financial instruments. Since they won't hold the loans, default risk will be shifted to buyers of the instruments, so there are obvious incentive problems. Second, credit enhancement techniques like credit subordination, excess spread and overcollateralization allow structured financial instruments (like private-label mortgage-backed securities), to have a tranche with an AAA credit rating even though it is structured on the basis of junk assets (Adelson, 2006). Thus, a high proportion of Ponzi financing may exist from the very beginning of the economic expansion; that is, a prolonged period of expansion may no longer be necessary to explain the dynamics of margins of safety. All that is necessary is a favourable trend for the prices of the assets underlying the Ponzi financing process. Recent developments in the housing market provide a clear example of this kind of dynamic, as discussed next.

4   The Financial Theory of Investment and the Current Global Financial Crisis[11]

Chapter 24 of Keynes's *General Theory* had identified two fundamental flaws of the capitalist system: an inability to achieve full employment and excessive inequality. Minsky emphasized a third flaw implicit in Keynes's theory: instability is a normal result of modern *financial* capitalism (Minsky, 1986, pp. 101, 250). Further, stability cannot be maintained – even with appropriate policy – because it changes behaviour in ways that promote evolution toward fragility. For this reason, Minsky rejected 'Keynesian' policy that promoted 'fine-tuning' of the economy – even if policy did achieve transitory stability, that would set off processes to reintroduce instability. Hence, '[t]he policy problem is to devise institutional structures and measures that attenuate the thrust to inflation, unemployment, and slower improvements in the standard of living without increasing the likelihood of a deep depression' (1986, p. 295). However, success could never be permanent; policy would have to continually adapt to changing circumstances.

Minsky argued that the relative stability of the post-war period had led to development of Money Manager Capitalism – a much more unstable version of modern capitalism. In a prescient paper written in 1987 (Minsky, 2008), Minsky predicted the explosion of home mortgage securitization that eventually led to the US sub-prime crisis in 2007. Indeed, he was one of the few commentators who understood the true potential of securitization, or, what came to be called the 'originate and distribute' model mentioned above. Rather than holding mortgages (and other types of loans), banks would simply originate the loans and then would sell them to investors such as pension funds and hedge funds. In principle, all mortgages could be packaged into a variety of risk classes, with differential pricing to cover risk. Investors could choose the desired risk-return trade-off. Thrifts and other regulated financial institutions would earn fee income for loan origination, for assessing risk, and for servicing the mortgages. Two decades later, Minsky's predictions were validated with a vengeance, as securitization spread far beyond mortgages to include student loans, credit card debt, auto loans and leases, and a range of other debts. By mid-2008, many of these markets were hit with rising defaults far exceeding what had been expected.

Minsky (2008) had argued that securitization resulted from two developments. First, it was due to the globalization of finance, as securitization creates financial assets sold to foreign investors with no direct access to American real assets. Minsky argued that the long depression-free period that followed WWII created a global glut of managed money seeking returns. (Previous to WWII, depressions had been associated with debt deflations that wiped out financial wealth.) Packaged securities with risk weightings assigned by respected rating agencies were appealing for global investors trying to achieve the desired proportion of dollar-denominated assets. When problems began in US sub-prime securities, the financial crisis quickly spread to the rest of the world because these were included in many global portfolios.

Second, over the post-war period, the importance of banks (narrowly defined as financial institutions that accept deposits and make loans) was rapidly eroded in favour of 'markets'. (The bank share of all financial assets fell from around 50% in the 1950s to around 25% in the 1990s.) This development, itself, was encouraged by the experiment in monetarism (1979–82, that decimated the regulated – bank and thrift – portion of the sector in favour of relatively unregulated 'markets', mostly large Wall Street investment banks), but it was also spurred by continual erosion of the portion of the financial sphere that had been ceded by rules, regulations, and tradition to banks. The growth of competition on both sides of the banking business – checkable deposits at non-bank financial institutions that could pay market interest rates; and the rise of the commercial paper market that allowed firms to bypass commercial banks – squeezed the profitability of banking. Minsky (2008) observed that banks appear to require a spread of about 450 basis points between interest rates earned on assets less that paid on liabilities. This covers the normal rate of return on capital, plus the required reserve 'tax' imposed on banks (reserves are non-earning assets), and the costs of servicing customers.

On the other hand, financial markets can operate with much lower spreads because they are exempt from required reserve ratios, regulated capital requirements, and much of the costs of relationship banking. At the same time, the financial markets were freer from the New Deal regulations that had made financial markets safer. Not only did this mean that an ever larger portion of the financial sector was free of most regulations, but that competition from 'markets' forced policy-makers to relax regulations on banks. As bank competitivity was damaged, firms turned directly to managed money for finance of activities. The managed money owned by pension and hedge funds was subject to far less oversight, and did not have the same capacity to assess creditworthiness. Further, managed funds operated with far greater leverage ratios (a bank can typically leverage its own equity by a factor of about 10, while hedge funds operate with leverage ratios of 30 and sometimes much more; this means they use one dollar of their own funds and borrow \$29 to increase the size of bets). All of this greatly increased fragility of the financial system. In normal expansions, high corporate profits mean that firms can rely more on relatively safe internal funds to finance activities. However, over the expansions of the 1990s and 2000s, firms greatly increased their use of external funds, so that debt ratios grew. While the 1980s are well-known for leveraged buy-outs and use of 'junk bonds', there was actually much more 'junk' issued during the Bush, Junior, expansion after 2005.

By the time of the real estate boom in the US from the mid-1990s through 2007 that eventually led to the sub-prime mortgage crisis, there was no longer any essential difference between a 'commercial bank' and an 'investment bank'. Minsky argued (1986, p. 45) that the New Deal reforms related to home finance had been spurred by a common belief that short-term mortgages, typically with large balloon payments, had contributed to the Great Depression; ironically, the 'innovations' in home mortgage finance leading up to the speculative boom largely recreated those conditions, running the US housing sector like a huge global casino.

As we write, the US financial sector remains in a crisis that is spreading around the world. Many commentators have referred to the crisis as a 'Minsky moment', questioning whether we have become a 'Ponzi nation' (e.g. Whalen, 2008). At this point, we can surmise that the financial innovations of the past decade greatly expanded the availability of credit, which then pushed up asset prices. That, in turn, not only encouraged further innovation to take advantage of profit opportunities, but also fuelled a debt frenzy and greater leveraging. The Greenspan 'put' (belief that the Fed would not allow bad things to happen, with evidence drawn from the arranged Long-Term Capital Management rescue, as well as the quick reduction of interest rates in the aftermath of the dot.com bust), plus the new operating procedures adopted by the Fed (the New Monetary Consensus, examined in several other chapters of this volume), which include gradualism, transparency, and expectations management (meaning, no surprises) tipped the balance of sentiments away from fear and toward greed. The Clinton mid-1990s boom and the shallow 2001 recession led to a revised view of growth according to which expansions could be more robust without inflation and that recessions would be brief and relatively painless. All of this increased the appetite for risk, reduced risk premia, and encouraged ever more leverage. Much of the rosy analyses conducted during the boom relied on modern orthodox finance theory, incorporated into complex models of market behaviour based on past experience. These models appeared to show that risk was systematically reduced and shifted to those best able to bear it. With the benefit of hindsight, we can now say that risks were neither shifted nor reduced.

It is no surprise that many analysts have looked back to Minsky's writings in order to understand the nature of the current crisis. It is now commonplace to find references to Minsky's financial instability hypothesis. It is also easy to find many commentators blaming mainstream efficient markets theory for the complacency that led to the systematic underpricing of risk over the past decade. One even finds mainstream economists pronouncing that 'stability is destabilizing' – a statement that runs contrary to the whole stream of neoclassical economics, which emphasizes the supposed equilibrium-seeking nature of the market economy. Minsky argued that there *could* be forms of capitalism that would tend toward a stable equilibrium, but he insisted that modern financial capitalism with complex and expensive capital equipment would tend toward fragility, with bouts of instability. In order to understand our form of capitalism, it is necessary to recognize how investment is financed and how this can generate cyclical behaviour – that can degenerate to a debt deflation and great depression in the absence of government intervention and apt policy-making.

Notes

1. More formally, $\Delta Y/\Delta I = 1/(1 - b(1 - t) + j)$ with Y the level of national income, I the level of aggregate investment, b the marginal propensity to consume, t the income tax rate, and j the marginal propensity to import.
2. According to Keynes, money has three special properties. It has a near zero elasticity of substitution, which means that when the demand for money rises, there is little substitution into alternative assets. It also has a near zero elasticity of production, which means that when the demand for money rises, labour does not get diverted to its production (since labour is not required to produce money because it is neither mined like a metal nor grown like a crop). Finally, the carrying cost

of money is negligible – money doesn't spoil (like food), doesn't depreciate with use (like a machine), and doesn't entail huge storage costs (most money today takes the form of electrical charges on computer tapes, but even paper money is relatively cheap to store). For these reasons, an increased demand for money can become a 'bottomless sink' of purchasing power.

3. Orthodox interpretations of Keynes present this very simplistically as a relation between 'the' interest rate, and the marginal efficiency of capital. In his Chapter 17, Keynes insisted that there are as many 'own rates of interest' as there are assets. Hence, the comparison is not simply between one return to capital and one interest rate, but rather across a whole spectrum of expected returns on assets, with different components $(q - c + l + a)$ making up the returns.

4. We want to emphasize here that Keynes's notion of equilibrium is not the same as that used in orthodox analysis. For Keynes, equilibrium implies a 'state of rest' in which there is no further inducement to change one's behaviour (in this case, a position in which firms are satisfied with the level of investment and of employment and production); it does not imply that all markets have cleared. Most importantly, Keynes's notion of equilibrium does not imply full employment of labour resources, which is the key implication of the orthodox identification of equilibrium as simultaneous clearing of all markets since involuntary unemployment is ruled out by assumption. Note also that for Keynes, equilibrium is a device used to analyse the forces that determine the aggregate levels of income, employment, and output, as well as the prices of assets. There is no expectation that we will ever observe a 'state of rest' in the real world. This is why Keynes's Chapter 12, which is chock full of colourful analogies – such as 'whirlwinds of speculation' – is so important. Expectations play a critical role in determining asset prices (thus, also in determining effective demand) and these are liable to disappointment and to fluctuation. Thus, even if we ever achieved a position in which every member of the economy were satisfied with her portfolio of assets, it would be a fleeting instant. Attempts to adjust portfolios cause asset prices to change which generates shifts of spending and employment from one sector to another, and also affects the total levels of spending and employment (Kregel, 1976, 1986).

5. Currency does not pay interest, so does not generate any q. Other forms of money, including bank demand deposits, might pay a small interest rate (hence, q is above zero); what is important is that liquid assets such as money of all types are expected to pay lower yields than more illiquid assets such as corporate bonds or capital assets. Hence, where exactly we draw the dividing line between 'money' and other types of assets is not important for this analysis. We can think of a spectrum of liquidity, with currency at one end, and factories with machinery at the other end.

6. Note that if these two curves are horizontal (no lender's or borrower's risk), then there is no intersection unless they lie on top of one another. For all other situations, investment would be either infinite or non-existent.

7. Following national accounting identities one has:

$$W + \Pi + T \equiv C + I + G + X - J$$

with Π the gross profit of firms after corporate tax, W employees' disposable wage income, T taxes, C the consumption level (of capitalists and workers), I the level of investment, G the level of government spending, X exports and J imports. Subtracting W and T from each side, and defining C_C the consumption of capitalists (so that consumption is divided between capitalist consumption and worker consumption out of wages, C_W) one gets:

$$\Pi = C_C - S_W + I + DEF + NX$$

With S_W the saving level of wage earners ($S_W = W - C_W$), *DEF* the government fiscal deficit, and *NX* net exports. Kalecki (1971, pp. 78–9) derived a causal relation out of the identity (thus transforming the identity into an equality) by arguing that Π is not under the control of firms whereas variables on the right side depend on discretionary choices.

8. The government spending multiplier is exactly analogous to the investment spending multiplier.

9. Friedman argued that money is the primary driving variable of nominal output; if the central bank would keep money growth constant, nominal GDP growth would also be stabilized. This led to his famous money rule: target money growth at some low and stable rate such as 4% per year, which the central bank could supposedly achieve by restraining growth of bank reserves.

10. According to neoclassical theory, capital earns a return equal to its marginal productivity – a physical, technologically determined, output. Keynes and Minsky reject this relation, arguing that in a capitalist economy what is important is the monetary return, that is, the expected money profits to be generated by owning and operating capital assets. According to Keynes, the productivity theory of asset pricing only applies to a co-operative economy – and as Keynes argued, this is one in which money might exist, but it doesn't matter.

11. Note that this section draws heavily on Wray (2008).

References

Adelson, M. (2006), 'MBS basics', Nomura Securities International Inc., Research Paper, March 31.

Chancellor, E. (2007), 'Ponzi Nation', *Institutional Investor*, 7 February.

Fama, E.F. (1970), 'Efficient capital markets: A review of theory and empirical work', *Journal of Finance*, 25 (2), 383–417.

Friedman, M. (1969), 'The optimum quantity of money', in M. Friedman (ed.), *The Optimum Quantity of Money and Other Essays*, 1–50, Chicago: Aldine.

Galbraith, J.K. (1961), *The Great Crash*, 3rd edn, Cambridge, MA: Riverside Press.

Gertler, M. (1988), 'Financial structure and aggregate economic activity: An overview', *Journal of Money, Credit and Banking*, 20 (3), Part 2, 559–88.

Goodhart, C.A.E. and Tsomocos, D.P. (2007), 'Analysis of financial stability', seminar paper presented at the Fondation Banque de France, 20 February, 2008.

Kalecki, M. (1971), 'The determinants of profits', in Kalecki, M. (ed.), *Selected Essays on the Dynamics of the Capitalist Economy*, Cambridge: Cambridge University Press, 78–92.

Keynes, J.M. (1936), *The General Theory of Employment, Interest and Money*, London: Macmillan

Kregel, J.A. (1976), 'Economic methodology in the face of uncertainty: The modelling methods of Keynes and the Post-Keynesians', *Economic Journal*, 86 (342), 209–25.

Kregel, J.A. (1986), 'Conceptions of equilibrium: The logic of choice and the logic of production', in Kirzner, I. (ed.), *Subjectivism, Intelligibility, and Economic Understanding*, 157–70, New York: New York University Press; reprinted in P. Boettke and

D. Prychitko (eds) (1998), *Market Process Theories*, vol. 2, 89–102, Northampton: Edward Elgar.

Kregel, J.A. (1997), 'Margins of safety and weight of the argument in generating financial crisis', *Journal of Economic Issues*, 31 (2), 543–8.

Kregel, J.A. (2008), 'Minsky's cushions of safety: Systemic risk and the crisis in the U.S. subprime mortgage market', Levy Economics Institute, Public Policy Brief no. 93/2008.

Lahart, J. (2007), 'In time of tumult, obscure economist gain currency', *Wall Street Journal*, 18 August, page A1.

Lavoie, M. (2008), 'Taming the New Consensus: Hysteresis and some other Post-Keynesian amendments', in this volume.

McCulley, P. (2007), 'The plankton theory meets Minsky', Global Central Bank Focus, PIMCO Bonds, March 2007, www.pimco.com/leftnav/featured+market+ commentary/FF... (accessed 3/8/2007).

Minsky, H.P. (1963), 'Discussion', *American Economic Review*, 53 (2), 401–12.

Minsky, H.P. (1981), 'Financial markets and economic instability, 1965–1980', *Nebraska Journal of Economics and Business*, 20 (4), 5–16.

Minsky, H.P. (1986), *Stabilizing an Unstable Economy*, New Heaven: Yale University Press.

Minsky, H.P. (2008), 'Securitization', Levy Economics Institute, Policy Note no. 2008/2.

Orléan, A. (1999), *Le Pouvoir de la Finance*, Paris: Odile Jacob.

Tobin, J. (1958), 'Liquidity preference as behavior towards risk', *Review of Economic Studies*, 25 (2), 65–86.

Tobin, J. (1969), 'A general equilibrium approach to monetary theory', *Journal of Money Credit and Banking*, 1(1), 15–29.

Weise, C.L. and Barbera, R.J. (2008), 'Minsky meets Wicksell: Using the Wicksellian model to understand the twenty-first century business cycle', in this volume.

Whalen, C.J. (2008), 'Understanding the credit crunch as a Minsky moment', *Challenge*, 51 (1), 91–109.

Wray, L.R. (1992), 'Alternative theories of the rate of interest', *Cambridge Journal of Economics*, 16 (1), 69–89.

Wray, L.R. (2008), 'Lessons from the subprime meltdown', *Challenge*, 51 (2), 40–68.

Part IV
The Real Interest Rate, Income Distribution, and Alternative Views of Stabilization Policies

13
Teaching the New Consensus Model of 'Modern Monetary Economics' from a Critical Perspective: Pedagogical Issues

John Smithin

1 Introduction

The evolution of the textbook treatment of macroeconomics and monetary economics would be a fascinating subject in its own right, for anyone with the time and energy to pursue it. From the publication of the first modern textbooks in the late 1940s, up to the early 1970s, so-called 'Keynesian' models,[1] stressing the importance of aggregate demand, were the order of the day (even if some bore little resemblance to anything in the writings of J.M. Keynes). Then, from roughly the late 1970s to the early 1990s, standard textbook fare was clearly based on monetarism,[2] the twentieth-century version of the quantity theory of money, actually with something of a lag compared to events in the real world, as in practice central banks had been forced to abandon the monetary targeting experiments of the 1979–82 period almost as soon as they had started. Finally, from the mid-1990s onwards a new textbook orthodoxy has developed in the form of a simple three-equation neo-Wicksellian model, the most salient features of which are that the monetary policy instrument is an interest rate (the 'policy rate'), and that the supply of money and credit becomes endogenous. The reason for this latest change is that it became impossible for textbook orthodoxy to go on making statements to the effect that central banks 'cannot control interest rates' and so on, at a time when the central banks themselves were saying and doing the opposite (for example, by posting interest rate targets on their websites and publicizing any changes), and questions of interest rate policy had become close to an obsession in the news media dealing with financial affairs. It is the Wicksellian element in 'modern monetary economics' that is meant to be the face saver. There is still supposed to be a 'natural rate' of interest somewhere in the model that eludes control of the central bank, and even though, admittedly, this cannot be observed in reality, it is still supposed to exert a decisive influence behind the scenes. Economic outcomes are made to hinge on any discrepancy between the policy rate and the quasi-mythical 'natural rate'.

The current state of textbook orthodoxy provides a number of difficult pedagogical challenges for those remaining economics instructors who teach their material from a critical perspective, not least because some heterodox schools of thought, such as the Post Keynesians, have been insisting on such issues as the endogeneity of money for many years. The belated acceptance of this point by orthodoxy should not, however, take the wind out of their sails, as there is still the issue of the natural rate of interest to deal with. (There is a difference, that is to say, between Wicksellian economics and Keynesian economics.) There are, however, two remaining issues of pedagogy that do seem to require attention. First, note that the standard expositions of the textbook material are themselves typically not very effective; they do not draw attention to what to a more critical eye would seem to be the key points. Their authors do not seem to be particularly comfortable or familiar with notions of endogenous money and credit creation, even though they have now been forced upon them. There is, therefore, a need for a more informed exposition even of the orthodox approach. Second, it also seems necessary to put forward an explicit alternative approach, ideally also in the form of a three-equation model, that directly confronts the standard model and shows the ways in which it can be modified to achieve more realistic results. This is a more effective strategy for a potential critic than simply harping on the weaknesses of the orthodox approach itself. In what follows, therefore, the objective of this chapter is to set out a simple line of approach that achieves both these aims.

2   The 'New Consensus' on Monetary Policy

Following on from the above remarks, the purpose of this section is to present a modified or revised version of the New Consensus model. This will illustrate the main points, but will be free from some of the expositional deficiencies identified above. The model is based on material previously presented in Barrows and Smithin (2006, pp. 191–8), a short textbook for MBA students.

Obviously, to call any theoretical tendency a consensus does run the risk of exaggeration. As mentioned, other terms that have been used in early twenty-first century textbooks are phrases such as 'modern macroeconomics' (Taylor, 2000, 2007), 'modern monetary economics' (Cecchetti, 2006), or similar. Essentially, it means the approach to macroeconomics that was widely accepted in academia, central banks, finance ministries and research institutes, for policy-making and theoretical discussion, around the beginning of the twenty-first century. It goes without saying that a 'consensus' on any topic does not necessarily imply that is it 'true', scientifically accurate, or not subject to rational criticism. It just means that it has majority support within the relevant peer group at a particular point in time. From the point of view of the student, it is necessary to learn this material simply to get some idea of the thought process that is currently going in mainstream academic and policy-making circles.

In terms of first principles, and in spite of the advertised break with monetarism, the current consensus is not all that much different from its predecessor or, for that matter from the whole traditional lineage of classical and neoclassical economic thinking. It is simply the latest development of this current of thought. Low inflation, 'sound money' and fiscal prudence are given pride of place over other possible economic objectives. Economic growth itself is thought to depend entirely on 'supply side' factors that determine another supposedly 'natural' rate, a natural rate of real GDP growth for each economy. This natural growth rate is admittedly not immutable. It may possibly be changed or improved upon in any particular case, but *only* as a result of technical change or improvements in productivity. Changes on the demand side, for example, those due to changes in monetary or fiscal policy, may be allowed to have some strictly temporary effects on the business cycle, but are nonetheless confidently believed to have *no* lasting impact on the underlying growth rate. All this is, of course, very familiar. The implication is that the main difference from traditional ideas is really only the recognition that central banks conduct monetary policy via changes in interest rates rather than directly setting the quantity of money. The central bank sets the 'policy-related' interest rate, and the money supply then adjusts endogenously as a result of the subsequent lending and borrowing activities of the commercial banks and the public. This idea may not have been a revelation in the financial markets, or to heterodox economists such as the Post Keynesians, but it did require some adjustments to what had become conventional academic economic thinking. In particular, it required the construction of an economic model making no reference to some deeply ingrained traditional concepts, money demand and supply, the *LM* curve, the velocity of circulation of money, etc.

For most economists with a conventional academic training a major problem with the idea that the interest rate, as such, can be a *policy* variable, is that, according to the usual way of looking at things, interest rates should be determined in a market just like any other price (the market for 'loanable funds'). If, on the contrary, we are arguing that the central bank is setting the interest rate, there is no guarantee that their target will conform to the theoretical market equilibrium. It will typically either be lower or higher than this hypothetical benchmark. In the latter case what is happening is that the central bank is directly or indirectly making additional funds available by credit creation to satisfy the demand for finance at that level, regardless of the amount of current saving. This is bound to cause difficulties for most economists with a conventional academic training, as it was a basic tenet of orthodox economics to deny that this was possible (Humphrey, 1993, pp. 35–44). Nonetheless, if they are to subscribe to the New Consensus economists must reluctantly accept something like this analysis. This is the main reason why it is also deemed necessary to bring back the concept of the Wicksellian natural rate of interest, in spite of the additional confusion that this causes. The idea is to salvage at least *something* of the notion of a market-determined interest rate.

There are other possible caveats to the idea that the central bank rather than the 'market' determines the general level of interest rates. It is true, for example, that the central bank only controls one specific interest rate, and a very short-dated one at that. For monetary policy to be the decisive factor, it must therefore be argued that there is some well-defined 'transmissions mechanism', whereby changes in the policy rate eventually feed through to other rates in the system. Also, it can always be claimed (and is sometimes claimed) by the central banks themselves that they only follow rather than lead the market in interest rate changes. As against both of these arguments, however, in the modern world a brief glance at the business press or internet sites dealing with financial matters will soon reveal headlines about the central bank 'hiking' (increasing) or 'cutting' (decreasing) interest rates, apparently of their own accord, or simply leaving them unchanged (which is also newsworthy).

Once the doctrinal difficulties have been overcome, the basic framework for policy analysis in the New Consensus model is revealed to consist of just three macroeconomic relationships. First, a demand function that resembles a traditional *IS* curve, namely:

$$y = d - \varepsilon r, \qquad \varepsilon > 0 \qquad (13.1)$$

stating that output growth depends positively on a demand parameter d, that can be defined as 'autonomous demand' as a percentage of GDP, and negatively on the real rate of interest. For policy analysis, the demand parameter can be taken to include fiscal policy actions, and the negative interest rate effect arises because a higher real interest rate will cause a decrease in investment expenditure as a percentage of GDP. One important point to notice about this specification is that it relates the growth rate to the real interest rate, rather than just the level of output to the interest rate, as in a standard *IS* curve. This difference is important if the objective of the exercise is to comment on the real world policy debate. Typically, research reports on the economy from financial institutions or brokerage houses will *not* refer to the behaviour of either the price level or the level of output, but rather precisely to the inflation rate and the rate of economic growth. A forecast will say something like 'growth will pick up in the next quarter (or year)', or 'inflationary pressures are rising', and so on. The typical textbook model is therefore unrealistic to the extent that it works in levels rather than rates of growth in the derivation of concepts like the *IS* curve. Equation (13.1) recasts the discussion in dynamic terms, i.e. in language more familiar to 'market watchers' in the real world. The details of how equation (13.1) is derived are given in the appendix below.

The second important relationship in the New Consensus model is a short-run supply function that is essentially a short-run Phillips curve (SRPC), or rather (if it relates inflation to output growth rather than unemployment), an 'accelerationist' inflation equation. The version used here, in equation (13.2) below, states that inflation in the current period will increase if the rate of GDP growth in the previous period was greater than the supposed natural rate, and that inflation will continue to increase as long as the discrepancy is maintained. Once again, it is important to note that equation (13.2) specifically relates inflation to growth, rather than (e.g.) the price level to the level of output, and can therefore be related directly to the expression explaining demand growth in equation (13.1):

$$p - p_{-1} = \beta(y_{-1} - y^N), \qquad \beta > 1 \tag{13.2}$$

An important technical point to notice is that is if inflation depends only on past events, as it does in equation (13.2), the dynamic short-run supply curve (SRAS) will actually come out flat, thus giving the model at least some Keynesian properties, if only in the short run. However, equation (13.2) also makes it clear that the SRAS will not stay in place in subsequent periods, so that these features will always disappear in the long run.

The third and final element of the New Consensus model is a central bank reaction function, such as:

$$r = r_0 + \gamma(p - p^*), \qquad 0 < \gamma < 1 \tag{13.3}$$

This is a simplified or truncated version of the much-discussed 'Taylor rule' for monetary policy (Taylor 1993), and states that the central bank will increase the *real* policy rate if the inflation rate is higher than some arbitrary target level p^* (and *vice versa*). In effect, the monetary policy is one of inflation targeting. As the actual policy instrument must be a nominal interest rate (as mentioned usually a nominal overnight rate), in practice 'increasing the real policy rate' must therefore mean increasing the policy instrument by more than one-for-one whenever there is an increase in observed inflation. Mankiw (2001), for example, has called this the 'Taylor principle' (as opposed to Taylor rule), and this willingness to actually *increase* real rates when deemed necessary (rather than simply respond to inflation) plays a crucially important role in the political economy of the new consensus.

Substituting (13.3) into (13.1), re-arranging (13.2), and invoking the equilibrium condition that the actual growth rate of real GDP converges to the natural rate in the long run, it is possible to construct a simple aggregate demand and supply model (in inflation-growth space), for both the short run and the long run as follows:

$$p = [(1/\varepsilon\gamma)d + p^* - (1/\gamma)r_0] - (1/\varepsilon\gamma)y \qquad \text{(AD)} \qquad\qquad (13.4)$$

$$p = p_{-1} + \beta(y - y^N) \qquad\qquad\qquad \text{(SRAS)} \qquad\qquad (13.5)$$

$$y = y^N \qquad\qquad\qquad\qquad\qquad \text{(LRAS)} \qquad\qquad (13.6)$$

The model therefore consists of an aggregate demand relationship (*AD*) between the growth rate and the inflation rate, a flat short-run supply function (SRAS), and a vertical long-run supply function (LRAS) that is simply the equilibrium condition.

The derived demand relationship in (13.4) shows a downward sloping demand-side relation in inflation/growth (p, y) space obtained by substituting the monetary policy reaction function into the dynamic *IS* curve. It is important to note that this implies that the negative relation between growth and inflation is therefore due *solely* to the assumed response of monetary policy. It only occurs because whenever (e.g.) inflation increases, the central bank will raise interest rates and thereby reduce demand.

Altogether there are three 'shift variables' for the constructed demand function in equation (13.4). First, there is the demand parameter, d, taken to include such things as fiscal policy (changes in the government budget deficit), as well as the 'animal spirits' of the private sector. An increase in d increases overall demand growth. Second, the inflation target itself, p^*. A lower (more stringent) inflation target must reduce demand because the central bank will need to raise real interest rates in the attempt to achieve it (and *vice versa*). The inflation target itself is therefore one indicator of the stance of monetary policy. Another such indicator, potentially, is the intercept term in central bank reaction function r_0, which we now label the 'base interest rate'. This is the third shift variable in the demand function. Note, however, that the r_0 term has a rather ambiguous status in the modern textbook treatments. Most of the textbooks seem to think of this as representing the Wicksellian natural rate of interest itself, meaning by this the real rate of interest that supposedly would exist even in a barter capital market in the absence of any such things as money and central banks. *If* that were true, then it obviously could not be changed by monetary policy, and from the point of view of the central bank would just have to be taken as given. This textbook interpretation of the r_0 term, however, seems far removed from reality. There is no way for central banks to know beforehand what the hypothetical natural rate should be, and also serious questions as to whether it is even a meaningful concept in the first place. In any practical application of equations (13.3) or (13.4), therefore, the r_0 term can only be some number that is chosen by the central bank on the basis of experience, 'rules of thumb', political expediency, or similar. As such it can always be changed, and the r_0 term itself then becomes simply another indicator of the overall monetary

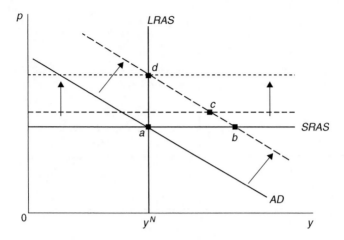

Figure 13.1 The effects of a demand expansion

policy stance. Whenever the base rate is lowered (raised) this represents an expansionary (contractionary) monetary policy, as actual real interest rates must also be lowered (raised) in order to accommodate the change in view.

As an illustration of how demand changes will work out in this framework, the graph in Figure 13.1 shows the impact of an increase in the parameter d, for example. This figure looks quite similar to those that have been used in the textbook analysis of fiscal policy for many decades now (actually since the first academic reaction against Keynesian ideas dating from the late 1970s). Moreover, this is not surprising, as the basic economic philosophy remains unchanged. The main difference in the New Consensus model is really only in the interpretation of what is occurring behind the scenes as far as the monetary policy response is concerned. It must now be conceded that some part of the response to a demand expansion is actually deliberately caused by the monetary policy reaction, rather than just by the 'market'. The argument remains, nonetheless, that a demand expansion may cause an initial boom in the economy, shown here by an outward shift of the demand function from point 'a' to point 'b', but that this will inevitably fade away over time, leaving only higher inflation as the end result. The *SRAS* curve will gradually shift upwards, and with each shift the growth rate will fall back and the inflation rate will rise, for example as at point 'c' in the first instance. The central bank is raising interest rates with each increase in the inflation rate, which slows the economy at each stage. The process will continue until the new long-run equilibrium is reached at point 'd', with no lasting effect on the growth rate, but only higher inflation. In terms of political economy, the point of this argument is obviously to suggest that that there should be no attempt to stimulate the economy in the first place.

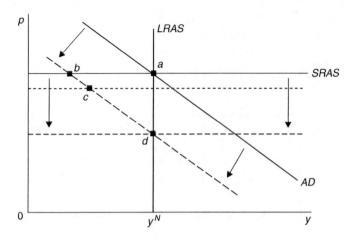

Figure 13.2   A lower inflation target

A second graphical example, in Figure 13.2, shows what occurs in the New Consensus model when the inflation target itself is revised downwards. Figure 13.2 is therefore an example of a 'tight' monetary policy in this context.

Evidently, as a result of this policy stance, the central bank will first need to raise the real policy rate in the attempt to hit the target. The demand schedule moves back and to the left, and there will be a monetary policy-induced recession at point '*b*'. But, then, however, or so the argument goes, a downward adjustment of expectations must take place. The *SRAS* will begin to shift downward, inflation will fall, and the central bank will be able to reduce the interest rate once again. Thereafter, the growth rate will begin to increase from its low point, and there will be series of ever more favourable temporary equilibria, such as that at point '*c*'. The process will continue until a new long-run equilibrium is reached at point '*d*'. The end result will indeed be a lower actual rate of inflation, and there need be no permanent reduction in the rate of economic growth. One interesting point, however, is that the original inflation target itself is never actually achieved. A lower target does reduce the final inflation rate, but, unless the r_0 term is adjusted as well, the target itself will be elusive. The final equilibrium rate of inflation in Figure 13.2, although lower than before, still does not conform to the target (see equation 13.8 below). Nonetheless, the political economy behind the narrative is evidently to convince the public that inflation targeting is a desirable policy objective, in spite of the initially depressing impact on jobs and employment. In the long run, it is argued, there will be no such negative effects.

We can summarize the basic equilibrium results of the new consensus model as follows. In the long run, the growth rate will always conform to the natural rate. That is:

$$y = y^N \qquad (13.7)$$

meanwhile, the equilibrium inflation rate will be determined by

$$p = (1/\varepsilon\gamma)d - (1/\gamma)r_0 + p^* - (1/\varepsilon\gamma)y^N \qquad (13.8)$$

Therefore, any demand expansion, such as an increase in the budget deficit, will ultimately only lead to inflation. Conversely, a 'tougher' inflation target will always lead to a one-for-one decrease in the actual inflation rate, even if the target itself is not actually achieved. A tighter monetary policy as a result of an increase in base rate of interest r_0, also reduces the inflation rate, again without any long run negative impact on the growth rate. The final influence on inflation is the natural rate of economic growth itself. An increase in the natural rate of growth (e.g., as a result of technical progress), will reduce the inflation rate.

The model also determines the actual level of the real interest rate that will prevail in equilibrium. This is given by

$$r = (1/\varepsilon)(d - y^N) \qquad (13.9)$$

Hence, a demand increase always tends to raise interest rates, and this result is consistent with some traditional arguments in neoclassical economics (e.g.) about the 'crowding out' effect. However, the mechanism by which this occurs is not so much a question of 'market forces' (as would have been argued in traditional theory), but actually the deliberate monetary policy response of the central bank. The increase in the real rate of interest would not occur if the central bank did not respond, and it is therefore only the response of the central bank that is 'validating' the neoclassical result in this instance. The other main determinant of the real rate of interest is the natural rate of growth itself, and an increase in the natural growth rate will tend to reduce the real rate of interest. Although a more traditional argument might have been that a higher natural rate of growth would justify a *higher* interest rate, the opposite occurs here simply because an increase in growth will reduce inflation, and hence 'allows' the central bank to reduce interest rates.

A final question to ask of the New Consensus model is what would actually be required to occur to achieve a *zero* inflation rate, that is, stable prices, in this setting. From (13.7) and (13.8), it can be seen that not only must p^* (the target) be set at zero, but *also* the intercept term in the monetary policy rule must continuously be adjusted, so that in the end:

$$r_0 = (1/\varepsilon)(d - y^N) \qquad (13.10)$$

Comparing (13.10) with (13.9), the implication is that the base rate of interest and the actual equilibrium interest rate must be equal if price stability is to be achieved. It is in this sense only that the final value of the r_0 term in equation (13.10) could be called a 'natural rate', that is, only if we *define* the natural rate as the rate consistent with zero inflation. However, it cannot be called a 'natural' rate in the other sense discussed above, that is a rate somehow uniquely determined outside of the monetary model via barter exchange. It is true that, if and when r_0 and r coincide (and if the inflation target is zero), then the inflation rate will also be zero. However, there is nothing in the system that prevents either the equilibrium interest rate, or the equilibrium inflation rate, from taking on quite different values at any time.

3   An Alternative Monetary Model

There are obviously a number of features about the new consensus model that many students will find unsatisfactory. Although it may be conceded that the exposition here has smoothed off some of the more obvious rough edges, the main objection that will occur to the intelligent layperson still remains. This is simply the incongruity of treating a *social* system, such as economy, as if it were actually a mechanical device that always springs back to some pre-determined equilibrium position. This problem may actually be invisible to the trained economist because of many years of study of mathematical methods drawn from the history of the natural sciences, but it frequently is very puzzling to the thoughtful beginning student, who will most likely initially approach the economic problem not from the standpoint of something like 19th-century theoretical physics, but from the commonsense viewpoint of either historical experience or of current affairs.

As it happens, however, it is a reasonably straightforward exercise to come up with an alternative framework that (while still using a 'mathematical' three-equation system as an expository device and for comparison purposes) is nonetheless able to get away from the idea of supposed 'natural rates' of either real economic growth, the real interest rate or the unemployment rate. The following system, for example, is readily comparable to the earlier one from equations (10.5) to (10.7) above, but does not have the natural rate feature:

$$p = [(1/\varepsilon\gamma)d + p^* - (1/\gamma)r_0] - (1/\varepsilon\gamma)y \quad \text{(AD)} \tag{13.11}$$

$$p = p_0 - a + w_0 + \eta y_{-1} \quad \text{(SRSI)} \tag{13.12}$$

$$p = p_0 - a + w_0 + \eta y \quad \text{(LRSI)} \tag{13.13}$$

In the new system, equation (13.11) is the same aggregate demand relationship as in equation (13.4) above, and, although it would have been possible to derive a more comprehensive description of the demand side from various sources in the heterodox economics literature (see, for example, Atesoglu and Smithin (2006, 2007) and Smithin (2009), for the present exercise the same AD function as before is retained for comparison purposes.

Equations (13.12) and (13.13), on the other hand, are quite different from their counterparts in the system of equations in (13.4) through (13.6), and are also labelled differently. Instead of referring to the long-run and short-run supply of *output*, the terminology is changed to refer the long-run and short-run supply of *inflation* (LRSI and SRSI). The starting point for both (13.13) and (13.14) is a simple mark-up pricing equation at the aggregate level, such as:

$$P = kWN/Y \qquad (13.14)$$

Here P is the aggregate price level, k is the average mark-up or profit share, WN is the aggregate nominal wage bill, and Y is real GDP. Instead of being derived from neoclassical microeconomics, this representation of the 'supply side' is therefore essentially similar to that found in the Kaleckian and Post Keynesian literatures. The macro pricing equation in (13.14) is conceived of as an aggregation or summation of the separate pricing equations of the individual firms, and the implication is that the dominant market structure is best characterized as an environment of generalized 'imperfect competition', rather than the textbook notion of 'perfect competition'. As recently explained by Smithin (2007, 112–13) this simple, but realistic, change in the premises of the model is actually all that is necessary to remove any question of the long-run neutrality of money, or of the existence of supposed natural rates of any of the economic variables.

Next, suppose that the wage bargaining process is such that that the average level of money wages, W, is given by:

$$W = P_{-1}(W/P)^* \qquad (13.15)$$

This means it is assumed that those involved in the wage bargaining process have a target real wage $(W/P)^*$ they ultimately wish to achieve, but in practice all they can do is negotiate a current money wage that 'catches up' to any increase in the price level that occurred in the previous period. The aim therefore is to set W/P_{-1} always equal to $(W/P)^*$. This is a similar sort of specification of the wage bargaining process to that often seen in the 'conflict inflation' literature,[3] and explains the use of the phrase 'supply of inflation' in describing equations (13.12) and (13.13) above. The conflict between the different parties to the wage bargaining process is what is causing ('supplying') the inflation that occurs in an endogenous money environment. By substituting (13.15) into (13.16), it is then possible to derive an explicit expression for the evolution of the price level, as:

$$P = [kP_{-1}(W/P)^*N]/Y \qquad (13.16)$$

The price level is therefore determined by the conflict over income shares between firms, trying to achieve a mark-up k, and workers, aiming for a real wage of $(W/P)^*$. Taking logs of (13.16) gives the inflation equation itself as:

$$p = p_0 + w^* - a \qquad (13.17)$$

where $p = lnP - lnP_{-1}$, $p_0 = lnk$, $w^* = ln(W/P)^*$, and $a = ln(Y/N)$.

A final step is then to include a 'wage curve' to explain the evolution of the target real wage itself, such as:

$$w^* = w_0 + \eta y_{-1}, \quad \eta > 0 \qquad (13.18)$$

which suggests that the target real wage will be revised upwards for the current period if the economy was experiencing a positive rate of growth in the previous period. The wage bargainers are therefore counting on an increased demand for labour in such circumstances. The intercept term in the wage curve, w_0, can now be called the 'base real wage rate' symmetrically with the notion of the 'base interest rate' in equation (13.11). To complete the model, substitute (13.18) back into (13.17) to yield the SRSI curve, (13.13). The LRSI curve, (13.12), is then simply the same relationship without time subscripts (that is, it is the long-run relationship between growth and inflation on the supply side).

The best way to sharpen the comparison between the alternative monetary model and the New Consensus version is now to repeat the analysis of the two graphical examples previously studied, that is, a demand expansion versus a 'tight money' policy in the form of a tougher inflation target. Figure 13.3, for example, illustrates the case of a demand expansion.

Once again, a demand expansion causes an initial boom in the economy in the short run. The demand function shifts outwards, and the economy moves from point 'a' to point 'b'. It remains true that the boom will soon start to put upward pressure on the inflation rate, and that, therefore, the high growth at 'b' cannot be sustained. The SRSI curve will shift upwards over time, and with each shift the growth rate will fall back and the inflation rate will rise, as initially at point 'c'. The *short-run* behaviour of the alternative model is therefore quite consistent with that of the 'modern macroeconomics' model discussed above. However there is difference in the longer term, because now the boom caused by a demand expansion is never *entirely* dissipated in inflation. The final equilibrium is at point 'd' (not back to the original starting point), which does imply a higher inflation rate than there was originally (essentially because of the unavoidable impact on costs of increased economic activity), but also a permanently higher growth rate. The demand expansion therefore has had a lasting effect on growth, though the final growth rate is not as high as at the peak of the boom. Nonetheless, the long run 'Phillips curve' is *not* vertical and we are back in a realm in which there does exist a

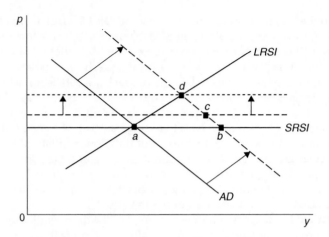

Figure 13.3 A demand expansion in the alternative monetary model

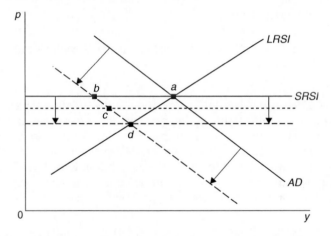

Figure 13.4 A lower inflation target in the alternative monetary model

long-run 'trade-off' between inflation and economic growth. To this extent, therefore, the model restores basic 'Keynesian' insights for the longer term as well as in the short run.

The graphical example in Figure 13.4, meanwhile, shows the impact of a tougher inflation target in the alternative model. The effect of a more stringent inflation target will certainly be to lower the actual inflation rate, even though, as was the case in the new consensus model, the target itself p^*, will not be achieved. It can now also be seen, however, that the price of pursuing this policy is that the economy will fall back to a lower long-run growth path. A reduction in p^* shifts the AD curve back and to the left, and there is initially a growth recession along the SRSI to point 'b'. It is true that the recession itself will then start to reduce wage pressures, the inflation rate will fall, and the growth rate will start to pick up again, e.g. back to point 'c' to start with. Also, as inflation begins to fall, the central bank will 'feel able' to lower real interest rates once again and hasten the recovery on its way. However, in spite of the recovery from the extreme low point, the final equilibrium growth rate never does recover back to its original level. The end result of the inflation targeting exercise is therefore not only lower inflation, but *also* a lower average growth rate, as the economy moves along the path 'a', 'b', 'c', 'd'. If the problem came to be understood in this way in the political arena, it is obvious that inflation targeting policies might not be as high on the agenda as they seem to have been in recent years.

As illustrated by these two graphical examples, the final equilibrium results of the alternative monetary model typically differ from those of the new consensus, even if the short-run behaviour of the economy looks much the same. There is *no* 'natural' rate of growth, and the equilibrium growth rate of the economy is given by

$$y = [1/(1 + \varepsilon\gamma\eta)]d - [\varepsilon/(1 + \varepsilon\gamma\eta)]r_0 + [\varepsilon\gamma/(1 + \varepsilon\gamma\eta)](a - w_0)$$
$$+ [\varepsilon\gamma/(1 + \varepsilon\gamma\eta)](p^* - p_0) \tag{13.19}$$

Therefore, a demand expansion, a relaxation of the inflation target, and an improvement in productivity, will all permanently increase the growth rate (that is, in the long run as well as in the short run). An increase in the base rate of interest, the base real wage rate, or the average mark-up (as reflected in the p_0 term), will all tend to reduce the equilibrium growth rate.

The equilibrium inflation rate in the alternative model is seen to be influenced by many factors other than just monetary policy, and is given by

$$p = [\eta/(1 + \varepsilon\gamma\eta)]d - [\varepsilon\eta/(1 + \varepsilon\gamma\eta)]r_0 + [1/(1 + \varepsilon\gamma\eta)](w_0 - a)$$
$$+ [\varepsilon\gamma\eta/(1 + \varepsilon\gamma\eta)]p^* + [1/(1 + \varepsilon\gamma\eta)]p_0 \tag{13.20}$$

Inflation will increase if there is either a demand expansion, or if the inflation target is relaxed. Combined with the results for growth reported above, this restores the notion of a long-run Phillips curve trade-off in these particular cases. On the other hand, an improvement in productivity will reduce the inflation rate, and if this occurs, there would therefore be higher growth with lower inflation, contrary to the Phillips curve logic. An increase in either the base real wage rate or the mark-up will increase inflation (conflict inflation), but an increase in the base interest rate will reduce it (as is assumed in traditional discussions of monetary policy).

As already suggested, one advantage of the alternative monetary model is that there is now somewhat more information about the distribution of income than in the case of the new consensus model. In that context really only the value of the real interest rate could be discussed. In the alternative model, its value is determined in the long run by

$$r = [\gamma\eta/(1 + \varepsilon\gamma\eta)]d + [1/(1 + \varepsilon\gamma\eta)]r_0 + [\gamma/(1 + \varepsilon\gamma\eta)](w_0 - a)$$
$$- [\gamma/(1 + \varepsilon\gamma\eta)](p^* - p_0) \tag{13.21}$$

There is no natural rate of interest, and the final value of the actual real interest rate is influenced as much by deliberate policy initiatives of various kinds as by pure market forces. An increase in the base interest rate will ultimately increase the final equilibrium interest rate, as will a demand expansion, an increase in the base real wage rate, an increase in the mark-up and a relaxation of the inflation target. Moreover most of these results come about essentially because of the central bank's 'automatic' response to inflation. An improvement in productivity, meanwhile, will tend to reduce the real interest rate, for the same reason in reverse.

In addition it is also now possible to say something about the impact of the various policy options on real wages. The equilibrium value of the real wage rate is given by

$$w = [\eta/(1 + \varepsilon\gamma\eta)]d - [\varepsilon\eta/(1 + \varepsilon\gamma\eta)]r_0 + [1/(1 + \varepsilon\gamma\eta)]w_0$$
$$+ [\varepsilon\gamma/(1 + \varepsilon\gamma\eta)]a + [e\gamma\eta/(1 + \varepsilon\gamma\eta)](p^* - p_0) \tag{13.22}$$

Therefore, all 'expansionary' policies, a demand expansion, a reduction of the base interest rate, and a relaxation of the inflation target, each tend to increase real wages (and *vice versa*). An improvement in productivity, and an increase in the base real wage rate, will also tend to increase real wages. On the other hand, an increase in the mark-up, (reflected in an increase in the value of the p_0 term) will tend to reduce real wages.

The mark-up itself has been treated here as an exogenous variable (firms using their market power to enforce the level of k at all times), and this may be defended as a not unrealistic assumption once the discussion has moved beyond the theoretical perfectly competitive model. In this case, therefore, by definition all of the distributional impact of any policy changes must be on either the real interest rate or on real wages. In a somewhat more complicated model, such as that outlined in Atesoglu and Smithin (2006, 2007) and Smithin (2009), it would also be possible to discuss in more detail how the entrepreneurial profit share itself gets determined. Even the current framework, however, has provided enough information content to point out the contrast with usual textbook treatment of distributional issues.

4   Conclusion

This chapter has presented a somewhat revised/refined version of the current textbook model of 'modern monetary economics', and also an alternative simple three-equation model with which to compare it. To teach a similar sequence in the university or college setting would surely represent a more legitimate pedagogical exercise than the usual one-sided textbook approach, in which only one macroeconomic theory is ever presented as the 'truth' at any point in time. The New Consensus model is the current economic orthodoxy, but the naiveté of representing this as simply the latest results of diligent scientific research into economic issues (in a manner similar to that of textbooks in the natural sciences) is soon revealed merely by a backward glance at any one or other of the remarkably similar economics textbooks from 20, 30 or 40 years ago, each of which would have uncritically presented the orthodoxy of their own day with a similar dogmatic confidence. The fact is that the New Consensus itself is 'nothing new'. It is essentially the same approach to economic theory as that set out by Wicksell (1898) more than a century ago, and for that matter by Thornton (1802) nearly one hundred years before that (more than two centuries before our own time). Current macroeconomic theories are just the latest period of ascendancy of this line of approach, as compared with the parallel rise and fall of their main ortho-dox rival in the shape of the quantity theory of money. However, there has always been another rival lurking in the wings, that is, a genuine monetary macroeconomics, the best-known statement of which is perhaps the work of Keynes (1936). In effect, the comparison made in this chapter has shown the relationship of the new consensus approach to this *second* type of challenge.

Acknowledgements

I would like to thank both Giuseppe Fontana and Mark Setterfield for detailed comments and discussion that have been important in clarifying the argument and the main issues at stake in this chapter. Any remaining errors are, of course, my own responsibility.

Appendix: interest rates and aggregate demand growth

The relationship between interest rates and the demand growth in equation (13.1) above can be derived from the familiar '$Y = C + I + G + (X - IM)$' breakdown of GDP from the national accounts. Here, we illustrate using only a simplified version of the GDP breakdown, one that eliminates government and the foreign sector, and reduces simply to:

$$Y = C + I \qquad (A1)$$

Now, add a Keynesian-type consumption function, slightly modified by making consumption depend on last period's income rather than on current income. This gives:

$$C = cY_{-1}, \qquad 0 < c < 1 \tag{A2}$$

Next, substitute A2 into A1;

$$Y = cY_{-1} + I \tag{A3}$$

and then divide through by Y_{-1}:

$$Y/Y_{-1} = c + (Y/Y_{-1})(I/Y) \tag{A4}$$

At this point, introduce the notation that $x = I/Y$. Also, recall that $c = 1 - s$, and that the growth rate, y, is given by $y = (Y - Y_{-1})/Y_{-1}$. Therefore:

$$(1 + y)(1 - x) = 1 - s \tag{A5}$$

which is approximately the same as:

$$y = x - s \tag{A6}$$

Finally, we can argue that investment as a percentage of GDP will depend negatively on the real interest rate as in:

$$x = x_0 - \varepsilon r, \qquad 0 < \varepsilon < 1 \tag{A7}$$

Then, substituting (A7) into (A6) we then arrive at:

$$y = d - \varepsilon r \tag{A8}$$

where the demand parameter, d, is given by $d = x_0 - s$. Equation (A8) is the same as equation (13.1) above.

Notes

1. One of the better and more informative examples of this type of material is the book by Ackley (1978). This is the second edition of a work first published in 1961.
2. Compare, for example, the treatment in Dornbusch and Fischer (1978) with that of Mankiw (1992).
3. See Isaac (1999) for a survey of this literature.

References

Ackley, G. (1978), *Macroeconomics Theory and Policy*, New York: Macmillan.

Atesoglu, H.S. and Smithin, J. (2006), 'Inflation targeting in a simple macroeconomic model', *Journal of Post Keynesian Economics*, 28, 4, 673–88.

Atesoglu, H.S. (2007), 'Un modelo macroeconomico simple', *Economia Informa*, 346, May–June, 105–19.

Barrows, D. and Smithin, J. (2006), *Fundamentals of Economics for Business*, Toronto: Captus Press.

Cecchetti, S.G. (2006), *Money, Banking, and Financial Markets*, New York: McGraw-Hill Irwin.

Dornbusch, R. and Fischer, S. (1978), *Macroeconomics*, New York: McGraw-Hill.

Humphrey, T.M. (1993), *Money, Banking and Inflation: Essays in the History of Monetary Thought*, Cheltenham: Edward Elgar.

Isaac, A.G. (1999), 'Inflation: conflicting claims approach', in O'Hara, P. (ed.), *Encyclopedia of Political Economy*, Volume 1, London: Routledge, 508–10.

Keynes, J.M. (1936), *The General Theory of Employment Interest and Money*, London: Macmillan.

Mankiw, N.G. (1992), *Macroeconomics*, New York: Worth.

Mankiw, N.G. (2001), 'US monetary policy during the 1990s', NBER Working Paper no. 8471, September.

Smithin, J. (2007), 'Aggregate demand and supply', in Forstater, M., Mongiovi, G. and Pressman, S. (eds), *Post Keynesian Macroeconomics: Essays in Honour of Ingrid Rima*, London: Routledge, 108–28.

Smithin, J. (2009), *Money, Enterprise and Income Distribution: Towards a Macroeconomic Theory of Capitalism*, London and New York: Routledge.

Taylor, J.B. (1993), 'Discretion versus policy rules in practice', *Carnegie-Rochester Conference Series on Public Policy*, 39, 195–214.

Taylor, J.B. (2000), 'Teaching modern macroeconomics at the principles level', *American Economic Review*, 90, 90–4.

Taylor, J.B. (2007), *Principles of Macroeconomics*, 5th edn, Boston: Houghton Mifflin.

Thornton, H. (1962 [1802]), *An Inquiry into the Nature and Effects of the Paper Credit of Great Britain*, New York: Augustus M. Kelley.

Wicksell, K. (1965 [1898]), *Interest and Prices: A Study of the Causes Regulating the Value of Money*, New York: Augustus M. Kelley.

14
A Post Keynesian Alternative to the New Consensus Model[1]

Eckhard Hein and Engelbert Stockhammer

1 Introduction

When it comes to economic policy analysis, mainstream macroeconomics today is dominated by New Consensus Models (NCMs).[2] In these models aggregate demand impacts on output and employment, but only in the short run. Due to nominal and real rigidities, for which microfoundations based on imperfectly competitive markets are delivered, the short-run Phillips curve is downward sloping. In the long run, however, there is no effect of aggregate demand on the 'Non Accelerating Inflation Rate of Unemployment' (NAIRU), which is exclusively determined by structural characteristics of the labour market, wage bargaining institutions and the social benefit system. An inflation-targeting monetary policy using the interest rate is able to stabilize output and employment in the short run, but in the long run it is neutral and only affects inflation (Fontana and Palacio-Vera, 2007). Fiscal policy is downgraded and is restricted to supporting monetary policies in achieving price stability (Arestis and Sawyer, 2003).

Teaching models based on these features of NCMs are becoming increasingly common in macroeconomics textbooks. This chapter aims at presenting a teachable Post Keynesian (PK) macro model that illustrates the various criticisms that have been voiced against the NCM.[3] These can be broadly summarized as follows. First, there are reasons to expect the short-run equilibrium (the NAIRU) to be unstable without policy interventions. Second, monetary policy will, under some important circumstances, most importantly deflation, not be able to stabilize the system. Third, in the medium run the NAIRU is endogenous to economic activity and monetary policy. PKs therefore derive a very different policy package from that of the New Consensus. We outline an alternative policy package where monetary policy aims at stabilizing the distribution of income by setting the real interest rate equal to the growth rate of labour productivity. Nominal stabilization is addressed by incomes policy and mediation of distributional conflicts through coordinated collective bargaining, while fiscal policy aims at real stabilization.

2 A Basic Post Keynesian Model

2.1 Production, finance, distribution and the inflation generation process

2.1.1 Production, finance and rentiers' income

We assume a closed economy with only rudimentary economic activity on the part of the state. There are no taxes and no state employment in the model, but only deficit-financed government demand. Technical conditions of production are fixed, there is no overhead labour, and labour productivity is therefore constant up to full capacity output given by the capital stock. The supply constraint is only reached by accident and the economy usually operates below the maximum capacity given by the capital stock.

Economic activity and the pace of accumulation are determined by entrepreneurs' decisions to invest, independently of prior saving because firms have access to credit generated by a developed banking sector. We assume that long-term investment finance is supplied by firms' retained earnings or by the long-term credit of rentiers' households (directly or through banks). Introducing interest payments into the model, capital income or gross profits (Π) splits into the (net) profit of the enterprise (Π_F) and rentiers' income (R):

$$\Pi = \Pi_F + R \tag{14.1}$$

With respect to the interest rate and credit, we follow the PK 'horizontalist' monetary view pioneered by Kaldor (1982), Lavoie (1992, pp. 149–216, 1996b) and Moore (1989) and assume that the interest rate is an exogenous variable for the production and accumulation process, whereas the quantities of credit and money are determined endogenously by economic activity. The central bank controls the base rate of interest, commercial banks mark up the base rate and then supply the credit demand they consider creditworthy at this interest rate. In what follows we consider just one interest rate as representative of the whole term-structure of interest rates.

Writing i_n for the nominal rate of interest, we can define the real interest rate for given inflation expectations ($\hat{p}^e$), the 'ex ante' real interest rate (i^e), as:

$$i^e = i_n - \hat{p}^e \tag{14.2}$$

The 'ex post' real interest rate (i) becomes endogenous to unexpected inflation ($\hat{p}^u$):

$$i = i_n - (\hat{p}^e + \hat{p}^u) = i^e - \hat{p}^u \tag{14.3}$$

Firms' payments to rentiers are given by the stock of debt (B) at issue prices and the nominal rate of interest. Expected rentiers' interest income (R^e) can therefore be decomposed into a part compensating for the expected inflationary devaluation of the stock of nominal assets held by rentiers ($\hat{p}^e B$), and expected real net income determined by the 'ex ante' real rate of interest ($i^e B$):[4]

$$R^e = i_n B = (i^e + \hat{p}^e)B = i^e B + \hat{p}^e B \tag{14.4}$$

Firms' 'real' interest payments and rentiers' 'real' income (R) are affected whenever unexpected inflation occurs:

$$R = (i_n - \hat{p}^u)B = (i^e + \hat{p}^e - \hat{p}^u)B \tag{14.5}$$

Positive unexpected inflation therefore redistributes real income from rentiers to firms, but there is further redistribution as will be seen below.

2.1.2 Conflicting claims, employment, unexpected inflation and distribution

Unexpected inflation in our model is systematically generated by the inconsistent income claims of rentiers, firms and workers.[5] The target gross profit share of firms (h_F^T), which has to cover retained earnings and interest payments to rentiers, is given by mark-up pricing on unit labour costs in incompletely competitive goods markets. In the short run, we assume the target mark-up to be constant up to full capacity output. Therefore, the firms' target profit share is simply a constant in the short run:

$$h_F^T = h_0, \quad 0 < h_0 \leq 1 \tag{14.6}$$

If unexpected inflation arises, the realized profit share becomes:

$$h = h_0 - h_2 \hat{p}^u, \quad 0 < h_0 \leq 1, \ 0 \leq h_2 \tag{14.7}$$

with h_2 denoting the effect of unexpected inflation on the realized profit share. The higher is h_2, the less effective are firms in protecting the profit share against unexpected inflation caused by external shocks or workers' wage aspirations. The actual mark-up will therefore fall short of the target mark-up.

The target wage share of workers [$W_W^T = (1 - h)_W^T$] depends on the rate of employment, e (or alternatively unemployment, u), because lower unemployment improves workers' or labour unions' bargaining power. Unemployment functions so as to contain the distributional claims of labourers (Kalecki, 1971, pp. 156–64). At this stage, we assume that workers and labour unions do not consider the inflationary macroeconomic effects of their nominal wage demands and the potentially restrictive monetary policy reactions. There is neither coordination between unions in different firms or industries, nor between wage bargaining parties and monetary policy, with an eye to avoiding the macroeconomic externalities of wage bargaining:

$$(1 - h)_W^T = W_0 + W_1 e, \quad 0 < W_0 \leq 1, \, 0 \leq W_1 \tag{14.8}$$

Whenever there is unexpected inflation, the realized wage share becomes:

$$(1 - h) = W_0 + W_1 e - W_2 \hat{p}^u, \quad 0 < W_0 \leq 1, \, 0 \leq W_1, W_2 \tag{14.9}$$

with W_2 denoting the effect of unexpected inflation on the realized wage share. The higher W_2, the less effective are workers in protecting the wage share against unexpected inflation caused by external shocks or firms' profit aspirations.

With adaptive expectations $(\hat{p}_t^e = \hat{p}_{t-1})$, we obtain the following short-run Phillips curve from equations (14.7) and (14.9):

$$\hat{p}_t^u = \Delta \hat{p}_t = \hat{p}_t - \hat{p}_{t-1} = \frac{W_0 + W_1 e + h_0 - 1}{W_2 + h_2} \tag{14.10}$$

As in the NCM we have, at each point in time, a short-run inflation barrier, a NAIRU. With consistent income claims: $(1 - h)_W^T + h_F^T = 1$, we obtain from equations (14.6) and (14.8) the stable inflation rate of employment (e^N):

$$e^N = \frac{1 - W_0 - h_0}{W_1} \tag{14.11}$$

and hence the NAIRU $u^N = 1 - e^N$. Whenever unemployment falls short of the NAIRU associated with e^N, inflation will accelerate because the sum of the income claims exceeds output, and unexpected inflation will arise, fuelling future inflation expectations. Whenever unemployment exceeds the NAIRU, inflation will decelerate.

Figure 14.1 shows the target wage shares of workers and firms as well as the realized wage share as a function of employment (in the upper part of the figure), and the related unexpected inflation (in the lower part of the figure).

Our model is therefore a three-class model with distributional conflict between wage earners, firms and rentiers ('financial capitalists'). The distribution of income between firms and wage earners depends on employment and hence on the level of economic activity, as does unexpected inflation. The distribution of profits between firms and rentiers depends on the interest rate and also on unexpected inflation and hence on employment. These distributional effects are usually ignored by the NCM.

2.2 The income generation process

In our model, the goods market equilibrium (Y_{IS}), and hence capacity utilization and employment (unemployment), is determined by effective

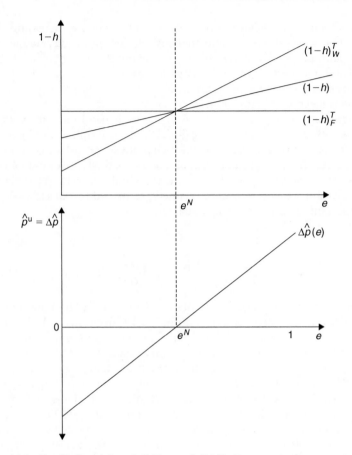

Figure 14.1 Conflicting claims, inflation and distribution

demand, consisting of firms' investment demand (I), rentiers' and workers' household consumption demand (C_R, C_W) and deficit financed government demand (D):

$$Y_{IS} = I + C_R + C_W + D \qquad (14.12)$$

For the analysis of consumption (saving), investment and the related goods market equilibrium we also assume that firms, rentiers and labourers form adaptive expectations, i.e. inflation expectations are given by actual inflation in the previous period. We assume a classical saving hypothesis, i.e. labourers do not save. The part of profits retained by firms is completely saved by definition, and profits distributed to rentiers' households (i.e. interest payments) are used by those households according to their propensity to save, which is assumed to be positive but below unity. Therefore, increasing interest payments by firms will stimulate consumption and aggregate demand, ceteris paribus. Regarding investment, we follow the arguments in Kalecki (1954) and assume that firms' investment decisions are positively affected both by expected sales and by retained earnings. Deficit financed government demand is taken to be exogenous in real terms.

'Ex ante' aggregate demand (Y_{IS}^e) will mainly depend on three variables which are of interest in the ensuing discussion: the nominal and hence the expected real rate of interest, the (expected) profit share and the government deficit (these are the exogenous variables of the income generation process). The consumption propensities of wage earners and rentiers and the elasticities of investment with respect to retained profits and to expected sales are the important parameters of the model:

$$Y_{IS}^e = Y_{IS}^e(i_n, h, D),$$

$$\frac{\partial Y_{IS}^e}{\partial i_n} < 0, \quad \frac{\partial Y_{IS}^e}{\partial h} < 0, \quad \frac{\partial Y_{IS}^e}{\partial D} > 0 \qquad (14.13)$$

The partial effects of changes in the interest rate and the profit share are as follows. With a given target mark-up in firms' pricing decisions, a change in the rate of interest means a redistribution of expected income among firms and rentiers. Assuming debtors' (firms) propensity to spend to be higher than that of lenders' (rentiers), a rising expected real rate of interest will have a dampening effect on the goods market equilibrium and hence on employment.[6] A change in the (expected) profit share affects distribution between firms and labourers. An increase in the profit share has a retarding effect on the goods market, because it depresses consumption and – via expected sales – it also has a retarding effect on investment. A rising profit share may improve firms' internal means of finance but we suppose that this positive effect is insufficient to compensate for the retarding effects, especially in a closed economy. Recent empirical studies have shown that in large and even medium-sized open economies, aggregate demand tends to be wage-led.[7] Deficit financed government demand in real terms has a positive effect on the goods market equilibrium.

Aggregate demand in the goods market determines the 'ex ante' goods market equilibrium and hence the 'ex ante' goods market equilibrium rate of employment (e_{IS}^e) when we take the labour supply as given. We call these equilibria 'ex ante equilibria', because they are based on expectations which need not be fulfilled, as will be seen below:

$$e_{IS}^e = e_{IS}^e[Y_{IS}^e(i_n, h, D)],$$

$$\frac{\partial e_{IS}^e}{\partial Y_{IS}^e} > 0, \quad \frac{\partial Y_{IS}^e}{\partial i_n} < 0, \quad \frac{\partial Y_{IS}^e}{\partial h} < 0, \quad \frac{\partial Y_{IS}^e}{\partial D} > 0 \qquad (14.14)$$

3   Is the NAIRU a Strong Attractor in the Short Run?

In a decentralized market economy, the 'ex ante' goods market equilibrium rate of employment in equation (14.14) which is determined by decentralized consumption and investment decisions may deviate from the stable inflation rate of employment determined in equation (14.11). Such a deviation will trigger unexpected inflation which will change the distribution of income between profits and wages, on the one hand, and between firms' retained profits and rentiers' income, on the other hand. The interesting question is now whether unexpected inflation will adjust the goods market equilibrium towards the NAIRU.

With unexpected inflation, the 'ex ante' goods market equilibrium rate of employment from equation (14.14) changes in the following way (deficit financed government demand in real terms is considered to be exogenous and therefore not treated explicitly here):

$$e_{IS} = e_{IS}\{Y_{IS}[i(\hat{p}^u), h(\hat{p}^u)]\} = e_{IS}(\hat{p}^u)$$

$$\frac{\partial e_{IS}}{\partial Y_{IS}} > 0, \quad \frac{\partial Y_{IS}}{\partial i} < 0, \quad \frac{\partial Y_{IS}}{\partial h} < 0, \quad \frac{\partial i}{\partial \hat{p}^u} < 0, \quad \frac{\partial h}{\partial \hat{p}^u} < 0$$

$$\Rightarrow \frac{\partial e_{IS}}{\partial \hat{p}^u} > 0 \tag{14.15}$$

Since unexpected inflation causes a deviation from the 'ex ante' goods market equilibrium employment rate in equation (14.14), equation (14.15) does not constitute an equilibrium in which expectations are fulfilled. Rather, it is a temporary 'ex post' goods market equilibrium. Since there is no positive or negative excess demand in the goods market, economic agents will not change the activity level defined in equation (14.15). However, they will adjust inflation expectations in the next period. The equilibrium will thus not reproduce itself over time. Unless the employment rate determined by the 'ex post' goods market equilibrium (e_{IS}) matches the stable inflation rate of employment, unexpected inflation will occur again, causing another deviation of the 'ex post' from the 'ex ante' goods market equilibrium, and so on.

Unexpected inflation affects distribution and therefore the goods market equilibrium. First, there is redistribution between gross profits and wages, as has been shown above, with unexpected inflation (disinflation) reducing (raising) the profit share and increasing (reducing) the wage share. Through this channel unexpected inflation (disinflation) has a positive (negative) effect on economic activity and employment, because we assume our model economy to be wage-led. Second, unexpected inflation causes redistribution among gross profits, with inflation (disinflation) reducing (raising) the share of rentiers' income in gross profits. Through this channel unexpected inflation (disinflation) is also expansionary (contractionary), because we assume that firms' propensity to spend exceeds rentiers' propensity to consume.

Unexpected inflation (disinflation) will therefore move the 'ex post' goods market equilibrium farther away from the distribution equilibrium, as is shown in Figure 14.2. The initial 'ex ante' goods market equilibrium rate of employment (e_{IS1}^e) exceeds the short-run stable inflation rate of employment (e^N) which triggers unexpected inflation. Since unexpected inflation has a positive effect on the 'ex post' goods market equilibrium rate of employment, this moves the goods market equilibrium even farther away from the distribution equilibrium. With adaptive expectations, economic agents make the new inflation rate the expected rate in the next period, the 'ex ante' goods market equilibrium moves to (e_{IS2}^e), and the 'ex post' goods market equilibrium curve shifts accordingly. Unexpected inflation is triggered anew and, as a result, the goods market equilibrium diverges monotonically from the stable inflation rate of employment. The NAIRU in our model is therefore not self-stabilizing. Therefore, monetary policy interventions are required in order to stabilize the system.

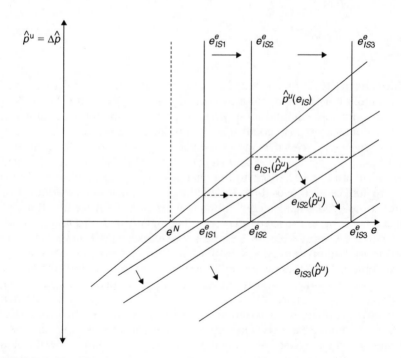

Figure 14.2 The NAIRU: a non-attractor

4 An Inflation Targeting Central Bank and the NAIRU as a Short-Run Attractor?

Applying the NCM idea of inflation targeting by the central bank, we have to bear in mind that it is the nominal rate of interest that an inflation targeting central bank can manipulate in order to achieve some target rate of inflation ($\hat{p}^T$). Here it is sufficient to assume that the only aim of the central bank is to erase unexpected inflation from the system. Therefore, we assume that the central bank's inflation target equals expected inflation ($\hat{p}^T = \hat{p}^e$). The central bank reaction function becomes:

$$i_n = i_0^e + \hat{p}^e + \hat{p}^u + i_1(\hat{p} - \hat{p}^T) = i_0^e + \hat{p}^e + \hat{p}^u + i_1(\hat{p} - \hat{p}^e)$$
$$= i_0^e + \hat{p}^e + (1 + i_1)\hat{p}^u, \quad 0 \le i_0^e, \quad 0 < i_1, \tag{14.16}$$

with i_0^e being the central bank's estimation of the 'equilibrium real interest rate' and i_1 the reaction parameter with respect to unexpected inflation. Introducing an inflation targeting central bank, we obtain the following effects on the goods market equilibrium rate of employment:

$$e_{IS}^{cb} = e_{IS}^{cb}\{Y_{IS}^{cb}[i_n(\hat{p}^u), h(\hat{p}^u)]\},$$

$$\frac{\partial e_{IS}^{cb}}{\partial Y_{IS}^{cb}} > 0, \quad \frac{\partial Y_{IS}^{cb}}{\partial i_n} < 0, \quad \frac{\partial Y_{IS}^{cb}}{\partial h} < 0, \quad \frac{\partial i_n}{\partial \hat{p}^u} > 0, \quad \frac{\partial h}{\partial \hat{p}^u} < 0 \tag{14.17}$$

Note that with an inflation targeting central bank, positive unexpected inflation triggers an increasing nominal and also real interest rate. And since an increasing interest rate has an inverse effect on the goods market equilibrium, following the interest rate rule in equation (14.16) may have the required stabilizing effects on economic activity and employment. The NAIRU may therefore be turned into an attractor by inflation targeting monetary policies, if the effects of changes in the nominal interest rate can overcome the destabilizing effects of unexpected inflation operating via the distribution of income between profit and wages and between firms and rentiers. This is unlikely to be a problem when unemployment falls short of the NAIRU, giving rise to positive unexpected inflation. The central bank can always increase its instrument variable, the nominal interest rate, according to equation (14.16) and wipe out unexpected inflation by means of erasing 'excess employment' from the system. For these adjustments to be stabilizing, however, it is necessary for the absolute value of the slope of the goods market equilibrium employment curve incorporating monetary policy responses (e_{IS}^{cb}) to exceed the slope of the short-run Phillips curve. Therefore, central banks have to be careful in their responses. This is shown in Figure 14.3.

There are further limitations on monetary policy if unemployment exceeds the NAIRU and unexpected inflation is negative, especially in a climate of low

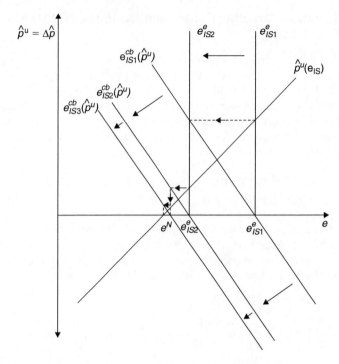

Figure 14.3   An inflation targeting central bank stabilizing the NAIRU

inflation and hence low nominal interest rates. With unexpected disinflation or even deflation, a negative nominal interest rate might be required in equation (14.16) in order to stabilize the system. This is something that central banks cannot achieve due to the zero lower bound on their instrument variable.[8] Central banks' capacities to adjust actual unemployment towards the NAIRU are thus asymmetric and an inflation targeting monetary policy strategy will be ineffective in periods of persistent disinflation and finally deflation. Central banks are therefore helpless when intervention is needed most urgently.

5   Medium-Run Endogeneity of the NAIRU

In the medium to long run the inflation barrier becomes endogenous to actual unemployment in our model. Here, we concern ourselves only with the effects on the distribution equilibrium and ignore the associated effects on the goods market equilibrium rate of employment, which may give rise to complex interacting dynamics between these two equilibria in the long run. Therefore, what follows has a medium-run time horizon. Whereas the first three channels we are discussing arise whenever the goods market equilibrium rate of employment persistently deviates from the stable inflation rate of employment, and hence from the failure of monetary policies to stabilize the system, the fourth channel will be associated with successful short-run monetary policy stabilization.

5.1 Persistence mechanisms in the labour market

Labour market related mechanisms for unemployment persistence have already been suggested by Blanchard and Summers (1988) and Ball (1999). Applying union wage bargaining or insider–outsider models, persistent unemployment and an increasing share of long-term unemployment in total unemployment, with the associated loss of skills and access to firms by the long-term unemployed, will decrease the pressure of a given rate of unemployment on labour unions' or insiders' target wage share and hence on nominal wage demands.

This can be integrated into our model as follows (see Figure 14.4). Assume that the share of the long-term unemployed in total unemployment increases when the unemployment rate exceeds some threshold, which is given by frictional unemployment caused by the 'normal' working of the labour market in the face of changing demand patterns and structural as well as regional change. Suppose now that the employment rate falls short of the 'full employment' rate (e^f) associated with this rate of unemployment. Since the share of long-term unemployment in total unemployment will now increase, the workers' target wage share for a given total rate of employment will increase. In Figure 14.4, the workers' target wage share curve rotates upwards, the stable inflation rate of employment decreases, the NAIRU thus rises, and the Phillips curve rotates upwards, too.

5.2 Wage aspirations based on conventional behaviour

We now assume that workers' distributional targets are affected by the actual distribution of income (Stockhammer 2008). If there is persistent deviation of the actual wage share from the target wage share, caused by a deviation of the goods market equilibrium rate of employment from the stable inflation rate of employment, wage earners will adjust their targets accordingly. Simply put, workers will get used to the actual distribution of income and incorporate it into their distributional target. As can be seen in Figure 14.5, a positive deviation of the actual wage share from the workers' target share, caused by unemployment exceeding the NAIRU, shifts workers' target real wage curve upwards. The stable inflation rate of employment decreases, the NAIRU rises, and the Phillips curve shifts upwards, too.

5.3 The effect of investment in the capital stock

The effects of investment in the capital stock on employment and the NAIRU have been stressed by Rowthorn (1995, 1999), Sawyer (2002) and Arestis and Sawyer (2004a, pp. 73–99; 2005). The size of the capital stock in relation to

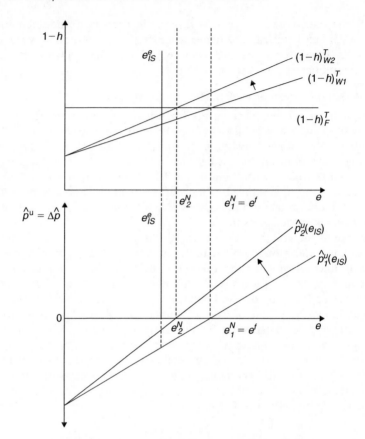

Figure 14.4   Labour market persistence mechanisms and the NAIRU

output, and hence the medium-run capacity utilization rate, may directly affect the stable inflation rate of employment and hence the NAIRU in our model, if firms' target mark-up is positively related to capacity utilization in the medium run. The lower the growth rate of capital stock, the higher will be medium-run capacity utilization, if the growth rates of the exogenous components of demand remain constant, and the higher will be firms' target profit share. As can be seen in Figure 14.6, weak investment, low demand and hence a rate of employment below the stable inflation rate makes firms' target wage share curve shift downwards, the stable inflation rate of employment decreases, the NAIRU rises, and the Phillips curve shifts upwards.

5.4   Persistent changes in the 'ex ante' real rate of interest

Changes in the 'ex ante' real interest rate associated with successful short-run inflation targeting monetary policies will have medium-run effects on

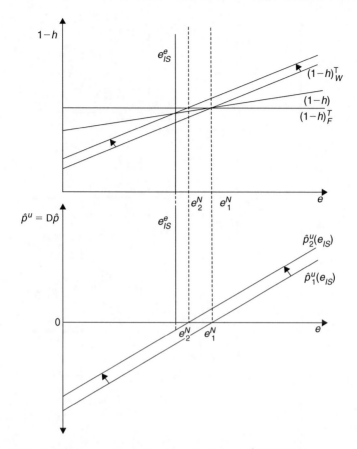

Figure 14.5 Endogenous wage and profit aspirations and the NAIRU

the inflation barrier (Hein 2006, 2008, pp. 133–52).[9] Since interest payments are costs from the perspective of the firm which have to be covered by the mark-up on unit labour costs, persistent changes in the 'ex ante' real interest rate will cause medium-run changes in the firms' target mark-up and hence in their target wage share.

If employment exceeds the stable inflation rate, as in Figure 14.7, applying the inflation targeting interest rate rule (equation (14.16)) will stabilize inflation in the short run. However, in the medium run higher interest rates will cause firms to raise target mark-ups and the firms' target real wage share curve will shift downwards. The stable inflation rate of employment will hence decrease, the NAIRU will increase, and the Phillips curve will shift upwards. At the new, lower level of economic activity the problem of inflation might arise again, inducing central banks to raise interest rates even further, which will depress real activity still further.

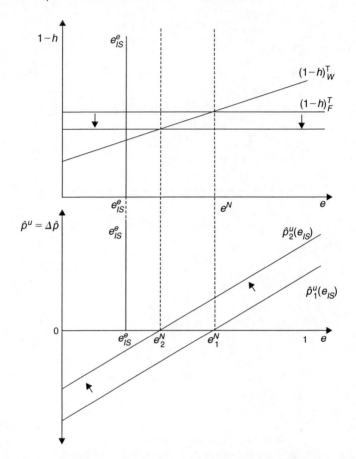

Figure 14.6   Low investment, slow capital stock growth and the NAIRU

5.5   Some empirical evidence on the endogeneity of the NAIRU

There are thus strong theoretical reasons to expect that there is a high degree of persistence in unemployment and, consequently, that the NAIRU is endogenous in the medium to long run. But there is also a substantial amount of empirical evidence to support such a view. Stanley (2004) provides a meta-analysis of the rich empirical literature on hysteresis and concludes that the available evidence indicates a rejection of the hypothesis that the NAIRU is exogenous. Logeay and Tober (2006) find that with the Kalman filter techniques which are now widely used in the (ex post) calculation of the NAIRU by the OECD and others, the endogeneity of the NAIRU cannot be rejected (for the Euro area).

However, the four channels of the endogeneity of the NAIRU discussed above have not received equal attention in empirical research. Ball (1999) has

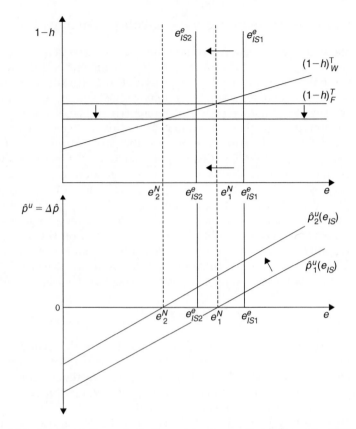

Figure 14.7 Persistent change in the 'ex ante' real rate of interest and the NAIRU

performed careful investigations of the different effects of monetary policies on medium-term unemployment and concludes that 'differences in monetary policy help explain unemployment successes and failures' (Ball 1999, p. 219) and 'whether hysteresis arises depends largely on the response of monetary policy to the recession' (Ball 1999, p. 192). However, he treats changes in monetary policy as demand shocks rather than distributional shocks. Ironically, the IMF (2003) finds a long-run effect of real interest rates on unemployment (without drawing policy conclusions). The capital shortage argument has been investigated extensively by Rowthorn (1995), Arestis and Biefang–Frisancho Mariscal (2000), Alexiou and Pitelis (2003), Arestis *et al.* (2006, 2007), and Palacio-Vera *et al.* (2006). They all find evidence that capital accumulation has strong effects on unemployment. The case for medium-run endogeneity is thus not only theoretically plausible, but is also backed by empirical evidence. Economic policy should not, therefore, treat the NAIRU as a given.

6 A Post Keynesian Macroeconomic Policy Assignment

From our analysis of inflation targeting monetary policies above it follows that, in the short run, this monetary policy assignment and the related monetary policy strategy may be adequate, but limited in their effectiveness. In the medium to long run, inflation targeting by means of an interest rate rule seems to be inappropriate. Therefore, central banks should refrain from attempting to fine-tune the economy by means of interest rate policies, and instead follow a 'parking it' strategy with respect to the interest rate (Rochon and Setterfield, 2007). Central banks should focus on the medium-to long-run distributional effects of interest rate variations and stabilize the rate of interest at a low level. Different interest rate targets have been proposed (Rochon and Setterfield, 2007; Smithin, 2007; Wray, 2007). Following Pasinetti's (1981) 'fair rate of interest', which allows rentiers to participate in real growth and keeps distribution between rentiers, on the one hand, and firms and labourers, on the other hand, constant, requires central banks to set the real rate of interest equal to productivity growth (Lavoie, 1996a; Setterfield, 2006b). Hence, we obtain the following monetary policy rule:

$$i_n = i_0^e + \hat{p}^e + \hat{p}^u \tag{14.18}$$

with i_0^e being given by medium-run productivity growth. Central banks will have to adjust their policy instrument, the nominal interest rate, so that a constant expected real rate of interest equal to medium-run productivity growth emerges. This implies adjusting the nominal interest rate to unexpected inflation at the end of each period.

Although monetary policies in this approach should neither pursue an inflation target nor make any attempt at adjusting the employment rate to some target value, central banks remain responsible for the orderly working of the monetary and financial system. This includes the definition of credit standards for refinance operations with commercial banks (credit controls), the implementation of compulsory minimum reserves of different types to be held with the central bank, the role of a 'lender of last resort' in the case of systemic crises, and so on.

The NCM view on the role of wage formation and wage bargaining, demanding nominal and real wage flexibility by means of structural reforms in the labour market and decentralization of wage bargaining in order to accelerate adjustment towards the NAIRU and reduce the NAIRU itself, cannot be sustained on the basis of our model. Nominal wage flexibility generates unexpected inflation whenever unemployment deviates from the NAIRU. This affects distribution between firms and rentiers, on the one hand, and between capital and labour, on the other hand, and is hence associated with real wage flexibility. And this will make actual unemployment diverge further from the NAIRU in wage-led economies, as our model has shown.

In order to avoid the destabilizing effects of nominal and real wage flexibility, PKs advocate rigid nominal wages and allocate the role of *nominal stabilization* to incomes or wage policies. Therefore, nominal unit labour costs should grow at a rate similar to the country's inflation target, which means that nominal wage growth should equal the sum of the medium-run rate of growth of labour productivity ($\hat{w}_0$) and the target inflation rate:

$$\hat{w} = \hat{w}_0 + \hat{p}^T \tag{14.19}$$

As the source of inflation is an unresolved distributional conflict between labour and capital, the optimal way to achieve nominal stabilization is to make the target wage shares of workers and firms compatible with each other for a relevant range of employment rates. As is shown in Figure 14.8, the

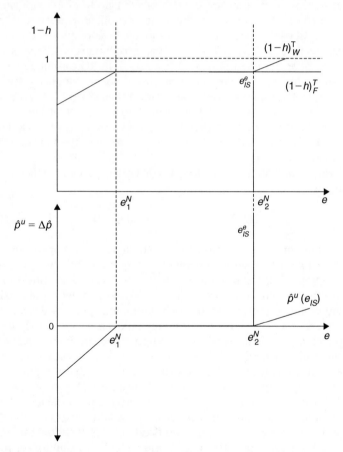

Figure 14.8 Result of the Post Keynesian macroeconomic policy mix

stable inflation rate of employment and hence the NAIRU becomes a corridor and the Phillips curve has a horizontal part between e_1^N and e_2^N. Variations in the employment rate between e_1^N and e_2^N do not trigger any unexpected inflation and hence no cumulative processes will set in. In this case, demand management is free to choose a high level of employment close to e_2^N without violating stable inflation rates. In particular a high degree of wage bargaining coordination at the national level, strong labour unions and employer organizations, and hence organized labour markets should be suitable for pursuing this nominal stabilization role of wage bargaining.[10] The government can contribute by mediating the conflict, by encouraging coordinated collective bargaining (so as to internalize inflationary spill-overs arising in un-coordinated bargaining systems) and through tax incentives.

Because of the problems associated with real and nominal stabilization by means of monetary policies, the complete neglect of discretionary fiscal policies in the NCM turns out to be a major problem (Arestis and Sawyer 2003, 2004a, 2004c). Therefore, PKs have argued in favour of real stabilization by means of fiscal policies. This again has two dimensions. First, since an adjustment of actual unemployment towards a NAIRU cannot generally be expected, neither from market forces nor from monetary policies, fiscal policies are required for short-run real stabilization. And second, since the NAIRU is endogenous to actual unemployment and hence to effective demand in the medium to long run through the channels discussed above, fiscal policies do not only have short-run real effects but also affect the long-run rate of employment.

Real stabilization should therefore be delegated to fiscal policies in the following way:

$$D = D_0 + D_1(e^T - e), \quad D_1 > 0 \qquad (14.20)$$

with D_0 representing permanent government deficit spending (or surpluses), which is required to keep employment at target (e^T) in the medium run, and D_1 representing the reaction coefficient in the case of short-run deviations of employment from target. The employment target is the maximum employment rate achievable without triggering unexpected inflation.

The effects of a PK assignment or policy-mix can be seen in Figure 14.8. Wage policies, and hence wage bargaining parties, are mainly responsible for stable inflation rates, and hence for nominal stabilization. Fiscal policies are responsible for the management of demand, maintaining effective demand at high employment levels, and hence for real stabilization in the short and in the medium to long run. The central bank should neither aim at fine-tuning the economy in real nor in nominal terms, and should thus not interfere with the tasks of wage and fiscal policies. It should rather focus on maintaining low real interest rates and a stable distribution of income between rentiers, on the one hand, and firms and labourers, on the other hand, in order to avoid the destabilizing distributional effects of changes in the interest rate.

7 Conclusions

We have shown that, in the short run, inflation targeting monetary policies (the main stabilization tool in the NCM) may be appropriate in the case of accelerating inflation, but ineffective in the case of decelerating inflation and finally deflation. Taking into account the medium-run cost and distribution effects of interest rate variations, however, renders monetary policies inappropriate as an economic stabilizer. Based on these results, we have argued that the NCM macroeconomic policy assignment should be replaced by a PK assignment. Enhancing employment without increasing inflation is possible if macroeconomic policies are coordinated along the following lines: the central bank targets distribution between rentiers, on the one hand, and firms and labourers, on the other hand, and sets low real interest rates; wage bargaining parties target inflation; and fiscal policies are applied for short- and medium-run real stabilization purposes. Taken as a whole, our model, provides an alternative to the NCM that emphasizes both the need for a richer array of policy interventions in the economy, and the neglected role of income distribution in macroeconomics. These are important issues for students to consider as they learn about the workings of the economy and the usefulness of macroeconomic policies.

Notes

1. This chapter is a revised, simplified and shortened version of Hein and Stockhammer (2007). There, a more formal and extensive treatment of the issues can be found. The major part of this chapter was written while Eckhard Hein was a visiting professor at Vienna University of Economics and Business Administration (WU). The hospitality of the WU is gratefully acknowledged. Many thanks go to Giuseppe Fontana and Mark Setterfield for very helpful suggestions to make the chapter more readable.
2. See Clarida, Galí and Gertler (1999) and Carlin and Soskice (2006, pp. 27–172) for NCMs.
3. For a critique of the NCM and its main elements, the NAIRU and an inflation targeting central bank, as well as for PK amendments see, among others, Arestis and Sawyer (2004a, 2004b, 2005, 2006), Atesoglu and Smithin (2006), Davidson (2006), Fontana (2006), Fontana and Palacio-Vera (2007), Hein (2002, 2006, 2008, pp. 133–152), Kriesler and Lavoie (2007), Lavoie (2006), Palacio-Vera (2005), Palley (2007), Rochon and Setterfield (2007), Sawyer (2002, 2006), Seccareccia (1998), Setterfield (2004, 2006a, 2006b), Smithin (2007), Stockhammer (2004, 2008), Wray (2007).
4. Repayment of debt is not considered explicitly.
5. Of course, there may also be exogenous shocks generating unexpected inflation.

6. This is the so-called 'normal case' for the effect of a change in the interest rate on the goods market equilibrium. In Hein and Stockhammer (2007) we also discuss the 'puzzling case' in which a rising interest rate has expansive effects on the goods market. This requires a low rentiers' propensity to save and a weak effect of internal funds on firms' investment. The complications arising from this case are eliminated from the discussion in this chapter.
7. See Naastepad and Storm (2007), Stockhammer, Hein and Grafl (2007), Hein and Vogel (2008), and Stockhammer, Onaran and Ederer (2009).
8. See the situation in the US during the Great Depression or in Japan in the 1990s.
9. The idea that lasting variations in interest rates may affect the functional distribution of income and hence the share of wages and gross profits in total income goes back to Sraffa (1960, p. 33) and has been proposed, in particular, by Neo-Ricardian authors (see for example Pivetti, 1991), but it can also be found in earlier PK work (Kaldor, 1982, p. 63; Pasinetti, 1974, pp. 139–41). See also Lavoie (1995).
10. See Hein (2006) and Kriesler and Lavoie (2007) for the incorporation of coordinated wage bargaining into PK models and Hein (2002) for a review of the related literature.

References

Alexiou, C. and Pitelis, C. (2003), 'On capital shortages and European unemployment: a panel data investigation', *Journal of Post Keynesian Economics*, 25, 613–31.

Arestis, P. and Sawyer, M. (2003), 'Reinventing fiscal policy', *Journal of Post Keynesian Economics*, 26, 3–25.

Arestis, P. and Sawyer, M. (2004a), *Re-examining Monetary and Fiscal Policy for the 21st Century*, Cheltenham: Edward Elgar.

Arestis, P. and Sawyer, M. (2004b), 'Monetary policy when money is endogenous: going beyond the "New Consensus"', in Lavoie, M. and Seccareccia, M. (eds), *Central Banking in the Modern World. Alternative Perspectives*, Cheltenham: Edward Elgar.

Arestis, P. and Sawyer, M. (2004c), 'On fiscal policy and budget deficits', *Intervention. Journal of Economics*, 1(2), 61–74.

Arestis, P. and Sawyer, M. (2005), 'Aggregate demand, conflict and capacity in the inflationary process', *Cambridge Journal of Economics*, 29, 959–74.

Arestis, P. and Sawyer, M. (2006), 'The nature and the role of monetary policy when money is endogenous', *Cambridge Journal of Economics*, 30, 847–60.

Arestis, P., Baddeley, M., and Sawyer, M. (2006), 'Is capital stock a determinant of unemployment?', in Hein, E., Heise, A., and Truger, A. (eds), *Wages, Employment, Distribution and Growth. International Perspectives*, Basingstoke, Palgrave Macmillan.

Arestis, P., Baddeley, M., and Sawyer, M. (2007), 'The relationship between capital stock, unemployment and wages in nine EMU countries', *Bulletin of Economic Research*, vol. 59(2), 125–48.

Arestis, P. and Biefang-Frisancho Mariscal, I. (2000), 'Capital stock, unemployment and wages in the UK and Germany', *Scottish Journal of Political Economy*, 47, 487–503.

Atesoglu, H.S. and Smithin, J. (2006), 'Inflation targeting in a simple macroeconomic model', *Journal of Post Keynesian Economics*, 28, 673–88.

Ball, L. (1999), 'Aggregate demand and long-run unemployment', *Brooking Papers on Economic Activity*, no. 2, 189–251.

Blanchard, O. and Summers, L.H. (1988), 'Beyond the natural rate hypothesis', *American Economic Review*, 78(2), 182–7.

Carlin, W. and Soskice, D. (2006), *Macroeconomics. Imperfections, Institutions and Policies*, Oxford: Oxford University Press.

Clarida, R., Galí, J. and Gertler, M. (1999), 'The science of monetary policy: a New Keynesian perspective', *Journal of Economic Literature*, 37, 1661–707.

Davidson, P. (2006), 'Can, or should, a central bank target inflation?', *Journal of Post Keynesian Economics*, 28, 689–703.

Fontana, G. (2006), 'The "New Consensus" view of monetary policy: a new Wicksellian connection', *Intervention. Journal of Economics*, 3, 263–78.

Fontana, G. and Palacio-Vera, A. (2007), 'Are long-run price stability and short-run output stabilization all that monetary policy can aim for?', *Metroeconomica*, 58, 269–98.

Hein, E. (2002), 'Monetary policy and wage bargaining in the EMU: restrictive ECB policies, high unemployment, nominal wage restraint and inflation above the target', *Banca Nazionale del Lavoro Quarterly Review*, 55, 299–337.

Hein, E. (2006), 'Wage bargaining and monetary policy in a Kaleckian monetary distribution and growth model: trying to make sense of the NAIRU', *Intervention. Journal of Economics*, 3, 305–29.

Hein, E. and Stockhammer, E. (2007), *Macroeconomic policy mix, employment and inflation in a Post-Keynesian alternative to the New Consensus model*, Department of Economics Working Paper no. 110, Vienna University of Economics & B.A.

Hein, E. (2008), *Money, Distribution Conflict and Capital Accumulation. Contributions to 'Monetary Analysis'*, Basingstoke: Palgrave Macmillan.

Hein, E. and Vogel, L. (2008), 'Distribution and growth reconsidered – empirical results for six OECD countries', *Cambridge Journal of Economics*, 32, 479–511.

IMF (2003), *World Economic Outlook. Growth and Institutions*, April, Washington, DC: IMF.

Kaldor, N. (1982), *The Scourge of Monetarism*, Oxford: Oxford University Press.

Kalecki, M. (1954), *Theory of Economic Dynamics*, London: George Allen.

Kalecki, M. (1971), *Selected Essays on the Dynamics of the Capitalist Economy, 1933–70*, Cambridge: Cambridge University Press.

Kriesler, P. and Lavoie, M. (2007), 'The New Consensus on monetary policy and its Post-Keynesian critique', *Review of Political Economy*, 19, 387–404.

Lavoie, M. (1992), *Foundations of Post Keynesian Economic Analysis*, Aldershot: Edward Elgar.

Lavoie, M. (1995), 'Interest rates in post-Keynesian models of growth and distribution', *Metroeconomica*, 46, 146–77.

Lavoie, M. (1996a), 'Monetary policy in an economy with endogenous credit money', in Deleplace, G. and Nell, E. (eds), *Money in Motion*, Basingstoke: Macmillan.

Lavoie, M. (1996b), 'Horizontalism, structuralism, liquidity preference and the principle of increasing risk', *Scottish Journal of Political Economy*, 43, 275–300.

Lavoie, M. (2006), 'A Post-Keynesian amendment to the New Consensus on monetary policy', *Metroeconomica*, 57, 165–92.

Logeay, C. and Tober, S. (2006), 'Hysteresis and the NAIRU in the Euro area', *Scottish Journal of Political Economy*, 53, 409–29.

Moore, B.J. (1989), 'The endogeneity of credit money', *Review of Political Economy*, 1, 65–93.

Naastepad, C.W.M. and Storm, S. (2007), 'OECD demand regimes (1960–2000)', *Journal of Post Keynesian Economics*, 29, 211–46.

Palacio-Vera, A. (2005), 'The "modern" view of macroeconomics: some critical reflections', *Cambridge Journal of Economics*, 29, 747–67.

Palacio-Vera, A., Martínez-Cañete, A. R., Márquez de la Cruz, E., and Pérez-Soba Aguilar, I. (2006), *Capital Stock and Unemployment: Searching for the Missing Link*, Working Paper no. 475, Levy Economics Institute of Bard College.

Palley, T. (2007), 'Macroeconomics and monetary policy: competing theoretical frameworks', *Journal of Post Keynesian Economics*, 30, 61–78.

Pasinetti, L. (1974), *Growth and Income Distribution*, Cambridge: Cambridge University Press.

Pasinetti, L. (1981), *Structural Change and Economic Growth*, Cambridge: Cambridge University Press.

Pivetti, M. (1991), *An Essay on Money and Distribution*, Basingstoke: Macmillan.

Rochon, L.-P. and Setterfield, M. (2007), 'Interest rates, income distribution and monetary dominance: Post-Keynesians and the "fair rate" of interest', *Journal of Post Keynesian Economics*, 30, 13–42.

Rowthorn, R.E. (1995), 'Capital formation and unemployment', *Oxford Review of Economic Policy*, 11(1), 26–39.

Rowthorn, R.E. (1999), 'Unemployment, wage bargaining and capital-labour substitution', *Cambridge Journal of Economics*, 23, 413–25.

Sawyer, M. (2002), 'The NAIRU, aggregate demand and investment', *Metroeconomica*, 53, 66–94.

Sawyer, M. (2006), 'Inflation targeting and central bank independence: we are all Keynesians now! Or are we?', *Journal of Post Keynesian Economics*, 28, 639–52.

Seccareccia, M. (1998), 'Wicksellian norm, central bank real interest targeting and macroeconomic performance', in Arestis, P. and Sawyer, M. (eds), *The Political Economy of Central Banking*, Cheltenham: Edward Elgar.

Setterfield, M. (2004), 'Central banking, stability and macroeconomic outcomes: a comparison of New Consensus and Post-Keynesian monetary macroeconomics', in Lavoie, M. and Seccareccia, M. (eds), *Central Banking in the Modern World. Alternative Perspectives*, Cheltenham: Edward Elgar.

Setterfield, M. (2006a), 'Is inflation targeting compatible with Post Keynesian economics?', *Journal of Post Keynesian Economics*, 28, 653–71.

Setterfield, M. (2006b), *Macroeconomics Without the LM Curve: An Alternative View*, Paper presented at the 9th Post Keynesian Conference 2006, Kansas City.

Smithin, J. (2007), 'A real interest rate rule for monetary policy?', *Journal of Post Keynesian Economics*, 30, 101–18.

Sraffa, P. (1960), *Production of Commodities by Means of Commodities*, Cambridge: Cambridge University Press.

Stanley, T.D. (2004), 'Does unemployment hysteresis falsify the natural rate hypothesis? A meta-regression analysis', *Journal of Economic Surveys*, 18, 589–612.

Stockhammer, E. (2004), 'Is there an equilibrium rate of unemployment in the long run?', *Review of Political Economy*, 16, 59–77.

Stockhammer, E. (2008), 'Is the NAIRU a Monetarist, New Keynesian, Post Keynesian or Marxist theory?', *Metroeconomica*, 59, 479–510.

Stockhammer, E., Hein, E. and Grafl, L. (2007), *Globalization and the effects of changes in functional income distribution on aggregate demand in Germany*, Department of Economics Working Paper no. 114, Vienna University of Economics & B.A.

Stockhammer, E., Onaran, Ö, and Ederer, S. (2009), 'Functional income distribution and aggregate demand in the Euro area', *Cambridge Journal of Economics*, 33, 139–59.

Wray, L.R. (2007), 'A Post Keynesian view of central bank independence, policy targets, and the rules versus discretion debate', *Journal of Post Keynesian Economics*, 30, 119–41.

15
The Central Banker as 'Regulator of Conflict': A 'Reversed' Reading of the Solow and New Consensus Models

Emiliano Brancaccio[1]

1   A Teaching Method Based On the Choice of Exogenous Variables

Macroeconomics has undergone numerous changes over the last 30 years as regards both research and teaching. With respect to the trends prevailing since the 1970s, the field of theoretical and applied studies has seen enormous growth in the influence of the neoclassical school as against very limited dissemination of alternative approaches. In the sphere of teaching, the consolidation of a neoclassical mainstream has led to significant standardization of study programmes. Unlike the situation in the past, these appear to be increasingly based on the adoption of American manuals, which are characterized by clarity of exposition and abundance of information but also by systematic acceptance of the dominant neoclassical paradigm. One of the reasons prompting numerous 'non-orthodox' teachers to use this type of course book is the conviction that students must receive a preliminary grounding in the mainstream and should be introduced to heterodox approaches only at a later stage. While this view is understandable and indeed acceptable to a large degree, there is some risk of stunting the growth of a critical spirit. The major American manuals prove in fact to be characterized by a typically 'progressive' approach to the discipline based on the simplistic idea of macroeconomics undergoing practically linear development toward an increasingly precise and unanimous understanding of reality.[2]

The need to offer students in their first year of economics a preliminary grounding of the mainstream type thus evidently clashes with the need to sharpen rather than blunt their critical spirit. This is a considerable problem because it is no easy matter to sum up the basic differences between the schools of heterodox thought and neoclassical theory in a handful of remarks. There is in fact a deep rift between the dominant approach and its critics. For example, while neoclassical economists always tend to identify the roots of their analyses in the paradigms of methodological individualism and of scarcity and utility, the critical schools – be they classical, Marxist, Kaleckian or Post Keynesian – reject methodological individualism, the principle of consumer sovereignty, and the paradigm of scarcity and utility, and prefer instead an aggregate and class-based reading of economic phenomena.

Fortunately, there exists one way out of the contradiction between teaching constraints and the primary goal of 'opening up the minds' of budding scholars. A particular method allows comparison of orthodox and heterodox approaches in a very simple way. This is based on the possibility of obtaining completely different results from the same mathematical structure depending on the choice of exogenous and endogenous variables. The analytical and political implications of a model can in fact be turned completely upside-down by reversing the positions of the variables determined within and outside the model. This teaching method obviously presents some limitations. Many of the radical differences in approach between the various schools of thought are inevitably overlooked. However, this procedure has its advantages and has already been adopted by various scholars.[3] The basic reason is that it allows students to see from the very outset of their contact with the discipline that economics is not a 'linearly progressive' field of research but on the contrary, by its very nature, a conceptual terrain of perennial dispute in both theoretical and political terms.

The teaching method of switching exogenous and endogenous variables will be adopted in this chapter for the purpose of examining the factors determining the distribution of income between wages and profits. As we shall see, income distribution is regarded as endogenous by neoclassical economists, always depending in the final analysis on the scarcity of goods and factors of production available in relation to the preferences of economic agents (given the technology available). This is a typical result of the paradigm of scarcity and utility, which characterizes both the traditional and the modern versions of the neoclassical approach.[4] For contemporary exponents of critical approaches, including those continuing the classical and Marxist traditions (but also some Kaleckians and Post Keynesians), the distribution of income between wages and profits should instead be regarded as an exogenous variable to be determined outside the mathematical cores of the models.[5] The basic idea underpinning this view is that the distribution of income depends on complex political and institutional factors, and ultimately on the outcome of conflict between social classes. Therefore it should not be enclosed within an overly rigid structure of formal logic.

Our analysis will take as its starting point two well-known models of mainstream neoclassical thought, namely the Solow growth model (1956) and the more recent macroeconomic model of the New Consensus, which exists in various versions (here we consider Taylor, 2000).[6] Though sometimes alluded to,[7] the connection between the two models has never been formally stated in the literature. However, the connection is evident from a neoclassical viewpoint. The Solow model makes it possible to determine the full-employment equilibrium and its long-term path of development, and it is around this equilibrium that the short-run fluctuations examined by short-period macroeconomic models develop. The New Consensus model constitutes a particular variant of the latter, taking expressly into account the way in which the central bank sets the interest rate. We can therefore state that the equilibrium of the Solow model is the pivotal point of reference for the New Consensus model. This is why we will make reference here to a combined 'Solow–New Consensus' model. Taking the mathematical structures of the two models as our starting point, we shall show how switching the positions of the exogenous and endogenous variables leads to very different results as regards both interpretation of the facts and political implications. In particular, we shall see that in the traditional versions of the Solow and New Consensus models, distribution is endogenous and the role of the central bank is simply to ensure that the economic system converges on its long-term equilibrium, where full employment and a specific inflation target are achieved. These results will then be turned completely upside-down through an operation confined almost exclusively to the choice of exogenous and endogenous variables. As we shall in fact see, the role of the monetary authority is totally different in the alternative version of the two models based on exogenous determination of the distribution of income, where the central bank becomes a crucial 'regulator' of distributive conflict between the social classes and the full-employment equilibrium no longer constitutes an inescapable point of reference. The chapter will end with some arguments in support of this alternative version of the models rather than the traditional neoclassical framework.

The technical difficulties of the chapter are within the grasp of students who have mastered the basic characteristics of the neoclassical model of growth and the use of the mathematics is limited to the bare essentials.

2 The 'Solow–New Consensus' Neoclassical Model

In this section we make explicit the logical connection between two well-known models of mainstream neoclassical thought, namely the Solow growth model (1956) and the more recent macroeconomic model of the 'New Consensus' (focusing on the version elaborated by Taylor, 2000). In this way we shall build an original 'Solow–New Consensus' model. We start with a description of the technology of the system put forward by Solow. We examine a capitalist system in which a single good is produced by means of labour and itself. Let K be the quantity of the good available as capital and therefore used as productive input, L the quantity of homogeneous labour employed, and X the quantity of the good produced. We thus obtain the following production function:

$$X = F(K, L)$$

Let us assume that capital tends to be exhausted within the space of a single cycle of production and must therefore be replenished every time continuously (this means that the rate of depreciation of the capital stock is equal to one). We shall further assume that the function has constant return to scale, so that:

$$\alpha F(K, L) = F(\alpha K, \alpha L)$$

for all $a > 0$. By defining $k = K/L$ and positing $a = 1/L$, we can therefore express the production function in per capita terms. In other words, we can identify the quantities of goods produced for every given input of labour:

$$x = f(k)$$

where $x = f(k) = X/L$. Let us finally assume that this function is continuous and differentiable, and that it satisfies the following customary conditions:

$$f(0) = 0, \quad f'(k) > 0, \quad f''(k) < 0$$

We shall now go on to the distribution of the income produced among the agents of production. We assume that all output is divided between wages and interest payments (which are supposed to be equal to profits). Letting w be the real wage and r the real rate of interest, we can therefore write:

$$X = wL + (1 + r)K$$

In order to express this equation in per capita terms, we then divide the whole by L and obtain:

$$f(k) = w + (1 + r)k \tag{15.1}$$

Let us now introduce the hypothesis of perfect competition, from which Solow and the neoclassical school draw the inference that labour and capital are remunerated in relation to their respective marginal productivities. In per capita terms, this can be expressed as follows:

$$f'(k) = 1 + r \tag{15.2}$$

Finally, we shall introduce another typical neoclassical hypothesis, namely that the income produced and saved is entirely transformed into investment (i.e. the replenishment and growth of the capital stock) and into expenditure that does not generate productive capacity (e.g. public spending). Letting s be the population's propensity to save, g the rate of accumulation of capital, and Z the real autonomous expenditure that does not generate productive capacity, we have:

$$sX = (1 + g)K + Z$$

In order to express this in per capita terms, we once again divide the whole by L. By defining $z = Z/X$, we obtain:

$$sf(k) = (1+g)k + z \qquad (15.3)$$

The Solow model is completely encapsulated in the system of equations (15.1), (15.2), (15.3). It enables us to understand how the model determines the growth and distribution of income endogenously on the basis of scarce factor endowments and the preferences of economic agents. The solution procedure of the model is as follows. It starts from the exogenous endowments of capital K and labour L. Once the endowments are known, competition ensures that the equilibrium levels of wages and interest determined are those corresponding exactly to the marginal productivity of the factors and therefore guaranteeing that firms make full use of the same. Given K and L, the ratio $k = K/L$ at which they will be employed by firms is also given. Moreover, the autonomous expenditure that does not generate additional productive capacity, z, is regarded as exogenous, as is the propensity to save s, which expresses the preferences of the population with respect to consumption choices. Given k, z and s, only three endogenous variables are left, namely r, w and g, for three equations. The system is therefore determined, in that r is obtained from equation (15.2), w from (15.2), and g from (15.3). At the same time, from the ratio k it is also possible to determine $f(k)$ and to obtain the degree of utilization u of productive capacity in conditions of full employment. This degree of capacity utilization represents the optimal level of output per capita y which can be obtained from a given level of capital per capita k. It is given by:

$$u = \frac{f(k)}{k}$$

In line with the neoclassical paradigm of scarcity and utility, the model therefore starts from endowments (and preferences) and endogenously determines the optimal degree of their utilization, the rate of accumulation and the distribution of the income produced.

The above situation is described in the jargon of development theory as an equilibrium of non-proportional growth, in that there is no guarantee of labour and capital growing at the same rate. Solow demonstrates, however, that the system does converge on an equilibrium of proportional growth under certain assumptions.[8] In any case, what matters here is the fact that both equilibria assume endowments and preferences as exogenous variables, and both generate endogenously the single distribution of income between wages and profits that ensures the full utilization of capital and labour, which gives rise in this model to the optimal degree of utilization of productive capacity and the absence of involuntary unemployment. Given that some authors speak in this connection of a *natural* equilibrium, a subscript will be added from now on to the equilibrium levels of the real rate of interest and the degree of utilization deriving from the Solow model (r_n and u_n).

We shall now go on to consider the New Consensus model, which will make it possible to examine fluctuations around the full-employment equilibrium discussed above. This model is distinguished from the traditional short-period macroeconomic models for the following reason. The models of the *neoclassical synthesis* traditionally assumed that the central bank decided autonomously on the amount of money to be put into circulation and then left the rate of interest to be determined by the market.[9] On the contrary, the New Consensus model assumes that the interest rate is set directly by the central bank. This model is favoured today because it appears to reflect more closely the way in which markets and monetary institutions really function. Ignoring the old question as to whether the economic system is capable of converging spontaneously on the full-employment equilibrium, the new consensus regards it as the task of the central bank to act so as to make the system converge on an equilibrium in which a specific 'inflation target' is achieved and full utilization of resources is ensured at the same time.

There are already a great many versions of the New Consensus model. The one adopted here is based primarily on the contributions of Taylor (2000) with some elements drawn from Kriesler and Lavoie (2007). The equations of this model are as follows:

$$r = r_n + \delta(\pi - \pi^T), \tag{15.4}$$

$$u = u_0 - \beta r \tag{15.5}$$

$$\Delta\pi = \gamma(u - u_n) \tag{15.6}$$

First of all, it has to be noted that these equations can only be determined if the levels of r_n and u_n are already known, which highlights the close logical relationship of dependency between this and the Solow model. We shall now go on to examine the meaning of the individual equations. Relation (15.4) is a simple version of the so-called 'Taylor rule' and constitutes a hypothesis about the behaviour of the central bank. It is assumed that the monetary authority sets a real interest rate r that is higher than the rate r_n, corresponding to the full-employment equilibrium, to the extent that the current rate of inflation π is higher than a target rate of inflation π^T (set by the central bank or the political institutions of the country). In other words, the central bank believes that it can influence economic activity and hence also price dynamics through action on the interest rate r. This conjecture is borne out by the other two equations of the model. Equation (15.5) is a simple expression of the traditional *IS* curve. It tells us that the interest rate has a negative influence on aggregate demand and hence also on the degree of effective utilization u of productive capacity. The effective degree u indicates deviations from the rate u_n deriving from more or less intensive utilization of capital and thus implying variations in per capita output y with respect to per capita capital k. In examining this equation, it should also be borne in mind that only the rate r_n is capable of generating demand and a degree of utilization u corresponding to the level u_n consistent with full-employment equilibrium. Finally, (15.6) is a simple derivation of the Phillips curve indicating that upward or downward variation in inflation depends on the difference between the effective degree of utilization, u, and the degree of utilization corresponding to the full-employment equilibrium (u_n).

The system therefore comprises three equations and three unknowns, r, u, and $\Delta\pi$. The rate of interest r_n and the full-employment degree of utilization u_n are given by Solow's equations and all the other variables are regarded as exogenous (it should be borne in mind that the effective rate of inflation π is also considered exogenous). The system is therefore fully determined. For example, let us assume an initial situation in which the effective rate of inflation is higher that the rate set as a target. In this case, the central bank will be able to set a particularly high interest rate, thus giving rise to a degree of effective utilization below the equilibrium level and hence to a negative variation in inflation. In this way, the effective inflation rate will tend toward the target rate. It can also be assumed that the central bank will take the opposite course of action in cases where effective inflation is below the desired level. On this view, the monetary authority acts on the system constantly with a view to attaining a situation of $\pi = \pi^T$, which unsurprisingly corresponds precisely to the Solow full-employment equilibrium. If the effective and target rates of inflation coincide, the model's equations tell us in fact that the interest rate and the degree of utilization of productive capacity will prove equal to their respect levels at full employment.

The following conclusions can thus be drawn from the complete 'Solow–New Consensus' neoclassical model. The equilibrium levels of wages and interest are the only ones guaranteeing full employment of the factors of production, and especially the available labour, L. Any action aimed at adjusting the distributive variables will necessarily involve deviation from the full-employment equilibrium. Moreover, spontaneous convergence towards equilibrium does not appear to be guaranteed. This is why the central bank is called upon to guide the system toward an equilibrium that ensures full employment and the simultaneous attainment of a target rate of inflation.

3   A 'Reversed' Reading of the Two Models

Let us now abandon the neoclassical paradigm of scarcity and utility and introduce some hypotheses typical of the heterodox literature. We shall assume that the available labour L is always surplus to the productive requirements of the system and that the utilization of capital can vary to a large degree without necessarily generating tension as regards prices. This means that scarce endowments no longer play a crucial role in determining the system's endogenous variables and thus involves a shift in perspective with two consequences at the formal level. First, it is established that the rate g of capital accumulation is no longer determined by saving but set exogenously in relation to the autonomous investment decisions of firms. Second, it is assumed that the interest rate r_n is also exogenous and depends essentially on the outcome of the conflict between social classes. These hypotheses obviously imply that the subscript attached to the interest rate and the capacity utilization rate can no longer indicate the *natural* full-employment equilibrium; at most, one can speak of a *normal* position, which can correspond to a situation of high unemployment of labour and has to be understood as a position established in a given historical phase. As a result of this change in exogenous variables, the Solow–New Consensus model will undergo a logical 'reversal' and lead to conclusions very different from those described above. In order to show the basic consequences of this reversed reading, let us re-state equations from (15.1) to (15.6), for ease of reference:

$$f(k) = w + (1 + r_n)k \tag{15.1}$$

$$f'(k) = 1 + r_n \tag{15.2}$$

$$sf(k) = (1 + g)k + z \tag{15.3}$$

$$r = r_n + \delta(\pi - \pi^T) \tag{15.4}$$

$$u = u_0 - \beta r \tag{15.5}$$

$$\Delta\pi = \gamma(u - u_n) \tag{15.6}$$

Furthermore, remember that $u_n = f(k)/k$. We shall start by examining equations (15.1), (15.2) and (15.3). On the assumption that r_n and g are exogenous, it will be necessary to identify three new endogenous variables if the model is to be determined. These will be k, w and z. The solution procedure of the model is therefore altered as follows. Equation (15.2) represents the condition that firms must respect if they are to choose the method of production that minimizes costs. In other words, it determines the ratio k in terms of which firms will combine the means of production with labour. Once r_n and k are known, the per capita output $f(k)$ is also determined as well as u_n. Once r_n, k and $f(k)$ are given, it is possible to obtain the real wage w residually through (15.1). In other words, the quota of production that goes to labour is determined by the difference with respect to the quota already assigned exogenously to the recipients of interest. Finally, given the accumulation rate g, it can be assumed that (15.3) is observed on the basis of the change in the ratio z between autonomous expenditure that does not generate additional capacity and income produced.[10] The final result is therefore radically altered with respect to the original Solow model. Factor endowments can in fact be seen to have lost their primary role. Labour in particular is now assumed to be abundant rather than scarce, which means that for every given level of demand, firms will employ only the number of workers needed to produce the total output demanded. Others will, however, remain unemployed. The distributive variables therefore no longer perform the task of ensuring the absorption of scarce endowments by firms. Distribution only determines the technical composition of labour and means of production which will be chosen by firms in order to maximize profits. But in this framework distribution is exogenous and does not change in the presence of unemployed labour. This does not mean, however, that distribution is left hanging in midair. On the contrary, it is regarded as the result of the relations of strength between the social classes and the outcome of the conflict inevitably arising between them.[11]

What function will the central bank perform in this new scenario? In order to answer this question, it is necessary to examine equations (15.4), (15.5) and (15.6) of the New Consensus model. It should be noted from a strictly formal viewpoint that the solution of the system does not change. The endogenous variables are in fact still r, u and $\Delta\pi$, determined on the basis of the same original procedure and as a function of the same exogenous variables and the levels of r_n and u_n already determined by equations (15.1), (15.2) and (15.3). There is, however, a substantial difference with regard to these last two variables, which no longer correspond to a full-employment equilibrium but simply reflect the balance of power between the social classes. The fact that the central bank seeks to guide the system toward r_n and u_n therefore necessarily takes on a completely new meaning.

Two different hypotheses can be put forward as regards the behaviour of the central bank. In the first case, it could be argued that the presence of a given exogenous level of r_n in equation (15.4) indicates the monetary authority's acceptance and defence of a certain distribution of income between the social classes. It should in fact be remembered that, as indicated by equations (15.5) and (15.6), the central bank can act indirectly through the interest rate r on the effective degree of utilization of capacity u and hence also on variations in inflation $\Delta\pi$. Its policy could therefore be aimed at making the exogenous distribution r_n compatible with the desired rate of inflation π^T. For example, if workers do not accept this distribution of income, they will put pressure on wages, which will obviously give rise to an increase in inflation. The central bank could in this case act as follows: it could put into effect a restrictive policy to weaken workers and cause them to moderate their demands by reducing the degree of utilization of productive capacity and thus generating unemployment.

This alternative interpretation of the model thus emphasizes the role of the central bank as a 'regulator of distributive conflict'. It is, however, a reading based on two equations, namely equations (15.5) and (15.6), about which the heterodox literature has always harboured great misgivings. In particular, economists adopting a critical stance toward the neoclassical mainstream have always raised doubts as to the existence of a strong and stable relationship between the interest rate and the degree of utilization of productive capacity. Moreover, they have always opposed the idea of an analogous relationship existing between the degree of utilization and variations in inflation.[12] This is why various heterodox economists would claim that in reality the parameters β and γ of the model could be equal to zero, thus making equations (15.5) and (15.6) wholly superfluous. The logical conditions are therefore created for a second alternative interpretation of the model.

4   Another Alternative Interpretation: The Central Banker and the Drain of Capital

If we eliminate equations (15.5) and (15.6), what meaning could an equation such as 15.4 – describing the behaviour of the central bank – possibly have? If we assume an open economy, it is possible to give an original answer to this question: a central bank reaction function could reflect the desire of the monetary authority to ensure that the national rate of interest does not diverge from the one prevailing in other countries so as to avoid any drain of capital. In other words, the central bank's reaction function could reflect the well-known condition of *uncovered interest rate parity*.[13] Hence using an F superscript to denote the foreign value of a variable, note that if the central bank is to avoid a disparity between the national rate of interest and the interest rate prevailing in other countries, its reaction function must become:

$$r = r^F$$

from which it follows that:

$$i - \pi = i^F - \pi^F$$

given the definition of the real interest rate $r = i - \pi$. Re-arranging this last expression yields:[14]

$$i = i^F + (\pi - \pi^F) \tag{15.4'}$$

Now let $\Delta E/E$ be the expected variation in the nominal exchange rate.[15] If the *purchasing power parity* condition[16] is assumed to hold, so that exchange rates reflect in some way the trends in rates of inflation, then $\Delta E/E = (\pi - \pi^F)$. Equation (15.4') therefore corresponds exactly to the uncovered interest rate parity. If this condition is respected, there should be no drain of capital.

On the basis of this interpretation, the behaviour of the central bank is therefore designed to keep the flows of capital under control by ensuring that internal interest rates are in line with those prevailing in other countries. It should be borne in mind that the central bank can still be seen here as a 'regulator' of distributive conflict. In this case, internal distribution will be determined by the situation prevailing at the international level, and the central bank no longer seeks to set the rate of inflation but confines itself to reacting to foreign inflation (it could be said that the internal distributive conflict is dominated by 'globalization'). But this complication does not change the basic role of the central banker, which is wholly concerned with the regulation of distributive conflict and has nothing to do with any consideration regarding a hypothetical full-employment equilibrium.

5   How to Choose Between Neoclassical and Alternative Formulations

As compared above, the 'Solow–New Consensus' neoclassical model and its reversed, heterodox version reveal some interesting analogies with *stereograms*, images that undergo a radical change in meaning in relation to the viewpoint from which they are observed. In our example, depending on the choice of exogenous variables, the central bank will be regarded in two very different ways: either as a 'driver' that brings the economy toward the full-employment equilibrium or as a sort of 'gendarme' of distributive conflict. Therefore, the choice of exogenous variables can be seen in the same way as the crucial moment at which model builders define their point of view and bring one or the other type of representation of the economic system into focus. The conceptual universe in which an economic model is embedded can of course never emerge simply from the system of equations and the choice of exogenous variables characterizing it, but must instead be tracked down in the 'meaning' attributed to these equations and variables. The problem of the choice of exogenous variables is, however, a crucial stage for the purposes of determining the 'sense' of a theory. This holds not only for teaching but also for the broader sphere of research, and not only in economics but also in all other fields of application of deductive logic.

The crucial question now is the following: what criteria should be adopted in the choice of exogenous variables? It is clear that if there is no scientific criterion for the selection of exogenous variables, we run the risk of falling into the solipsistic view that 'anything goes' in the choice of premises provided that the propositions derived in the subsequent stage of research are logically consistent with respect to the initial decisions (Feyerabend, 1975). However, the drift toward solipsism is not unavoidable. It should be remembered that the neoclassical theory has been subjected to many criticisms, which can be also extendend to the neoclassical 'Solow–New Consensus' model. One of them is that this scheme seems logically consistent only in an unrealistic world with just one good. While this problem, long identified by Sraffa (1960) and his successors, now appears to have been somewhat forgotten in the literature, the neoclassical theorists do not seem to have fully succeeded in solving it.[17] The 'reversed' and heterodox version of the two models described here therefore seems to conform better to the observable reality of a multi-good world. There is thus some logical reason for the curiosity of young scholars to be aroused by it.

Notes

1. DASES – Università del Sannio. Address for correspondence: Via delle Puglie 82, 82100 Benevento, Italy. Email: emiliano.brancaccio@unisannio.it. I would like to thank the editors of this book, Guglielmo Forges Davanzati and Antonella Stirati, for their helpful comments. Any remaining errors are my own.

2. The American textbooks of Blanchard (2005), Mankiw (2007) or Stiglitz (1997), for example, make almost exclusive reference to the debate developed within the so-called 'neoclassical synthesis'. Marxists, Classical economists or Post Keynesians are rarely cited.

3. Marglin (1984), Dutt (1990), Kurz and Salvadori (1995, pp. 46–8) among the others. See also Brancaccio (2008).

4. Samuelson (1970), Koopmans (1975). For a criticism of the neoclassical paradigm of scarcity and utility, see Pasinetti (1993).

5. Sraffa (1960), Garegnani (1990). The assumption of an exogenous distributive variable is not an exclusive prerogative of the Sraffian Surplus approach. For example, it is possible to show that this hypothesis is compatible with the so-called Circuit approach (Graziani 2003). For a demonstration of this compatibility, see Brancaccio (2005, 2009).

6. See also Clarida *et al.* (1999), Taylor (1997, 1999), Woodford (2001, 2003), Carlin and Soskice (2006). For a critical view of the New Consensus, see among others Arestis and Sawyer (2004), Setterfield (2004, 2006), Fontana and Palacio-Vera (2007), Fontana (2006), Kriesler and Lavoie (2007).

7. Taylor (2000, p. 91), quoted also in Kriesler and Lavoie (2007).

8. Let l be the growth rate of the working population. On the assumption that l is exogenous, the equilibrium of proportional growth will be determined when the ratio k arrives at such a level as to comply with the following condition (3'): $sf(k) = (1 + l)k + z$, i.e. when the rate of saving (or capital accumulation) coincides exactly with the exogenous rate of growth of labour and thus generates development leaving the ratio k between the endowments of capital and labour unchanged. In this case, the model proves to consist of equations (1), (2) and (3'). The exogenous variables of the model are therefore l, z and s. While (3') determines k, (2) and (1) determine r and w respectively. The absolute scale of activity will depend in every period on the endowment of labour L, which remains exogenous in this case.

9. Modigliani (1944), Patinkin (1965). For a current textbook which can be associated to the tradition of 'neoclassical synthesis', see Blanchard (2005).

10. The macroeconomic implications of autonomous expenditure that does not generate additional capacity are examined in Serrano (1995).

11. For a thorough analysis, see Garegnani (1990). See also Kurz and Salvadori (1995, pp. 26–7).

12. Kriesler and Lavoie (2007), among others.

13. Gandolfo (2001).

14. Equation (15.4') can also be derived directly from equation (15.4) as follows. Starting from equation (4), we assume for the sake of simplicity that $\delta = 1$. We also begin

by hypothesizing that the current rates of inflation π^T and π^F are equal, respectively, to the national and foreign target rates of inflation. Let i and i^F be the domestic and foreign nominal rates of interest and π the expected effective rate of internal inflation, which can differ from the respective target rate π^T. Now, it is known that the real interest rate is generally given by the difference between the nominal interest rate and the rate of inflation. However, it may happen that the expected effective rate of inflation differs from the target rate. In this case the real interest rate will be given by $r = i - \pi^T - (\pi - \pi^T)$, that is $r = i - \pi$. Furthermore, the real foreign rate of interest will be given by $r^F = i^F - \pi^F$. Once the relevant substitutions are made, equation (15.4) becomes equation (15.4'), as stated above.

15. The nominal exchange rate E is defined here as the domestic price of foreign currency, so that $\Delta E/E > 0$ denotes a depreciation of domestic currency.
16. Gandolfo (2001).
17. According to Garegnani (2003), it is possible to address the Sraffian criticism not only to the old long period Wicksellian models but also to the short period neo-Walrasian versions of neoclassical capital theory.

References

Arestis, P. and Sawyer, M. (2004), 'Monetary Politicy when Money is Endogenous: Going Beyond the New Consensus', in Lavoie, M. and Seccareccia, M. *Central banking in the modern world. Alternative perspectives*, Cheltenham: Edward Elgar.

Blanchard, O. J. (2005), *Macroeconomics*, Upper Saddle River, NJ: Prentice Hall.

Brancaccio, E. (2005), 'Un modello di teoria monetaria della produzione capitalistica', *Il Pensiero economico italiano*, 13, 1.

Brancaccio, E. (2008), *Anti-Blanchard*, Elementi di macroeconomia critica, University of Sannio, lecture notes.

Brancaccio, E. (2009), 'Solvency and labour effort in a monetary theory of reproduction', *European Journal of Economic and Social Sciences*, 1.

Carlin, W. and Soskice, D. (2006), *Macroeconomics. Imperfections, Institutions and Policies*, Oxford: Oxford University Press.

Clarida, R., Galí, J. and Gertler, M. (1999), 'The Science of Monetary Policy: a New Keynesian Perspective', *Journal of Economic Literature*, 37.

Dutt, A. K. (1990), *Growth Distribution and Uneven Development*, Cambridge: Cambridge University Press.

Feyerabend, P. K. (1975), *Against Method*, London: NLB.

Fontana, G. (2006), 'The New Consensus View of Monetary Policy: a New Wicksellian Connection?', Levy Economics Institute, Working paper 476.

Fontana, G. and Palacio-Vera, A. (2007), 'Are Long-Run Price Stability and Short-Run Stabilization Policy All That Monetary Policy Can Aim For?', *Metroeconomica*, 58.

Gandolfo, G. (2001), *International Finance and Open-Economy Macroeconomics*, New York: Springer-Verlag.

Garegnani, P. (1990), 'Sraffa: Classical versus Marginalist Analysis', in Bharadwaj and Schefold (eds), *Essays on Piero Sraffa*, London: Routledge.

Garegnani, P. (2003), 'Savings, investment and capital in a system of general intertemporal equilibrium', in Petri, F. and Hahn, F., *General Equilibrium: Problems and Prospects*, London: Routledge.

Graziani, A. (2003), *The Monetary Theory of Production*, Cambridge: Cambridge University Press.

Koopmans, T. C. (1975), 'Concepts of Optimality and Their Uses', Nobel lecture.

Kriesler, P. and Lavoie, M. (2007),' The New Consensus on Monetary Policy and its Post-Keynesian Critique', *Review of Political Economy*, 19, 3.

Kurz, H. and Salvadori, N. (1995), *Theory of Production*, Cambridge: Cambridge University Press.

Mankiw, N. G. (2007), *Principles of Economics*, Florence, KY: South Western.

Marglin, S. A. (1984), *Growth Distribution and Prices*, Cambridge, MA: Harvard University Press.

Modigliani, F. (1944), 'Liquidity Preference and the Theory of Interest and Money', *Econometrica*, 12.

Pasinetti, L. (1993), *Structural Economic Dynamics*, Cambridge: Cambridge University Press.

Patinkin, D. (1965), *Money, Interest and Prices*, 2nd edn, New York: Harper & Row.

Samuelson, P. A. (1970), Maximum Principles in Analytical Economics, Nobel lecture.

Serrano, F. (1995), 'Long Period Effective Demand and the Sraffian Supermultiplier', *Contributions to Political Economy*, 14.

Setterfield, M. (2004), 'Central Banking, Stability and Macroeconomic Outcomes: a Comparison of New Consensus and Post-Keynesian Monetary Macroeconomics', in Lavoie, M. and Seccareccia, M. (eds), *Central Banking in the Modern World: Alternative Perspectives*, Cheltenham: Edward Elgar.

Setterfield, M. (2006), 'Is Inflation Targeting compatible with Post Keynesian Economics?', *Journal of Post Keynesian Economics*, 28.

Solow, R. (1956), 'A Contribution to the Theory of Economic Growth', *Quarterly Journal of Economics*, 70.

Sraffa, P. (1960), *Production of Commodities by Means of Commodities*, Cambridge: Cambridge University Press.

Stiglitz, J. (1997), *Principles of Macroeconomics*, New York: W.W. Norton & Company.

Taylor, J. B. (1997), 'A Core of Practical Macroeconomics', *American Economic Review*, Papers and Proceedings, 87 (2).

Taylor, J. B. (2000), 'Teaching Modern Macroeconomics at the Principles Level', *American Economic Review*, Papers and Proceedings, 90, 2.

Taylor, J. B. (ed.) (1999), *Monetary Policy Rules*, Chicago: University of Chicago Press.

Woodford, M. (2001), 'The Taylor Rule and Optimal Monetary Policy', *American Economic Review*, Papers and Proceedings, 91.

Woodford, M. (2003), *Interest and Prices: Foundations of a Theory of Monetary Policy*, Princeton: Princeton University Press.

16
Institutions, Expectations and Aggregate Demand

Jesus Ferreiro and Felipe Serrano

1 Introduction

The concept of rational expectations is the cornerstone of orthodox economic theory. As Minford and Peel (2002) argue: 'in its modern guise macroeconomics is based entirely on the idea that agents are rational. Hence rational expectations are central to the subject today' (p. 41). Although the conclusions reached by the mainstream about, for instance, the reasons for and duration of economic disequilibria, the causes of economic cycles, and the impact of economic policy are based on this way of analysing the economic behaviour of individuals, in most undergraduate textbooks, this way of representing how individuals make their economic decisions is not made explicit. In fact, in most textbooks that discuss competing schools of economic thought and their main differences, it is not explained that these schools can be grouped into two main approaches, according to their treatment of the information problems: schools that identify information problems with situations of risk, and schools that treat information problems in terms of uncertainty.

Both in the case of the New Classical Macroeconomics, which argues that rational expectations exist at every moment, and the New Keynesian Economics, which argues that rational expectations only exist in the long term, the existence of rational expectations guarantees the existence of a competitive equilibrium outcome, that is, an outcome that clears all markets, and where individuals make optimizing decisions. From a dynamic perspective, rational expectations help individuals to make optimal intertemporal allocations of their lifetime resources, and, consequently, the economy evolves along a long-run sustainable path of economic growth, consistent with a non-accelerating inflation rate of economic growth. This is equivalent to a non-accelerating inflation rate of unemployment (NAIRU) and a vertical Phillips curve (at least in the long run). In this approach, long-run economic activity is determined only by the endowment of productive factors (capital and labour) and their productivity (technology) and by institutional elements mainly related to the labour market.

In this mainstream view, the role of economic authorities as regulators of the economic process is downgraded. Since in the long term agents have rational expectations, their decisions about the creation and use of productive factors will always be optimal, and consequently, any public intervention will reduce the volume of these inputs or will reduce their productivity. In either case, the level of economic activity and the welfare of society will fall.

By accepting that in the short run agents cannot have perfect information, the existence of mistakes by agents and the subsequent deviation of current levels of economic activity from those prevailing in the long term (i.e. the existence of an output gap) is accepted. In this situation, the implementation of transitory policy measures that bring current levels of economic activity back into equilibrium are justified.

Focusing on macroeconomic policy, the orthodox view implies that, first, fiscal policy must focus on avoiding fiscal imbalances and reducing the size of the public sector (usually measured as public expenditures and tax revenues as a percentage of GDP), and, second, that monetary policy must concentrate all its efforts in the achievement of an environment of low and stable inflation. There is no room for an active macroeconomic policy designed to alter the (long-term) level of economic activity. Keynesian demand-side policies would be ineffective. Indeed, discretionary demand-side policies are seen as the main source of the recurrent shocks that separate current economic activity from the path of long-term growth. In the long-run, economic activity is determined by the aggregate supply curve, where the relevant expectations (that is, those related to the inflation) are always correct.

Focusing our attention on the long run, the existence of an optimizing equilibrium outcome assumes that individuals have access to complete information and have the capacity to process this information. As a result, agents do not make systematic errors, that is, errors are always stochastic, due to events about which agents do not have past information, and that, consequently, cannot be predicted. Nevertheless, agents learn from their mistakes, and do not repeat their errors. Competitive markets with flexible prices are the only institutions that agents need. Interaction in the market guarantees that agents are coordinated: all agents behave in the same manner, that is, making decisions that maximize their individual utilities, which, in turn, leads to an equilibrium outcome.

Nonetheless, the existence of information problems in the short run as a consequence of an asymmetric distribution of information is accepted, although this is a transitory situation. In the short term, rigid prices mean that any unanticipated event will lead to errors in agents' predictions, thus leading to inefficient resource allocations. Therefore, any transitory change in one relevant variable will have real consequences, affecting real variables, such as employment or the level of economic activity. However, in the long run, this effect will disappear and the economy will return to its natural equilibrium point:

> [A]lthough classicals and Keynesians disagree about whether the Phillips curve relationship can be exploited to reduce unemployment temporarily, they agree that policymakers can't keep the unemployment rate permanently below the natural rate by maintaining a high rate of inflation. Expectations about inflation eventually will adjust so that the expected and actual inflation rates are equal ... Thus the actual unemployment rate equals the natural rate in the long run regardless of the inflation rate maintained. (Abel and Bernanke, 2001, p. 446)

Only as a result of short-term prediction errors will economic activity depart from the long-run equilibrium level. The size and the sign of the deviation will be directly related to the size and the sign of the prediction error in the inflation rate. Therefore, changes in agents' spending and in aggregate demand are explained by differences between the expected and the actual inflation rates.

Since it is information problems that generate inefficient (that is, far from equilibrium) economic outcomes, the information problem must be addressed and solved at its source. At this point, it must be stressed that the problem is not the lack of information but the asymmetric distribution of information, that is, the fact that only some agents lack information and/or a group of agents have partial or mistaken information.

For mainstream economics, this asymmetry is the direct consequence of strategic behaviour by policy-makers. Public authorities lead private agents astray by announcing policy measures, mainly monetary policy interventions, that are not fulfilled. It is this time-inconsistency problem that generates prediction errors on the part of private agents.

Based on these premises, the achievement and maintenance of the desired equilibrium outcome is only possible if the institutional design of the public sector and policy-making guarantee the 'proper' working of public authorities – namely, credible and time-consistent policy compatible with the market-clearing equilibrium. Examples of these kinds of institutions are fiscal rules, the independence of central banks, the explicit setting of inflation targets and the implementation of strategies of inflation targeting.

As previously argued, this approach is based on the axiom that, in the long run, individuals do not face any information problem and that, consequently, rational expectations will always prevail. No other institution is needed but the market to reach and maintain the best possible outcome: the market-clearing outcome. However, in the short run, the assumption of rational expectations is relaxed, allowing for the existence of information problems in the form of an asymmetric distribution of information. It is in the short run that different kinds of institutions are required in order to return the economy to a situation of equilibrium.

The logical corollary is that not only active macroeconomic policy (based on the management of aggregate demand) but also the workings of any institutions that do not contribute to either solving the problem of asymmetric information or imposing rigid constraints on public authorities will have a negative impact on economic activity and the welfare of society.

Obviously, if the assumption of perfect information and rational expectations is relaxed, the above analysis of the role played by institutions and aggregate demand in the economic process collapses. The purpose of this chapter is to establish these propositions in a way that is accessible to undergraduates. As we will see in the following sections, accepting the existence of uncertainty involves recognizing the key role played by institutions both at a micro and macroeconomic level, and the importance of aggregate demand as a key determinant of economic activity both in the short and the long run. It is important that undergraduates are made aware in this way of the role played by Minford and Peel's (2002) 'rationality premise' in the orthodox views of how the aggregate economy works and how macro policy should respond to the economy.

2   Institutions and Information Problems

The analysis of the information problems that agents must solve in their decision-making processes is one of the most complex issues that economic theory, or to be more precise, the different economic theories and models that comprise the economics discipline, face. The particular ways that economic theories use to incorporate information problems into their analyses can be used as a guide to their differences.

The origin of the different treatment given to these problems can be found in two different concepts of economic science. For the neoclassical school, economics is the science that studies the distribution of scarce resources among alternatives uses. Consequently, the central problem is the study of the efficient allocation of resources through the mechanism of the market. In this view, there is no historical time, only logical time.[1] However, from an alternative perspective, the object of economic science is to study how individuals satisfy their needs through an economic process that changes through time. It is, therefore, historical time, not logical time, which plays a key role in economic analysis. Nonetheless, and despite the existence of these differences, all theories agree on linking the analysis of the institutional framework to the existence of information problems. Institutions are a source of information for individuals, and, consequently, an instrument that helps them to make decisions. Before expanding upon the relationship between institutions and information problems, we must clarify what we mean by institutions, and what are the most relevant information problems faced by individuals.

An institution can be defined as a set of formal and informal rules, including their enforcement arrangements. The general aim of institutions is to provide individuals with a set of rules that guide or determine their individual behaviour. Thus, as North (1990) argues, institutions help to reduce uncertainty. The concept of uncertainty usually encompasses the set of information problems that individuals face in their decision-making. Thus, we face uncertainty when we do not know what will happen in the future. We also face a problem of uncertainty when we do not know whether the person, or the agent/firm, with whom we relate has more information than we do, and consequently we do not know whether or not our decision is correct. Nonetheless, given the importance in all economic paradigms of the way in which the concept of uncertainty is interpreted, it is important to make a clear-cut distinction between differing treatments of the information problem.

Some of the decisions made by individuals in the present are influenced by events that will take place in the future. This means that individuals must attempt to foresee future events, something that is not always feasible. The economic process is not a continuous process but an evolutionary one. The articulation of the variables that characterize this process in a specific moment of time may be different than that existing at another point in time. This does not mean that it is impossible to distinguish economic analysis from historical analysis. What we mean is that it is not always possible to anticipate the future using probability calculations. The concepts of 'risk' and 'uncertainty' must always be present in economic analysis. Risk situations are those situations that can be anticipated using probabilities estimated from past frequencies. On the contrary, genuine 'uncertainty' (Davidson, 1991) means that an event cannot be anticipated by probability calculations due to the evolutionary (i.e. non-ergodic) nature of the economic process.

Information problems, however, are not limited to the above mentioned situations. The interaction of individuals through the market generates other kinds of information problems. Agents face information costs when they try to buy or sell their property rights. These costs can arise as a result of different elements. The search for the necessary information when a transaction is to be made involves costs in terms of time. These costs can take a commercial form if the information is bought in the market. The cost can also be the result of the bounded capacity that agents have to analyse available information, which can lead these agents to pay for the analysis of information by a specialized agent. There are also costs arising from the asymmetric distribution of information among the agents that participate in a market. In all cases, it is worth noting that when we work with these kinds of information problems, we are implicitly assuming that the information exists – that is, that the relevant problem is *access* to information and not the (non)*existence* of information. In some situations this assumption is not a restrictive one. However, there are situations, where we face a problem of genuine uncertainty, in which it is useless to argue the existence of a problem of access to information because this information simply does not exist.

If institutions help to solve information problems, then analysis of institutions should be directly related to the analysis of the economic process. We need to ask: Should institutions be considered an endogenous or an exogenous variable in economic models? And is the creation of institutions a process mainly determined by economic needs or, on the contrary, is it the result of other factors?

The endogenous nature of institutions is an old and new discovery of economic theory. Between both discoveries we find the neoclassical theory of economic equilibrium. The hegemony reached by this school after World War II led to a marginalization of the old American institutionalism. The neoclassical theory of equilibrium is a theory in which institutions do not exist, the only exceptions being those institutions compatible with economic equilibrium. Institutions are something outside the economic model: an exogenous variable whose working is determined by the hypotheses and axioms that lead to the existence of an equilibrium outcome.

The new institutionalism, although it shares some key elements with neoclassical theory, involves a rediscovery of institutions by economic theory. Like the neoclassical theory of equilibrium, its aim is the analysis of the process of resource allocation. Nonetheless, its macroeconomic analysis is deeper. Institutions are shown as a constituent element of the resource allocation process, that is, institutions are again an endogenous variable in economic models. Individuals are no longer agents facing an individual problem of utility maximization. Society as a whole influences the individual decision-making process and the opinions that individuals hold about what can or cannot be done. The rationality of agents is not unlimited, and, consequently, institutions can help to correct their bounded capacities of information processing. The transfer of property rights is determined by 'rules of the game' that limit the possibilities of exchange, and, therefore, markets are not abstract things but the outcome of collective decisions. Depending on how property rights, and especially the possibilities for exchanging these rights, are defined, markets can have different characteristics.

However, the new institutionalism is based on a very restrictive assumption: the existence and availability of information. The information problem above mentioned, although present, is not equivalent to that existing in the real world. Although this does not invalidate the theory, its results must be understood as involving certain caveats. An example will help the reader to understand what we mean. Agency models are one of the main developments of new institutionalism. However, these models are based on the assumption that the agent has all the information that the principal needs to make her decision. Therefore, the analytical problem focuses on the discovery of necessary and sufficient conditions that mean that the relationship between the principal and the agent is not dominated by the latter as a result of the asymmetric distribution of information. However, if because of the existence of uncertainty the necessary information is not available, the problem is not one of asymmetric information. This situation poses a different institutional problem. In this case, the relevant issue is not correcting the problem of asymmetric information, but the construction of institutions that redress the risks arising from the existence of uncertainty.

Are both analyses, that is, the problems of uncertainty and asymmetric information, compatible? Initially, one might be tempted to give a positive answer. The problems of the asymmetric distribution of information are different from those arising from the existence of uncertainty, and in the real world we can find examples of the existence of both information problems. Moreover, not all of the decisions that individuals make are necessarily influenced by events that can happen in the future. However, from a theoretical perspective, these two dimensions of institutional analysis are based on radically different theories of economic equilibrium, and it is not clear that both theories can incorporate both of the dimensions of institutional analysis alluded to above. Hence the neoclassical theory of equilibrium cannot easily incorporate the institutional dimension related to the existence of uncertainty, or, at least, cannot incorporate it in the terms in which it is currently formulated. Moreover, the idea of the existence of an equilibrium in a dynamic frame of economic analysis, similar to that argued by Keynes, is not clearly accepted, and, actually, many authors explicitly reject this possibility. Therefore, the question posed at the beginning of this paragraph would simply be a rhetorical question, lacking in analytical relevance. Nonetheless, in our opinion the question is relevant, and should lead to reflection about how the different information problems that agents face in their decision-making processes can be made compatible in a coherent way.

In sum, the neoclassical treatment of information problems warrants that, at least in the long term, the economy will reach an equilibrium outcome which is stable and optimal. The design of institutions and the working of the public sector must be directed towards achieving this outcome, by solving the potential problem of asymmetric information. However, what happens if this assumption is relaxed and it is accepted, as in the Post Keynesian approach, that individuals suffer from problems of genuine uncertainty? Can we keep arguing the existence of an equilibrium outcome with similar characteristics to those mentioned above?

3   What Role for Equilibrium in Economic Theory?

In a simplistic manner, it is tempting to divide the different economic theories and models into two broad categories. The first category would include models of neoclassical inspiration. The main characteristics of these models would be the existence of rational expectations, flexible prices, optimizing behaviour of agents and, consequently, the existence of a market-clearing equilibrium outcome. The second category would encompass alternative (heterodox) models. These models, by rejecting the existence of rational expectations and flexible prices, would seem to argue the absence of an equilibrium outcome, leading the economy to a situation of permanent instability. However, this is incorrect. The rejection of the existence of perfect information or rational expectations does not involve the rejection of the existence of an equilibrium outcome. Actually, the discussion about the existence of an equilibrium outcome is a recurrent debate, for instance, in the Post Keynesian school.[2]

One does not need to be a professional economist to realize that the real world is not characterized by the existence of absolute and permanent chaos. Despite the fact that we can argue that the economy will not stay (even in the short-term) in a stable equilibrium, the truth is that economic activity usually flows along a relatively stable path, where changes are small and, sometimes, predictable with a low margin of error.[3] Where, then, does debate among different economists and schools originate?

In our opinion, this debate arises because equilibrium is identified with the specific neoclassical concept of equilibrium. As we explained above, in neoclassical theory, equilibrium is the result of a set of hypotheses and axioms about the behaviour of individuals, the characteristics of markets and the nature of the information that agents handle. The normative criterion used to define equilibrium is that of 'market-clearing' and the criterion (also normative) used to choose between different equilibrium states (when the problem of efficient allocation is studied) is the concept of 'Paretian optimum'. In the neoclassical world, agents can always anticipate and predict the equilibrium outcome since this is predetermined before the economic process begins, there existing at each moment only one possible equilibrium outcome. Once equilibrium has been reached, in the absence of exogenous shocks, the economy will remain permanently at the equilibrium outcome. Any transitory change in the determinants of the individual process of resource allocation generates a transitory outcome that, nonetheless, returns to the point of origin (i.e., equilibrium) when the transitory shock disappears. This economic system is, therefore, homeostatic and time-reversible. A permanent shock, meanwhile, will generate a new, unique equilibrium outcome that will be known to agents when they have all the relevant information. In fact, under the hypothesis of perfect information or rational expectations, agents will always be able to anticipate the new equilibrium before it is reached.

To reject the existence of rational expectations involves putting emphasis on the evolutionary and non-ergodic nature of the economic process and, therefore, on the relevance of uncertainty in the economic analysis (Davidson, 1991, 2002, 2007). The existence of uncertainty places the notion of historical time at the core of the analysis (Robinson, 1962), which means that, from a theoretical perspective, events are not predetermined but contingent – that is to say, their probabilities are directly influenced by past events and, consequently, the current level of economic activity, or even the current equilibrium, is path-dependent. Therefore, any economic outcome is the result of a specific combination, historically determined, of economic and social forces.

In a world ruled by uncertainty, it would seem that economic processes should be unstable, subject to deep, sudden and permanent swings, and that the capacity of agents to predict and incorporate the future in their current decision-making process is nil (Setterfield, 2003). This kind of world, where agents do not have information about future events, about the behaviour of other agents or about the consequences of their own decisions, poses, however, a number of methodological problems for the analysis of the decision-making processes of individual agents and of the macroeconomic performance of the economy. Thus, in this kind of economy, it would not be possible:

- to include expectations of future events or results that influence agents' current decisions in a specific way
- to model the economy, in the sense of specifying stable causal relations and predicting the consequences of any shock-induced change in the variables included in those relations
- to argue the existence of certain key determinants of economic activity (aggregate demand as the determinant of economic activity, for example, or the relevance of profit expectations for current investment decisions)
- to make qualitative valuations of current outcomes
- to set objectives and targets for economic policy.

Moreover, the historical evidence 'demonstrates that capitalist economies move through time with a substantial degree of order and continuity that is disrupted only on occasion by bursts of disorderly and discontinuous change' (Crotty, 1994). We can say that in these periods the economy evolves in a cyclical way around a 'stable' trend or path (Crotty, 1992, 1994).

In our opinion, the concept of equilibrium involves the idea of the existence of an economic outcome that can be considered as stable, predictable and desirable. This notion involves the existence of stable functional relations among economic variables and of stable individual behaviours, which permits the theorist to incorporate such relations and behaviours into economic models. Thus, economic analysis is not limited to a simple ex-post explanation of past events, but is enlarged to include the possibility of predicting future behaviours and results depending on changes in certain values of the relevant variables or changes in the parameters of the model.

In this sense, both in the mainstream and Post Keynesian approaches, the concept of equilibrium plays a similar role in economic analysis – that of a benchmark to evaluate current behaviour and outcomes and the workings of economic policy. However, the content of the notion of equilibrium is not the same in the two approaches. There are two key distinctions: the capacity to predict economic results, and the normative content of these results.[4]

In a neoclassical economy, given the rational-optimizing behaviour of individuals, any equilibrium is, by definition, always desirable. Thus, the equilibrium outcome is only determined by economic-technical criteria. In the neoclassical model, equilibrium is, therefore, a laboratory result, a game of relations which are built ignoring the most obvious aspect of reality – the existence of historical events which determine the nature of relations among variables. On the contrary, for non-neoclassical approaches (like Post Keynesian economics) the concept of equilibrium has a clear normative content since it includes criteria which permit individuals in a society to assess how desirable these outcomes are. These criteria are not immutable, being subject to change in so far as the interests of different agents and their interrelationships evolve across time and space.

This approach involves not only a different concept of equilibrium and a different role played by institutions in the real world, but also a different criterion to evaluate economic results and the working of institutions.[5] In opposition to the notion of neoclassical efficiency, whose benchmark is the market-clearing equilibrium, we can talk of an objective of *social efficiency* based on the values shared in a society in each historical period. We understand by social efficiency a historical situation in which the desirable economic objectives and the procedures for reaching these objectives are clearly determined and shared by the majority: i.e. a certain distribution of competences between the state and the market; certain institutions working as sources of information in the generation of expectations; and even certain public and private actions to correct undesirable outcomes of the economic process.[6]

Moreover, the existence of this kind of equilibrium is not based on the existence of perfect information, but on the existence of a set of stable expectations in the short and in the long run. It must be stressed that the stability of expectations can be reached at any level of economic activity. In this sense, Kregel (1976) explains how Keynes, in his lecture notes on the *General Theory*, presents a model of stationary equilibrium where both short-term and long-term expectations are fulfilled, but where these expectations do not guarantee that the economy reaches a point of equilibrium with full employment. Therefore, the stability of expectations is a necessary but not sufficient condition to attain full employment equilibrium.

Institutions are, therefore, a key instrument for solving, or palliating, the information problems faced by the agents, both the problems related to the bounded rationality and those related to the lack of information about the future and the problems of coordination with other agents. It is in this sense that institutions are a key determinant of economic activity in market economies. The stability of economic outcomes is related to the existence of stable institutions that help individuals to behave in a specific way. Consequently, if economic outcomes are to be changed in a specific and permanent way, current institutions must also be reformed, or even replaced with, new institutions that contribute to the creation of a new set of expectations, and so modify the economic decisions made by individuals.

4   Institutions, Aggregate Demand and Demand-Side Economic Policies

As we have argued, the level of economic activity prevailing at any point in time is contingent on the current set of expectations that rule individual decision-making processes. In turn, these expectations are provided by the current set of conventions and institutions.

As mentioned in previous sections, in mainstream economics there is no need for institutions besides the market and those institutions that help to solve the problems of asymmetric information. In this framework, the resource allocation decisions will lead to an optimizing equilibrium outcome. However, in a world with uncertainty there is no a priori outcome or technical solution to the problem of resource allocation. The level of economic activity will depend, also, on individual expenditure decisions and hence on the level of aggregate demand, and will thus depend on information about the behaviour of other agents and about the future value of the determinants of individual spending decisions.

In so far as there is no predetermined outcome, any level of economic activity can constitute an 'equilibrium' outcome; i.e. economic activity can be managed to reach a certain stable level of economic activity or a certain path of economic growth. The necessary and sufficient condition is that the short- and long-term expectations be compatible with that level of economic activity. The common recipe in textbooks is that a Keynesian equilibrium outcome, which would usually be identified with a full employment level of activity,[7] simply involves setting the full employment level of aggregate demand through fiscal and monetary policy. Thus, a well-designed macroeconomic policy is a necessary and sufficient condition to reach and maintain full employment.[8]

However, these measures do not guarantee that expectations will be permanently stabilized at a point compatible with the full employment level of activity. Agents' expectations cannot be determined in such a precise way. Only with the design of institutions oriented to the attainment of full employment can that outcome be effectively reached (Stockhammer, 2006–7): 'To make sure that there is never a persistent lack of effective demand, the government must develop institutional arrangements that encourage some decision makers to spend in excess of their current income so that aggregate spending on the products of industry will offset any excess savings propensity at full employment' (Davidson, 2007, p. 23). Policies oriented to institutional design are not in direct competition with macroeconomic policies, however. On the contrary, by emphasizing the relation between expectations and institutions, a new field for reflection for Keynesian thought is opened, bringing about a reconciliation with classical institutionalism.

This is one lesson that we can learn from the 'golden age' of capitalism. The implementation of a Keynesian economic policy, based on the management of aggregate demand via demand-side policies, was possible thanks to the existence of national institutions (for instance, the Welfare State) and international institutions (for instance, the Bretton-Woods institutions, such as the IMF and World Bank) that helped individuals to create and maintain the expectations that, in the long-term, the economy would be close to a full employment level of activity. Since the mid-1970s, however, the new, or reformed, institutions have helped to create a new environment where long-term expectations may have emerged (for instance, those related to low inflation rates). The achievement of low and stable inflation rates might be considered an equilibrium situation. Whether or not this outcome is socially optimal or desirable is another question, however. If the answer is no, then new institutions will need to emerge, allowing the implementation of a different strategy of economic policy focused on a new economic objective.

5   Conclusions

In the current mainstream, the role played by demand-side policies is downgraded. Aggregate demand only matters in the short term, and in a negative sense. Hence deviations from the long-term path of economic growth are the result of prediction errors made by agents, and, thus, the result of inefficient decisions, errors that are, in turn, explained by the existence of problems of asymmetric information. To get an optimal-equilibrium outcome, the problems of asymmetric information must be solved. These are the grounds for the existence of certain institutions that correct this information problem, involving the implementation of rules that limit and constrain the behaviour of public authorities.

This approach is based on the axiom that, at least in the long term, agents have rational expectations and that, therefore, they do not suffer a problem of uncertainty. If the axiom of perfect information is abandoned, there is no equilibrium outcome in neoclassical terms. This, however, does not mean that the economy will be unstable. In fact, market economies are characterized by a substantial degree of order and stability. Institutions play in the real world a key role as a coordination mechanism of individual behaviours, and as a source of information about the future that helps individuals to plan their decisions.

Any level of economic activity can be reached. The current state of short- and long-term expectations will determine the economic outcome existing at any point in time. Thus, public authorities can tame the economic process through the design of institutions and the adoption of the appropriate macroeconomic policy. What this chapter has tried to illustrate, and what is important for students of macroeconomics to understand, is the way in which our conception of the economy – including the level of economic activity that will ordinarily be achieved, the role of institutions, and the purpose of macroeconomic policy – is shaped by the initial assumptions we make about decision-making and the availability of information about the future.

Notes

1. Logical time is a situation where the relevant variables in the economic analysis are stable, and, therefore, the relationships among them can be studied in terms of causal relations. Historical time is a (long-term) situation where the relationships among variables lose stability, and, consequently, in econometric terms, the correlation coefficients are weaker.
2. See Ferreiro and Serrano (2007), Lang and Setterfield (2006–7, 2008), Lawson (2005) or Sardoni (2008), among others.
3. A good example is the turbulence in the financial sector since 2007. It is obvious that the current situation cannot be defined as an equilibrium. However, we cannot but argue that for long periods, the financial sector (at least in the developed economies) works quite smoothly, and that agents in these economies can foresee with a low margin of error, for instance, the conditions of access to bank credit.
4. Thus, for instance for mainstream economics the objectives of economic growth or employment/unemployment have a pure technical content. It is talked of as a long-term sustainable growth pact or a non-accelerating inflation rate of unemployment. These, and no others, are the only objectives in the long term. However, the Post Keynesian economics, for instance, identifies the objective of unemployment with a certain rate of unemployment, and objective and target defined by economic but also social and political elements.
5. In this sense, our notion of equilibrium is closely related to a notion of balance of forces, a balance of forces that represents the existing social order (Lawson, 2005).
6. Therefore, the prevailing definition of equilibrium at any point in time, like the modelling-theory of the economic process itself, is institutionally specific and historically contingent (Crotty, 1990, 1992).
7. It must be noticed that the concept of full employment has a deep normative content. For the neoclassical economy, full employment is identified with a situation of market-clearing, and, thus, full employment is understood as a situation where the current real wage equals the labour market clearing wage. At this point, all workers willing to work at the equilibrium wage find a job. This definition means that the equilibrium in the labour market can be reached at any level of employment. In the case of a New Keynesian economy, full employment is identified with the NAIRU or the NAWRU, that is with a level of (un)employment that guarantees a certain rate of growth of prices or wages. In Post Keynesian economics, full employment is identified with a certain (and low) rate of unemployment, let us say, 3%. And finally for Beveridge, a full employment situation would be identified as one where the number of unemployed workers is equal to or below the number of vacant jobs.
8. Thus, for instance, it is often argued, as the European Central Bank usually does, that keeping a low and stable inflation rate helps to foster economic growth and employment: 'Over the last few decades there has been a remarkable convergence on the need to make price stability the main or primary objective of monetary

policy. Price stability has taken central stage because it is both an achievable medium-term goal for central banks and a pre-condition for a well-functioning market economy. In preserving price stability, monetary policy facilitates economic growth and the efficient use of resources' (European Central Bank, 2001, p. 7).

References

Abel, A.B. and Bernanke, B.S. (2001), *Macroeconomics*, Boston: Addison-Wesley.

Crotty, J. (1990), 'Keynes on the stages of development of the capitalist economy: the institutionalist foundation of Keynes' methodology', *Journal of Economic Issues*, 24, 761–80.

Crotty, J. (1992), 'Neoclassical and Keynesian approaches to the theory of investment', *Journal of Post Keynesian Economics*, Summer, 14(4), 483–96.

Crotty, J. (1994), 'Are Keynesian uncertainty and macrotheory compatible? Conventional decision making, institutional structures and conditional stability in Keynesian macromodels', in Dymski, G. and Pollin, R. (eds), *New Perspectives in Monetary Macroeconomics: Explorations in the Tradition of Hyman P. Minsky*, Ann Arbor: University of Michigan Press, 105–39.

Davidson, P. (1991), 'Is probability theory relevant for uncertainty? A Post Keynesian perspective', *Journal of Economic Perspectives*, 1, 129–43.

Davidson, P. (2002), *Financial Markets, Money and the Real World*, Cheltenham: Edward Elgar.

Davidson, P. (2007), 'Strong uncertainty and how to cope with it to improve action and capacity', in McCombie, J. and Rodriguez Gonzalez, C. (eds), *Issues in Finance and Monetary Policy*, Basingstoke: Palgrave Macmillan, 8–27.

European Central Bank (2001), *Why Price Stability*, Frankfurt: European Central Bank.

Ferreiro, J. and Serrano, F. (2007), 'New institutions for a new economic policy', in Hein, E. and Truger, A. (eds), *Money, Distribution and Economic Policy. Alternatives to Orthodoxy*, Cheltenham: Edward Elgar, 141–57.

Kregel, J. (1976), 'Economic methodology in the face of uncertainty: the modelling methods of Keynes and the Post-Keynesians', *Economic Journal*, 86, 209–25.

Lang, D. and Setterfield, M. (2006–7), 'History versus equilibrium? On the possibility and realist basis of a general critique of traditional equilibrium analysis', *Journal of Post Keynesian Economics*, 29(2), 191–209.

Lang, D. and Setterfield, M. (2008), 'Stability, equilibrium and realism: a response to Sardoni', *Journal of Post Keynesian Economics*, 30(3), 491–5.

Lawson, T. (2005), 'The (confused) state of equilibrium analysis in modern economics', *Journal of Post Keynesian Economics*, 27(3), 423–44.

Minford, P. and Peel, D. (2002), *Advanced Macroeconomics: A Primer*, Cheltenham: Edward Elgar.

North, D. (1990), *Institutions, Institutional Change and Economic Performance*, New York: Cambridge University Press.

Robinson, J. (1962), *Essays in the Theory of Economic Growth*, London: St Martin's Press.

Sardoni, C. (2008), 'Some considerations on equilibrium and realism', *Journal of Post Keynesian Economics*, 30(3), 485–90.

Setterfield, M. (2003), 'Keynes's dialectic?', *Cambridge Journal of Economics*, 27, 359–76.

Stockhammer, E. (2006–7), 'Uncertainty, class and power', *International Journal of Political Economy*, 35(4), 31–49.

Author Index/Name Index

Key: f = figure; n = note; **bold** = extended discussion or word emphasized in the main text.

Subject Index